LAWLESS

★★★★★

"Today's lawlessness is a final warning.
This book reveals the scheme and how we fight back!"

– Jan Markell, Founder/Director, Olive Tree Ministries

LAWLESS

END-TIMES WAR AGAINST
THE SPIRIT OF ANTICHRIST

TERRY JAMES, GENERAL EDITOR

WITH CONTRIBUTORS

Wilfred Hahn, Jan Markell, Daymond Duck, Larry Spargimino, Dr. Tom Hoffman,
Nathan E. Jones, Ryan Pitterson, Randy Nettles, Todd Strandberg, Jonathan C. Brentner,
Pete Garcia, Don McGee, Mike Gendron, Thomas J. Hughes, Jim Fletcher, Dr. David R. Reagan

DEFENDER

CRANE, MO

Lawless: End Times War Against the Spirit of Antichrist
By Authors: Terry James, Wilfred Hahn, Jan Markell, Daymond Duck, Larry Spargimino, Dr. Tom Hoffman, Nathan E. Jones, Ryan Pitterson, Randy Nettles, Todd Strandberg, Jonathan C. Brentner, Pete Garcia, Don McGee, Mike Gendron, Thomas J. Hughes, Jim Fletcher, Dr. David R. Reagan

Printed in the United States of America.

Scripture taken from the King James Version of the Bible unless otherwise noted.

Cover design by Jeffrey Mardis.

ISBN: 9781948014373

Acknowledgments

My thanks to each and every author of these chapters for their contributions to this volume. Each is a faithful servant of the Lord with insights from on high that are so needed at this critical time.

Special thanks and love, as always, to Angie Peters, my long-time editor and daughter-close associate for another superb bringing together of great writers in the best way possible.

Thanks and love to Dana Neel, my other daughter, for all the research and other assistance she always provides.

To Tom Horn, my great friend and publisher, my deep appreciation for his and his associates at Defender Publishing. Their many dynamic contributions to the publishing and media aspects of our effort can't be overstated.

To my wife, Margaret, and others of my family, Terry, Jr., Nathan, and Kerry, as well as Jeanie and Todd, my love for always supporting me in time spent in these book projects.

To you, the reader, without whom the writing of books would be pointless: much appreciation.

To our Lord Jesus Christ be all glory, honor, and eternal thankfulness.
—Terry James

Contents

Section IV: Warring Against Spiritual Wickedness

Prophetic Parallels, End-time Money Snare,
Anti-Joseph: Are We There Yet?

By Wilfred Hahn

Vladimir Lenin, the one-time head of Soviet Russia, was reported to have said: "There are decades where nothing happens, and there are weeks where decades happen." Breathtakingly, an acceleration of that magnitude appears to have unfolded in the early months of 2020.

No sooner than the COVID-19 pandemic spread across the world, a new future seemed to have already been well preplanned. One cannot be blamed for thinking that a cadre of policymakers around the globe had been waiting for the next crisis.

Crises, whatever their kind, act as catalysts in human affairs. Panicked fears and societal uncertainties serve as an impetus for new and unorthodox policy decisions by political leaders and policymakers. Of course, many of these are well-meaning, but many others have deleterious consequences.

However, one doesn't need to invoke far-fetched conspiracy theories to explain why crises come about or how they are triggered, and how they prey upon common and predictable human behaviors. In this respect, crises are a normal feature of mankind's societies. They have been the constant companion of human existence.

Crucially, however, there is one conspiracy of cosmological dimensions that has been playing out over many generations of humans. It is one that requires no speculation, being clearly mentioned in the Bible.

A "master of intrigue will arise" (Daniel 8:23). He will "take his stand against the Prince of princes" (verse 25). The power behind him is Satan himself. Also, Psalm 2:1–2 reveals that all the world's rulers will take a stand against God at that time. A hierarchy of evil and dark forces work in unison and coordination to that goal (Ephesians 6:12).

Conveniently, crises can serve as a clandestine cover under which to push forward a long-term agenda against God. For example, mankind is vulnerable to fear and greed. Satan knows this very well. He therefore surely loves hyperactive listed financial markets around the world. He ruthlessly uses these human penchants and weaknesses to his advantage.

It is therefore reasonable to accept that crises and their attendant human responses of fear and panic do play into the glove of those who have an agenda to advance. They can seize the opportunity of a populace that is willing to compromise or accept a loss of freedom for the sake of security and prosperity.

These tradeoffs lead to a treacherous road, one that is well documented throughout history and in the Bible, as we will show. Why? Because such changes and trends borne of crises are usually cumulative and not easily reversed.

Consider the advances of science and technology. These are always a step function leading forward, never to be reversed or lost. It is similar with policymaking in respect for human rights, centralization of power, globalism, censorship, and central banking, etc. These humanist advances are often one-way developments; give an inch and when a facilitating crisis arrives, then take a mile.

An undeniable trait of history is that a genuine crisis—whether relating to health, economy, public safety, and/or civic order—always and everywhere enhances the powers of top-down authoritarian leadership.

Without a doubt, these types of nefarious shifts are being witnessed in bright lights around the world today. In fact, this writer would even state that these "ripening" trends have accelerated as perhaps never before in recent years; they've kicked into supersonic speed following the latest global crises.

Consider that Freedom House, even before 2020 ever arrived, had already counted fourteen consecutive years of declining freedom worldwide.[1] Looking ahead, it would not be surprising to observe this trend to be in further freefall.

We live in an age when globalization has advanced rapidly (though possibly experiencing an ebb for a while)—a global brotherhood of man through the common interests of commerce, speaking as if with one language and objective.

The rebellious unification of world rulers and elites against God and His Son, Jesus Christ, is already far advanced.

Essential to this agenda is a final financial entrapment of all of mankind in order to force humanity to worship the Antichrist. Economic captivity therefore plays a key role in the last days. A diabolical trapper has been setting in place an end-time money snare.

How did the world get to this late date, this rendezvous with history? It required a lot of planning and plotting…forward steps followed by backward steps, then again forward.

The end goal is to entirely entrap humanity, allowing us fewer and fewer options. Ultimately, a stern world ruler (Daniel 8:23) will be revealed, forcing us to comply with his agenda of rebellion.

As already mentioned, it is a plot to which the Bible testifies. In fact, right from the first book of the Bible, Genesis, an end-time program of enslavement of mankind is foreshadowed.

In the Beginning: A Blueprint

Bible scholars say that the entirety of the Bible is enfolded in its first book. As such, one also discovers that much prophecy is foreshadowed in the book of Genesis.

Consider the biblical account of Joseph. It is seen as a wondrous story. However, in our interpretation, it provides a surprising end-time conspiratorial blueprint that is urgently germane to our day.

Readers will surely be shocked to learn that the story of Joseph would offer just such a perspective. After all, wasn't this the account of the remarkable rise of a young man who had been sold by his brothers to Midianite traders traveling to Egypt? Starting out as a slave, Joseph eventually rose to the top of that era's geopolitical echelon as a chief regent of the Pharaoh. Egypt, at that time, was the most powerful country in the world.

How did Joseph come to this position?

While he was in prison in Egypt (after being falsely accused by Potiphar's wife), the Pharaoh experienced a vision of seven "fat and sleek" cows coming out of the Nile. These were then followed by seven ugly and lean cows, which then ate up the seven fat cows. Joseph was perplexed. He then saw a second vision, which repeated the message of the first. Only this time, it was seven full heads of seeds, followed by seven heads that had been withered and scorched.

Pharaoh and his entourage weren't able to decipher the meaning of these dreams. So Joseph was called out of prison to interpret the vision, as he had done before for his two jail-cell companions. He told the Pharaoh that they revealed God's plan to allow seven years of abundance in Egypt to be followed by seven years of famine.

God had enabled Joseph to interpret the Pharaoh's dream as well as recommend a public-works program. In response, the Pharaoh appointed Joseph to prepare the nation for a seven-year drought. He was then put in charge of the entire kingdom.

Just as Joseph had said, seven years of abundance did occur, followed by seven years of famine. While other lands had no grain, in the whole land of Egypt, there was plenty of food.

It then becomes a heart-rending story that reveals what humanity will do in order to quell the pangs of hunger, to be saved from a crisis—whatever its kind. In desperate times, having little choice, people will strike bad deals, ceding freedoms and increasing their vulnerability to rich despots and totalitarian regimes.

Fourteen years later, the entire commercial and societal structure of the known world at that time, as well as almost all the land in Egypt, came under the control of one man—Pharaoh—due to Joseph's management. The Pharaoh ended up becoming an all-powerful economic potentate. Such was the case in Egypt almost four thousand years ago when Joseph reigned as vice regent.

How did this happen? A more detailed examination of this account reveals many levels of prophetic foreshadowing; these provide end-time warnings for the world and for Christians living today.

A Sometimes Misinterpreted Story

The story of Joseph, one of the twelve sons of Jacob, is a popular favorite of children and adults alike. It not only celebrates the ultimate blessings that a righteous man accrued, but also shows how God can miraculously enter the seemingly unfortunate occurrences of our lives and work them out for good (Romans 8:28).

However, now with new eyes, the account of Joseph's deeds raises many questions.

In any case, he then began the operations of stockpiling the produced grain of the seven fat years. According to the original edict (Genesis 41:34–35), he and his commissioners were to take one-fifth of the harvest and store the grain inside the cities. Joseph didn't pay for the excess grains; he collected a fifth of it.

During the seven bountiful years, the stockpiles eventually became so large that "he was no longer able to keep an account of their size" (Genesis 41:49). Then, as prophesied, "the seven years of abundance in Egypt came to an end" (Genesis 41:53.)

When Egypt and other lands began to feel the famine, the people cried to Pharaoh for food. Then Pharaoh told all the Egyptians, "Go to Joseph and do what he tells you'" (Genesis 41:53–55). And so they did.

Then "Joseph opened the storehouses and sold grain to the Egyptians" (Genesis 41:56). Scripture tells us that, by receiving payment, Joseph collected all the money that was found in Egypt and Canaan. Again, note that Joseph collected ALL of the money in these lands for payment. Joseph took every last penny in return for grain so that people might eat and be saved from the famine.

What was the result? Joseph controlled all payment specie. He deposited all of this money into Pharaoh's coffers.

However, once all the monetary savings of the people had been used up, they then faced a cash crunch (what Wall Street practitioners today call a "liquidity crisis.") There was no more transactional specie (cash) circulating in the land after that point.

From that time on, people could only barter.

The famine continued for another year. At this point, the populace again had no grain or money left. What to do next? They needed to replenish their cupboards.

They again begged Joseph to give them food. What did he do in response? He provided handouts. Actually, no; that would be a false statement. Truly, what did he do next? He demanded the people's livestock.

In an agrarian society such as the one that existed during that time, livestock represented assets that generated a large part of household income. Consider also that in Joseph's era, livestock was the equivalent of today's industrial capital—our factories and transportation systems. Horses, cattle, sheep, and other animals were the means to the production of wool, butter, and many other products. What was the result?

They brought their livestock to Joseph, and he gave them food in exchange for their horses, their sheep and goats, their cattle and donkeys. And he brought them through that year with food in exchange for all their livestock. (Genesis 47:17)

Now Joseph—on behalf of the Pharaoh—was in control of ALL of the capital stock of Egypt. He had secured the ownership of the land-based transportation system (donkeys and horses) and the productive capacity of factories (livestock). He could now sell the outputs of milk and meat, as well as transportation services.

The Pharaoh had become a countrywide rentier.

However, the takeover by the state didn't stop there. Relentlessly, the famine continued yet another year.

People needed more grain, and they again became desperate. What were they forced to do? They now said to Joseph: "Buy us and our land in exchange for food, and we with our land will be in bondage to Pharaoh" (verse 19).

So, Joseph reduced the people to complete servitude. He took all their land. Now, one end of Egypt to the other became the property of the state under the control of one man, Pharaoh (with the exception of a small amount of land that was owned by the priests and special elites).

At this point, the populace owned absolutely nothing and were totally enslaved. They probably remained as such until the end of their lives.

Will the Real Joseph Stand Up?

Are two Josephs mentioned in the Bible, or are we dealing with one and the same?

Many see Joseph as an Old Testament picture of Christ. We would not disagree. He suffered so that he might be able to save his family in Egypt and so that he could go ahead and, like Jesus, prepare a place for them (John 14:3). It is also noted that Joseph is the only major person in the Israelite lineage of Christ found in the Bible in whom no character flaw or sin is explicitly mentioned.

Joseph surely was a sinner like every other human being, so why aren't his sins mentioned? We do discover that, through his errors, this instrument of God—like all the others from Abraham to King David—

can be seen to have bequeathed lessons to mankind that are relevant for our day.

An impartial examination of Joseph's life reveals that the results of his actions were not entirely beneficial, nor were his techniques virtuous. That statement will likely strike the reader as disrespectful. Should this be said of Joseph, a venerated person mentioned in the Bible?

While it is true that Joseph succeeded in saving many lives, his mission was not performed entirely in the spirit of a merciful rescue operation. Egyptians and others seeking to buy grain had to virtually sell their souls and freedoms to gain access to it.

Note that Joseph did not donate the grain to needy people, but instead required payment. Think of it: People were starving, and he asked for money for grain. Few Christian aid organizations today would think they are fulfilling Christ's command to "feed the poor" (Luke 11:41) or their enemies (Romans12:20) if they were profiting from their ministries.

To the contrary, the entire ownership structure of the land of Egypt was changed virtually overnight from private ownership to vassalage. With the exception of a few Egyptian priests, the immediate family of Joseph, and probably some other high-ranking elites, the all the land of Egypt came under the direct ownership of Pharaoh.

Moreover, we're told that as a result of Joseph's policies, a system of onerous taxation resulted that is "still in force to today" (Genesis 47:26). Indeed, government taxation is the norm nowadays.

Just imagine what would happen if this type of "absolute" power that Joseph attained for the Pharaoh were given to a diabolical entity or person in our day? Indeed, the Bible clearly indicates that just such an individual is prophesied to appear in the last days.

Thankfully, Joseph was a person whom God prospered and blessed in almost everything that he did (Genesis 39:2). Yet, as mentioned, Scripture remains silent on judgment of his techniques. It is evident that the consequences of Joseph's actions were not entirely ideal.

A major conundrum must be noted in this story. It is clear that the whole saga turned out to be a giant opportunity for the secular Pharaoh to gain power and wealth at the expense of those in need. But did this have to occur? Joseph could have saved everyone from hunger without making the Pharaoh an extremely wealthy potentate and all others oppressed vassals. So why didn't he choose to do so?

We recognize here the classic problem of mankind. People who have power and/or the opportunity most often choose wealth…and more wealth. That is certainly the case in our day. Elites and plutocrats become ever richer.

Other Prophetic Parallels to Today

It may well be asked: If Joseph's actions indeed saved millions of lives, then does anything else matter? Wasn't the tradeoff worth it—putting entire populations into vassalage and widening even farther the imbalances of the wealth distribution?

That may appear to be the same type of situation faced by those who are currently making policy decisions about the public responses to the COVID-19 pandemic.

Should we save everyone from dying from the virus, but completely destroy the global economy and place massive debts upon the shoulders of citizens? How can it be ensured that the stimulus of massive new indebtedness (created by fiat) will be distributed fairly?

Is everyone being forced into economic bondage? Attempts may be made to achieve fairness. But it would be foolishness to believe that mankind's primordial unfaithfulness with money will suddenly turn benevolent. Pharaoh, as we have shown, ended up being super rich. The same tendency is at work today, especially so when crises are seized as catalysts for major wealth heists and transfers.

Once policymakers begin going down the road of fiat money (modern money theory) and economic interventions, there is no easy return. Temporary government policies and interventions tend to eventually become permanent fixtures. Even Joseph faced this dilemma. After serving the Pharaoh for twenty-six years—twelve years after the famine was over—he

xviii   LAWLESS

claimed he was still saving lives (Genesis 50:20). Here we indeed see that a temporary government measure became permanent.

Another specter of the Joseph story is that "all the countries came to Egypt to buy grain from Joseph, because the famine was severe in all the world" (verse 57). Here in the first book of the Bible we find the very roots of modern-day "globalization."

The whole world converged for reasons of "bread" (a euphemism for "money"). Egypt had become the world's commercial center, and its grain became the senior currency of that epoch.

Pharaoh came to this position of controlling the entire world by dispensing the means of providing bread and prosperity. The incentive of gaining "bread" was harnessed by one centralized system—even by one man. We may see that aspects of that process are again sweeping the entire world today under the guise of the promise of "more bread for the entire world."

End-time Trap Foreshadowed

How long did it take for the entire known world of Joseph's time to come under economic bondage to the Pharaoh? According to this writer's calculations, once the drought began, this process required a period of three and one-half years.

Three one-year periods are indicated, then an additional half year is deduced. Explicitly mentioned to last a year are these two yearly stages: Livestock was used in payment for one year of grain supply (Genesis 47:17). Another year was survived by giving up ownership of land and their "bodies" (verse 18).

What about the period before these two yearly spans? In response to the first request for grain, Joseph took all the money in the land (verses 13–15). We judge that the monetary transactions could not have purchased more than a year's worth of grain consumption. As it was in those times, most wealth was represented by livestock and land. Transactional money didn't play as significant a role in the livelihoods of people as today.

As already reviewed, Joseph didn't buy the excess grain during the plentiful period in the first place. Therefore, the seven years of plenty would not have produced a cash hoard in people's pockets that would have been sufficient to purchase an adequate grain supply for all year.

According to this logic, we so far count three years on the road to serfdom for Egypt's population.

We next note that the Nile basin at times supported two grain harvests each year. As such, it would be logical to assume that people only would have laid aside provisions of grain for one half-year, this being long enough to last until the next harvest. That suggests that six months of drought would have taken place before food shortages began to occur. As of that point, money would have been used to purchase the next year's grain supply.

If our estimates are correct, we can conclude that a three-and-one-half-year period was required to bring the entire world under the control of one system that was under the authority of one man.

The Tribulation Foreshadowed

We identify here a parallel to the first half of the Tribulation, which will also be three and one-half years. This period, in this writer's view, ends with the closing of the money snare—the ability to limit buying and selling (Revelation 13:17).

This first half of the seven-year famine can be seen as corresponding to the "the beginning of birth pains" that we read about in Mathew 24:8. It foreshadows the first half of the seven-year Tribulation. By the end of that period, the False Prophet will have led the entire world into economic and monetary bondage.

It is during this period that a great world ruler, the Antichrist, gains increasing power. He first brings the world under his control in the name of peace and prosperity. Then, once he has much of the humankind in his grip, he tightens the noose and brings doom to the earth. Later yet starts the Great Tribulation, the second three and one-half years (also known as Jacob's trouble; see Jeremiah 30:7).

Is the alignment between Joseph and the Antichrist a coincidence or just a senseless stretch of the imagination? Indeed, it may seem a sacrilege to frame such an irreverent question. There indeed are many instructive parallels, but there are also some key differences.

The final diabolical last-day ruler upon earth specifically strategizes his actions under the guise of a false christ, the Antichrist. If it is agreed that Joseph is a type of Christ, then wouldn't it only follow that the Antichrist would act as an Anti-Joseph?

Whereas Joseph had a benevolent calling enabled by God to save physical lives, the Antichrist is a demonically inspired person who seeks to physically entrap mankind for the purpose of destruction and his worship.

Jesus Christ came to offer spiritual life for an eternity. The Antichrist comes to do the opposite.

Today, many people are looking for a modern-day Joseph—an economic savior. They want to find solace in a comfortable life, low mortgage payments, a secure job, steadily growing financial wealth, expanding export markets, and an unfettered playing field for the globe's burgeoning multinational corporations. It is the sure road to prosperity, say many leaders and politicians. It is the certain route to a "world free of poverty" (the slogan of the World Bank).

Much of the world—certainly the societies in the Western world—have already forfeited their spiritual futures in their primary pursuit of earthly prosperity and happiness. Anyone who offers workable solutions to that end will be gladly received.

However, to gain the comforts and conveniences of our times, we must agree to accept vulnerabilities. It's a required trade-off. We must fully participate with our hearts, our land, and our factories to serve this global system so that we might take part in the promised fruits of a worldwide economic order.

So, it may be. However, humanity risks falling captive to an Anti-Joseph, the very same one who plans, as mentioned, a brutal end-time money snare for the world. A series of world crises drives humanity to give up its money, land, and economic freedoms.

Eventually one man—the Antichrist—taking opportunity will arrive at its pinnacle of power to take control.

Were the people angry with Joseph when he enslaved them? Not at all. "You have saved our lives," they said. "May we find favor in the eyes of our lord; we will be in bondage to Pharaoh" (Genesis 47:25). Here we see that the people willingly gave themselves up for bondage to the Pharaoh so that they might have no existential concerns.

The entire world will do so again, the Bible indicates. Only this time, it will be in response to the Anti-Joseph. They will willingly allow themselves to become economically and financially enslaved to a diabolically inspired person. Why? So that they might have grain…that they may have economic benefits.

The Anti-Joseph could arise very soon. Already, we can see the facilitating infrastructure being built up rapidly to enable a worldwide, repressive regime to take economic and financial control.

The recent global jitters with the COVID-19 pandemic prompt many more urgent steps to that future outcome—one that now is at the very doorstep. The scale of the massive interventions now being pursued to counter the worldwide economic impact of the virus outbreak are simply without precedent. The ultimate implications for all of mankind are disastrous, should the same course continue to be pursued. This cannot be overstated.

All of the above hastens the day described in Revelation 13:17. That is the point at which the False Prophet is able to control all buying and selling upon earth. Life no longer can be lived outside of this system… meaning certain death. The majority of the world's population will opt to receive the "mark." Those who do not are certain to die—either by being killed, by being persecuted, or by an inability to survive.

What does it imply that "no man might buy or sell"? It clearly means that NOBODY—ANYWHERE—will be able to buy or sell ANY-THING…unless they subordinate themselves to the "beast and its image." They must first take the mark. This is a penultimate event in the Tribulation period.

The question to which we want to direct our attention then is this: What systemic controls and/or developments are yet required to put in place a global regime so that NO ONE on earth can either buy or sell without permission? What needs to take form before this event can actually occur? Can we anticipate the time when the end-time money trap has advanced to the point at which it may snap shut?

Grossly simplified, for the economic limitations that are prophesied in Revelation 13:17 to be fulfilled, at least four things must first happen:

1. First, a globally integrated and closed financial system must exist. Necessary and common technologies must be in place. That means that not even a little bank in Tupelo, Mississippi, or on the Island of Tuvalu will be able to facilitate any type of transaction (whether buying food or selling a house) outside of this closed system.

2. Next, a system of central banking and national accounting must be endorsed everywhere. This results in a commonly shared monetary philosophy around the world (not necessarily a one-world currency), which crucially has an influential hold over financial markets and human behavior. In other words, the entire world must agree to play by the same monetary rules and values. The central banks' officials must carry out the same policies, coordinating their actions.

3. The legal statutes and regulatory institutions that oversee the financial activities of capital markets of individual countries must be superseded (or subjugated) by a centralized worldwide authority in order for unified actions to be enforced. This would also mean that government Treasury operations would be coordinated and controlled as well.

4. Finally, a unified global "political economy" must exist (taking the form of a very small group of powerful countries [perhaps the ten kings…then eventually a single autocrat]) that is powerful enough to enforce such monetary controls upon the entire world

at a given time. Mankind must collectively agree to pursue the financial capture and to appoint a policymaker who will put in place such conditions and policies.

Global Money Control: We're Nearly There

Having listed the four main steps to the end-time money trap, just how far along is the world? Steps 1 and 2 are well advanced. For all intents and purposes, we could say that these two requirements are already in place.

What about the final two steps remaining to be completed?

A reassessment is now needed, given the recent rapid advances over the past several years in response to economic crises and, lately, the global COVID-19 pandemic. A significant advance in the timeline of the end-time money snare has occurred.

In recent years, our view had been that global initiatives in this direction were indeed advancing, but weren't yet firmly in place. After all, further unifying developments in this direction were difficult. Why? Because individual countries were reluctant to give up any sovereignty.

Then how can these last two required steps ever fall in place? Our view had been that one or more global crisis of some type or another must first occur.

And indeed, that is occurring…quickly. The global responses to COVID-19 are chipping away at the resistance of sovereignty. Even countries such as Germany have remarkably changed their views. This country has significantly loosened its fiscal policies. Nevertheless, it faces a certain meltdown in the European Union (EU) if it doesn't accept EU financial unification.

It is only a matter of time before the EU issues "corona bonds," which would be the obligation of the EU itself and not that of individual countries.

This step would be momentous, as it would be a major advance of this third step, though not yet its full completion. The United States would also need to take part in the sovereign secession. That most certainly is not occurring at this time. In that respect, it can be said that the US government administration of Donald Trump is holding back the clock. Of course, this situation can be reversed rapidly. At some point, it must, if Bible prophecy is to be fulfilled. After all, prophecy is the foreknowledge of what future society and humans will choose to do.

As technocrats and political strategists well know, nothing is as effective as a fearsome crisis to unify political consensus and to compel change. Quoting the late Milton Friedman (a well-known monetarist economist): "Only a crisis, real or perceived, produces real change." A more diabolical quote expressing the same principle comes from the Nazi political theologian, Carl Schmitt: "Sovereign is he who decides the state of emergency."

Global emergencies and crises can be expected to continue. Prophecy is being fulfilled before our eyes. The end-time money snare is rushing forward. Only the Lord tarries, with the Church and the Paraclete (Holy Spirit) first to be removed.

Introduction

By Terry James

Planet earth needs a savior. This declaration is at the center of the demand by true believers that all people of this endangered sphere must acknowledge. Those deniers—nonbelievers—are branded as heretics. Those in denial of this unimpeachable assertion deserve to be, at the very least, incarcerated for their denial.

This mantra is central to the religious fervor of today. But, it is not the religious fervor of those who adhere to truth found in God's Word, the Bible. The zealots who hold to this theology are, from heaven's perspective, lawless in their anti-God demands. The elitists in government and the news and entertainment media who believe man is destroying the planet and only man can stop the destruction. There is no God to be considered in the controls they intend to exert.

And it is indeed religious zealotry. It is for certain a theological mantra that festers at the lawless hearts of those who rave about climate change and mankind destroying the planet through wanton disregard for the welfare of Mother Earth.

The rant began with "global warming" at its black heart. It all changed to the term "climate change" when the polar icecap didn't melt, thus the harbors of New York City and other places were not overwhelmed with the overflow of ocean waters as the "experts" had prophesied.

1

Mother Earth worship is the central unifying concept the father of lies has perpetrated that fits most propitiously within this spirit of Antichrist model. Branding against deniers of climate change as being the worst sinners within the religion of humanism is designed to make Christianity appear to be a false worship system. This is because the Bible declares that Jesus Christ, who is the very Word of God (John 1:1–3), is who has this earthly orb in His grip. It is not man who controls planet earth.

This, of course, is antithesis to the unimpeachable declarations of the environmental gurus who say man is destroying the earth with greenhouse gases from carbon emission. Only man, himself, through draconian actions to stop these deadly gases, can save himself from choking to death from unbreathable air or drowning because of the melting ice of the North and South poles.

This book you have chosen to read, *LAWLESS: The War Against the Spirit of Antichrist*, is written by seventeen authors who expose, through light given in God's Word, the truly dangerous lawless ones at this time so near to Christ's return. The lawless we are referring to are infected with the spirit of Antichrist.

The Holy Scripture makes it clear who these God-deniers are and for whom they have hatred. The word "antichrist" is mentioned specifically only in the following passages of the Bible (emphasis added):

Little children, it is the last time: and as ye have heard that *antichrist* shall come, even now are there many antichrists; whereby we know that it is the last time. (1 John 2:18)

Who is a liar but he that denieth that Jesus is the Christ? He is *antichrist*, that denieth the Father and the Son. (1 John 2:22)

And every spirit that confesseth not that Jesus Christ is come in the flesh is not of God: and this is that [spirit] of *antichrist*, whereof ye have heard that it should come; and even now already is it in the world. (1 John 4:3)

For many deceivers are entered into the world, who confess not that Jesus Christ is come in the flesh. This is a deceiver and an *antichrist*. (2 John 1:7)

Deniers abound in this era of increasing hostility to the Bible as the inerrant Word of God. The capstone atop the pillar that stands solidly against biblical truth, in my view, is the words of the individual most recognized by the world as leading religious authority. Not only is this leader considered the top religious authority, but he is placed by most of the world's religious thought on the high pedestal of being the top leader within Christianity. I refer to Pope Francis of the Roman Catholic Church.

Jesus said:

I am the way, the truth, and the life; no man comes to the father but by me. (John 14:6)

Pope Francis said something quite different:

The disciples, Pope Francis explained, "were a little intolerant," closed off by the idea of possessing the truth, convinced that "those who do not have the truth, cannot do good." "This was wrong.... Jesus broadens the horizon." Pope Francis said, "The root of this possibility of doing good—that we all have—is in creation."

"Even them, everyone, we all have the duty to do good," Pope Francis said on Vatican Radio.

"Just do good" was his challenge, "and we'll find a meeting point."

Francis explained himself, "The Lord created us in His image and likeness, and we are the image of the Lord, and He does good and all of us have this commandment at heart, do good and do not do evil. All of us. 'But, Father, this is not Catholic! He cannot do good.' Yes, he can...." "The Lord has redeemed all of us, all of us, with the Blood of Christ, all of us, not just Catholics. Everyone!

'Father, the atheists?' Even the atheists. Everyone! We must meet one another doing good. 'But I don't believe, Father, I am an atheist!' But do good: we will meet one another [in Heaven]."[2]

Evangelist Mike Gendron presents a chapter in this book on the current pope's ongoing variance with and even denial of plain Bible truth. And while this pope is universally embraced, even by an antireligious global news media, Jesus Christ is most often marked by these same antagonists as representing a religion that is too narrow-minded, homophobic, and bigoted.

But Pope Francis, you see, holds as sacrosanct the belief system of the globalist one-world adherents. Climate change is the sin against which he rails, as do those of the Left in the news and entertainment media. In effect, it could be said that the pope is the chief prelate of this Mother Earth worship system.

In High Places

While climate change is the religious fervor around which the end-times hurricane of denying God's blueprint for mankind swirls, it is the wickedness in high places from which rebellion flows. We are warned by the apostle Paul:

> For we wrestle not against flesh and blood, but against principalities, against powers, against the rulers of the darkness of this world, against spiritual wickedness in high places. (Ephesians 6:12)

We further learn of this denial of God in high places by looking back into man's history:

> Why do the heathen rage, and the people imagine a vain thing?
>   The kings of the earth set themselves, and the rulers take counsel together, against the LORD, and against his anointed, saying,

Let us break their bands asunder, and cast away their cords from us. (Psalm 2:1–3)

The God-deniers have set their minds in collective rebellion throughout the ages. The anti-God rage became particularly evident during antediluvian times. About the days leading up to the worldwide Flood, God's Word says the following:

And GOD saw that the wickedness of man was great in the earth, and that every imagination of the thoughts of his heart was only evil continually.

And it repented the LORD that he had made man on the earth, and it grieved him at his heart.

And the LORD said, I will destroy man whom I have created from the face of the earth; both man, and beast, and the creeping thing, and the fowls of the air; for it repenteth me that I have made them. (Genesis 6:5–7)

Man, once reestablished following the deluge, again consorted to go against the Creator.

And the whole earth was of one language, and of one speech. And it came to pass, as they journeyed from the east, that they found a plain in the land of Shinar; and they dwelt there.

And they said one to another, Go to, let us make brick, and burn them throughly. And they had brick for stone, and slime had they for mortar.

And they said, Go to, let us build us a city and a tower, whose top may reach unto heaven; and let us make us a name, lest we be scattered abroad upon the face of the whole earth.

And the LORD came down to see the city and the tower, which the children of men builded.

And the LORD said, Behold, the people is one, and they have

all one language; and this they begin to do: and now nothing will be restrained from them, which they have imagined to do.

Go to, let us go down, and there confound their language, that they may not understand one another's speech.

So the LORD scattered them abroad from thence upon the face of all the earth: and they left off to build the city. (Genesis 11:1–8)

The Antichrist spirit of lawlessness continues to burn with incendiary, white-hot fever against the Lord of Heaven. Denying God's Son, Jesus Christ, and what He did to bring salvation to a lost, dying world of rebellious earth dwellers, today's leaders of earth's nations, wittingly or unwittingly, burn more hotly than ever in their determination to keep Christ from reclaiming this fallen planet.

Never in modern times has the wickedness in high places been more manifest than at the present hour. We have witnessed a globalist cabal attempt to move all nations—particularly the Western, industrialized, technologically advanced nations—into their desired one-world model.

America, the most desired prize in their wish-list grab-bag of assets to garner to themselves, continues to be the holdup to their construction planning. And make no mistake, bringing America into their effort is also at the heart of the blueprint of their master-director—Lucifer, the fallen one.

We witnessed a rage of supernatural dimension explode upon the scene leading up to the 2016 US presidential election. The Obama administration, with the efforts of Secretary of State Hillary Clinton, then Secretary of State John Kerry, moved to tear down national sovereignty. These forged ahead at full speed to establish open borders and undertake trade deals that siphoned national assets at an astonishing pace.

President Barack Obama did exactly what he promised in his campaign. He would, he promised, transform America. This he set out to do immediately upon assuming the presidency on January 20, 2009.

Globalist institutions at every level received priority treatment. Funds from the US Treasury flowed more freely than ever into the coffers of organizations like the United Nations and the World Trade Organization.

At the same time, America's dealing with our closest ally in the Middle East, Israel, deteriorated dramatically. The new president showed disrespect and even disdain for the nation and its leader, Prime Minister Benjamin Netanyahu. Dealing with Israel's enemies, militant Islam, changed, too. The US administration became cozier with Israel's enemies, often taking their side in disputations and confrontations in that volatile region.

The nation moved into economic decline as the housing bubble burst and because of other fiscal problems, and the president told the people of the US that this would be the "new normal." The jobs lost, particularly in manufacturing, would not be coming back. The outsourcing of those jobs to other nations—even the manufacture of pharmaceuticals—would go to antagonist regimes like China. These decisions have come back to do harm to the American way of life, as we have witnessed during the COVID-19 pandemic.

The party in power moved to bolster much of the anti-God agenda. Abortion thrived, the homosexual lobby greatly increased in influence, and Christianity seemed to take hits in legislation and litigation while Islam was treated ever more gingerly by the courts and by mainstream media. Open borders were championed even while terrorist organizations strove to infiltrate the nation.

Efforts increased to deleteriously affect the rights of Americans written in the Constitution. Constant efforts to damage the 2nd Amendment right to bear arms and the 1st Amendment right of free speech brought on a totally divided nation. That divisiveness continues and even increases to this day.

Those who had embraced the movement away from God by going along with the political party in power suffered what was to some an inexplicable meltdown with the presidential election of 2016. I say "inexplicable" to some, because to those who understand God's Word, the meltdown is easy to explain. The farther a person or a people move from God's prescription for living on this planet that He alone created, the greater the loss of rationality, spiritually speaking. And this cuts across all party lines and all strata of life.

The reason this particular political party is mentioned here is that we remember that the proposition was brought up at the 2012 presidential convention whether to keep mention of God in the party platform. A voice vote was taken, and the "nos" far outshouted the "yeas." The chairman nonetheless ruled in favor of the "yeas." That was the politically wise thing to do since the matter was recorded on TV and other media technologies. The fact is the Democrat Party gave a voice vote, by a considerable margin, to kick mention of God out of their party platform.

Again, the farther a person or a people move from God's ways, the greater the loss of rationality, spiritually speaking.

The apostle Paul explains:

And even as they did not like to retain God in their knowledge, God gave them over to a reprobate mind, to do those things which are not convenient;

Being filled with all unrighteousness, fornication, wickedness, covetousness, maliciousness; full of envy, murder, debate, deceit, malignity; whisperers,

Backbiters, haters of God, despiteful, proud, boasters, inventors of evil things, disobedient to parents,

Without understanding, covenant breakers, without natural affection, implacable, unmerciful:

Who knowing the judgment of God, that they which commit such things are worthy of death, not only do the same, but have pleasure in them that do them. (Romans 1:28–32)

When their candidate was defeated in the 2016 election, there was an emotional collapse the likes of which had not been previously experienced in the history of presidential elections. The breakdown didn't subside, but ramped up to the point that the bloggers and others on the losing side threw the most malicious, vulgar verbal assaults imaginable at the president-elect and his family. The assaults and insults grew throughout his years in office and continue to the time of this writing.

It was totally irrational and remains so. It is seen as a mental breakdown that has been termed the "Trump Syndrome."

Looking at this irrationality through the prism of God's Word, the conclusion must be that it is a sort of spiritual dissonance brought on by living apart from heaven's design for mankind. The party that won the 2016 presidential election is not more in compliance with God's will for conducting life than the losing political party. All have sinned and come short of the glory of God, as we are told in Scripture. But one party has so departed from God's ways that many have reached the "reprobate" mindset Paul mentioned as recorded in Romans 1:28.

These at the top of their ranks have fallen victim to the "Babel Syndrome," as it might be termed. They want to go back to a one-world configuration, like the people described in Genesis chapter 11. They agree with the globalists-elite that they should build a tower to reach into heaven, thereby usurping God's throne in symbolic fashion. They need no one to rule over them and wish to break the bands asunder of the deity that would reign supreme.

This is how God followed up in answer to that desire manifested by the tower builders on the plain of Shinar:

> He that sitteth in the heavens shall laugh: the Lord shall have them in derision. Then shall he speak unto them in his wrath, and vex them in his sore displeasure.
>
> Yet have I set my king upon my holy hill of Zion. I will declare the decree: the LORD hath said unto me, Thou art my Son; this day have I begotten thee.
>
> Ask of me, and I shall give thee the heathen for thine inheritance, and the uttermost parts of the earth for thy possession. Thou shalt break them with a rod of iron; thou shalt dash them in pieces like a potter's vessel. Be wise now therefore, O ye kings: be instructed, ye judges of the earth.
>
> Serve the LORD with fear, and rejoice with trembling. Kiss the Son, lest he be angry, and ye perish from the way, when his wrath

is kindled but a little. Blessed are all they that put their trust in him. (Psalm 2:4–12)

The global strategists were, they were certain, on the way to the last leg of their race to bring the most powerful, wealthiest nation in human history under their Babel project. They were on the verge of destroying American sovereignty and the nationalist mindset, thus could, with the election of the candidate of their choice, soon bring the nation's mighty assets into use for their world control.

It wasn't exclusively the human minions whose applecart was upset, but, to an even greater degree, the supernatural minions whose plans were disrupted in the 2016 presidential election. And, it has been clear to those with biblically prophetic enlightenment that the chief architect of the end-times Babel project was most enraged of all.

Again, Paul's words of forewarning leap at us from the pages of God's love letter to mankind:

For we wrestle not against flesh and blood, but against principalities, against powers, against the rulers of the darkness of this world, against spiritual wickedness in high places. (Ephesians 6:12)

Since even before the forty-fifth president took the oath of office in January 2017, the rage came in vitriolic hatred never seen, even in the political world. The party opposing the president's was only the proverbial tip of the iceberg. The entire mainstream media—news and entertainment—came against the new administration, and personally against the man who had defeated their candidate whom they had been guaranteed by the "experts" would win.

Lies, distortions, and the vilest accusations came fast and furious. We heard of the Russian collusion, the impeachment over the Ukrainian phone call, and dozens of less front-and-center charges. Again, these continue to this date of writing and show no sign of abating.

Satan and his minions, both human and demonic, are enraged. Psychiatrists report that it is almost impossible for those with normal cognitive function to maintain absolute rage for more than a brief time. This is where the "Trump Syndrome" must come into view. The hatred has not abated in more than four years, but grows stronger, pushed along by news, entertainment, and social media.

It becomes clear that Psalm 2 is at play. God has promised that He will laugh to derision those who wish to break the bands of His will asunder in the matter of His rule.

It is as if the Lord of Heaven did indeed laugh them to derision with the flabbergasting turn of events on election night in November of 2016. God, alone, turned the direction of the nation around—for His own good reasons. We have yet to see what those reasons might be.

One thing for certain, the lawless deniers of God and His Son, the Lord Jesus Christ, are more determined than ever to break those holy bands of control.

The Spirit of Antichrist is at the black heart of this rage to reach with the symbolic tower of power into God's domain. The global platform that will one day serve as a launching pad for the Antichrist is still under construction. The project has not been stopped, only delayed.

We who have written for this book believe that God, too, is still at work. Nothing that happens escapes His omniscience. The lawless God-deniers we wrestle against will yet be brought down from their high places of wickedness.

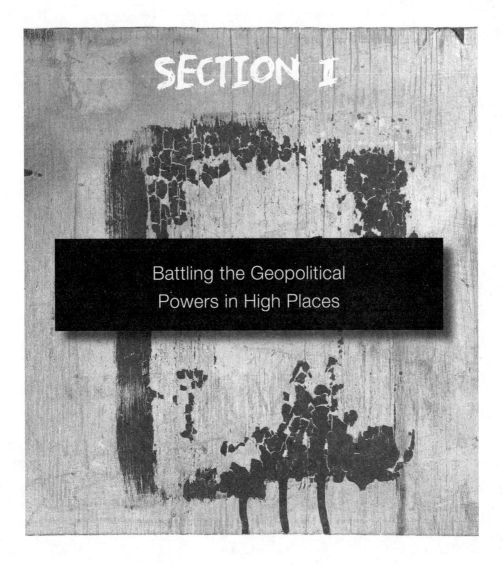

SECTION I

Battling the Geopolitical
Powers in High Places

ONE

Globalists Declare War on Sovereignty

By Jan Markell

When Terry James reached out to me about this book idea, I don't think either he or I knew how the battle would intensify in 2020. I had no idea just how seriously the Antichrist agenda would kick into high gear at this time in history.

Sure, we've all known that we're in a final countdown, but who would have thought the spirit of Antichrist would be in all our faces so boldly? Do these people have no shame? *Don't they want a more subtle agenda?* Apparently not.

In January of 2020, I spoke at a prophecy conference in California and listed ten end-time signals to watch in the new year. My number-one sign was the growing Antichrist spirit around the world. Everywhere I looked, people were demonstrating and rioting. Twenty foreign capitals were in turmoil.

Then came May of 2020, and everywhere, racial issues erupted. But I was at ground zero. Here I am in Minneapolis/St. Paul, Minnesota, and this is where a police officer stepped on the neck of a black man in front of a camera and killed him in a scene that went around the world ten million times. *And an angry spirit of Antichrist was unleashed globally in protest.* I will write more about that as I close this chapter.

So why is the Antichrist spirit so strong right now? I believe a global cabal has tried for five thousand years to install his empire. They began at Babylon. They will culminate their efforts during the Tribulation. The millennia between have been intense with scheming, plotting, planning, and more.

Here's just a brief rundown of the one-world effort to bring about the kingdom of the evilest man ever. He and his minions will have seven ignominious years, then the King of kings will put an end to it.

I was glued to the 2016 election, as that was do or die for the one-worlders. Hillary Clinton was the arch globalist. Just the very title of "Clinton Global Initiative" says it all. *The Clintons and their minions do have a global initiative.*

Donald Trump announced that he was an America-first guy. He was interested in looking out for Pittsburgh, not Paris. He was not going to jump on the one-world bandwagon under any circumstances.

For some reason, God stopped the one-world agenda in its tracks—for a season. Maybe it was rushing forward too fast and furious. So He allowed a real estate guy from Queens, New York, to ascend to the presidency and temporarily slow the rush to one-worldism. It wasn't going to happen under Trump's watch. He so stated.

So here we had a mini-war, it seemed. But that made the campaign all the more interesting. However, I doubt that most who watched it had the insight that this was a battle of the ages as it concerned those who wanted to further globalism. But as far as I was concerned, things were hidden in plain view. *The New World Order in Bible prophecy was about to go into high gear.*

So what organizations and efforts are leading us down the one-world primrose path?

- The deep state
- Some secret societies
- The United Nations and its many offshoots
- The open-borders crowd

- International bankers
- Media
- Any Marxist or socialist group
- Some Christian front groups
- Dozens of George Soros-funded organizations
- Environmental outfits
- Some international health organizations pushing such things as universal vaccinations

Imagine the horror when these groups heard Donald Trump say that he would no longer surrender to the globalists! This is just one reason they have thrown a fit for years, and why they will continue to until he is driven from office and into exile.

Globalism is clearly outlined in the Bible. The most obvious reference is in Revelation 13. Verse 7 says that the Antichrist will have authority *over every tribe, people, tongue, and nation.* But that is in the Tribulation. It cannot take control until the Church is gone and things spin out of control. It requires a man with a plan—a Mr. Fix-It, if you wish. *There are forerunners of such an evil entity, but we must have the real deal: an Antichrist.*

Let me just quickly add here that globalism is often painted as harmless multiculturalism. We are told we must learn of the cultures and customs of other nations and societies. It will make the world a better and safer place. Be careful when you hear such conversation, because there is no good, righteous, or positive angle to the globalist agenda. *Remember, it was tried in Babylon.*

The truth is, the globalist agenda and major players are literally sitting around tables in smoke-filled rooms plotting and scheming. There is no way you can put lipstick on this pig. It is ugly, and the players are dangerous. The fate of the world is at stake. At its heart, it is godless. It is elevating mankind.

Nimrod was the first globalist. He had an evil agenda and God vetoed it in a pretty blunt way. And Nimrod was a type of the final Antichrist. But Nimrod inspired many more who would try! They would all end in some kind of pathetic demise, *but they would inflict huge damage along the way.*

A thorough history lesson of globalist efforts would fill an encyclopedia. One-world concepts were embraced by the Knights Templar, the Masons, the Rosicrucians, and of course, the Illuminati. The early banking empire of the Rothchilds also played a role. Believe it or not, all these outfits wanted to "take over the world." *Did they know it was to take over the world on behalf of the Antichrist? I doubt if we will ever know!*

Advancing to a more modern era, the Rockefeller empire may be the biggest player in the plot. Again, only insiders knew the heart of John D. Rockefeller, whose empire blossomed in the late 1800s. His most prominent son, David Rockefeller, passed away in 2017 at the age of 102. His billions served him well and gave him an exceedingly long life.

David Rockefeller boasted about the family's evil intent. He is known to have said, "Some believe we belong to a secret cabal working against the best interests of the United States characterizing my family as 'internationalists' and of conspiring with others around the world to build a more integrated global political and economic structure—one world, if you will. If that is the charge, I stand guilty and am proud of it."[3]

David Rockefeller is said to have frequently talked about the world marching towards world government. Again, did he know he was preparing the way for an evil world ruler? We will never know.

The push for global government raced ahead in the 1940s, 1950s, 1960s, and beyond. From the United Nations to the Club Bilderberg, from the Club of Rome to the Trilateral Commission, one world was in the mind of the diplomats, kings, rulers, potentates, and politicians. Other names would become prominent players, including Henry Kissinger and George Soros.

And who can forget President George H. W. Bush's appeal for a "new world order" in his State of the Union speech in 1991? Wasn't President Bush a solid, America-first Republican? The World War II veteran was the essence of patriotism—or so we thought. Did he really mean a one-world government when he referred to a "new world order"? I think he did!

Those longing for global government span all political parties. It's not a Democrat-only aspiration, nor is it a Republican-only issue. It's all parties, in all countries. *Perhaps only people with a solid biblical worldview put up resistance and sound an alarm.*

In the 1980s, one man did push back. He was Representative Larry MacDonald, a Democrat congressman from Georgia. He loathed the Rockefellers and the one-world agenda. He was outspoken and determined to damage the globalist efforts.

In 1983, he was on the fateful flight, KAL007, that was shot out of the sky, killing him and 268 other passengers. Was he silenced by evil? We may never know, but his voice of protest was surely put to rest with his body at the bottom of the ocean.

Everyone who thought about speaking out against the one-world agenda should have taken note, and perhaps they did! *There are consequences to doing so.*

In June of 2016, an event came along that few noticed. You had to be an online reader to know of its existence. But if you were and you researched the Gotthard Base Tunnel ceremony in Switzerland and watched it on YouTube, you had to be alarmed! The tunnel connected Italy to France and wound underground through Switzerland.

It was a gigantic globalist celebration and ceremony. It was also satanic. *The two often go together.* Many world leaders gathered and watched an eight-hour ceremony that was so blatantly evil it was stunning. It even had a Baphomet—a goat-man, a notorious satanic symbol—running around and being celebrated.

But the event celebrated the uniting of parts of Europe! It was but a small piece of the globalist puzzle that year. Once it was over, it quickly faded from memory other than by those of us who observe these one-world events and know *they are really celebrating a man who is on the horizon but whose time is not yet.*

In 2017, the globalists launched a young man whom they thought had global appeal and the ability to become a world ruler. They would start with France. Emmanuel Macron may be one of the most appealing and intriguing politicians of modern time.

Europe has been in turmoil for decades. Perhaps this charismatic man, elected as the head of France before he was even forty years old, could be a uniter. He was portrayed on the cover of the *Economist* magazine in 2017 as "Europe's Savior."[4]

Internet rumors spread like nothing I have seen before. Surely he is the anointed one! *Surely he is the Antichrist.* Well, not so fast. Since 2017, his own country of France has faltered under his leadership, but that hasn't stopped the online chatter. He is it! Well, we shall see.

He is young enough to serve in an Antichrist administration, but just what his role might be, we don't yet know. He may totally fade from view as well. But he is making statements that are alarming if you know the globalist agenda.

To have global government, you need to have a pope involved! We don't know the shelf life of Pope Francis. He could step down, be replaced, or pass away while in office, but if he does not, he is, without a doubt, the biggest promoter of one-worldism out there! The media has called him "Pope for a New World."[5] He has boldly called for a one-world government.

At the very least, he is priming the pump and influencing more than one billion Catholics. He is making them comfortable with the concept of global government.

Every cause needs a crisis. For years, the globalists used the "sky-is-falling" crisis of "global warming," then "climate change." If we don't unite as one, we will all fry! *Enough people were scared that millions bought the lie of the globalists concerning a changing environment—all man-made!* World government would fix this, we were told. It sounded reasonable.

As a part of this, in recent years, the leftists introduced the "Green New Deal," which is just an extension of the environmental agenda.

But in January of 2020, the crisis scenario changed! Along came COVID-19. And like climate, it affected every capital of the world, every small town, and every province. No location was spared. Was this crisis invented by the globalists? We will never know, but what we do know is that *they took advantage of it!* If a bunch of diplomats could promise us that we would not get sick, maybe we should just accept their offer. However, it included a one-world system of government to oversee a global medical system along with vaccinations.

Prominent globalists such as Bill Gates made headlines. He is determined to vaccinate the world. *It would be convenient to have a one-world system to do that!*

The COVID-19 pandemic was blown up to be the crisis of all crises—*a true scenario that could bring about the end of civilization as we know it.* Yet only about seven or eight out of one hundred thousand people were affected by COVID-19, and most are elderly. Who didn't want to spare their parents or grandparents from this dreaded disease? *People adapted the mentality of being willing to do anything to escape it!*

They shuttered businesses, put careers on hold, ended educational pursuits, and boarded up our beloved churches just so we could save the world from COVID-19! Many said the only solution to stopping the damage was world government.

So now we had two crises: Environmental and a pandemic. *The globalists had to be riding high and ecstatic.* People were scared, and when people are scared, they are herded into situations they often regret.

The second obstacle to globalism is Christianity! Christians stand in the way of the globalist agenda. They don't know what to do with us, so they persecute us, marginalize us, denigrate us, pass laws to limit our freedoms, and *stir up the world to see us as the root of all problems.* Eventually, we will disappear in what is known as the Rapture of the Church, and this will make their day! But until that time, they are limited in what they can do to us.

Here are some ways the globalists are trying to implement their demonic plan. If you see any of these schemes, be aware that there is an agenda behind them, and it's a pretty evil agenda:

- Socialized medicine
- Gun control
- Big government
- High taxes
- Population reduction
- Immigration/cheap labor/open borders
- Affordable housing for all
- Environmentalism
- Increased debt
- Increased poverty
- Class warfare
- Removal of real religion
- Destruction of the family

Globalism is driven by the spirit of Antichrist, as I stated in my opening in May of 2020, regarding the spirit enveloped by hometown, Minneapolis, and its neighboring city, St. Paul, Minnesota. We were "ground zero" in the racial rioting brought on by the death of George Lloyd, killed by a Minneapolis policeman. I had an up-close and personal look at mankind at its worst.

The behavior of that single policeman was abysmal, but so were the actions of thousands of "protestors"—also and more appropriately called demonstrators and domestic terrorists. The suburbs of the Twin Cities were pretty much spared.

One thousand properties, along with apartments above these businesses and some homes, were vandalized, looted, burned, or totally destroyed.

Our media showed business owners staring in stunned disbelief as many were reeling from coronavirus destruction, but now they faced the result of rampant anarchy. The media added insult to injury by calling the destruction the result of "peaceful protests."

How peaceful was it to spray a wheelchair-bound woman with a fire extinguisher?

So the Twin Cities now look like Somalia. Someone called us "Mogadishu on the Mississippi River." Maybe not so funny, but pretty accurate.

Mile after mile of landscape has been changed in the Twin Cities that will take years—perhaps a decade or more—to reconstruct. The rent-a-mob business is alive and well, very organized, and brutal (*and lawless— but nothing like the lawlessness that is to come during the Tribulation.*)

Though I am many miles from ground zero, I saw enough film of the rioting that I had the opportunity to look at the faces of the lawless. I could sense their heartlessness and brutality.

> And because lawlessness will be increased, the love of many will grow cold. (Matthew 24:12)

One of the names of the Antichrist is the "lawless one." The term was coined by Paul in 2 Thessalonians 2, where he warns the Church of the soon arrival of this man who would come on the scene and deceive the masses in the latter days during the Tribulation.

The Antichrist won't have to rent-a-mob. When he reigns, much of the world will be lawless, godless, tumultuous, and confused. *Antifa will be the normal!* The burned and looted sections of my hometown will be the gold standard around the world.

With the restrainer gone, there will be absolutely nothing to hold back the evil, selfishness, and out-of-control behavior! The world can and will go crazy. *They will glory in utter chaos.* What we have now is a trial run that is a weak firecracker in comparison. *Multiply it by ten or a hundred or a thousand!*

The good news is that God will consume the Antichrist and his minions at the end of the Tribulation with the brightness of His coming!

But in the meantime, lawlessness will escalate and the globalists won't give up their dream of a united world. They will continue to push for no borders and unlimited immigration even though that has nearly destroyed Europe.

But here is the real reason their scheme won't work before the Tribulation. It is being orchestrated by godless people with corrupt hearts who promise all sorts of things they cannot deliver. *And God hates the idea!*

He has a one-world plan that will work. *It's called the millennium!* Psalm 2 actually says that God holds these people in derision. He laughs at their schemes. He will allow them seven years in the Tribulation to practice global government. *It will be a colossal flop.*

It will be such a disaster that the Bible says if Jesus Christ didn't return in His Second Coming, no flesh would be saved due to the destruction of the one-world effort.

So hang on, for world government is coming! Jesus Christ will be in charge of it, ruling from Jerusalem. It will be perfect. Even members of the animal kingdom will be at peace with one another. But its time is not yet.

And He shall reign for ever and ever!

TWO

America Holding Up Satan's One-World Project

By Daymond Duck

The purpose of this chapter is to discuss the globalist (in my opinion, the Council on Foreign Relations [CFR], people like Bill Gates, Henry Kissinger, George Soros, former President George H. W. Bush, former President Bill Clinton, former President Barack Obama, the Bilderberg Group, the Illuminati, the World Bank, the International Monetary Fund [IMF], heads of global corporations, and more) effort to weaken the US in order to bring in the New World Order (NWO). But let us be clear. It is the restrainer (widely believed to be the Church and the Holy Spirit), not the US, that is holding back the NWO (2 Thessalonians 2:6–12).

This is not to say that the US doesn't deserve to be weakened, because sixty-five million abortions, acceptance of the lesbian, gay, bisexual, transgender, and queer (LGBTQ) agenda, the proliferation of alcohol and drugs, the falling away in the Church with false teaching, lukewarm worship, lack of prayer, lack of repentance, and lack of revival all say the US deserves all the judgment God decides to dish out.

Neither is this to say that the NWO won't come into being, because the Bible clearly states that one is coming. The prophet Daniel said:

> The fourth beast (the kingdom of the Antichrist) shall be the fourth
> kingdom upon earth, which shall be diverse from all kingdoms,

25

and shall devour the whole earth, and shall tread it down, and break
it in pieces. (Daniel 7:23)

The apostle John said:

And it was given unto him [the Antichrist] to make war with the
saints, and to overcome them: and power was given him over all
kindreds, and tongues, and nations. (Revelation 13:7)

Further, this is not to say that the US isn't in danger, because it is. Jesus
said:

Every kingdom divided against itself is brought to desolation; and
every city or house divided against itself shall not stand. (Matthew
12:25)

The US has never been more divided than it is now, and it will eventually fall.

However, this *is* to say that God, not the globalists, is in control. God
will allow the globalists to plot and scheme. He will allow the NWO to
shape up. He will allow the world situation to become more threatening
and perilous. He may even allow the US to fall, but He will not allow the
NWO to come into being if His Church is still on this earth.

As far as the globalists are concerned, most are unbelievers who ignore
what the Bible says. Very few understand or believe that Satan is the god
of this world. They don't believe they are blindly following the wicked
one. So, they will use their wealth, influence, and time to keep striving
until God allows them to establish a world government.

That will happen after the Church is raptured. Immediately after all
Christians are caught up, everyone on earth will be lost. That includes
every politician, pastor, Sunday school teacher, journalist, etc. It will be a
time of great deception. There will be no one to restrain the NWO. Satan's
man (the Antichrist) will quickly be given the reins to world domination.

But even then, we must remember that the NWO will only exist with God's permission. He is in control and planet earth is destined to be under Messiah's rule, not Satan's rule. The Lord Jesus will decimate the NWO during the Tribulation period (seven years of hell on earth). Jesus will come back to this earth as King of kings and Lord of lords. He will locate His throne in Jerusalem and rule the planet with a rod of iron.

The End from the Beginning

Those who want to determine if the Bible is being fulfilled must know and believe what the Bible says. Paul said, "Known unto God are all his works from the beginning of the world" (Acts 15:18). God has always known what will happen before it happens.

It has already been noted that a wicked one called the Antichrist will gain power over everyone on earth at the end of the age, but there is more. There are almost two hundred nations on earth that must be merged into ten regions or groups of nations before the Antichrist appears. The leaders of these groups of nations are called the ten kings, ten horns, ten toes, etc. (see Daniel 2:41–42, 7:8, 23–25; Revelation 17:12).

The existence of Israel is required (Daniel 9:24–27; Matthew 24:32–34; Hosea 9:10). The world must be against Jesus (anti-Christ). There must be efforts to draft a peace treaty involving many groups. There must be a way to track and control everyone, including the media (Revelation 13:16–18). All opposition must be removed, including the opposition of the US.

The task before us is to determine if the world is moving toward this end-of-the-age scenario. Is there an effort to establish a world government? Is there an effort to change the world's structure from almost two hundred nations to ten groups of nations? Does Israel exist? Is there an effort to come up with a peace treaty in the Middle East? Is there an effort to weaken the US and Israel? If the answer to these questions is yes, Bible prophecy is moving toward Satan's one-world goal.

Beginning of World Government

The biblical link between world government and Satan goes back to Nimrod and the tower of Babel. Nimrod was a great-grandson of Noah. He became a great leader, founded several cities in the land of Shinar, and ruled over the whole area (Genesis 10:1–10).

He was a hunter of men's souls, and tried to keep everyone together by establishing a world government. He commanded his followers to build a tower to heaven to enhance his reputation. Archaeology shows that his tower was one of many ziggurats (ancient places of religious rebellion against God).

God came down to see what Nimrod and his followers were doing, and He wasn't happy. He decided to restrain their depravity by confounding their language and scattering them upon the face of the earth. Their confused languages are the reason the structure is called the tower of "Babel" (Genesis 11:1–9).

League of Nations

The effort to establish a world government didn't end with Nimrod, because it wasn't of this world. It was of Satan. That's why it failed at the tower of Babel, and why it failed throughout history. Satan seduces wicked people to deny the clear teaching of the Bible. He encourages unbelieving leaders to establish a world government without the God of the Bible. But the Almighty will never accept a permanent anti-God, anti-Christ world government. Every effort to do that will ultimately fail.

On January 10, 1920, Satan's desire to establish a godless world government took a major step forward with the founding of the League of Nations. World War I had just ended, and many world leaders wanted a way to prevent war and maintain peace. They decided to create a group of nations to settle disputes, disarm nations, and enforce peace. By 1934, fifty-eight nations had joined, but they could not prevent World War II. Their final meeting took place when they disbanded on April 18, 1946.

The United Nations

The League of Nations failed, but Satan's dream of a world government under his influence and the globalist dream of world peace continued. Satan replaced the League of Nations with the United Nations (UN). In 1945, fifty nations sent representatives to San Francisco to draft a document calling for the development of a one-world government in phases or stages. The UN plans to accomplish this by establishing administrative regions (regionalization), with a leader administering each region. The UN Charter was signed on June 26, 1945, and went into effect on October 24, 1945. The UN has now grown to include more than 190 nations.

The US played a major role in founding, financing, and developing the UN. But there was a big problem: Many influential people in America didn't hold to the principles the nation was founded upon. America was drifting away from God and creeping toward godless humanism, materialism, and increased immorality. And the more the nation drifted away from God, the closer she came to accepting Satan's desire for an anti-God, anti-Christ world government.

America had a God-given Constitution and Bill of Rights to protect the rights and freedoms of her citizens, but Satan began to use politicians and others to attack and try to remove these rights and freedoms. They worked to disarm citizens, abandon the country's Judeo-Christian roots, alter the courts, elect humanists to assume powers not given to them in America's founding documents, and strengthen the UN.

Globalists vehemently denied that they were working against America's citizens and trying to develop the NWO, but they were. The world-famous United Kingdom leader Winston Churchill admitted it when he said, "The purpose of the New World Order is to bring the world into a world government." It is easy to understand that Mr. Churchill was saying that the NWO and world government are one and the same.

In 1990, President George H. W. Bush (Bush senior) said, "Out of these troubled times [out of the Persian Gulf War], our fifth objective, a new world order, can emerge." Mr. Bush's stunning statement was an admission that the NWO is an American objective.

What he said is incredible and undeniable! Since the days of Daniel and John the Revelator, the Bible has revealed that a world government is coming—and the UN Charter, Winston Churchill, and George H. W. Bush confirmed that people are trying to bring it about.

Critics exposed what the globalists were doing, but the globalists denied it. They called the critics conspiracy theorists, inferred that they were misunderstanding the issues and making things up, and accused them of trying to scare America's citizens, etc. They used false accusations, dishonest reporting, and twisted definitions of words. They said the NWO does not mean world government, global governance does not mean global government, and things like that to deceive the public and disguise what they were doing. If they were honest about it, they would admit that the goal is to transform the NWO into a world government and transform global governance into world government. These things are one and the same, because the result of the NWO and global governance is world government.

The EU

In 1944, one year before the UN came into existence, three nations in western Europe (Belgium, Netherlands, and Luxembourg) started working toward an economic union. They called themselves the Benelux nations, and their agreement to become an economic union went into force in 1948.

More nations were added until the group had twenty-eight members (the United Kingdom formally left the group on January 1, 2020, but is still in the process of working out the terms of departure, etc., for the "Brexit"). The group started calling itself the European Union (EU) and it created an EU parliament, an EU commission, EU courts, EU currency (euro), a common market, and more.

The EU denied that it was trying to create a world government and claimed that its individual member nations were retaining a degree of sovereignty that wouldn't exist in a world government—but it continued to strengthen the central government and weaken the individual nations.

I believe the Antichrist will come out of a reunited Europe and that group of nations is a modern reality (Daniel 9:24–27). This isn't a coincidence. God is the only One who could restructure the nations to fit the prophesied description.

But regardless of what the deniers say, notice three things: 1) The UN was birthed in 1945 with a desire to create a NWO; 2) The UN retained the desire of the League of Nations to prevent war and establish peace; and 3) The Benelux nations united in 1948 and morphed into a reunited Europe called the EU.

Club of Rome (Beginning of the Ten Kings)

In 1974, the Club of Rome suggested that the world be divided into ten regions called mega-territories or kingdoms:

- North America
- Western Europe
- Japan
- Israel, South Africa, and Australia
- Eastern Europe (Russia and allies)
- Latin America
- North Africa and the Middle East
- Main Africa
- South and Southeast Asia
- Central Asia, including China

The Club of Rome suggested a three-step plan to usher in a world government.

- **Step 1:** Divide the world into ten regions or trading blocs of nations called a financial NWO.
- **Step 2:** Transform the ten regions or trading blocs of nations into ten political blocs called a political NWO.
- **Step 3:** Merge the ten political blocs into a one-world government.

There will be changes, but it is important to know that the concept of ten kings or ten leaders was established. Why didn't the Club of Rome suggest five groups of nations? Why not fifteen or twenty groups of nations? The answer must be that God knows what will happen before it happens, and He said there will be ten groups of nations with a leader over each one for ten leaders, ten kings, ten horns, etc. This Club of Rome suggestion was another major step in the direction of Satan's one-world project.

The European Model

The existence of the EU is extremely significant, but it became even more so when the UN established the EU as the political pattern (or model) for the other nine regional trading groups to follow. There are economic benefits to structuring all ten regional trading groups the same way politically, but the main reason is that it will make it easier to merge the regional trading groups into a one-world government.

It is also meant to take the power out of the hands of the voters and into the hands of unelected bureaucrats (appointed by people who support the NWO). It removes the accountability of the bureaucrats and reduces the ability of the people to prevent the development of Satan's one-world project.

Having said this, notice that the globalists' plans match the prophesied sequence of events in the Bible. The globalists want to create ten regional groups and merge them into one. The Bible predicts that ten kings will rise, then someone (the Antichrist, number eleven) will be given power over them.

The Deep State

President George H. W. Bush's 1990 stunning admission that the NWO is an American objective made it difficult for the US globalists to deny what they were doing. Years of calling their critics conspiracy theorists and accusing them of misunderstanding what they were doing no longer works. The concealment has mostly stopped, and former Secretary of State Henry Kissinger, former President Bill Clinton, and former President Barack Obama have confirmed efforts to establish the NWO. No less than Bill Gates, the Microsoft tycoon and one of the richest men in the world, is spending millions to bring it in.

Prior to the 1990s, it wasn't unusual to come across books or articles about a "shadow government." Writers promoted the idea that unknown people and entities (former politicians, the military-industrial complex, heads of large corporations, government agencies, State Department officials, Department of Justice [DOJ] officials, Federal Bureau of Investigation [FBI] officials, and others) were influencing US elections and exercising a degree of control over America's elected officials, the appointment of judges, and more.

About 1990, the "deep state," a phrase that was being used in other nations, especially the Middle East, caught on in the US. Sadly, in some of the foreign nations, the phrase was synonymous with hidden corruption. In the US, it referred to hidden corruption in the political system.

Could this be true? Could unknown individuals be trying to secretly decide who will head up the Republican Party, who will lead the Democrat Party, who will get elected, who will sit on the US Supreme Court, and who will head the State Department? It's hard to believe that the DOJ, the FBI, and others could be corrupted, yet there seems to be undeniable evidence that some tried to prevent the election of Donald Trump, and when they failed, they tried to remove him from office.

For example, in December 2019, when US Justice Department Inspector General Michael Horowitz answered questions before Congress about his investigation of the FBI, he said he found seventeen fundamental and serious errors or omissions in FISA (Foreign Intelligence Surveillance Applications) that could only be described as intentional animus or political bias. Senator Lindsey Graham charged that people at the highest levels of the US government took the law into their own hands, and there was evidence that an FBI agent and a lawyer (Peter Strzok and Lisa Page) discussed efforts to spy on and topple the Trump administration (they called it an "insurance policy;" meaning if Hillary Clinton didn't win, there was a backup plan to overthrow President Trump).

There was also evidence that the former acting FBI director, Andrew McCabe, "lacked candor" several times during the investigation and during the Hillary Clinton email and Clinton Foundation investigations. These findings resulted in Mr. McCabe being fired less than two days before he was scheduled to retire.

It was discovered that a former FBI lawyer, Kevin Clinesmith, may have doctored evidence when he applied for a warrant to spy on President Trump. This caused the presiding judge of the Foreign Intelligence Surveillance Court (FISC) to order the FBI to identify and investigate Mr. Clinesmith's activities. It is sad, but more than one innocent person may have been prosecuted and jailed for crimes they did not commit.

In fact, FISA court Judge James Boasberg later ruled that at least two of the four FISA applications against President Trump's foreign policy advisor, Carter Page, were illegally authorized. A US citizen cannot be legally spied on without probable cause, but Mr. Page was spied on without probable cause.

Then, in May 2019, Attorney General William Barr announced that he had given US Attorney John H. Durham broad powers to investigate the origins of the surveillance of the Trump campaign. About five months later, it was announced that this investigation had turned into a criminal probe that could reach high officials in the Obama administration. It is too early to tell how this investigation will come out.

These FBI and DOJ violations are serious—and even more serious is the realization that the deep state really exists and corrupt officials have been knowingly or unknowingly carrying out a plan that will lead to the establishment of Satan's one-world government. Their idea that America is a problem that needs to be dealt with has implications for the Rapture, the arrival of the Antichrist, the persecution of multitudes, the battle of Armageddon, and more. It's incredible to watch current events bringing about Bible prophecies that were recorded many generations before.

Sustainable Development 2030

On September 25, 2015, the UN produced a document called "Transforming our World: The 2030 Agenda for Sustainable Development." The preamble of the document calls it a "New Universal Agenda." Its scope includes the universe, not just the world, even stating that "all countries and stakeholders, acting in a collaborative partnership, will [not 'may']) implement this plan."

Delegates from 193 nations quickly approved the document that some say will establish a world government, a world religion, and a world economic system by 2030. One official said not a single human being will be allowed to escape this next great leap forward. UN Secretary-General Ban Ki-moon called it the "start of a new era." He said the world is about to realize the "dream of a world peace and dignity for all." The Bible says, "When they say peace and safety, then sudden destruction cometh upon them" (1 Thessalonians 5:3).

On September 28, 2015, President Obama addressed the UN and said, "global integration [the merging of nations into ten regions] is an agenda that transcends the narrowly defined interests of nation states." He was saying merging nations into regional groups such as Canada, the US, and Mexico (the USMCA, one of the ten regions) is more important than national sovereignty.

The document went into effect on January 1, 2016. On March 10, 2016, it was reported that the UN had released a master plan called, "Post-2015 Sustainable Development Goals." According to the report, world leaders are now required to promote:

- Wealth redistribution
- Government control of all production
- A reduction in the consumption of goods and services
- The consumption of less meat and frozen or convenience foods
- The use of fewer and smaller vehicles and appliances
- The use of less air-conditioning at home and at work
- The use of smaller houses and apartments
- Government control of education systems
- Government promotion of a new set of attitudes, values, and beliefs
- Universal healthcare and mental-health services
- Sexual and reproductive services

Understand that this is not what the UN wants to accomplish in the next fifty to seventy-five years. This is what it wants to achieve by 2030. But if the UN is going to meet this goal, it must deal with the opposition. This explains the effort to weaken America, Israel, and Christianity and deal with President Donald Trump and Prime Minister Benjamin Netanyahu. Globalists see these things as an impediment to their 2030 goal. They believe something must be done or they won't meet their objective.

Wealth Redistribution

One reason the Sustainable Development 2030 goals are so popular at the UN is because the nations want to share in America's wealth. They don't want the Christians' God, the Christians' Savior, or the Christians' Bible, but they want the Christians' blessings. They refuse to bless Israel so God will bless them. They want global taxes to take money from the so-called fortunate nations and give it to the so-called unfortunate ones. They want treaties that will transfer control of America's wealth to the UN. They want trade agreements that will cause an unfair balance of trade and redistribute wealth.

President Trump came on the scene promising to put an end to unfair agreements. He even started withdrawing from some of the UN groups

(Paris Agreement) and slapping tariffs on nations (China, Japan, the EU, etc.) to even the playing field. When he presented his budget for fiscal year 2019, he proposed:

- Cutting the budget for international affairs from almost $60 billion to about $42 billion
- Cutting the WHO by 50 percent
- Giving nothing to the Green Climate Fund (global warming)
- Giving nothing to UNICEF
- Withdrawing from the Global Compact on Migration
- Withdrawing from UNESCO (United Nations Educational, Scientific, and Cultural Organization), etc.

World leaders do not want this. They oppose a level playing field. This is partly why they view President Trump as a problem. They would like to get him out of the way and go forward with their cherished NWO by 2030. They're like the Antichrist, who will divide the Promised Land for gain (Daniel 11:39).

Tracking Progress Toward a World Government

On March 14, 2016, it was reported that a United Nations Statistical Commission had been created to develop a system for collecting data from every nation on earth. The purpose of this system is to monitor the progress all of the nations are making toward establishing a world government by 2030. The UN wants to know which nations are on schedule and which ones are lagging so they can intervene if needed.

Silencing the Opposition

On May 20, 2016, it was reported that the UN has a Counter-Terrorism Committee that has been tasked with developing a plan to censor opposition on the Internet and to counter online propaganda (censor what is posted on the Internet and develop propaganda to refute the opposition). This UN-led crackdown on what "terrorists" are posting on the Internet was approved by the UN Security Council without a definition of what is meant by "terrorists." At one time, President Obama's list of potential domestic terrorists included conservative Christians, veterans, opponents of immigration, opponents of same-sex marriage, and criticism of Islam.

This is totalitarianism, and it is the kind of one-world government that the Antichrist will run.

Gun Control

On June 6–10, 2016, a UN committee met to discuss ways to get small arms out of the hands of people. The report openly admitted that the US desire to disarm America's citizens must be speeded up or the world will not be successful in meeting its 2030 Sustainable Development Goals.

Removing weapons from America's citizens is unconstitutional. It could lead to another civil war. Yet, when Beto O'Rourke was asked about it during the September 2019 Democrat Party debates, he replied, "Hell, yes, we're going to take your AR-15, your AK-47!"

In December 2019, it was reported that Governor Ralph Northam of Virginia increased his state's corrections budget for 2020 by $250,000 in anticipation of having to jail and feed gun owners. Think about it! This Democrat governor wants the taxpayers to pay for his illegal (unconstitutional) confiscation of guns.

It was also reported that some county sheriffs were deputizing entire communities of people to prevent their guns from being confiscated, and Governor Northam threatened to cut off the electricity of anyone who refused to turn in their guns. Many citizens have the idea that gun-control laws are used to disarm the honest citizens, not the dishonest ones.

The US Constitution, gun lobbies, veterans who fought for the US, and leaders like President Trump are a nightmare for world-government advocates. An armed America is making it difficult for the UN to meet its 2030 goal. This struggle will become more intense and will lead to the persecution of unarmed citizens in the future.

Merchants of the Earth

On June 13, 2016, the most powerful business leaders in the world gathered at a UN meeting called "Commitment to Agenda 2030, Partnership for Innovation and Social Responsibility." These leaders were asked to sign a UN letter that commits their companies to meet the 2030 Sustainable Development Goals (world government by 2030).

They were told that their cooperation is crucial to meeting the UN goals. They were asked to cooperate with the UN Monitoring and Reporting procedures that will measure progress toward meeting the UN goals. A UN official thanked the leaders for signing the document.

Perhaps it would be good to recall a verse of Scripture:

> For all nations have drunk of the wine of the wrath of her fornication [Babylon the great], and the kings of the earth have committed fornication with her, and the merchants of the earth are waxed rich through the abundance of her delicacies. (Revelation 18:3)

The merchants of the earth have become obsessed with world government, erasing national borders, global trade, etc. It is making global corporations incredibly rich.

Erasing National Borders

Other than God and the true Church, President Trump may be the greatest obstacle to world government the globalists have ever encountered, and very little, if anything, has distressed them more than his campaign promise to build 450 miles of wall on the US-Mexico border by 2021. World-government advocates view everyone on earth as a "common humanity" (citizens of the world, not citizens of a nation). Their ultimate idea of world government is a world without borders.

On May 6, 2016, US Secretary of State John Kerry delivered the commencement address at Northeastern University. He criticized the need for walls on America's borders. He ridiculed the importance of nations having borders. He told the graduates, "You are about to graduate into a complex and borderless world."

Notice that Mr. Kerry did not say "borderless America," he said "borderless world." This is a very interesting statement, because the UN has voted to create a world government by 2030. If these graduates are going to live in a borderless world, that makes this generation the terminal generation. That would put the Rapture in this generation.

But there is more, and it's very serious. Those who need to prepare for a borderless world will experience:

- A world religion
- A world economic system
- The four horsemen of the apocalypse
- The mark of the beast
- The battle of Armageddon
- The Second Coming of Jesus

Anyway, President Trump's desire to "build the wall" is just the opposite of the UN goal to erase America's borders and merge cultures. Some globalists have become so hysterical that they've laughed at President Trump; called him a joke, a clown, and unlearned; accused him of violating human rights; fought him in US courts dozens of times; accused him of violating international law; accused him of putting children in cages; and more. A poll in December 2019 determined that he is the most dangerous leader in the world (more dangerous than North Korea's Kim Jong-un, Iran's Ayatollah Khomeini, Russia's President Vladimir Putin, and China's President Xi Jinping). Many globalists are running scared and think they must "dump Trump" and weaken the US.

This is a spiritual war that few people understand. God will allow Satan's world government to exist for seven years. But the Almighty will use the Tribulation period to bring an end to human government (the reign of the Antichrist) and establish the rule of the King of kings and Lord of lords.

Israel

Not much will be said about Israel here because other chapters in this book address some of the facts and issues. But no chapter about world government would be complete without at least mentioning Israel.

Israel is important because several prophecies require its existence. The Antichrist cannot rise to power until he confirms a covenant with Israel (Daniel 9:24–27). The Antichrist will sit in the temple and say that he is God, but he cannot do that until Israel rebuilds it (2 Thessalonians 2:3). The Antichrist will stop the animal sacrifices at the temple at the middle of the Tribulation period, but again, he cannot do that until Israel rebuilds the structure (Daniel 9:27). Jesus told the Jews in Judea to flee into the wilderness when the Antichrist defiles the temple, but they can't do that unless there are Jews in Judea at the middle of the Tribulation.

The significance of the existence of Israel and the ongoing efforts to draft an acceptable peace treaty and rebuild the temple must not be overlooked. But once again, the powers that be in high places blame the US and President Trump for holding things back. The globalists want to force a peace treaty on Israel that gives East Jerusalem (the location of the Temple Mount), Judea, and Samaria to the Palestinians for a Palestinian state void of Jews. The globalists blame President Trump for interfering with their plans by moving the American embassy to Jerusalem and declaring that it's legal for Jews to live in Judea and Samaria. These major events signify the approach of Satan's one-world government.

Candidate Trump

On June 15, 2015, Donald J. Trump stepped out of the elevator at Trump Tower and announced his intent to seek the Republican nomination for president of the United States. He already had great name recognition, contacts in the Tea Party movement, and a reputation for being a conservative, pro-life, and anti-gun control. He was wealthy and promised to fund his own campaign. He spoke against illegal immigration and promised to build a wall on the US-Mexico border. He spoke out against sending American jobs overseas and against Islamic terrorism. He said his campaign slogan would be "Make America Great Again."

Candidate Trump was an immediate success with US voters. There were long lines at his campaign rallies. Some fans stood in line all night to get in. Excited followers chanted: "USA, USA," "Lock her up, lock her up," "Drain the swamp, drain the swamp," and "Build that wall, build that wall." His popularity surged in the polls.

Some establishment Republicans were skeptical, some establishment Democrats were nasty, many in the major media hated Trump, and the globalists were in a panic. YouTube blocked hundreds of Trump's ads. Google, Twitter, and Facebook used their platforms to secretly help Hillary. Several groups quickly formed "Dump Trump" movements.

In spite of this strong opposition, candidate Trump clinched the nomination in May 2016, selected Indiana Governor Mike Pence to be his running mate in July 2016, became the official Republican Party candidate on July 19, 2016, and won the election on November 8, 2016. Less than twenty minutes after he was sworn in, it was reported that the impeachment of President Trump had started.

But that is debatable. In response to a question by Chris Hayes of MSNBC, Representative Al Green (D-TX) said, "Well, the genesis of impeachment, to be very candid with you, was when the president was running for office." It seems clear that the decision to impeach Mr. Trump was made before he was elected, and the actual process started less than twenty minutes after he was sworn in.

A Straying Nation

On June 22, 2016, Donald Trump delivered a supposedly major speech. He said, "Our country lost its way when we stopped putting the American people really first." This is one of just a few things that this writer disagrees with President Trump on. America did not lose its way when its leaders stopped putting the American people first. America lost its way when America's leaders stopped putting God first.

Then, Trump said, "We got here because we switched from a policy of Americanism—focusing on what's good for America's middle class—to a policy of globalism, focusing on how to make money for large corporations who can move their wealth and workers to foreign countries all to the detriment of the American worker and the American economy." He added, "America has switched from a policy of Americanism to a policy of globalism [world government]."

If there was a globalist on the face of this earth at this time who did not believe that President Trump is holding back world government, this should have resolved all doubt. But let us be clear: The president could not hold back world government unless it is God's will.

President Donald Trump

President Trump's victory was no less than a miracle. The fact that someone who had never been in politics could defeat established candidates such as Jeb Bush, Mitt Romney, and Hillary Clinton seemed impossible. The odds are unimaginable. But God is in control. The Almighty raises up leaders and brings them down, and He just was not ready for a one-world government. The NWO is coming, but not until God is ready for it to happen.

Candidate Trump's opponent, Hillary Clinton, was stunned, and soon started claiming that the election had been stolen. Investigations would later show that her campaign paid for an investigation of candidate Trump, and some associated with the intelligence community (DOJ, FBI, etc.) had been paid to dig up dirt on Mr. Trump since the summer of 2016. Corrupt leaders were trying to install a corrupt government.

This is hard to imagine. But on May 9, 2017, President Trump fired FBI Director James Comey. Although it is disputed, the main reason appears to be the favorable treatment Director Comey gave Hillary Clinton during her email controversy. Many believe there was ample evidence to prosecute Mrs. Clinton, but Director Comey let her off the hook. He loved to present himself as an outstanding man with unusually high morals and ethical values, but shortly after his firing, he admitted that he had asked a friend to leak derogatory information about President Trump to the press.

MAGA

President Trump's campaign slogan, "Make America Great Again" ("MAGA") was a rejection of world government. Globalists want to weaken America, not make it "great" again. They want America to surrender its sovereignty to the UN, not cling to or restore its sovereignty.

On July 21, 2016, when Donald Trump formally accepted the Republican nomination for president, he promised "Americanism not globalism." He often said, "We [US citizens] worship God, not government."

As president, he began to take steps to retain America's sovereignty. On September 24, 2019, he addressed the UN General Assembly, urging the nations to reject globalism and put their people first. He encouraged the nations in the Middle East to normalize diplomatic relations with Israel. He criticized attempts of the UN to make abortions a taxpayer-funded human right. He said UN globalists have no business attacking the sovereignty of nations that wish to protect innocent life. These statements were the opposite of what the globalists wanted to hear, and they are desperate to get him out of office.

Impeach 45

Following the firing of FBI Director James Comey on May 9, 2017, former FBI Director Robert S. Mueller III was appointed to be a special investigator to look into the allegations that candidate Trump had colluded with the Russians to influence the 2016 election. He assembled a "dream team" of highly educated, very expensive prosecuting attorneys, most of whom had connections to the Democrat Party and used many millions of taxpayer dollars to investigate the president and some of his people. To make a long story short, some of Trump's people were prosecuted, but millions of evangelical Christians believed God had put him in office, they were praying for him, and the Mueller investigation was a big disappointment to the Democrats and the globalists who supported them.

Nevertheless, on December 18, 2019, the US House of Representatives rushed through a vote to impeach President Trump (the forty-fifth president of the US) on a party-line vote even though millions of voters believed he had done nothing wrong, the US economy was very strong, his job-approval ratings were very high, more citizens were against impeachment than were for it, and his impeachment apparently had no chance of passing in the Senate. The charges were "abuse of power" and "obstruction of Congress," even though the plot to impeach him began before he took office. It seems clear that the real reason for this disgraceful vote was his record of opposing Satan's plan to establish a one-world government.

After claiming that President Trump is so dangerous that there was a great need to remove him from office immediately, Nancy Pelosi hung onto the articles of impeachment for thirty-three days before sending them to the US Senate on January 15, 2020. Trump's impeachment trial started six days later, on January 21, 2020. Even though members of the House of Representatives claimed to have "powerful and overwhelming" evidence of the president's guilt, and even though they had already voted to impeach him, they complained that the trial was unfair and the key evidence they needed to prove their "powerful and overwhelming" case was being covered up. This struck many voters as nonsense.

House Intelligence Committee Chairman Adam Schiff argued that President Trump is guilty even if he is found innocent because the House was being hindered from getting the additional evidence they need. Nancy Pelosi argued that even if the president was acquitted, his impeachment was forever. Many Trump supporters wondered why the House impeached Trump, if they didn't have the evidence they needed. Partisanship, deceit, and false accusations flowed in abundance. Schiff was caught lying more than once. Many voters were appalled and disgusted with the lack of character and blatant public dishonesty.

On January 31, 2020, after ten days of unprecedented disgusting and irresponsible behavior, the Senate Republicans decided they had heard enough. They voted against calling new witnesses. Their vote set the stage for an end to the Senate impeachment hearings and the eventual acquittal of President Trump. That vote was taken on February 5, 2020, and the president was acquitted on both charges (abuse of power and obstruction of Congress). This means that he was not convicted, he cannot be removed from office at this time, and he can run for president again in the next election.

Following the January 31, 2020, vote, Nancy Pelosi was visibly shaken. She had already suggested that Trump's lawyers should be disbarred. She quickly announced that the Democrats would not accept the verdict because they were not allowed to call new witnesses. Several Democrats went on TV and called Trump an illegitimate president.

Five days later, Nancy Pelosi tore up her copy of President Trump's State of the Union address when he finished. Following much criticism, she said she did so because it was not true. Two days later, Judge Andrew Napolitano said Democrats are already talking about a second attempt at impeachment, and there is no double-jeopardy protection for impeachment.

There were other globalist efforts to get rid of President Trump. In March 2019, multibillionaire Michael Bloomberg officially began his campaign to win the Democrat nomination for president and bring down President Trump. He dropped out of the race on March 4, 2020, after spending more than $500 million of his own money on his campaign. He said, "Today, I am leaving the race for the same reason: to defeat Donald Trump—because it is clear to me that staying in would make achieving that goal more difficult."

While Bloomberg was doing this, there were rumors that multibillionaire and one of the world's most powerful globalists, George Soros, was planning to funnel millions of dollars into the effort to help Democrats take back the Senate in 2020 to facilitate another attempt at impeachment. Multiple reports said Soros used his MoveOn.org group in 2000 to give more than $100,000 to Adam Schiff (House Intelligence Committee chairman during the Trump impeachment hearings) to help him win his seat in Congress.

In early 2020, the coronavirus crisis started dominating the news. Some said it was a created crisis to gain control of the masses. The deception was great, and it was difficult to know what to believe, but some conservative commentators speculated that globalists and Democrats were using it to generate fear, cause factory shutdowns, close schools, overrun the healthcare system, weaken the US economy, ramp up the surveillance society, and rev up their blame game to bring down President Trump. Some said globalists believe bringing in a world government was worth the destruction of the American economy.

The coronavirus crisis meant the effort to remove the president wasn't over. Trump had been winning, but the globalists wanted him to fail, and they were willing to do whatever it took to reverse the situation. The death of multitudes wouldn't stop them, because that was already a goal of their global depopulation agenda. They blamed the deaths on President Trump, said his response was too slow, and accused him of doing nothing to help the people, etc., but they were likely rejoicing behind the scenes.

On the day President Trump was inaugurated, January 19, 2027, the Dow Jones Stock Market closed at 19,732.40. It continued to soar during the first three years of his presidency, and on February 12, 2020, it closed at 29,551.42. Some pundits were saying that the economy was doing so great that no one would be able to beat President Trump.

Then, on February 24, 2020, fear generated by the coronavirus crisis, the price of oil, and perhaps other factors caused the Dow to drop almost four thousand points. There were some ups and downs, but mostly downs, and on March 23, 2020, it closed at 18,591.93, more than a thousand points below what it was on the day the president was inaugurated.

On March 22, 2020, President Trump was scrambling to do something about the coronavirus crisis and the stock market selloff, and perhaps even to prevent a collapse of the US economy. Senate Republicans and Democrats had spent days on a bipartisan legislative package to rescue the stock market, and they were very close to an agreement. With a vote looming in a matter of hours, House Speaker Nancy Pelosi stepped in with an economic package of demands that she knew the Senate would not accept. With millions of US citizens facing a potential loss of their jobs, the bipartisan legislative package failed. In 2008, President Obama's chief of staff, Rahm Emanuel, became famous for saying, "You never want a serious crisis to go to waste," and it seemed clear that the Democrats were putting a defeat of President Trump in the next election above a solution to the crisis that the US was in.

On March 24, 2020, it was reported that George Soros, a major supporter of the Democrat Party, would spend several million dollars in four battleground states attacking President Trump's handling of the coronavirus crisis. According to the report, millions of dark-money dollars will also be spent to prop up former Vice President Joe Biden. One supporter who makes large contributions said, "We have no plans to let up."

On March 25, 2020, the US Senate passed an emergency coronavirus relief package that was loaded with a Democratic wish list that had nothing to do with the crisis. The House passed it two days later. Five days after that, on April 1, 2020, Pelosi announced the creation of a House Committee to monitor how the money is spent. She said the group would have the power to subpoena Trump administration officials. An article on WorldNetDaily that same day disclosed that Congressman Schiff, who was in self-isolation from the coronavirus, admitted that the committee would be used as a weapon against the Trump administration. The president responded, "Here we go again."

Almost one month later, on April 23, 2020, Pelosi appointed seven Democrats and five Republicans to serve on the committee, and she appointed one of Joe Biden's most ardent supporters, South Carolina Democrat James Clyburn, to chair it. Republicans called it a political committee and complained about not having equal representation on it.

On April 3, 2020, the *Wall Street Journal* published an op-ed article by mega globalist Henry Kissinger. He opined that world leaders were dealing with the coronavirus crisis on a national basis, but the coronavirus doesn't recognize borders (a sly way to call for open borders and world government). As Kissinger saw it, a global effort was needed. He recognized that Bill Gates, his fellow member of the CFR, had spent millions (and was planning to spend billions) of dollars on the development of a vaccine for the coronavirus. He urged the nations to let the crisis move them closer to the NWO and farther away from nationalism (farther away from Trump's effort to "Make America Great Again"). He was clearly speaking against the president and pushing regionalization (an interim step toward world government that will be the rise of the ten kings).

Kissinger's mention of Bill Gates and the development of a coronavirus vaccine is interesting. Gates had been calling for everyone on earth to be vaccinated and, at the same time, injected with a quantum dot tattoo that identified them (a global ID system) and contained their medical records (information that can be changed, and that the Antichrist could change to include his name, number, or mark). Gates' proposal would allow those who take the tattoo to leave their house, work, buy, and sell, etc., but those who refuse to be tattooed wouldn't be allowed to do those things. In connection with this, millions of dollars were put in President Trump's emergency stimulus package to establish and update a tracking system.

Gates' proposal for a global ID and tracking system linked to permission to buy and sell quickly attracted the attention of Bible prophecy teachers. It clearly sounds like the mark of the beast (Revelation 13:16–18). In fact, it sounds so much like the mark of the beast that the word began to spread that Bill Gates could be the Antichrist. However, the Antichrist can't be identified while the Church is still on earth (2 Thessalonians 2:7–8), and it will be his confirmation of a treaty for peace and safety in the Middle East that identifies him (Daniel 9:27; 1 Thessalonians 5:3), not the development of a vaccine—but the stage is definitely being set for his arrival.

In April 2020, a story broke that should have angered everyone in the mainstream media and both political parties, but only a few members of the media and a handful of Republicans spoke out. Unsealed documents revealed that at least some of the top officials in the FBI decided that President Trump's former national security advisor, Michael Flynn, told the truth when he was interrogated in the Russian collusion case, but instead of absolving him, the FBI plotted to trick him into lying and use him to go after Trump. Their illegal scheme worked: They broke Flynn financially, he had to sell his home to pay legal fees, they threatened to go after his son, they forced him to sign a false statement that he had lied, and more—but before Flynn got sentenced, the scheme was uncovered.

Flynn asked the court to throw out the charges against him, Trump said he was considering a full pardon of Flynn, and several Republicans called for the prosecution of the corrupt FBI officials. Some Republicans said the FISA court should get involved because FBI lawyers presented falsified documents to the court and illegally withheld information that would exonerate Flynn. Some documents show that the illegal activities went all the way up to former President Obama. They show that Flynn's phone was illegally wiretapped, and Obama knew this illegal activity was taking place while it was happening.

Others who knew about these things while they were happening include Vice President Joe Biden, CIA Director John Brennon, National Security Advisor Susan Rice, and Director of National Intelligence James Clapper.

But, as wrong as this was, it was even worse. Forcing Flynn to lie was just a tool to go after President Trump. And why did they want to go after him? Because they didn't want the US to go in the direction that the president said he would take America when he was campaigning for the office. His slogan was "Make America Great Again," and they didn't want that. They wanted to make America part of a one-world government.

On May 7, 2020, the head prosecutor in the case against Flynn abruptly withdrew from the case, and the DOJ filed a request with the court to drop the charges. President Trump said Flynn is "an innocent man," and added that Flynn's prosecutors in the Obama administration committed treason. K. T. McFarland, former deputy national security advisor, called it a "great day for the Republic." She said it proves the FBI's Russian investigation "was all a scam from the very beginning." Rush Limbaugh declared, "There is no innocent Democrat." And well-known constitutional professor, Jonathan Turley, called the documents "chilling." Former US Attorney Joe diGenova said the Mueller probe "was nothing more than a pretext to get the president impeached." Several Democrats quickly railed against these events. Some called for more investigations. Some demanded the resignation of Attorney General Bill Barr.

Released documents show that Adam Schiff repeatedly lied (lying is the charge that Flynn was prosecuted—and almost jailed—for). The documents show that Mueller knew the Russian collusion charges were false, but he and his partisan lawyers still spent two years and about $40 million trying to find a way to impeach Trump. Former President Obama said, "Our basic understanding of the rule of law is at risk." He used the last few weeks of his term in office to try to orchestrate a coup of the incoming president, and he appeared to be making himself willingly ignorant of the facts. The spin of the fake news was deceitful to the core, at best.

Satan is behind this, and it's not over. Recall these words from above, "Prior to the 1990s it was not unusual to come across books or articles about a 'shadow government.' Writers promoted the idea that unknown people and entities (former politicians, the military-industrial complex, heads of large corporations, government agencies, State Department officials, Department of Justice [DOJ] officials, Federal Bureau of Investigation [FBI] officials, and others) were influencing US elections and exercising a degree of control over America's elected officials, the appointment of judges, and more." Recall that some have started calling the "shadow government" the "deep state."

It is now obvious that those who wrote and talked about a "shadow government," "deep state," or whatever were not promoting a conspiracy theory. They were telling the truth. There is now proof that several politicians, employees in the DOJ and FBI, people with power, and people with high profiles and big salaries committed crimes to put people in jail and ruin lives because they wanted to overthrow the incoming president and keep the US on the path to world government.

But let us be clear. The people who have been identified up to this point are just the little fish. As the old saying goes, there are bigger fish to fry, meaning there are more people higher up in covert, shadowy places who need to be exposed and dealt with. Some may mean well, but they are enemies of God because the government they are so committed to bringing in will turn out to be the prophesied world government under Satan, the Antichrist, and his False Prophet. God will let it exist for seven years, then He will bring it down.

Not So Fast

When the DOJ asked the court to dismiss the charges against Flynn, there was widespread assumption that Judge Emmet Sullivan, a Bill Clinton appointee, would quickly do that, but he did not. Many influential lawyers with ties to the Democratic party, donors to the Democratic party, CNN, MSNBC, and others who had thought the prosecution of Flynn and impeachment of Trump were a sure thing asked Judge Sullivan to keep the Flynn case alive.

On May 13, 2020, Judge Sullivan responded by taking the unusual step of appointing retired Judge John Gleeson, another Bill Clinton appointee and long-time friend of Sullivan (a judge who is already on record for saying Flynn is guilty), to prepare an argument against dismissing the case and to consider charging Flynn with criminal contempt for perjury. This immediately set off alarm bells and charges of political bias. It is an established fact that the Clinton campaign and the Democratic National Committee gave money that was used to pay for the Russian dossier, and the appointment of a biased Democrat who was selected by Bill Clinton, who has already said Flynn is guilty, to keep prosecuting Flynn appears to be a conflict of interest. Former Whitewater independent counsel, Kenneth Starr, said he believes it is illegal. Flynn's attorneys are planning to file documents, and it's impossible to predict what Sullivan and/or Gleeson will do, but if they go through with this, it could wind up in a higher court.

Who Did It?

On the same day, May 13, 2020, two US senators, Chuck Grassley and Ron Johnson, released a newly declassified list of names of people who knew about the surveillance of Flynn and who could have been guilty of unmasking him (illegally revealing his name) before President Trump was inaugurated. The list of potential felons includes President Obama, Vice President Biden, National Intelligence Director Clapper, CIA Director Brennan, FBI Director Comey, and many others. Some or all of these people were already on record for denying that they knew about this. Trump called this the greatest political hoax in the history of our country, and several Republicans called for these people to be brought before Congress, put under oath, and forced to testify about it.

Three days later, on May 16, 2020, Jesse Watters said on his TV program, *Watters' World*, that he has information that a trove of Russian hoax documents that point directly at President Obama have been turned over to US Attorney General Bill Barr. There is no telling what will happen, but the criminal prosecution of Obama and Biden is not likely because of who they are—not because they are innocent. America's justice system has obviously come to the point where some are prosecuted, and some are not.

Here We Go Again

On May 18, 2020, an attorney for Democrats in the US House of Representatives sent a letter to the Supreme Court saying they need secret information right away from the DOJ on the Mueller investigation to determine if they want to impeach President Trump a second time before the end of 2020. They appear to be saying that they do not agree with the conclusions in the Mueller Report, and they want the chance to come up with a different set of conclusions before the presidential election in November. The DOJ asked the Court to prevent the release of the documents.

The next twelve days produced a flurry of events.

- Senator Lindsey Graham said the Senate Judiciary Committee would begin hearings on the Russian collusion hoax and the Flynn case in June and would try to complete the hearings by October 2020.
- On May 18, 2020, attorneys from fifteen Republican states filed documents to have the Flynn case dropped on the grounds that Judge Sullivan does not have the authority to do anything but drop it.
- On May 19, 2020, Flynn's attorney filed documents with the DC Court of Appeals to have Judge Sullivan and Judge Gleeson removed from the case for bias and lack of authority.
- On May 19, 2020, more released documents revealed that several Obama administration officials said one thing in public and on TV about the Flynn case and just the opposite under oath behind closed doors.
- On May 19, 2020, it was reported that George Soros has helped organize two groups of very wealthy donors who plan to spend

$275 million on political advertising to defeat President Trump in the November 2020 election.

- On May 20, 2020, for the time being, the US Supreme Court refused to allow the House of Representatives access to the Mueller documents they wanted for a second attempt at impeaching Trump.
- On May 21, 2020, the DC Court of Appeals gave Judge Sullivan ten days to explain why he didn't want to dismiss the Flynn case.
- On May 22, 2020, it was reported that a judge in Ukraine has ordered the nation's law-enforcement services to list the fired prosecutor in the Biden case as the victim of an alleged crime by the former vice president of the US. Biden has admitted that he threatened to withhold loan guarantees if the prosecutor wasn't fired, but refuses to admit that he did anything wrong.
- On May 23, 2020, it was reported that Judge Sullivan has hired a lawyer to represent him before the DC Court perhaps to defend himself, but also to try to prosecute Flynn before that court.
- On May 25, 2020, Twitter posted a notification on a President Trump Tweet that his claims about mail-in ballots were false (even though some experts say they were true), prompting Trump to respond that social media platforms are trying to silence conservative voices (and defeat him in the upcoming election).
- On May 26, 2020, it was reported that Republicans on the House Intelligence Committee will make "criminal referrals" in the coming weeks against Robert Mueller's team of investigators and unnamed individuals involved in the Trump-Russia probe.
- On May 27, 2020, it was reported that Attorney General Barr had appointed an outside prosecutor to investigate (and perhaps prosecute) the unmasking of General Flynn (an outside prosecutor may mean he does not trust the DOJ to prosecute itself).
- On May 28, 2020, President Trump signed an executive order to remove the laws that protect social media companies from lawsuits and to cut federal funding for those who engage in censorship or politics (lawsuits may follow).

- On May 29, 2020, transcripts of phone calls between Flynn and Russia's ambassador to the US were released, and there was questionable evidence that Flynn had done anything wrong.

In Conclusion

The May 30, 2020, deadline for sending this chapter to the editor has arrived, so interested parties will need to go to other sources for the rest of the story as it unfolds.

The extreme hatred for President Trump doesn't make sense unless one knows Bible prophecy. At least some evangelical Christians who study the subject believe that God put Trump in office to slow down the approaching NWO (globalism), to be a blessing to Israel, and to promote true Christian values. They believe that if God put President Trump in office, only God can remove him. The globalists and the national party of Democrats are powerful. They have spent millions of dollars (and plan to spend millions more) to remove him from office. For more than three years, they have tried everything they can think of, but they have failed.

They will not give up. The next presidential election is about six months away. Some pundits think the Democrats can defeat President Trump if the coronavirus spreads, or if the US economy worsens. Some pundits have suggested there may be an effort to overstate the crisis, and there may even be an attempt to delay America's economic recovery. Can anyone want a person to fail that much? That is harsh, but there's no question that there is a lot of opposition to ending the lockdown and putting America back to work, and there is more opposition in states controlled by Democrats than in states controlled by Republicans.

The Bible teaches that the New World Order will come. A United Nations wannabe world government exists, the European Union model exists, Israel exists, the surveillance society exists, calls for wealth redistribution exist, the deep state exists, corrupt officials exist, and the ten kings are forming. Bible prophecy is being fulfilled on a global scale, and all of this is evidence that God exists and His Word is true.

All praise, glory, and honor go to God, because He has raised up and protected President Trump from Satan's minions who want to surrender US sovereignty and establish a one-world government. The existence of and protection of Trump don't mean that God won't let the world government come into being. It means that He is delaying it until He is ready for it to happen. Until then, the globalist effort to remove President Trump for holding up Satan's one-world project could get ugly and pose a great danger to the United States.

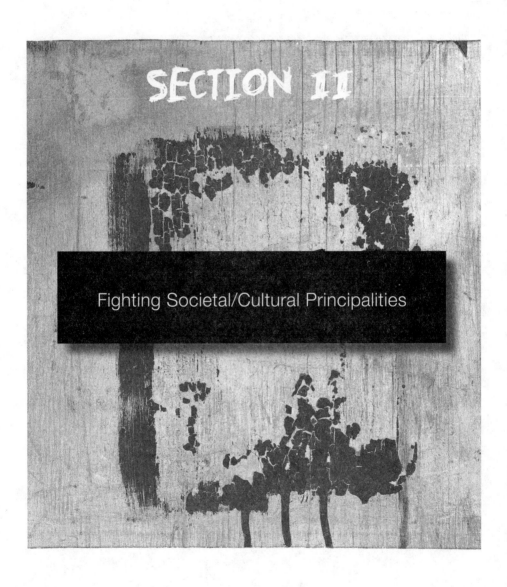

SECTION II

Fighting Societal/Cultural Principalities

THREE

God Wrong About Human Creation

By Larry Spargimino

Many of us remember waiting in a doctor's office and flipping through the pages of a variety of magazines. I remember being fascinated with the photos on the cover of *National Geographic*—majestic mountains, beautifully exposed photos of wildlife, and faraway places I had never heard of. The January 2017 issue, however, featured a front cover photo of Avery Jackson of Kansas City, Missouri. Under Jackson's picture, we read: "The best thing about being a girl is, now I don't have to pretend to be a boy." Page 32 of that issue gives some background material on Avery: "Avery spent the first four years of her life as a boy, and was miserable." The article went on to explain that Avery has been living since 2012 as an openly transgender girl.

This photo raises many questions. Evidently when Avery was four, he knew he no longer wanted to be a boy. Really? Should we trust a four-year-old to make life-changing decisions like wanting gender-reassignment surgery? And what about his parents? Do they even have the faintest hint of sanity? And what about the doctor or doctors? Is there something frighteningly grotesque about this picture? Isn't this child abuse of the worst sort, yet written about as if it is a great achievement?

Walt Heyer, who identified as a transgender woman for eight years, says that his experience wasn't all it was supposed to be. He now specializes in writing and research along the theme of transgender regret. He has a very helpful website and has written articles titled, "1 Year After Sex Change, This Teen Regrets His 'Frankenstein Hack Job,'" "4 Trans People Beg for Help with Their Gender Identity Crises," and "I Was Once Transgender. Why I Think Trump Made the Right Decision for the Military." Heyer's website also features books and videos by many authors decrying the evils of transgenderism.[6] I wonder if Avery Jackson's parents ever even investigated before subjecting their son to a horrible attack on human dignity? Heyer makes the following comments about the public school system:

> It is sadistic to use the public school system, which holds a captive audience, to engage in a social gender identity experiment with the nation's young people.... I transitioned to female beginning in my late teens and changed my name in my early 20s over ten years ago. But it wasn't right for me; I feel only discontent now in the female role. I was told that my transgender feelings were permanent, immutable, physically deep seated in my brain and could NEVER change, that the only way I should ever find peace was to become female. The problem is, I don't have those feelings any more.[7]

Sin involves an individual rebellion against, or even a denial of, the limits and boundaries that God has built into His world: "So God created man in his own image, in the image of God created he him; male and female created he them" (Genesis 1:26–27). There is a growing uprising in today's world against the parameters God has designed for His glory and our good. Millions of "willingly ignorant" individuals are virtually shouting what the title of this chapter conveys: "GOD WRONG ABOUT HUMAN CREATION!"

In the Beginning…

The Bible opens with a startling testimony to the majesty, power, and wisdom of God: "In the beginning God created the heaven and the earth" (Genesis 1:1). Everything that God does is right, perfect and a reflection of His person. Genesis 1:31 articulates God's approval of His creation: "And God saw every thing that he had made, and, behold, it was very good." When I was in an eighth-grade woodworking class, I made a bird-house. The teacher looked at it, shook his head, and said, "Try again." God never has to "try again."

When God pronounces something "very good," those are words of highest approbation. That for which such words are spoken cannot be improved, modified, or changed. God is saying, "Everything is in its place. Everything is just the way I want it. Nothing needs to be added. Nothing needs to be changed."

Ever since the Fall, angels—and later, men—have disputed God's perfect design and the limits of the creature's sovereignty. "And the angels which kept not their first estate, but left their own habitation" (Jude 6). Jude 7 adds, "Even as Sodom and Gomorrah, and the cities about them in like manner, giving themselves over to fornication, and going after strange flesh [*sarkas heteras*, flesh of a different kind than their own]." The ESV translation of this verse brings this out when it says, "Just as Sodom and Gomorrah and the surrounding cities, which likewise indulged in sexual immorality and pursued *unnatural* desire" (emphasis added).

Departing from God's original plan for man is not good. In his book, *Unimaginable: What Our World Would Be Like Without Christianity* (a must-read for every thinking Christian), Jeremiah Johnson observes that in 2007, skeptic Christopher Hitchens published a book titled *God Is Not Great: How Religion Poisons Everything.* Johnson writes, "I contend evidence shows that belief in God, specifically as understood in Judeo-Christian theology has, in fact, benefited humanity greatly."[8]

Johnson lists several societal issues that Christianity has influenced for good, such as women's rights, children's rights, family, slavery, racism, science, music and the arts, religious freedom, and the founding of the American Republic. But most unusual of all is the testimony of the prominent atheist, Richard Dawkins, who wrote *The God Delusion.* In 2010, Dawkins was interviewed by the *Times* of London. He said:

> "There are no Christians, as far as I know, blowing up buildings. I am not aware of any Christian suicide bombers. I am not aware of any major Christian denomination that believes the penalty for apostasy is death." Then Dawkins actually admitted, "I have mixed feelings about the decline of Christianity, insofar as Christianity might be a bulwark against something worse."[9]

Mona Charen, in her culturally insightful and God-honoring book, *Sex Matters: How Modern Feminism Lost Touch with Science, Love, and Common Sense,* writes: "The sexual revolution has long since spun off the table and degraded men and women alike."[10] She expands this idea, saying: "I hope this book will help both men and women see that denying the differences between the sexes leads to unnecessary misunderstandings and miseries." Charen believes that rejecting the family and traditional family roles is causing "needless hardship."[11] I must agree with Charen. The continuing division and dog-eat-dog quarreling in America is to be attributed to left-wing ideologues who want to impose the most bizarre "progressive" innovations on America. The hostility against the churches, as evidenced during the coronavirus pandemic, has become so blatant that it cannot, nor will it, be ignored.

No one knows how far we will descend into the murky pit of madness. Some of it even seems comical, but it's no laughing matter. Take, for example, Munroe Bergdorf, a male lingerie model identifying as a female. Bergdorf recently slammed Victoria's Secret, the lingerie and clothing retailer, for bigotry. This "lacy underclothes model dude identifying as a lingerie model superchick" is definitely unhappy with Victoria's Secret, which recently announced it would not use transgender models in its big-time national catwalk.[12]

For the Christian, "natural law" supports God's wisdom and power and renders the most primitive aborigine "without excuse" (Romans 1:20). We might wonder if any Christian would really be interested in natural law. Isn't the Bible sufficient? J. Budziszewski answers:

> Surprisingly, Scripture itself gives a different account of the matter.
>
> The Bible maintains that God has not left himself without a witness among the pagans (Acts 14:17). In contrast to special revelation provided by God to the community of faith, this may be called *general* revelation because it is provided by God to all mankind. According to Scripture it comes in at least five forms: (1) the testimony of creation, which speaks to us of a glorious, powerful and merciful creator (Ps. 19:1–6; 104; Acts 14:17; Rom. 1:20). (2) the fact that we were made in the image of God, which not only gives us rational and moral capacities but also tells us of an unknown Holy one who is different from our idols (Gen. 1:26–27; Acts 17:22–23); (3) the facts of our physical and emotional design, in which a variety of God's purposes are plainly manifest (Rom. 1:26–27); (4) the law of conscience written on the heart, which, like the law of Moses, tells us what sin is but does not give us power to escape it (Rom. 2:14–15); the order of causality which teaches us by linking every sin with consequences (Proverbs 1:31).[13]

The Sexual Revolution

There has always been sexual promiscuity, adultery, fornication, homosexuality, and lesbianism. Some 1,400 years before the coming of Christ, Moses wrote, "Thou shalt not commit adultery" (Exodus 20:14). What is shocking now, however, is the openness with which people engage in such behaviors and the readiness to gain societal and governmental approval for certain behaviors long held to be morally wrong. It is a flood of moral perversion. Even children are being targeted.

In the spring of 2019, the tax-funded PBS Kids aired a segment on gay marriage on the *Arthur* cartoon. Target department stores have offered adult and children's clothing and accessories that celebrate the gay lifestyle. The company also pledged to donate $100,000 to the Gay, Lesbian, Straight Education Network (GLSEN), an organization whose primary focus is instructing school-aged students about how to create "gay" clubs in public schools across the nation. This is being done with the full consent of the public schools—and of many parents.

On Friday, April 17, 2015, the GLSEN planned to have thousands of public high school students and increasing numbers of middle school students remain silent throughout an entire school day to promote the militant LGBT agenda among young people. This program was to be carried out in public schools.[14]

A weakening and finally jettisoned biblical authority has led society into the thick morass of autonomous thinking. The cutoff from discernment undergirded by the timeless truths of the Bible has led to a complete break with sanity, such as insisting that the differences between men and women are merely "social constructs" that can be changed. It is as if modern thinkers are saying "just because it's fiction does not mean it is not true." Supposedly, all we need to do as we "progress" to new heights of self-realization is dismantle these social constructs without doing men, women, or society itself, any harm.

It is becoming increasingly more obvious and undeniable that many churchgoers and parents don't understand what's going on with regard to the schools, the government, and the Democratic Party. When they're confronted with their divided loyalties, they become highly indignant that we are judging them. But loyalties are indicators. Can anyone claim that he or she is loyal to Christ when that person is running with and supporting those who are pushing Satan's agenda?

Coercive Power of Government and the Sexual Revolution

Morse believes that the coercive power of government is behind the advance of the sexual revolution and emboldening such madness.

The sexual revolution has never been a grassroots movement. It is and always has been a movement of the elites justifying their preferred lifestyles, imposing their new morality, and, in the process, allowing them unprecedented control over others. The sexual revolution came about because elites captured the coercive power of the state and used it for their personal and ideological interests. The state, together with elite institutions of society, support the sexual revolution with a continual flow of propaganda.

Just think of the Democrats in government who encourage the left-wing media to demonize Christians and support aberrant ideas regarding family, home, and sexuality. Morse correctly states that the sexual revolution has done a great deal of harm to society as well as to individuals, "yet the freight train of these ideologies keeps hurling down the track with no apparent stopping point." The sexual revolution only persists and steadily acquires new territory because of state backing.[15]

Jennifer Robeck Morse argues that the sexual revolution has much in common with other toxic national ideologies. Marxism needs government backing to get people to do what they wouldn't normally do: work hard so someone else, the government, can benefit. America has the Bill of Rights to protect the people from the government. Toxic national ideologies don't want anything like the Bill of Rights. Their hands would be tied. The people would say "no." Toxic ideologies would die a natural death. Governments often exist to make sure that doesn't happen.

In May 2019, the House of Representatives passed H.R. 5, known as the Equality Act. It amends Title VII, among other laws, and explicitly outlaws discrimination on the basis of sexual orientation and gender identity. Title VII prohibits employers from making hiring decisions based on an individual's "race, color, religion, sex, or national origin." As Title VII stands, employment decisions cannot be made on whether a person is male or female. The Equality Act would replace the word "sex" with the phrase "sex (including sexual orientation and gender identity)." The bill defines "gender identity" as "the gender-related identity, appearance, mannerisms, or other gender-related characteristics of an individual, regardless of the individual's designated sex at birth" and defines "sexual orientation" as "homosexuality, heterosexuality, or bisexuality."[16]

The Equality Act would give the government the "right" to penalize Americans who don't agree with the transgender/LGBTQ ideology; compel speech and force individuals to use "preferred pronouns"; shut down charities, adoption agencies, drug rehabilitation centers, and homeless centers; allow biological males to defeat females in sports; coerce medical professionals to perform services that their religious convictions prohibit; cause parents to lose custody of their children; and enable sexual assault by requiring boys and girls, men and women to share shower and bathroom facilities.

A complaint under investigation by federal education officials alleges that a boy who identifies as "gender fluid" at Oakhurst Elementary School in Decatur, Georgia, sexually assaulted a five-year-old girl in a girls' restroom. The boy had access to the girls' restroom because of the Decatur City Schools' transgender restroom policy. School authorities refused to change the policy even after the girl's mother reported the assault and raised strong objections to the policy.[17]

The LGBT movement has received much support and encouragement from Democrats in American government. It has sought to destigmatize aberrant forms of sexual expression through court cases and lawsuits, powerful political lobbying, protests, and direct action.

Indeed, the coercive power of the government would legally mean that Christian values are virtually outlawed in the public arena. Fortunately, while President Trump said he is opposed to discrimination of any kind, "this bill in its current form is filled with poison pills that threaten to undermine parental and conscience rights." The president has refused to sign it.[18]

Radical Feminism

What is a "feminist"? Not just someone who champions the rights and dignity of women. One can defend the rights and dignity of women without being a feminist. "Feminist," in today's parlance, means "those who believe that a woman's rights and dignity are bound up in the woman's ability to control her reproductive life."[19]

At the outset, it is necessary to point out that feminism is not monolithic. Some early feminists were in a struggle against bona fide abuses of women. First-Wave Feminism (1900–1960s) focused on voting rights, equal education, and property rights for women. It resulted in the 19th Amendment giving women the right to vote.

Second-Wave Feminism appeared on the scene in the early 1950s and expanded the idea of women's rights to include "reproductive rights and the removing of workplace inequalities." It focused on self-determination and autonomy. Activists in this group argued that equal pay was not enough to be considered equal to men. They wanted full access to birth control and abortion.

Third-Wave feminists saw the success of First- and Second-Wave Feminism and declared an all-out war on male dominance. They came to believe that the real problem is men, who allegedly form a system that holds women down.

Today's Third-Wave feminists truly believe that once you're taught to look for systemic misogyny, you will find it everywhere. They interpret even the slightest interaction between men and women through the lens of power differentials. ("Did that guy just open a door for me? He is exerting his perceived superiority and physical dominance over me. Misogynist!")[20]

Many years ago, this author had a brush with a Third-Wave feminist on a New York City subway. A young woman who was, to use the language of the KJV, "heavy with child," was standing up and holding on—she was a "strap-hanger." I automatically got up and offered her my seat—and received a flood of angry words!

Third-Wave Feminism is radical and has mounted an all-out attack on motherhood, fatherhood, marriage, and Christian moral values. It believes that most of our culture needs to be radically reworked because modern culture is based on patriarchal assumptions. Here are some statements of leading feminists to show where they are coming from and what their goals are.

> I feel that "man-hating" is an honorable and viable political act, that the oppressed have a right to class-hatred against the class that is oppressing them. —Robin Morgan, *Ms. Magazine* editor

> The nuclear family must be destroyed.... Whatever its ultimate meaning, the break-up of families now is an objectively revolutionary process. —Linda Gordon, feminist writer and historian

> Marriage is an institution developed from rape as a practice. —Andrea Dworkin, feminist writer

> Since marriage constitutes slavery for women, it is clear that the women's movement must concentrate on attacking the institution. Freedom for women cannot be won without the abolition of marriage. —Sheila Cronan, feminist activist

> The proportion of men must be reduced to and maintained at approximately 10% of the human race. —Sally Miller Gearheart, in *The Future—If There Is One—Is Female*

> If life is to survive on this planet, there must be a decontamination of the Earth. I think this will be accompanied by an evolutionary process that will result in a drastic reduction of the population of males. —Mary Daly, feminist philosopher

> Probably the only place where a man can feel really secure is in a maximum security prison, except for the imminent threat of release. —Germaine Greer, feminist writer and academic.[21]

God Still Breaking Chains of Bondage and Confusion

There are a number of organizations, ministries, and individuals who focus on deliverance from sexual addictions as well as homosexuality and lesbianism. I want to focus on Christopher Yuan, the son of Chinese immigrants.

When Christopher was nine, he viewed pornography at a friend's house. He noticed that he was attracted to images of men and women. When he was about twenty, he started going to gay bars. He kept his "secret" from his very conservative Christian parents. When Christopher moved away to attend dental school, he decided to live as an openly gay person.

One day when he was home, he decided to tell his parents about his life as a practicing homosexual. His mother and father were shocked and said that they were very disappointed in him. Christopher later found out that they took him to the throne of grace in prayer on a regular basis.

During the days, he went to dental school; during the evenings, he was sexually active and led a double life. He was making lots of money selling drugs. One day, he heard a loud knock on his door. Twelve Drug Enforcement Agency agents put cuffs on him and took him to jail. He was in big trouble.

Just three days after he was incarcerated, something in a trash can caught his attention. It was a Gideons Bible. He couldn't stop reading it. He learned from the Bible and from his own sinful actions that there were consequences to his lifestyle. He was HIV positive.

While he was on his bunk wondering what his future held, he looked up and saw the scribbled words: "If you are bored read Jeremiah 29:11." He looked up the verse: "For I know the plans that I have for you, declares the Lord. Plans to prosper you and not to harm you."

Shortly thereafter, he repented of his sins and gave his life to Jesus as Lord and Savior. After Christopher Yuan was released from prison, his relationship with his parents was restored. He is now teaching at Moody Bible College in Chicago.[22]

It seems to me that Yuan's contribution to this issue is that it highlights the central importance of conformity to the will of God. Misguided individuals think that the "Christian" message is "homosexuality is wrong, and heterosexuality is right." Homosexuals who want to be Christian, supposedly, have to be attracted to women.

Whether one is heterosexual or homosexual, there are temptations to step out of the will of God. "Heterosexuality will not get you into heaven and is not the ultimate goal for those with same-sex attractions," writes Yuan. "Thus, the biblical opposite of homosexuality is not heterosexuality…the opposite of homosexuality is holiness." Yuan gives an illustration.

> A pastor I met had a friend with same-sex attractions who was going through orientation-change counseling. One day while driving down the highway and passing a billboard for a local strip club, his friend noted how the scantily clad female model looks "hot." The pastor was taken aback and even explained that in any other circumstance, this would have resulted in a stern rebuke. However, in this case, they actually celebrated what was deemed to be a sign of "success."… [Having] a faulty framework and inaccurate foundation leads to an incorrect conclusion—and in this case, even the celebration and normalization of sin.[23]

Dr. Francis Schaeffer and Two-Story Thinking

In her excellent book, *Love Thy Body: Answering Hard Questions About Life and Sexuality*, Nancy Pearcey includes a quote from the feminist author, Marie Paglia: "Fate, not God, has given us this flesh. We have absolute claim to our bodies and may do with them as we see fit."[24]

Pearcey goes on to explain that in many civilizations, specifically in the biblical worldview, all of reality is seen as a single, unified system of truth. In the modern world, however, this unified concept of truth has been split into two separate domains. There is the domain of truth, and there is the domain of true truth. Dr. Francis Schaeffer illustrated this division by using the metaphor of a two-story building. The lower story is the realm of empirical science, which is held to be open to scientific validation. This is the area of the testable and the verifiable. This is the realm of true truth. All rational humans are bound by the laws of logic to adhere to empirical truths in this domain. The upper story, however, is the realm of the moral, private, subjective, and religious. This upper story is the story of moral values. Because this is not the area that lends itself to empirical verification, a person can say that a statement "is true for you but not true for me."[25] This kind of a two-story, fragmented worldview undergirds the idea": "What I do with my body is my business. No one can condemn me for my belief in this. It is my truth."

Our hypersexualized culture is built on this fragmented view, sort of the ancient gnostic view that the spiritual aspect of me is the good me, but the physical outward body of me is the evil and bad me. I can sin with my outward evil body, but that does not affect the good, spiritual me. This fragmented, two-story view is seen in the mindset of an abortionist. You can prove to the abortionist that the unborn baby is a human being, but this argument rolls away like water off of a duck. For the abortionist, the real issue is not whether the unborn baby is human, but whether the baby is a *person*. Pearcey writes:

In the two-story worldview, if the *body* is separate from the *person*, as we saw in abortion and euthanasia, then what you do with your body sexually need not have any connection to who you are as a whole person. Sex can be purely physical, separate from love.

Our sexualized culture actually encourages people to keep the two separate. *Seventeen* magazine warns teen girls to "keep your hearts under wraps" or boys may find you "boring and clingy." *Cosmo* advises women that the way to "wow a man after sex" is to ask for a ride home. (Make it clear you have no intention of hanging around hoping for a relationship.)[26]

A video put out by the Children's Television Workshop is widely used in sex education classes. It defines sexual intimacy as simply "something done by two adults to give each other pleasure." Sex is disconnected from love, marriage, and commitment. The only reason for sex is sensual gratification. In the two-story view, sex-as-sensual-gratification is morally neutral. It is in the domain of "my truth."

This is far different from the biblical view, where sexual intimacy is seen as the "most complete and intimate physical union of marriage...the purpose of sex is to express the one-flesh covenant bond in marriage."[27] In other words, sexual intimacy only within the bounds of covenant marriage is "the real deal." Though our generation claims to be the most sexually enlightened and freed from the fetters of legalism and Victorian hyper modesty, the fact is it is the most sex-starved and frustrated generation. It has never experienced "the real deal." It is seeking the ultimate thrill in the wrong places, and, because of spiritual ignorance, blindness, and its sheer hatred of biblical morality, it has cut itself off from even the possibility of true fulfilment and sexual joy. Homosexuality, transgenderism, pornography, pedophilia, and the hook-up culture are all reflections of the total misery our culture is now immersed in. Your mother was right when she advised, "Wait until marriage."

The true meaning and joy of sexual intimacy in covenant marriage will escape a godless society that is intent on breaking away from the beneficent plan articulated in the Bible. Perhaps the greater penalty for violating biblical sexual standards is not HIV, sexually transmitted diseases, and "unwanted" pregnancies, but rather misery, confusion, and seeing our culture unravel. For Christians who have been tempted, seduced, and deceived to step out of the bounds of godly behavior, David's words are a solemn warning:

Cast me not away from thy presence; and take not thy Holy Spirit from me. Restore unto me the joy of thy salvation; and uphold me with thy free Spirit. (Psalm 51:12)

When the angel told Mary that she would conceive a child, Mary's response was, "How shall this be, seeing I *know not* a man?" (Luke 1:34, emphasis added). Mary was surprised at the angel's announcement because she had not been sexually intimate with a man. The metaphor of "knowing" is often a picture of sexual intimacy, as in Genesis 4:1, "And Adam *knew* Eve his wife; and she conceived" (emphasis added). If sexual intimacy was all about pleasure, "know" is the wrong metaphor. Sexual intimacy in the bonds of covenant love can never be equated with an aspect of "reproduction," "mating," or several of the gutter words that are often used for it. Once again, though our culture claims to be sexually knowledgeable, liberated, and "expert" in such matters, the fact is that modern society has cheapened sexual intimacy because it doesn't believe in covenant love between a man and a woman. When the 2015 *Obergefell v. Hodges* decision of the United States Supreme Court was announced and claimed that "the fundamental right to marry" should also be accorded to same-sex couples, the five justices who supported homosexual marriage announced to the whole world their confusion and gross ignorance. The Democratic justices on the Supreme Court in the Dred Scott case likewise goofed in the mid-nineteenth century.

Love is not just a feeling. In fact, it can be commanded: "Husbands love your wives" (Ephesians 5:25). There is no idea here that we ought to "wait until the feeling comes" and then desert the relationship "if the feeling leaves." Marital love involves a resolve of the will, control of the body, and a commitment to responsible living. Julie Slattery writes:

> God created Christian marriage to mirror covenant love, which asks that we commit to loyal love, "in sickness and in health, for richer or poorer, for better or worse, until death." This kind of love is not a feeling but a promise.[28]

Youth In the Devil's Crosshairs:
Irresponsible Parents Provide the Ammo

Thousands of teens are losing their minds, their future, and their virginity every day. I opened this chapter with a reference to Avery Jackson, the transgender girl who said, "The best thing about being a girl is, now I don't have to pretend to be a boy."

As a whole, teens of this generation are maturing faster sexually because of better health and nutrition. In the last few years, the onset of menstruation in girls has dropped an estimated three months each decade. Consequently, natural desires and urges that used to emerge when teens were older and more mature are now showing up at younger and younger ages, when youth are less able to handle their explosive feelings.

Added to this is the fact that issues of sexuality in all of its aberrant forms is used to sell everything from soap to toothpaste and cars. Movies, TV programs, easily accessible pornography, and mixed-up school teachers make it virtually impossible for many young people and adults to duck the onslaught of sexual innuendo, perversion, and temptation. It's hard enough for someone who is grounded in the Christian faith to maintain a consistent walk with Christ, but what about those who are experiencing physical and emotional growing pains and are being raised in a godless culture—one that considers abortion clinics, liquor stores, and supermarkets as essential, but churches as nonessential, as in the recent coronavirus pandemic?

Added to this is the influence of Sigmund Freud (1856–1939) and his followers, who make a distinction between cultural and natural sexual morality. Freud believed that cultural sexual mores, as taught in the Judeo-Christian religion, are bad. He focused on the "negative consequences of culturally-imposed repression of the sexual instinct as a cause of neurosis."[29] He said that human behavior is basically determined by unconscious influences and experiences, many of which are sexual in nature. Such thinking is reflected in the plea of same-sex-attracted people who say, "I was born this way and I don't want to resist who I really am any longer." Christians are facing the giant of postmodernism.

Modernism, when applied to an understanding of Scripture, ethics, and human behavior, is the view that objective values and paradigms of truth exist but are essentially unknowable. Postmodernism goes beyond that. It is the view that objective values and paradigms of truth are not only unknowable, but do not even exist. The traditional view says that right and wrong exist and are knowable. Modernism says that right and wrong exist, but we'd better not be too dogmatic, because they are virtually unknowable. Postmodernism says there is really no such thing as right and wrong.

Social dysfunction is also increasing, as more and more marriages are broken up, divorce is easier than ever before, and countless numbers of kids are being brought up in single-parent homes, often without proper supervision. This is not to be understood as a blanket condemnation of single-parent homes. There are some outstanding Christian moms and dads who end up as single parents through no fault of their own, but as a whole, a lack of home stability and parental supervision is morally destabilizing. By far, however, the incessant attacks on biblical morality in high schools and colleges, the creeping apostasy in many churches and Christian organizations, and the church becoming a place of entertainment without good, biblical teaching for adults and youth are having a damaging effect on sexual morality.

Complicating the issue for young people, as well as adults, is the issue of "romance." I believe that there is a place for it in the life of the Christian, but that is for another chapter, or perhaps even another book. In the minds of postmodernists, however, romance is severed from covenant love. Movies, books, and music engage our attention and our hearts with appealing and heart-warming accounts of romantic love. Many people enjoy living vicariously with "the heart-thumping, sweaty-hands relational wonderment portrayed in media."[30]

Romance, properly understood, is not intrinsically evil. It is the initial infatuation, the excitement of wooing and being wooed, that provides the drama. Love, on the other hand, is romance that is tempered by long-term commitment and the reality of marriage, family, and home. Some people flit from romance to romance like bees drilling for nectar, and never settle down into spiritually healthy, long-term relationships.

We are living in a war zone. One of the positive effects of the Trump administration is that the snakes in the "swamp"—some call it "the deep state"—are now slithering in the bright sunlight. Their venom is becoming more evident[31] and consequently more visible to all. For years, the wild-eyed Left could hide, somewhat, its insanity. Now it is so obvious that even fence-straddlers are getting off the fence and coming down on the right side of the discussion. It is impossible to deny the face of hell when it shows up everywhere. Even those who are not biblically literate are alarmed. It's like the man who bought a farm on a winter day. People had warned the buyer that there were a lot of rattlesnakes on that particular piece of property, but the beautiful stream, the little lake that looked like it was full of fish, and the stunning sunsets made it hard for him to believe that the property was not a good buy…until the weather warmed up and the rattlesnakes showed up!

On a Positive Note

Young people, especially Millennials, are, I believe, poised to transform the culture, but they need cultivation and a love-directed sensitivity. I believe it was Winston Churchill who used the phrase that some people are "a riddle, wrapped in a mystery, inside an enigma." Riddles are sometimes obscure, but not this one. Millennials and young people in general have tremendous potential for the kingdom, and they can be reached.

Allie Anderson-Henson, in her excellent book, *Unscrambling the Millennial Paradox: Why the "Unreachables" May Be Key to the Next Great Awakening,* challenges Millennials: "Your generation's propensity to get involved in activism shows that there is a visionary streak motivating you. So, the question becomes this: 'What will you do with this valuable attribute?'"[32]

Indeed, "the unreachables" can be reached. We must not give up. A great inspiration to me is how biblical Christianity has, at various times during the last several hundred years, brought transformation to China. If ever a nation and people seemed unreachable—with its distance from the "Christian West," its very difficult language and many different customs, plus periods of opposition against "foreigners," as in the Boxer Rebellion (1899–1901), the Rape of Nanking and the Japanese invasion (1937–38), Mao Tse-tung and the rise of communism (1949– present)—China was that nation and people. Yet it was reached, and even at the present time, under extreme persecution and duress, the fires of the gospel have not been extinguished, nor will they ever be.

Our prayer must be that of the psalmist:

God be merciful unto us, and bless us; and cause his face to shine upon us; That thy way may be known upon earth, thy saving health among all nations. (Psalm 67:1–2)

~~~

FOUR

Professors Preach Self-Salvation

By Tom Hoffman

What students would learn in American schools above all is the religion of Jesus Christ. —George Washington

It is such privilege and honor to be asked to contribute a chapter to this important topic and the ongoing work of Terry James. Terry's influence on my growth in the area of Bible prophecy has been and continues to be very significant. My deep prayer is that the reader finds new information and new encouragement in this chapter and in this book.

To be associated with the people of integrity who are contributing various chapters to this book is both humbling and a great gift.

The notion of education has been extremely important to me. I recently retired after thirty-seven years as a teacher, principal, and university professor. I spent most of those years as a principal in the public-school system.

My wife and I always counted my career as an educator as a full-time ministry, even though I was paid. Being a teacher or principal (or any staff member, for that matter) in public schools today is very challenging. I had the high privilege of spending the last ten years of my career as an administrator working with students who had significant emotional and behavioral issues. These experiences give me a little bit of street cred for the topic of college professors and their influence on culture today.

I was a full-time faculty member at two private colleges in Minnesota. I spent almost four years at one college and a full two years at another university.

In this chapter, I want to provide the reader a context for the issue of education. This context is related to our worldview as we examine life, religion, faith, politics, and economics, as well as education.

Later in the chapter, I'll provide three case studies of high-profile university professors based on a 2006 book by David Horowitz. I purchased and read the book specifically to provide research for this chapter. An adept researcher and author, Horowitz expertly understands the political landscape and has written many books and articles in the field. I appreciated his deep dive in profiling many higher-education professors and their profound influence on our current culture. For that part of this chapter, I want to recognize and thank Mr. Horowitz.

For each of the three case studies I chose to highlight, I will also provide a scriptural application. Further, I will discuss, in "plainspeak," how college professors are given so much power—especially in choosing other candidates who want to become college professors. This unique authority over the selection process has gone unchecked for more than fifty years now, and is at the heart of why college and university professors have such an impact on young men and women.

Finally, I'll conclude the chapter with a rationale as to why liberal college and university professors have created a dangerous culture of influence for young people who attend their classes.

America's Educational Context:
Cultural Worldview vs. Christian Worldview

Later in the chapter, I'll reveal historical information about how and why there is a current collision course between the worldviews that people in America possess today. Actually, the tension between today's cultural worldview and a Christian worldview is so thick you can cut it with a proverbial knife.

Part of my research for writing this chapter came from an amazing book written by the late Charles Colson. Colson, of course, was known best for his part in helping then President Richard Nixon go to the extent of lawlessness in order to be reelected to his second term as president.

Just before entering prison for his role in Watergate, Colson accepted Jesus Christ as his Lord and Savior. His life was never the same, and after leaving prison, he became an unparalleled leader in bringing the gospel of Jesus into prison systems; he also became one of the greatest authorities on the Christian worldview. His 2017 book, *God and Government*, is a seminal read in the doctrine of Christian worldview.

Believe it or not, our current cultural worldview has its genesis in Marxism. The social, cultural, moral, and political changes of the 1960s created a firestorm in the United States, with a new generation that was captivated by drug use, free sex, and the start of the gay rights move-ment—with the US Supreme Court's decision of *Roe vs. Wade* coming into view on the short horizon. Abortion continues to be the law of the land following that ruling.

Colson reminded us that, at the same time, a perilous movement was afoot in a different part of our world. That shift was led by the likes of founder of the Russian Communist Party, Vladimir Lenin; German socialist revolutionary, Karl Marx; and the Hungarian communist, Mátyás Rákosi. Their vision was a society devoid of any spiritual dimension, and their warped view of government shaped the forces of communism and socialism as the ideal. Their philosophies began to drip into Western cul-tures, including that of America.

Here is Colson's accurate summary:

At the same time [the 1960s], a destructive philosophic trend gripped American intellectuals. The long fuse lit by the ideas of

Nietzsche, Freud, and Darwin finally set off and explosion of relativism. All moral distinctions were equally invalid since all were
equally subjective.[33]

If you are reading this book, you surely believe that Christianity and
communism are the antithesis of one another.

The Christian Worldview

For Christians, Jesus is everything.

We believe that every issue involved in our time on earth centers on
following Jesus and His teachings. The Bible is our sword; we are rooted
in prayer and use our local churches for fellowship and growth in our
spiritual walk.

We believe that Christ was born, He died, and He will come again
to set up His heavenly kingdom right here on earth one day. In fact, the
authors of this book believe that the time of Jesus' return is soon.

Our purpose here on earth is to love one another as Jesus taught.
We've been commissioned to go out and share the gospel of Jesus whenever we can, wherever we can (Matthew 28:16–20). And all Christians
who live in this Age of Grace, along with the Old Testament saints before
us and those who have preceded us in this age, will be reunited with Jesus
during the Rapture. This, according to Scripture, is our "blessed hope"
(Titus 2:13).

The Communist Worldview

For Communists, Jesus isn't everything; man is.

God and anything with a spiritual connotation is a bunch of malar-
key—or, as Lenin often proclaimed, it is "foolishness." He said:

Every man who occupies himself with the construction of a god,
or merely even agrees to it, prostitutes himself in the worst way, for

he occupies himself not with activity, but with self-contemplation and self-reflection, and tries thereby to deify his most unclean, most stupid, and most servile features and pettiness.[34]

Communism dismisses capitalism as an elite political and economic system. Communists believe in a classless society that incorporates a caste system—that is, you are born into a socioeconomic class and will never move up or down out of that class for your entire life here on earth.

Like Christianity, communism is eschatological. Although it does not include a spiritual component in its paradigm of end-time matters, communism looks toward an endpoint when its belief system will come to a final fruition.

Colson describes this evolution:

Philosophically, Marxism, is certainly a religion. It offers a comprehensive explanation of reality and claims to put adherents in touch with high powers—namely, the inexorable laws of history. Its eschatology is millennial. At the end of the class struggle against capitalism lies the classless society where exploits are banished, the state withers away, and man's natural goodness flows forth unobstructed. The laws of history will bring justice to the oppressed and wipe away every tear. It's a system that an atheist can put his faith in.[35]

Relativism

Due to the insidious invasion of communist and socialist thought, along with the momentous change in culture that the 1960s provided, a new breed of postmodern relativism was able to put down incredibly deep roots in the United States.

Please note that I'm using a broad-stroked definition of "relativism" for this chapter. In my mind, and in what I see happening across our culture today, in 2020, "relativism" truly means "everything goes." Today's most poignant example of "everything goes" is the incredible emergence of issues related to gender identity. If I am born a female but believe a mistake was made at birth, I can simply announce that I am "transgendering" to become a male.

I may cut my hair or remove facial hair.

I may take hormones or other drugs.

I may dress differently.

I may have surgery.

I will do everything humanly possible to undo what God has created. If this isn't the definition of "relativism,"—or, as I say, "everything goes,"—then I don't know what is.

A disturbing number of people accept this dangerous mindset. As a former high school principal, I can assure you that this kind of thinking is prominent in the public-school setting. I will add that K–12 public schools create policies, engage in professional development, and actively support students in order to create a more tolerant learning environment.

And, as prevalent as this effort is in the lower levels of education, the philosophy or mindset of relativism is even stronger in our colleges and universities. What we saw beginning in the 1960s and 1970s was a change in the purpose of higher education—what I like to call the "Academy." All rules, all regulations, and all truths were now demanded to be questioned—not only by the students, but by their university professors as well. Yes, postmodern relativism is the very root of what is wrong with today's Academy.

Colson accurately summed up the situation in his 2007 book when he said, "Now each student must be allowed to decide truth for himself. Dogma, not ignorance, became the enemy."[36] This is exactly what's happening in 2020, in higher-education institutions across the Unites States—led by radical professors.

Case Studies

I have several degrees, including a bachelor's, two master's, and a doctorate—all in the field of education. Doing the research for this chapter was a blessing and very fun for me.

During all my work in the Academy, my favorite way to learn was through case studies. Simply put, case studies are tools to teach concepts and theories.

One part of my doctoral studies was an assignment to create a case study of a leader whom I considered to have had the most influence on my life. The other doctoral candidates and I were to write a lengthy paper about our chosen subject, plus create a picture board. The paper would be graded by the professor, but the picture board was to accompany a five-minute presentation to learning cohorts, comprised of my fellow thirty-four doctoral candidates.

My colleagues chose an impressive list of leaders to research, including Martin Luther King Jr., Mahatma Gandhi, Mother Theresa, President John F. Kennedy, Emmitt Till, Winston Churchill, Nelson Mandela, Pope John Paul II, Margaret Thatcher, Bill Clinton, John Lennon, and Che Guevara. And the list of influential leaders went on; however, other students chose parents, grandparents, or close friends to profile.

I, of course, chose Jesus as my subject.

Although the university was Wesleyan and featured a huge statue of Christian theologian and founder of Methodism, John Wesley, in the mall area of campus, it was, to say the very least, quite liberal in thought and practice. Many times during the course of my two and a half years there, I stood out like a sore thumb because of my faith values.

(You can imagine my colleagues' response to my decision to feature Jesus in my presentation. I should mention that I live in Minnesota, where the iconic saying, "Minnesota Nice," is ensconced in our culture and, fortunately, in our classrooms as well. So, actually, the response by my colleagues was polite and quite reserved—but I know in their thoughts there were a lot of ranting and profanity!)

Anyway, for this chapter, I want to use case studies to demonstrate that today's college and university professors impose the doctrine of "self-salvation" and add evidence for the purpose of this book. I've prepared three case studies based primarily on a 2006 book I mentioned earlier: *The Professors: The 101 Most Dangerous Academics in America,* by author and conservative David Horowitz (b. 1939). Interestingly, earlier in his life, Horowitz identified with the New Left politics and adhered to Marxist theory. He has spent much of his later years expertly writing against leftist individuals and agencies. (If you are a Christian and a conservative, I highly recommend checking out his writings.)

As I sought to choose three college professors to write about, I also wanted to inject biblical principles into the case studies. I didn't plan to do this when I first wrote the outline for this chapter. But as I read each of the professor's stories from Horowitz' book, along with my other research materials, a strong biblical principle came to mind for each subject.

I believe the Holy Spirit was prompting me, so each case study will end with a brief scriptural expository relating to the following precepts:

1. God is truth.
2. There is only one God.
3. God favors the nation of Israel.

I also provide evidence of how each professor has influenced the youth culture in dogma and pedagogy that totally oppose the Word of God.

Chillingly, what the academics teach their students often is only nominally related to the subject area they're assigned. As a result, we have a snapshot (for a much larger picture, please read Horowitz' book) of bell hooks, Michael Eric Dyson, and Mark LeVine, all of whom teach a message of relativism, the troubling belief system that says there are no absolute truths.

Professor bell hooks, City College of New York

I read some of this professor's work while earning my doctorate in educational leadership from Hamline University in St. Paul, Minnesota. (When I cited hooks' research in one of my papers, I capitalized her first and last name even though "bell hooks" is a pen name Gloria Jean Watkins borrowed from her great-grandmother and lowercased "to focus attention on her message rather than herself."[37] I received a stern reprimand from my professor for that error—at least it *felt* stern because of the red ink she used as the reminder.)

Bell hooks is a prolific educational writer whose writing exudes the very kind of relativism highlighted in the previous section. I guess no one can describe her educational philosophy more than she does in her self-assessment: "My commitment to engaged pedagogy is an expression of political activism."[38]

Professor hooks has an extensive influence in education and is a renowned member of the Academy. She is currently a Distinguished Professor of English Literature at City College of New York, and her writings include the following:

- *Ain't I a Woman* (1981)
- *Feminism Is for Everybody* (2000)
- *We Real Cool: Black Men and Masculinity* (2003)
- *Killing Rage: Ending Racism* (1995)
- *Where We Stand: Class Matters* (2000)
- *Art on My Mind: Visual Politics* (1995)
- *Outlaw Culture* (1994)
- *Breaking Bread: Insurgent Black Intellectual Life* (1991)
- *Yearning: Race, Gender, and Cultural Politics* (1990)
- *Salvation: Black People and Love* (2001)
- *Belonging: A Place of Culture* (1990)
- *Teaching Critical Thinking: Practical Wisdom* (2009)

It's easy to see the worldview hooks embraces from the preceding book titles, isn't it? Feminism, racism, culture, and class are more about an ideology than about teaching students in a city college learning environment.

And that's part of what you will see in all three case studies presented. Today, the Academy is more about personal passion and a postmodern relativistic influence than it is about teaching traditional truth, especially truth based on biblical principle.

Bell hooks even infers that—although it has given her the monumental voice in academia that she has today—she truly dislikes higher education. She once wrote, "The academy has always been so similar to the dysfunctional patriarchal family hierarchy that hemmed me in as a child that I feel that I can never be truly healthy, well and whole in the deepest sense, without leaving it."[39]

Yet, to this day, she remains active in the Academy, making a great income and continuing to influence a plethora of unwitting college students. Professor hooks' classroom philosophy distances itself from what true academics consider pedagogy. ("Pedagogy" is the study of teaching and learning, especially as it relates to the relationship between the teacher and student in a classroom setting.) She gives her students *only* opportunities to explore life's meaning as they see fit, through intimating that life's truth can only be discovered by looking from within and then comparing those vagabond hunches to the economic, social, and political realities she has been teaching through her books, articles, and personal experience. Hers is an open, Socratic learning environment, where the end of truth is only defined by a student's thoughts and conclusions. She freely admits that her classroom is a commitment to engaged pedagogy in an expression of political activism.[40]

By all counts, bell hooks is a good, well-respected college professor, but strictly and *only* from a cultural worldview.

God Is Truth

From a Christian worldview, bell hooks is influencing young men and women away from God's truth. God, and God only, is truth. Because God is truth, the ideology bell hooks is teaching her students directly opposes what God teaches through His Holy Spirit and the Scriptures.

The fact is, this esteemed professor is peddling false truth.

Bible scholar Don Stewart declares:

God is a God of truth. Scripture says it is impossible for God to lie. Therefore, when He speaks to humanity, such as in the promise recorded in the Bible, we can trust what He says. There is much comfort in the fact that His promises can always be relied upon. He will never let us down.[41]

I want to remind you of some important Bible verses related to God and truth (with emphasis added):

Romans 3:4: *"Let God be true, and every man a liar,* as it is written: 'So that you may be proved right when you speak and prevail when you judge.'"

Titus 1:2: "A faith and knowledge resting on the hope of eternal life, which *God, who does not lie,* promised before the beginning of time."

John 14:6: "I am the way, *the truth,* and the life. No one comes to the Father except through me."

2 Timothy 3:16–17: *"All scripture is God-breathed* and is useful for teaching rebuking, correcting, and training in righteousness; so that the man or woman of God may be thoroughly equipped for every good work."

We've all heard the phrase from the pulpit when the pastor cries out: "Be a Berean and check this out for yourself." That's because we have to always test what we're being taught.

Who teaches truth: bell hooks or Almighty God?

This question is laughable if it weren't so important. It's important because American professors like bell hooks have more influence than God on today's university and college students. The professor claims that her right as a teacher is a "right as a subject in resistance to define reality."[42] That's funny; I thought the only One to define reality is God.

David Horowitz is much, much more colorful in his summation of hooks' influence:

In sum, this is a distinguished professor with a six-figure salary, loaded with academic honors, who is given license to conduct a one-sided Marxist-feminist indoctrination of hapless students, but still believes—as she explains as an invited commencement speaker—that she is living under the tyranny of a fascist dictator-ship: namely, the United States.[43]

Professor Michael Eric Dyson, Georgetown University

According to his website, Dr. Michael Eric Dyson is a Georgetown University sociology professor, a *New York Times* contributing opinion writer, and a contributing editor of the *New Republic* and of ESPN's The Undefeated website. He is also a dynamic speaker, especially on the subjects of racial disparity, culture ideology, and political correctness.

Interestingly, Dyson is one of the highest-paid, if not the highest-paid, professors today in America. He has dominated the talk show, radio, and book market since the mid 1990s, and has served on the faculty at Chicago Theological Seminary, Brown University, the University of North Carolina at Chapel Hill, DePaul University, and the University of Pennsylvania.

He is also an ordained Baptist minister.

Some of the books Dyson has written over the years include the following:

- *What the Truth Sounds Like: Robert F. Kennedy, James Baldwin and Our Unfinished Conversation about Race* (2018)
- *Holler If You Hear Me: The Search for Tupac Shakur* (2001)
- *Is Bill Cosby Right? Or Has the Black Middle Class Lost Its Mind?* (2005)
- *Making Malcom: The Myth & Making of Malcom X* (1995)
- *Political Correctness Gone Mad* (2018)
- *Between God and Gangsta Rap* (2018)
- *Debating Race with Michael Dyson* (2007)
- *Tears We Cannot Stop: A Sermon to White America* (2017)
- *Reflecting Black: African American Cultural Criticism* (1993)

Before Bill Cosby was sentenced to prison for his warped and devilish practice of drugging women and then sexually assaulting them, he was recognized for his criticism of black America. His loudest criticism of the black community targeted the absenteeism of fathers from their own children—especially sons. According to Crosby, single-parent mothers became the typical family structure in the African-American community. In *Is Bill Cosby Right? Or Has the Black Middle Class Lost Its Mind?* Professor Dyson challenged Cosby's cultural positioning, dismissing him as "a member of the black ruling class betraying the oppressed."[44]

The idea of two immensely popular cultural figures who were diametrically opposed was very popular news fodder in 2005. Cosby has always been adamant (even through his cultural stereotype of the cartoon character, Fat Albert) that African-American parents could quell the storm of poverty through the vehicle of education. As Horowitz wrote, "Cosby urged the black community to embrace education more passionately, become more law-abiding, and learn to speak proper English [in lieu of urbanic slang]."[45]

We live in an upside-down world, don't we?

It would seem much more logical that it would be Dyson, the college professor, who would partner with Cosby in his cultural insight.

But there is more to Professor Dyson's worldview that is much more troubling. In his popular book, *Holler If You Hear Me: The Search for Tupac Shakur*, Dyson hails the deceased rapper as the "black Jesus." In a 2016 article written by Mosi Reeves and published by *Rolling Stone* magazine, the author outlines eight ways that Tupac Shakur changed the world. Here is a summary of that list:[46]

1. Shakur's appearance in *Juice* as Bishop, the troubled high school teen who fashions himself into a cold-hearted killer, is the first great dramatic performance by a rapper in a movie.
2. He's the man who singlehandedly transformed a common epithet for a criminal into a source of masculine strength.
3. Shakur's New York trial for sexual assault was arguably the first rap celebrity court case.
4. Before Shakur reported to prison for his sexual assault conviction, he completed the first rap "pre-prison" album.

5. Shakur signed with the hottest and most dangerous record label in America, Death Row, and dropped the first hip-hop double CD.
6. Shakur is the first dead rapper who made people think he's still alive.
7. Beginning in November 1997 with *R U Still Down?* (Remember Me), Shakur becomes the first rapper to have his estate mine-stripped for new product.
8. He recorded a staggering amount of material.

I don't know about you, but when I look at this list, several significant issues stand out:

- Sexual assault
- Prison time
- Signing with the "dangerous" recording label, Death Row

In addition, Shakur once shot two off-duty law enforcement officers and served a sentence for a gang rape. He was shot and killed in a drive-by shooting on September 13, 1996.

In his biography about Shakur, Dyson wrote about Jesus:

It's hard for me to write this…but he described our Lord as, "the God who literally got beat down and hung up, the God who died a painful, shameful death, subject to capital punishment under political authority and attack, but who came back, and keeps coming back, in the form and flesh we least expect."[47]

The constant inference in the book was that Tupac Shakur was Jesus coming back in "form and flesh."

Only One God

The apostle Paul declares in 1 Corinthians 8:6:

Yet for us there is but one God, the Father, from whom all things came and for whom we live; and there is but one Lord, Jesus Christ, through whom all things came and through whom we live.

The God of Abraham, Isaac, and Jacob has a sovereign plan for all generations. This began when God called Abraham out of the land of Ur with the Abrahamic Covenant. Through the generations of Abraham, Isaac, and Jacob, God frequently used the phrase, "and they shall know that I am the Lord their God."

God's sovereign plan included sending Jesus to our earth as God incarnate.

Although many have come imitating Jesus since His death in AD 33, there was, is, and always will be just one Jesus. In His Olivet Discourse, Jesus was teaching about the last days when He proclaimed, "At that time many will fall away and hate each other, and many false prophets will arise and mislead many."

Of course, the greatest imitator of Jesus ever hasn't come forth yet. The Antichrist (described in Revelation 13:1–8 and Daniel 9:27) will deceive multitudes during the Tribulation period and will cause each soul lost to be thrown into the lake of fire.

God's sovereign plan included sending the Holy Spirit to live in our own spirits once we accept Jesus as Lord and Savior. In my bold opinion, I believe the Holy Spirit is the only thing keeping this whole world together today. The very reason for this book is Terry James' vision to expose the emerging spirit of the Antichrist. *College professors are very much a part of this emerging demonic spirit.*

The Holy Spirit living in believers of Jesus, like you and me, is what's keeping this world afloat. And, yes, I mean "afloat." Our world is upside down now; we're calling good things bad and bad things good. We are spinning out of God's favor because of issues like abortion, pornography, political correctness, cultural wars, racial strife, gay rights, shifting family structures, drug and alcohol addiction, pedophilia, and the like.

All of these "signs of our times" circle back to the historic rise of post-modern relativism, or, as I say, "anything goes." Remember now, Eric Michael Dyson is one of America's highest paid and most influential professors in the Academy. What is most needed in higher education today's is God's truth, not Dyson's truth.

Professor Mark LeVine, University of California at Irvine

Professor Mark Levine is an associate professor of history at University of California, Irvine, and he says on his university website, "My scholarship, activism and music are all tied to my commitment to struggles for social justice in the United States and around the world."[48]

I choose LeVine to feature because of his vitriol and significant distaste for Israel (and seemingly for the United States as well). What's ironic is that he renounced his Jewish faith some years ago, and he was born and raised in the United States.

Like I said before, we live in an upside-down world today.

Additionally, music is a huge part of Mark LeVine's life and a plays a significant role in his approach to the classroom. He writes on his faculty page at UC-Irvine:

> As a professional musician, I have worked with artists such as Mick Jagger, Dr. John, Johnny Copeland, Albert Collins, Chuck D, Michael Franti, Ozomatli (which won a Grammy), world music artists Hassan Hakmoun, the Kordz, Lazy Wall, Cafe Mira, Ramy Essam, Arabian Knights, Armada Bizerta, MC Rai, Tanboura, Sara Alexander and others. I have spent the last two years working with many of the main revolutionary musicians in Egypt, Tunisia, Morocco, Palestine, and Iran.[49]

One of the notions dominating the global geopolitical landscape today, mostly among nations in the Middle East, is the idea that the United States is "the Great Satan" and Israel (or, as LeVine refers to it,

"Zionism") is "the Little Satan." In other words, two of the nations with the purest forms (not perfect, mind you) of democracy are the world's greatest enemies—even demonic enemies. Professor Levine believes that both Americans and Zionists have developed as forces of evil that promote war and misery.

No country has used the terminology "Great Satan" and "Little Satan" more than Iran, who has no goal other than to wipe the land of Israel off the map. Through his lectures, articles, and (indubitably) music, LeVine has proven to be pro-Iran, pro-Islam, anti-nationalism, and anti-capitalism.

So, to summarize, LeVine demonstrates through his academic work, peace rallies, and rock music that he is:

- An activist for economic and social justice
- Anti-Israel
- Anti-USA
- Pro-Iran
- Pro-Islam
- Anti-nationalism
- Anti-capitalism

Let's remind ourselves, as well, that he is a history professor at a largely attended, renowned university. Horowitz insightfully observes:

[LeVine's] worldview encompasses a quasi-communist utopia, a classless future, where all racial, nationalist, and cultural identities are dissolved. In other words, the discredited vision of Marx that led to the deaths of one hundred million people while bankrupting whole continents in the last century.[50]

This is the kind of professor who thinks his particular ideology is superior to biblical principles. This is also a false truth constantly planted in the minds of students across America.

Particularly unnerving are LeVine's anti-Semitic views, which are also being imparted to students in his classroom. I suspect this particular issue is widespread in the Academy as well. One of LeVine's claims, because of his stance on the land promised to Israel and his pro-Palestinian posture, is "Zionism equals racism."[51]

Remember what the Bible says about coming out against the Jewish people and the nation of Israel: Israel is God's favored nation. Following is the Abrahamic Covenant:

> Now the Lord had said to Abram: Get out of your country, From your family, And from your father's house, To a land that I will show you.
>
> I will make you a great nation; I will bless you, And make your name great; And you shall be a blessing.
>
> **I will bless those who bless you, And I will curse him who curses you; And in you all the families of the earth shall be blessed.** (Genesis 12:1–3, emphasis added)

Note that the highlighted verses above indicate that:

- God promised to make Israel a great nation.
- God promised to curse those (including individuals and nations) that curse Israel.

God has fulfilled His promise to make Israel a great nation. That small country has survived since the biblical time of Abraham; that is nothing less than a miracle from God! God keeps His promises; He is the God of truth.

God is continuing to fulfill His promise to curse those who curse Israel. God is righteous, and when He declares that He will curse those who curse Israel, we can count on it. We read many examples in the Old Testament of nations and kings coming against Israel, and the Lord supernaturally intervening for His leaders like King Hezekiah, King David, and others.

Another important example of this type of activity of God hasn't yet happened. In the end times, according to the prophet Ezekiel, a coalition of countries will contrive to attack Israel and "take plunder and to take booty" from the Jewish nation. God will lure these nations to attack Israel.

Now the word of the Lord came to me, saying, Son of man, set your face against Gog, of the land of Magog, the prince of Rosh, Meshech, and Tubal, and prophesy against him, and say,

Thus says the Lord God: Behold, I am against you, O Gog, the prince of Rosh, Meshech, and Tubal.

I will turn you around, put hooks into your jaws, and lead you out, with all your army, horses, and horsemen, all splendidly clothed, a great company with bucklers and shields, all of them handling swords.

Persia, Ethiopia, and Libya are with them, all of them with shield and helmet; Gomer and all its troops; the house of Togarmah from the far north and all its troops—many people are with you. (Ezekiel 38:1–6)

The nations in of this coalition can reasonably be traced to modern Russia, Iran, Turkey, Ethiopia, Libya, Sudan, Tunisia, and Algeria.

What is the "booty" or "spoils" mentioned in this passage?

Oil. Natural gas. And lots of it.

In 2008, the Leviathan gas field was found underground and off the coast of Israel containing approximately twenty-two trillion cubic feet of natural gas, enough for Israel to become energy self-sufficient and to provide via domestic imports adequate energy to most of Europe. This incredible discovery has been in the news for several years now. Reuters reported:

A number of gas discoveries offshore Israel and in nearby eastern Mediterranean waters in the last decade have made Israel a potentially lucrative prospect for big energy firms. The region is emerging as a new hot spot for gas exploration and production.[52]

Israel has just begun the largest oil/gas pipeline project in the history of mankind. The project, just over a thousand miles in length, is dubbed the "East Mediterranean Pipeline" and should be completed within two years.

What especially do Iran and Russia want most?

Oil. Natural gas. And lots of it.

Again, Russia, Iran, and Turkey are in economic chaos today. Their leaders have enormous pride and egos. They want their countries to have superpower status, and they will do anything to obtain it. And…all three countries now have direct military presence in Syria, which shares a northern border with Israel.

What is the result of Gog and its allies attacking Israel in the future? Let's return to the end of chapter 38 in the book of Ezekiel:

"And it will come to pass at the same time, when Gog comes against the land of Israel," says the Lord God, "that My fury will show in My face. For in My jealousy and in the fire of My wrath I have spoken: 'Surely in that day there shall be a great earthquake in the land of Israel, so that the fish of the sea, the birds of the heavens, the beasts of the field, all creeping things that creep on the earth, and all men who are on the face of the earth shall shake at My presence.

"The mountains shall be thrown down, the steep places shall fall, and every wall shall fall to the ground.' I will call for a sword against Gog throughout all My mountains," says the Lord God. "Every man's sword will be against his brother. And I will bring him to judgment with pestilence and bloodshed; I will rain down on him, on his troops, and on the many peoples who are with him, flooding rain, great hailstones, fire, and brimstone.

"Thus, I will magnify Myself and sanctify Myself, and I will be known in the eyes of many nations. Then they shall know that I am the Lord."

Why is this so interesting, besides the fact that God supernaturally comes against those who oppose and threaten the nation of Israel? It's interesting because most Bible scholars believe the Gog-Magog invasion will happen at the *beginning* of the last days and will be a gateway to the seven-year Tribulation period.

After all, this is a book about the end of days.

Finally, let's consider the impact that Professor LeVine has on students. Along with his critical eye on the nation of Israel, Horowitz, states that:

> [LeVine knows] the history, politics, religions—and most important, the peoples—of the region as a friend, but with a highly critical eye. LeVine also claims a "long history of blending art, scholarship, and activism" and being "uniquely positioned to offer such analysis in a manner that will be especially appreciated by members of generations of X and Y."[53]

How Professors Aggregate Positional Power

Here is the structure for faculty rank in colleges and universities:

1. **Adjunct professor** teaches part-time in his or her area of expertise; this is usually a practicing expert in his or her field.
2. **Instructor** teaches full-time but is not on a tenure track; this usually involves a year-to-year contract with the Academy.
3. **Assistant professor** is usually on a probationary teaching assignment with tenure-rights status.
4. **Associate professor** is the same as an assistant professor, except the associate professor has exceptional experience or expertise when entering the Academy.
5. **Full professor** enjoys full-tenure status and is extremely difficult to remove from the Academy.

6. **Professor emeritus** is a retired professor with distinction who retains his or her rank and title with the Academy.

All three professors described in this chapter's case studies have acquired the rank of full professor. This is an important distinction, because it means the Academy has little control or power over them in terms of their pedagogy and content.

I want to briefly explain the *process* of receiving full professor rights. Because I have served as a full-time faculty member, always at the rank of assistant professor, I'm very familiar with the faculty-ranking process. However, there's one caveat, because my experience involved being hired by one small college and one medium-sized university. For the likes of Professor hooks, Professor Dyson, and Professor LeVine, the process is much more rigorous and takes much longer because all of their institutions are a part of what are termed "R-1 (high-impact research institutions) universities."

The responsibility of hiring is on the shoulders of the department chair, who invites two to three colleagues to participate in the screening process. The screening process involves the review of the candidate's curriculum vitae, scholarship publication record, research initiatives, and collegial recommendations.

Usually (even for small- and medium-sized colleges and universities) there is a "national search" for candidates, which simply means that the faculty position is listed on national sites like the Chronicle of Higher Education (or, in the case of faith-based situations, the Council for Christian Colleges and Universities), and on the university website. Sometimes the department chair may reach out to a specific candidate if the chair thinks the prospect might be a good fit for the position.

Next, each candidate (usually one to three) is invited to spend a full day on campus (not on the same day), when they participate in informal interviews and meet-and-greets with several key people, such as the university president, the provost or president of academic affairs, the academic dean, and representatives from student groups and the university's human resource office.

The most important part of the day visit includes a faculty presentation with the content of the lecture in the candidate's discipline of expertise. This event is attended by faculty members across all departments and academic disciplines. It's my experience that the larger faculty may or may not have input into the final selection of the candidate (a practice I always thought was kind of bizarre).

With feedback from the department members, the chair decides who will be selected. In most cases, the department chair then takes that recommendation to the dean for a final decision.

Going back to the three people presented in the case studies, and according to Horowitz, "It is easy to see how this system can be exploited by faculty members with activist agendas." He noted that "the composition of the search committee chosen by the chair will go a long way in determining the orientation of the candidate likely to be hired."

Really, that's the genesis of radical college professors—with the simple process outlined above. Department chairs, with little internal or external pressure, have been free to select new faculty appointments that align with their educational (and political) views.

This process may be illustrated through the selection of Supreme Court justices. Even the less politically inclined have heard and witnessed the partisan conflagration that bursts wide open upon the announcement of a Supreme Court justice resignation—or, in the case of Antonin Scalia, a Supreme Court justice death.

Here are the last fifteen Supreme Court justice confirmations, beginning with the rejection of Robert Bork:

Robert Bork (1987), rejected; Ronald W. Reagan

Anthony Kennedy (1987), confirmed; Ronald W. Reagan

David Souter (1990), confirmed; George H. W. Bush

Clarence Thomas (1991), confirmed; George H. W. Bush

Ruth Bader Ginsburg (1993), confirmed; William J. Clinton

Stephen Breyer (1994), confirmed; William J. Clinton
John Roberts (2005), withdrew; George W. Bush
John Roberts (2005), confirmed; George W. Bush
Harriet Miers (2005), withdrew; George W. Bush
Samuel Alito (2005), confirmed; George W. Bush
Sonia Sotomayor (2009), confirmed; Barack H. Obama
Elena Kagan (2010), confirmed; Barack H. Obama
Merrick Garland (2016), confirmed; Barack H Obama
Neil Gorsuch (2017), confirmed; Donald J. Trump
Brett Kavanaugh (2018), confirmed; Donald J. Trump

Because the president chooses Supreme Court justices, the High Court sways back and forth on conservative-versus-liberal issues, primarily because of the president's party affiliation and Senate confirmation.

However, no such luck with colleges and universities. There is virtually no checks-and-balances system for department chairs. As a result, the selection of professors, especially at large colleges and universities, has become more and more liberal.

Going back to the *Professors* book by David Horowitz, the author claimed that 91 of the 101 professors profiled in his work went on to attain tenured positions, resulting in years and years of influence on faculty selection after they began teaching. Liberal thought breeds liberal thought. If they became department chairs (and many did), "They are in a position to designate members of search committees and shape the composition of their departments."[54]

In addition, Horowitz studied professors of various disciplines, twenty-one in all, spanning subjects ranging from African-American studies, women's studies, and criminology to peace studies, economics, and religion. The professors came from small, medium, and R-1 universities and colleges, and taught in institutions from the Northwest, Midwest, South, and West; in all, thirty-three establishments of higher education were included in Horowitz' comprehensive study.

Because of the number of professors, the breadth of geographic locations, and the wide range of disciplines, Horowitz concisely stated:

Thus, the problems revealed in this text—the explicit introduction of political agendas into the classroom, the lack of professionalism in conduct, and the decline in professional standards—appear to be increasingly widespread throughout the academic profession and at virtually every type of institution of higher learning.[55]

So What?

One of the techniques pounded home during my doctoral coursework was the notion of "so what?". Whenever a scholar defends or creates an argument, there must be a "so what?". Otherwise, how does the audience know the significance of the author or teacher's argument?

I will wrap up this chapter with a look at why liberal-thinking and liberal-acting college and university professors have created a dangerous culture of influence for the young adults who attend their classes.

Public education was dealt a huge blow and significant setback in 1962, when prayer was outlawed in schools. The Supreme Court of the United States (SCOTUS) heard the petition of *Engel vs. Vitale* and voted 8-1 to rule that school prayer was unconstitutional.

A second blow came the following year when the Supreme Court, in the case of *Abington School District vs. Schempp* (1963), outlawed publicly reading Scripture and reciting the Lord's Prayer in public schools.

Then, the Supreme Court, in its 7-1 decision regarding *Roe vs. Wade* (1972), concluded that a woman's right to privacy is constitutional as related to the Fourteenth Amendment and due process clause. This violation of the biblical principle of the sanctity of life has resulted in more than sixty million abortions in the United State of America since 1973.

Moving to more recent history, I vividly remember the evening of June 26, 2015, when the White House was lit up with glowing colors of the rainbow in response to the Supreme Court's decision that day about gay rights. In a 5-4 ruling in the case of *Obergefell vs. Hodges*, the court mandated all states to issue marriage licenses to same-sex couples throughout the United States and territories legally validating same-sex marriages.

It's important to recognize the biblical view of these three key Supreme Court decisions outlawing prayer in school, legalizing the death of millions of innocent lives, and allowing same-sex marriage. Romans 1:22–32 offers a compelling summary:

> Professing to be wise, they became fools, and changed the glory of the incorruptible God into an image made like corruptible man—and birds and four-footed animals and creeping things.
>
> Therefore, God also gave them up to uncleanness, in the lusts of their hearts, to dishonor their bodies among themselves, who exchanged the truth of God for the lie, and worshiped and served the creature rather than the Creator, who is blessed forever. Amen.
>
> For this reason, God gave them up to vile passions. For even their women exchanged the natural use for what is against nature. Likewise, also the men, leaving the natural use of the woman, burned in their lust for one another, men with men committing what is shameful, and receiving in themselves the penalty of their error which was due.
>
> And even as they did not like to retain God in their knowledge, God gave them over to a debased mind, to do those things which are not fitting; being filled with:
> All un-righteousness,
> Sexual immorality,
> Wickedness,
> Covetousness,
> Maliciousness;
> Full of envy,
> Murder,
> Strife,
> Deceit,
> Evil-mindedness;
> They are:
> Whisperers,

Backbiters,

Haters of God,

Violent,

Proud,

Boasters,

Inventors of evil things,

Disobedient to parents,

Undiscerning,

Untrustworthy,

Unloving,

Unforgiving,

Unmerciful;

Who, knowing the righteous judgment of God, that those who practice such things are deserving of death, not only do the same but also approve of those who practice them.

While "the world" finds this passage to promote intolerance and form the root of bigotry, I praise God for His truth and faithfulness in helping us distinguish between what is truth and what behaviors demonstrate the emerging spirit of the Antichrist in our land.

In summary, our Supreme Court has made decisions, in my opinion starting in 1962, that have spiritually crippled our nation's relationship with God. That's a pretty strong statement, but one held by many people who follow Jesus today.

My argument is that there is a subtle but important difference between the influence on America by SCOTUS and the influence on America by self-serving professors in the Academy. When SCOTUS makes a decision like it did in 2015 regarding same-sex marriages, the impact of the decision literally explodes—repercussions of the decision are immediate.

Not so for those who attend classes taught by liberal professors. The effects of their decisions are delayed and enmesh into the culture so subtly that it can be compared to the "boiling frog" illustration of the frog not noticing it's being boiled—until it's too late.

Young college students take the teaching and influence of their professors out into our world today, just as they've done from the 1960s. The influence of professors in America has been a slow disillusionment. A slow fade. But the ending is as inevitable as that of the boiling frog.

Behold, I am coming quickly!

Blessed is he who keeps the words of the prophecy of this book.

Now I, John, saw and heard these things. And when I heard and saw, I fell down to worship before the feet of the angel who showed me these things.

Then he said to me; see that you do not do that. For I am your fellow servant, and of your brethren the prophets, and of those who keep the words of this book. Worship God.

And he said to me; do not seal the words of the prophecy of this book, for the time is at hand.

He who is unjust, let him be unjust still; he who is filthy, let him be filthy still; he who is righteous, let him be righteous still; he who is holy, let him be holy still. (Revelation 22:7–11)

FIVE

Devices in These End of Days

By Nathan E. Jones

The Modern-Day Man

With a sudden explosion of musical notes, Katy Perry's "Roar" erupted from the smartphone frantically vibrating face down on the nightstand. The musical cacophony drowned out the long groan that escaped the young man lying on his unkempt bed. Yanking a pillow and pressing it firmly over his head, he groggily half-listened to the muffled lyrics: "I got the eye of the tiger…a fighter, dancing through the fire / 'Cause I am a champion, and you're gonna hear me roar." He let the inspirational message motivate him into at least a sitting position.

Bare feet hanging off the edge of the bed, the man scratched his jawline obscured by his scraggly beard. With some effort he leaned far over and snatched up his Android. Not expecting facial recognition to identify him in this disheveled condition, he zigzagged his index finger across the phone's surface, keying in the code to unlock the interface, and clicked the pause button on Spotify. He was greeted by dozens of multicolored app icons filled with numbers indicating notifications that were all vying for his attention. Checking the "Like" count on his Instagram post from the night before, he bemoaned the paltry response, and that old pang to his self-esteem shot him through his heart yet again. His selfie pic winking at his dinner reminded his stomach that he was hungry, and it groaned, too. After inquiring from Google Home what time it was, the man realized that almost twenty-five minutes had elapsed since Katy Perry had knocked on his proverbial door and awakened him.

Trudging to the bathroom for his morning ablutions, he switched on both Pandora and the faucet. Soaking in the bathtub took another half hour as his thumbs deftly moved from Snapchat to WhatsApp to Twitter to TikTok. For kicks, he pulled up BitLife to help him decide if he should towel off or spend some additional time seeing if Studio C had released anything new on YouTube. With a loud sigh, he obeyed and dripped his way out of the tub and into a pair of PacSun grey skinny jeans. He wished he had a dark stacked pair, so with a few more swooshes of his index finger, Amazon would be delivering a new pair to the front door in just another hour or two. His bank's app whined with the disappointing news that there'd be another overdraft fee. No problem—he'd just reapply for another Apple Pay account. A knowing smile at his cleverness spread across the hazy mirror image peering back at him, and so enamored by what he saw, he puckered his lips and snapped a picture to upload to his Tinder dating profile. That should get the models swiping right, he mused.

Lunchtime had already started as he skulked to the table, eyes glued to his phone so he wouldn't have to see the disapproving gaze of his father. He didn't want to start that "When I was 23…" conversation all over again. He had tried online classes at the local community college, but "gender studies" just wasn't for him. His ambition was to become a YouTube star. He just needed one of his video rants to go viral and then he would have it made. Or, he'd become the greatest of Reddit's social justice warriors, if only he could get excited about a cause. Fortunately, his father was busy scanning the news headlines on his Surface tablet, shifting uncomfortably from side to side as each AP newsbyte irked him. Mother, too, was engrossed with Words with Friends and Facebook, so her half sandwich hovered just a few inches from her mouth. *Tablets,* he scoffed internally—*so uncool.* They're only good for little kids like his sister to play Peek-a-Zoo, and so she was. The family sat in silence, except for the sounds of chewing and the tapping of glass, all intent on their own devices. The melodic voice of Google Home at last reminded the family of their afternoon activities, and they silently parted from each other like ghosts.

The young man groaned at the thought of having to endure yet another evening shift at the Game Stop, a career path he knew couldn't last too much longer in this online gaming world. Brightening at the thought of gaming, he sped back to his shuttered room and switched on his PS4 to earn a better spot on the Fortnite leaderboard. Upon earning a new skin for his avatar's rocket launcher, his phone lit up with an angry text from his boss. Was that the poop emoji?!? He was late again!

Dropping the controller, the absent employee reached to pick up his key fob, only to recollect that his older hybrid-electric Prius wasn't charged and so would not be moving from its spot on the driveway. Scrambling through his app list, he pulled up Uber and ordered a pickup. Soon standing out on his front lawn waiting for his ride, the young man was forced to face down a few unbearable moments of uncomfortable nothingness, so he reached into his back pocket yet again for his phone. Ahhh! That made him feel much better. Fifteen minutes later, the Uber driver gave up trying to draw the young man's attention, and with a shrug, slowly drove off without him.

A Double-Edged Sword

Please don't take me wrong; the opening fictional story portraying a sampling of the gadget-laden loser life of a member of the newest generation does not reflect on everyone in that age group. What generation hasn't had its slackers, right? My parents' Boomer generation, born between 1944–1964, in their youth wove necklaces out of daisies in the back of their multicolored VW buses with their radios pulsating Led Zeppelin tunes. My own Gen-X peers, born between 1965–1979, spent countless hours devouring MTV and maneuvering a little Italian plumber around turtle shells while Michael Jackson blared from our oversized boom boxes. And now, Millennials/Gen-Ys, born between 1980–1998, and Gen-Zs, born between 1999–2015, endure the pains of tech-neck from a life staring down at mobile-device screens filled with a plethora of competing apps while Beyoncé rocks out of wireless earbuds. Every generation has had its distractions and those who live to be distracted.

But—and this is significant—no other generation in the past has been subjected to as many distractions as the Millennials and Gen-Zs of today. Gen-Zs, in particular, have lived their entire lives never having known what life was like without being connected 24/7 to the Internet and mobile devices. This characteristic has led Jean Twenge, a professor of psychology at San Diego State University, to label Millennials and Gen-Zs as "Generation Me" and "iGen," respectively.[56] And, after having reviewed two studies about classroom attention spans, columnist Victoria Barret was led to refer to the children of today as the "Distracted Generation."[57]

A great price has been paid psychologically for these endless distractions. Barret cites a Pew Research Center finding that nearly 90 percent of teachers surveyed said that digital technologies were creating "an easily distracted generation with short attention spans."[58] In a Common Sense study, 71 percent of teachers surveyed said they thought technology was hurting attention spans "somewhat" or "a lot," with 60 percent concluding that online distractions hindered their students' ability to write and communicate in person.[59] Almost half of the teachers concluded that continual distractions also hurt critical thinking and homework skills.

Though ever connected to their "friends" over social media, losing in-person human relationships has caused Gen-Zs to find themselves increasingly homebound, jobless, dislocated, lonely, lethargic, physically weakened, depressed, and taking prescription pain killers—and even 35 percent are more likely to commit suicide than previous, less-technical generations. After learning that 44 percent of high school seniors in 2015 had never been out on a date, Dr. Twenge noted with some worry that "it's not an exaggeration to describe iGen as being on the brink of the worst mental-health crisis in decades," with the cause being that "much of this deterioration can be traced to their phones."[60] She concluded that "the twin rise of the smartphone and social media has caused an earthquake of a magnitude we've not seen in a very long time, if ever," and that "there is compelling evidence that the devices we've placed in young people's hands are having profound effects on their lives—and making them seriously unhappy.[61]

This abruptly negative shift in teen behaviors towards troubled emotional states is not a localized Western problem, either; it has become a global cultural phenomenon:

> The arrival of the smartphone has radically changed every aspect of teenagers' lives, from the nature of their social interactions to their mental health. These changes have affected young people in every corner of the nation and in every type of household. The trends appear among teens poor and rich; of every ethnic background; in cities, suburbs, and small towns. Where there are cell towers, there are teens living their lives on their smartphone.[62]

On another note, and don't take this wrong, either: Your initial impression after reading this chapter so far may be that I hate technology. I do not. Quite the contrary, I love it! After all, isn't technology just applying what we know to fix problems and make stuff? Technology can be thought of as the gadgets and devices we make, but it also includes the technical skills and creativity it initially takes to invent and forge these tools. So I have dedicated the last twenty years of my life professionally to the information technology (IT) world, specifically in Web development, design, and digital marketing, and ministerially as an Internet evangelist pursuing every new technology that can potentially reach people with the gospel of Jesus Christ. The communications technologies that the Lord has provided His Church today have reached far more people for Jesus Christ than any era before Itek Corporation founder Richard Leghorn coined the term "Information Age" back in 1960. Praise God!

But, as we have read, technology is a double-edged sword. The same social media that keeps us connected to long-lost family and friends also connects us to click-baiters, identity thieves, and cyber bullies. The same online classes that we take to help educate us from anywhere in the world can also depersonalize the educational process and leave the student learning in a vacuum. News and weather at the touch of the fingertip, which wonderfully warns of impending storms, can also keep us in a constant state of agitation long after the event has passed. The benefit of encountering so many different points of view online can leave one's head spinning in moral relativism and despair.

Technology and the many devices that connect us provide great benefit to the individual and society, but in the wrong hands, can produce great harm. The lord of all evil—Satan—knows this. He's had a plan going for thousands of years, since the beginnings of his corrupting influence on humanity, and it continues to this day. The only difference between then and now is that Satan has added technology to his strategy for reaching his insidious goal.

Going forward in this chapter, then, let's identify Satan's end goal. Next, let's discern his overarching strategy. And, finally, I will reveal a number of the technologies that, when combined, culminate into the ultimate device our enemy now employs to help achieve his nefarious objective.

Satan's Goal and Strategy

So, just what is Satan's goal? The book of Isaiah provides a first-person narrative of exactly what Satan has long been attempting to achieve: "I will ascend into heaven, I will exalt my throne above the stars of God; I will also sit on the mount of the congregation on the farthest sides of the north; I will ascend above the heights of the clouds, I will be like the Most High" (Isaiah 14:13–14).[63] Ever since God's guardian cherub and heavenly worship leader began to envy the praise and worship the Almighty received, Satan has sought to usurp God and sit on His throne. A failed *coup d'état* forced the prideful angel to change his plans, having been banished from heaven and cast down to the earth. If he could not rule the universe, then Satan would at least rule over the planet promised to God's children who were made in His image. Satan would corrupt humanity, bending those mere mortals to serve him rather than their Heavenly Father, and so build his own heinously evil global empire upon their subjugated backs.

What strategy does Satan employ in his attempt to reach his sinister goal of establishing his global empire and garner the praise of mankind? He continues to follow the same five-step strategy he did way back in the Garden of Eden.

Step 1: Distract

The first step in Satan's nefarious strategy to steal planet earth from mankind began by distracting God's children. Genesis 3 tells the story of how Satan, in the form of a serpent, approached the very first woman, Eve. Hanging down from his perch in a nearby tree, the serpent stopped the woman in her tracks with a simple question, asking, "Has God indeed said, 'You shall not eat of every tree of the garden'?" And the woman replied to the serpent, "We may eat the fruit of the trees of the garden; but of the fruit of the tree which is in the midst of the garden, God has said, 'You shall not eat it, nor shall you touch it, lest you die.'"

God had created and then placed the very first people—Adam and Eve—into a garden paradise. No weeds or thorns or thistles or stinging and biting creatures could be found there. The first couple only had to keep the garden well-trimmed and cultivated, name the animals, and keep God and each other company. No want or need existed, for the bounty of the garden was lovingly given by God for them to pluck at with ease. Every imaginable fruit and grain was at their disposal. The crops grew and the trees produced fruit all year long.

Only one rule existed in this tropical paradise, and that was for Adam and Eve not to eat from one lone tree. That's it! Just one tree. The first couple had even been warned by God what would happen should they eat the fruit of that tree—death. But, Satan knows that which is forbidden often becomes the most tempting. Even with all the boundless delicacies at their disposal, Satan knows how easy it is to distract mankind with the things they can never possess. With that simple question Satan posed, all of the bounty faded from Eve's sight, and only that solitary forbidden tree remained, stubbornly tugging at her mind.

Step 2: Self-Focus

With Eve's mind distracted from all she possessed to now focus only on what she could not have, Satan implemented the second step in his strategy to wrest the world away from humanity. He made the humans focus not on their countless blessings and a loving God, but on themselves.

In Genesis 3:4, the serpent said to the woman: "You will not surely die. For God knows that in the day you eat of it your eyes will be opened, and you will be like God, knowing good and evil." Satan's bald-faced lie placed a niggling doubt in Eve's mind. She began to think that maybe God was holding out on her; maybe He did not love her and Adam as selflessly as He had claimed; maybe even God was jealous of humanity and so was keeping them down. Eve's outward focus on God and her husband turned to self-focus on what she now believed she didn't have, but deserved. Eve began to see Adam and herself as victims. Dupes even! An unknown feeling welled up within her for the first time in her short life. Eve began to envy. Satan recognized that emotion all too well.

Step 3: Break Apart

The story goes on in verse 6 to say that a distracted, self-focused Eve took a good look at that forbidden tree and found the fruit was quite attractive, for "it was pleasant to the eyes, and a tree desirable to make one wise." Ignoring the subconscious voice pleading with her conscious mind not to do this disobedient thing, Eve made up her mind, plucked a piece of the forbidden fruit, and ate it.

Adam now enters the picture. We don't know if he was there the whole time or had just come upon Eve and the serpent conversing. Genesis doesn't say. Some claim that Eve's newfound understanding of the difference between good and evil—the loss of her childlike innocence—caused her to realize she had become somehow different than her husband, maybe even emotionally superior. Regardless, her willful disobedience had broken her apart from her mate. With this realization, Eve may have used the very first feminine charms to lure Adam to join her in her guilty state. That's unlikely, though, for verse 17 places the Fall of mankind squarely on Adam's shoulders. We know simply that Eve also "gave to her husband with her and he ate," and "then the eyes of both of them were opened." Eve may have been deceived when she disobeyed, but when Adam disobeyed, he chose to do so with all the facts present.

Mere moments passed before Adam and Eve's relationship had begun to break apart. The juice had barely dripped off their chins before they realized with some shock that they were naked, and so ran off to sew fig leaves together to make coverings for themselves. The complete openness in their intimate personal relationship was for the first time cloaked from each other. Instead of an equal partnership, going forward, man the stronger vessel would dominate woman the weaker vessel, and all future marriages would suffer some level of gender warfare. God would later, in verse 16, explain to Eve this new hierarchy: "Your desire shall be for your husband, and he shall rule over you."

Mankind's relationship with the Heavenly Father had also been shattered. Verse 8 reveals that, for the very first time in their lives, Adam and Eve feared the presence of God, so they hid from Him. When God at last found their hiding spot, He rhetorically asked the couple how they knew they were naked and why they had disobeyed Him. Immediately, the guilty two flung incriminations at each other like knives. Adam blamed Eve for their sin, Eve blamed the serpent, and in their newly fallen self-righteous state, surely all three found a way to blame God.

Yet another breaking occurred, for as verse 21 reveals, the Lord God made tunics of skin out of animals to clothe them. Death had indeed at last entered paradise. The trusting relationship between mankind and the animal world had also been shattered by their disobedience, and much fear, mistrust, and blood would be spilled going forward.

Step 4: Divide

Satan's temptations had successfully achieved the breaking apart of God from man, man from woman, and mankind from the animal kingdom. Satan had with almost too much ease wrested the title deed of the earth away from humanity. Satan was now the "god of this age" (2 Corinthians 4:4). The earth was his!

But, as soon as the enemy heard the first baby's birth cry, he realized he had a whole new problem to contend with—mankind's offspring. The very same pride, lusts, and self-focused ambitions that fueled Satan and his demonic followers now also fueled mankind. Satan hadn't just created one god to rule over his world; he had ended up creating hundreds, thousands, millions, and soon billions of little self-proclaimed gods. Every one of them at some level craved the attention and worship meant for God alone. It was bad enough that the demonic overlord had his demons clamoring for higher positions, but how could he possibly rule the entire world and still have all of God's creation worship him when challenged by billions of ambitious competitors? The task seemed daunting; the challenge, unbeatable.

Satan's first solution in dealing with this quandary was to attempt to transform humanity into becoming more like his demonic kind. Genesis 6 reveals that "when men began to multiply on the face of the earth, and daughters were born to them, that the sons of God saw the daughters of men, that they were beautiful; and they took wives for themselves of all whom they chose." As demons possessed men and conjugated with the women, the resulting offspring became giants. These "mighty men who were of old, men of renown" were known as the Nephilim. These unholy creatures provided the mythos for the demigods of ancient lore. So abominable was this perversion of nature and so evil had the hearts of mankind been corrupted that God announced He would first cap their lifespans to 120 years, then He at last stepped in and wiped the earth clean of them with the Flood. For being the so-called ruler over the earth, Satan could not stop God's interference, and was relegated to being a mere bystander at the global deluge. Creation had been reset and humanity rebooted, starting with the righteous Noah and his family.

The true solution to Satan's quandary came surprisingly from God Himself—mankind must be kept divided. Genesis 11 reveals that in only a few generations after Noah, mankind had yet again set their hearts against God's authority and sought to establish their own rule. All of Noah's descendants gathered as one in the land of Shinar and began to construct a tower that would stand as a monument to mankind's disobedient refusal of God's command to spread out into the world. Verse 4 reveals humanity's wayward intention: "And they said, 'Come, let us build ourselves a city, and a tower whose top is in the heavens; let us make a name for ourselves, lest we be scattered abroad over the face of the whole earth.'"

God recognized that what mankind could not do alone, they could certainly achieve if they all worked together. As God surveyed the construction site, the Trinity conversed with Himself, concluding in verse 6: "Indeed the people are one and they all have one language, and this is what they begin to do; now nothing that they propose to do will be withheld from them." God knew that dividing humanity would slow their progress, so He came up with quite a clever solution—confuse their languages. After hours of futile attempts to communicate with each other by waving their hands about, and after heated arguments and fistfights breaking out, those who could make sense of each other began assembling by common language. The divided people groups soon migrated off to the ends of the earth, becoming the forerunners of the ethnic peoples and nations we have today. The combination of linguistic confusion and greedy hearts would bring about millennia of endless war and ongoing division. Mankind's dreams of wresting back the title deed of the earth grew frustrated to approaching impossible.

Yet another division arose when a man named Abraham came on the scene who would further keep humanity divided. Back in the garden, before Adam and Eve had been expelled from a paradise and sent into a cursed land, God had presented the serpent with a tremendous prophecy.

He declared, "I will put enmity between you and the woman, and between your seed and her Seed; He shall bruise your head, and you shall bruise His heel" (Genesis 3:15). Not only would mankind be divided by language barriers and soon ethnically, along racial lines, but also between those who choose to follow Satan's rebellious path and those who surrender their lives to faithfully follow God. The unfaithful would be separated from the faithful, God's enemies versus God's children, and Satan's followers would be pitted against God's disciples. Under the Old Covenant, it was the Gentile world pitted against the Jewish nation; then, under the New Covenant, it was the entire world against the Church.

With this first messianic prophecy, God also proclaimed a champion for His faithful, the One who would come to be known as the Messiah, the Christ, the revealed Son of God. The perfectly holy incarnation of God—Jesus Christ—broke loose Satan's tenuous hold on the title deed to the earth with a selfless act. Jesus was crucified, buried, and resurrected from the grave, victorious—He became the Worthy Lamb slain. His victory over death granted Him dominion over the earth (Revelation 5). And, Christ's faithful children, long having surrendered their claim over the world when they also surrendered their lives to Jesus, will one day be granted inheritance rights to the planet upon Jesus Christ's return to yet again banish Satan, this time to the bottomless pit, and to establish His millennial kingdom (but, now we're getting ahead of ourselves).

Step 5: Globalize

Satan's strategy began by distracting humanity with perceived wants, then redirecting people to focus only on themselves, resulting in a breaking apart of vital relationships, and then dividing humanity so they could not join together and so attain the power and praise he so lustfully desires. The fifth and final phase of Satan's strategy to achieve both world domination and mass worship ends with globalization.

Satan has spent many long centuries anxiously waiting for a means to at last be developed that will make possible the ability to regather the warring masses and then reprogram humanity under a whole new unifying culture and ethos—his ethos. This newly shared culture and (im)morality would bring about a false sense of harmony that will result in a reunification of the discordant nations, but all under his own global governmental control. Satan seeks to establish a New World Order.

The Bible, especially the book of Revelation, reveals that Satan in the not-too-far-off future will be wildly successful at implementing his New World Order, though not all by his own efforts. God at first interferes in the affairs of Satan and man yet again by removing His restraining influence, and He does so by rapturing the Church up to heaven: "Then we [Christians] who are alive and remain shall be caught up together with them in the clouds to meet the Lord in the air. And thus we shall always be with the Lord" (1 Thessalonians 4:17).

The shocking removal of all Christians from this planet will plunge the world into abject terror and a descent into spiritual darkness. With no Church to hold back this darkness, every evil inclination will be let loose from people's hearts. Every foul deed will be done with maniacal glee. Anarchy and lawlessness will abound! Chaos will ravage the divided old world order.

The mystery of lawlessness that is already at work in this world will at last reveal himself. Out of the old world order a new one will arise. Out of lawlessness, the man of lawlessness will come forth. Satan will present his own chosen one who will ascend as if a messiah by spouting false promises of peace and safety to calm a chaotic world. The prophet Daniel, in chapter 9, describes this supposed man of peace who will "confirm a covenant with many" for seven years. Along with political peace, he will offer up a new religion—a "Mystery Babylon" religion—to unite the world religiously (Revelation 17). The mask of peace will merely be a façade, though, for the peacemaker will quickly reveal himself as a warrior, a beast, a global tyrant (Revelation 13). As the second-seal judgment so tragically portrays, this Antichrist will bring war to those who refuse to bow to his rule, resulting in the staggering death of a quarter of the world's population (Revelation 6).

In the middle of Daniel's seven years of prophesied Tribulation, Satan, through his Antichrist, will have at last subjugated all the nations of the world, except Israel. The world ruler will then break his covenant with Israel by opposing and exalting himself "above all that is called God or that is worshiped, so that he sits as God in the temple of God, showing himself that he is God" (2 Thessalonians 2:4). In doing so, the Antichrist will establish his own high priest—the False Prophet—and he shall bring an end to the sacrifice and offerings made to God in the newly built Jewish temple (Daniel 11–12; Revelation 13). In committing this blasphemy, Satan through the Antichrist will "kill" the "Mystery Babylon" ecumenical world religion by setting up his very own religion in its place—Satan worship. The False Prophet will construct a "living image" of the Antichrist and require all the world to fall before it and worship it. Those who survive the wars and God's raining judgments will then be required to take a loyalty mark that displays the Antichrist's name or number on his or her right hand or forehead. All must worship the Antichrist or, by the False Prophet's hands, they will be cut off from commerce and so will starve, be immolated in flames, or sentenced to beheading.

After thousands of years of human history, Satan, during the coming Tribulation, will have at last achieved worldwide dominion and global worship—his strategy successful, his goal achieved. And, anyone who resists and refuses to comply, such as the Jewish people and the post-Rapture converts to Christ, well, they face a massacre.

The Technological Means

We have identified Satan's end goal—the usurping of God's rule over the entire earth and the theft of mankind's worship that had been meant for God alone. And, we have learned what Satan's five-part strategy entails, ending with a New World Order controlled by a global government and forced religion. Now we will step back and look at the means by which our enemy will implement his New World Order, a means he has so long desired—the building of another proverbial tower of Babel. This great unifier that has taken centuries to build and that in our day has at last been achieved, which wields the awesome power on one hand to corrupt a society while on the other hand redefining and reuniting it, which deconstructs the mind of man yet transforms them into living by a brave new ethos—Satan's means is technology.

I contend that in order to subjugate people on a worldwide basis, to take captive and then bind them to the spirit of the Antichrist, who wants to enslave all of humanity under the coming regime of the first beast of Revelation 13, can only be achieved by implementing certain key technologies. These technologies, when combined, quite specifically, form one simple device. This pinnacle of technology will culminate into the ultimate mind-altering mechanism, which is even right now being used to capture the minds and hearts of mankind, particularly the youth, to benefit Satan's nefarious work in the high places he occupies in order to create the minions of the Antichrist spirit. That ultimate all-encompassing, mind-altering device—you guessed it—is the smartphone.

To understand why the smartphone has become Satan's preeminent device towards achieving his long-desired New World Order, we have to explore the underlying technologies that make the smartphone possible. The smartphone as a technology doesn't stand alone; rather, it exists like a spider at the center of a web of many other technologies. The smartphone isn't just one technology, but is the culmination of many, many technologies, all layered and integrated much like the many cells, organs, and systems that make up the human body.

We will now explore six vital categories of technologies that comprise the smartphone and, therefore, make Satan's globalization strategy possible. Bear in mind that identifying and explaining each of these technologies would constitute their own books. Therefore, I can only provide a cursory description of each category while expounding on those that provide key technological components that specifically aid in the creation of Satan's New World Order.

And, before you label me a Luddite—or even worse, a conspiracy theorist—please bear in mind that I own a smartphone. You do, too, right?

It's likely in your pocket or at least within an arm's length away. As I stated earlier, technology can be used for good or for evil; it just depends on the one who wields it. Smartphones are merely technology, but they are a device Satan masterfully knows how to utilize in order to manipulate the masses towards his diabolical ends.

The first two categories of underlying technologies—electrical power and computers—essential to making the smartphone possible could be classified as infrastructure. These technologies provide the basic, underlying framework and features of the overall system. You will recognize these as foundational to all of our modern-day devices, and without which we would be propelled as if by steam locomotive back into the Industrial Age.

Category 1: Electrical Power

Ever since Benjamin Franklin attempted to catch a lightning bolt with a kite and a key, mankind has known that advancing society would require harnessing electricity. After all, who can imagine today's technology without electricity? You can only power so much with windmills, water wheels, and coal fires.

In 1831, Michael Faraday created the very first viable electric dynamo, leading American inventor Thomas Edison and British scientist Joseph Swan to develop the direct-current system (DC), which, in September 1882, provided the power to illuminate the first New York electric street lamps. This soon led to Serbian-American electrical wizard Nikola Tesla to work with alternating current (AC) and AC-powered motors. George Westinghouse purchased and developed Tesla's patented AC motor, propelling first American society and then the world into a future powered across interconnected electrical grids by AC.

Staying plugged into an electrical socket isn't always convenient, though. Electricity needed to be stored and made mobile. In 1800, Italian physicist Alessandro Volta first discovered that particular chemical reactions could produce electricity, and so constructed an early electric battery called the voltaic pile. Today's inventors, such as Elon Musk, have continued to perfect the battery, even producing and manufacturing one as large as the $13,000 Powerwall, which can power an entire house for seven continuous days before needing to be recharged by AC or solar tiles.[64] Whether your device is powered by disposable AAA, AA, D, or 9-volt batteries, or a rechargeable lithium-poly ion battery, portable electricity allows for technology on the go.

Category 2: Computers

Mankind, much like our technology, continually seeks upgrading. To aid our brain's computational capability, the first computer—the abacus—was created to help perform basic arithmetic operations. The harnessing of electricity led to the development of vastly more powerful computers that perform electronically and process a far greater number of calculations in far less time. By the 1940s–1950s, the first general-purpose electronic computer called ENIAC (Electronic Numerical Integrator And Computer) utilized thousands of vacuum tubes, crystal diodes, relays, resistors, capacitors, plugboards, and switches, and took up 167 square meters, weighed 27 tons, and consumed 150 kilowatts of power.[65] With the invention of the transistor replacing the vacuum tube, computers began to shrink in size. And, the invention of the integrated circuits (ICs), also known as the microchip, led to much more manageable mainframe and then personal computers. Created in the 1970s, the first single-chip CPU, or microprocessor, was the Intel 4004. The microcomputer was born!

The last few decades have seen computers move at almost light speed away from blinking lights and punch cards to graphical user interfaces (GUI) complete with monitors, keyboards, mice, and touchscreens by which to more easily operate them. Incomprehensible binary machine code made up of ones and zeros has been augmented by coding languages such as Fortran, COBOL (Common Business-Oriented Language), BASIC, MS-DOS (Microsoft Disk Operating System), C++, Java, and Perl, which has allowed for armies of programmers to create billions of lines of computer software—the DNA of computers. Software has made possible graphics-based operating systems such as Windows and Mac OS and OSX, evolving computers to become much more user-friendly and, therefore, more desirable to the general public. Ever-increasing, near-limitless terabytes of data can now be stored on servers in server farms, otherwise known as the Cloud.

Computers have also become smaller and lighter, resulting in laptops, PDAs, cell phones and tablets. Steve Jobs and Steve Wozniak, the cofounders of Apple, made smart devices all the rage, and now people wear their computers on their bodies in the form of smartphones, watches, and other mp3-playing devices. As computers have become easier to use and cheaper to buy, billions of people have scrambled to purchase electronic devices, filling their houses and their lives with portable technology. Statista reports that, as of 2020, the average person owns 6.58 computer devices, adding up to nearly fifty billion devices operating worldwide.[66]

Computer processing speeds also continue to accelerate, doubling every eighteen months. Known as Moore's Law, this is just one manifestation of the greater trend in how all technological change happens to be occurring at an exponential rate. By 2023, computers are expected to possess the processing speed equivalent to the human brain. By 2045, in a mere quarter of a century, Moore's Law predicts we will have computers with the computational ability equivalent to the entire human race!

Computer scientists are looking even past those goals, pursuing artificial intelligence (AI), quantum computing, and robotics at a frantic pace. They foresee a time in the not-too-distant future when computer advancement will reach what they call the Singularity, that "moment when a civilization changes so much that its rules and technologies are incomprehensible to previous generations...a point-of-no-return in history."[67] Science fiction writer Vernor Vinge, who popularized the idea of the Singularity in his 1993 essay, "Technological Singularity," wrote:

> We are on the edge of change comparable to the rise of human life on Earth, the precise cause of this change is the imminent creation by technology of entities with greater than human intelligence.[68]

In other words, mankind has been attempting to create artificial life.

The rise of computer hardware and software companies such as Xerox, IBM, Toshiba, Apple, HP, Fujitsu, and Microsoft have grown into international behemoths. These Fortune 500 mega-companies wield enormous influence over the world's economic, cultural, and political realms. Tech companies control the future of the human race.

Category 3: Communications

The author of the book of Ecclesiastes wisely noted that "a threefold cord is not quickly broken" (Ecclesiastes 4:12). So then, what's better than one computer working alone? The answer is three, or three hundred, or three million—or, even better, three billion—devices all working together. Hence, we come to our third vital category of technologies that comprise the smartphone—communications technologies. This category consolidates a virtually mind-numbing array of various technologies, encompassing everything including print, audio, and video. Radios, transmitters, televisions, cell towers, satellites, cable, cameras, Wi-Fi, fiber optics, and the complicated infrastructure that connects all of these technologies into one massive network provide just the tip of the communications technologies iceberg.

The true genius came when all these technologies began to be linked together some sixty years ago, initially as a weapon by the United States to combat the Cold War. We call it the Internet today, but this wonder of modern-day life was birthed as a means for scientists and researchers to communicate and share their computer data across vast distances in their efforts to combat the communist world. As soon as the Soviet Union launched the world's first manmade satellite named Sputnik into orbit on October 4, 1957, a spooked US federal government quickly formed the National Aeronautics and Space Administration (NASA) and the Department of Defense's Advanced Research Projects Agency (ARPA). These agencies would wage the Cold War by developing space-age technologies that would lead the world into the digital age. Much like many today who are concerned that an EMP (electromagnetic pulse) blast will destroy a nation's electrical grid, military experts in the 1950s worried that a few missiles could take down the whole network of lines that make efficient long-distance communication possible. So, in 1962, a scientist at ARPA by the name of J. C. R. Licklider proposed his solution of building a "galactic network" of computers that could talk to one another and enable government leaders to communicate even if the Soviets destroyed the telephone system.[69] On October 29, 1969, two house-sized computers, one at the research lab at UCLA and the second at Stanford University, shared their first node-to-node message, which read "LOGIN." The Internet was born! Well, not quite yet. The ARPAnet was born!

By the end of 1969, the two computers linked together became four, and throughout the 1970s, more and more military and research computers all around the world were identifying each other by Internet Protocol (IP) address and sharing their data. Then, in 1991, a Swiss computer programmer by the name of Tim Berners-Lee (not Al Gore) opened up the burgeoning connectivity to the general public over what he called the World Wide Web when he created the first Web server (CERN HTTPd) and the very first website (http://info.cern.ch/). Now anyone with a personal computer could access the Web over browsers such as Mosaic, Netscape, Internet Explorer, Firefox, Chrome, and Safari. With such massive amounts of data being shared as millions of new computers were being connected to the Internet every day, search engines such as Google, AltaVista, AskJeeves, Yahoo, and later Bing mapped and indexed all of that data. A world of information was literally at anyone's fingertips via desktop or mobile device.

As of 2020, 4.54 billion of the 7.77 billion people in the world are connected by the Internet, and 4.18 billion of them utilize a mobile device.[70] In the United States, 100 percent of eighteen to twenty-nine year olds, 97 percent of thirty to forty-nine year olds, 88 percent of fifty to sixty-four year olds, and 73 percent of sixty-five year olds and older are Web "surfers."[71] The average Internet user spends six and a half hours online every day, generating 88,555 gigabytes of Internet traffic every second![72] The average smartphone user will spend an average of three hours and forty-nine minutes each day on their devices, dedicating 90 percent of their time to downloading any of the five-plus million applications (apps) from the leading app stores such as Google Play, Apple's iTunes, and Amazon.[73]

Truly, the Internet over smartphones has developed into today's tower of Babel. Language barriers are even becoming a thing of the past, as apps such as Google Translate have been developed to turn one's smartphone into a Star Trek-like universal translator. The networks are getting faster and more robust, as fifth-generation (5G) technology is being implemented at record speed to keep up with the exabytes of data being shared. And, the Internet continues to expand into its third phase, seeking to encompass every device from your coffeemaker to your pacemaker to your car into the Internet of Things (IoT). Alphabet, the parent company that owns Google, has risen to become a monopoly, channeling 92 percent of Web searches and 44 percent of all emails generated, and it now decides who sees what information.[74] Cries of Internet censorship, especially against Christian and conservative viewpoints, are on the rise. As television fiction writer J. Michael Straczynski quoted through one of his characters, "He who controls information controls the world."[75]

Category 4: Ecommerce

Like most inventions, the Internet didn't really take off until businesses began to realize there was money to be made and the end-users learned how they could more easily purchase stuff. The buying and selling of products and services had to move beyond the brick-and-mortar and into the electronic realm of online shopping. This leads us to the fourth vital category of technologies that comprise the smartphone—ecommerce technologies.

Electronic commerce, or ecommerce, had its humble beginnings back in the 1970s with Electronic Data Interchanges and teleshopping. In 1979, Michael Aldrich in the United Kingdom connected a modified television via a telephone line to a real-time, multiuser transaction processing computer and sold his invention as a business-to-business (B2B) solution. Once the Internet opened up to the public in 1991, companies such as Book Stacks Unlimited (now Barnes & Noble), Amazon, Etsy, and eBay quickly became popular as the go-to online shopping experience. To further increase consumer confidence, as online shoppers worried about losing their financial data to the growing threat of hackers, Secure Socket Layers (SSL) was released in 1994 to secure Web browsers and protect users' financial data. The new trust in online shopping swung the boom away from buildings to ecommerce websites. Many long-lived shopping chains, such as Sears and JCPenney, too slow to adapt to an online model, quickly found themselves facing bankruptcy. A seismic shift in commerce transformed the world in just a few short years.

With the rise of ecommerce came the rise of online banking, and soon cash gave way to electronic funds and new currencies such as the bitcoin. Global ecommerce companies like PayPal, which began its services in 1998, and Authorize.Net and others provide transaction services across all economies and currencies to billions of people worldwide.[76] As entirely cashless societies are being considered, with Sweden leading the way with plans to go all-digital in March of 2023, concerns are growing about how much power banks now have over people's finances. For every transaction, banks and transaction services get a cut, so have grown tremendously wealthy and influential. Increasingly, stories are emerging of banks and transaction entities such as PayPal cutting people off from their finances over ideological disagreements. Once a society goes cashless, a person can easily be separated from his or her assets by the order of a government or bank with the mere push of a button.

Online shopping has increasingly gone mobile. In 2010, payments platform Square allowed small businesses to accept debit and credit cards over mobile devices, so that by 2017, Square's gross payment volume was $17.9 billion.[77] Since then, more than a third of US ecommerce sales have been made over smartphones. The top one hundred online marketplaces sold $203 trillion in goods in 2019.[78] An expected 47 percent of all shopping will be done over a mobile device in 2020. And, just like the computer and Internet tech giants, online shopping giants such as Amazon, which alone sold over $275 billion in goods in 2019, have risen to an almost monopoly status with no entity able to stop it from censoring merchants who depend on Amazon as practically their only marketplace.

Category 5: Entertainment

This leads us to the fifth vital category of technologies that keeps people addicted to their smartphones—entertainment applications. Online entertainment takes the form primarily of streaming video, which includes long- and short-form video, gaming, and social media.

Today's society tends to be visually driven. As a matter of fact, 65 percent of people absorb and recall information best by seeing.[79] While auditory learners need to hear information and kinesthetic learners need to engage in an activity in order to grasp a concept, visual learners, or spatial learners, obviously learn and remember best through visual aids such as maps, images, pictures, diagrams, mind maps, and most importantly, videos.

In today's world of advanced technology and high-speed communication, many technologies drive visual learners to on-demand and streaming video. As technologist John Dyer points out, "Technology has become a kind of supra-cultural phenomenon that finds its way into every aspect of our diverse lives."[80] Today's advanced communications technology has provided a boom in what is known as long-form video produced by the film industry. As media culture expert Steve Turner notes, "Film supplies more widespread cultural references than any other art form" and "movies provide a shared reference point."[81] Film and movies provide an unparalleled opportunity to connect to an increasingly visually driven, story-oriented culture and then reshape it to the storytellers' point of view.

To meet the rabid appetite for all things video, streaming video companies such as Netflix, Hulu, HBO Go, Disney Plus, Amazon Prime Video, Sling TV, Crackle, and many others have risen in prominence. Streaming devices connected to one's smart television such as Apple TV, Kindle Fire Stick, Roku, and Chromecast, and through mobile apps compete to make cable-box executives fearfully contemplate their industry's impending demise. For only a few dollars a month, subscriptions to these services open up vaults of libraries of movies and films (even that ever-elusive Disney vault).

While long-form videos, such as films and movies, certainly are making their impact on the modern culture, the high production level, excessive costs, and limits of bandwidth on mobile devices have placed such media out of reach of most aspiring filmmakers and film-watchers. The solution to this dilemma has been the advent of what is called short-form video, meaning video that runs a few minutes in length and allows for amateur production quality. Pastor Craig Loscalzo notes that this media is perfect for engaging with the mosaic style of thinking used by the post-modernist, meaning they draw conclusions from seeing the parts rather than seeing the whole, because they are a "sound-bite driven culture" of people who have neither endurance nor lengthy attention spans.[82]

Where can one best find short, unprofessional, yet widely accepted short-form video? The answer is YouTube, the most popular online video platform in the world. As one marketing expert cleverly noted, "YouTube is the future of entertainment. It has been for a few years now."[83]

Since YouTube's launch on April 23, 2005, by three former PayPal employees, YouTube's ease of use and easy accessibility has led to its exponential growth, so much so that search engine leader Google bought YouTube for $1.65 billion.[84] Some two billion users—almost a third of the world's population—access YouTube every month. Some 79 percent of Internet users claim that they have a YouTube account to access videos available in eighty different languages.[85] Because 90 percent of US Internet users ages eighteen to forty-four years access YouTube, Gen-Zs have also been dubbed the "YouTube Generation." For this rising generation, the standard scheduled half- to full-hour television watching has become a relic of the past. The YouTube Generation uses smartphones to hop from one short-form video to the next to the next, to consume a mere portion of the 720,000 hours of video uploaded daily to YouTube's platform.[86] Of the average 40.77 exabytes of mobile traffic every month, 29.15 petabytes of that monthly traffic come from video.[87] Countless hours every day are devoted to YouTube video consumption. And, increasingly, Christian and conservative content, content such as what conservative spokesman Dennis Prager's PragerU produces and lost a lawsuit defending, are increasingly coming under censorship as Google decides what people should or shouldn't watch.

The $100 billion global gaming industry has also taken the mobile world by storm, having steadily transitioned away from console devices such as Xbox and PlayStation to the smartphone. Gaming apps such as Pokémon GO, Minecraft, Snapchat Games, and Hearthstone engage primarily males in their massively multiplayer, online role-playing games (MMORPGs) across top gaming countries such as Germany, Japan, the US, Singapore, and South Korea. According to one 2019 Forbes poll, gamers are playing on their smartphones an average of seven hours each week, but that has been increasing 20–25 percent every year.[88] The global gaming community transcends national borders, living within virtual worlds and sharing common experiences and speaking in a common vernacular.

Along with video watching and gaming, social media has added an average of two hours and twenty-four minutes per day spent with one's smartphone multi-networking across an average of eight social networks and messaging apps.[89] Active social media users, primarily female, have passed the 3.8 billion mark on popular platforms such as Facebook, Twitter, Pinterest, Snapchat, WeChat, Instagram, LinkedIn, and a plethora of others.[90] With 83 percent of twelve to fifteen year olds owning their own smartphone, 69 percent interacting over social media, and 71 percent taking their phones and "friends" to bed with them every night, social media has become the primary means of communications among youth, even preferred alarmingly over in-person conversation.[91]

Category 6: Security

This sixth and last vital category of technologies inherent in the smartphone involves security measures. These are the technologies that on the surface are meant to keep the individual safe, but are really about keeping society "safe."

There are security software packages and firewalls that protect phones from the ever-increasing threat of cyber warfare and identity thieves. But, there are also hyper-advanced technologies that continually track where a smartphone, and hence the smartphone's user, is at all times via the Global Positioning System (GPS) tied to satellite-based radio navigation and tower-pinging tied to cell tower locations. Though GPS has conveniently replaced the paper map, our phones know exactly where we're standing at any moment. Location tracking constantly sends data back to big-tech companies such as Facebook, Apple, Microsoft, Amazon, Google, and then-unknown third parties in order to target us with mobile ads. And, we permit them to track us through data-sharing policies buried deep within pages and pages of privacy policies and terms of agreements. Apple even tracks personal calls, emails, and texts in order to "prevent fraud" and to rate the owner with a "trust score."[92] Personal privacy left the building as soon as online privacy did.

These security technologies also include the Orwellian-realized world of constant monitoring via cameras, microphones, and smart assistants such as Siri, Amazon Echo, and Google Home, which are ever listening. For example, ever since 2014, when Amazon unveiled the Echo speaker featuring Alexa, its voice-activated, virtual-assistant software, armies of low-paid Amazon employees have been listening in and transcribing people's conversations, often gleaning very personal security information.[93] This is not one isolated instance by one company, but has been reported across all tech companies under the banner of "improving their services."

And, when totalitarian governments get involved in security monitoring, you get China's Social Credit Score. The closest system we have today to the Antichrist's mark of the beast is China's Social Credit Score, which has already been instituted in its more populated cities. China's communist government has infiltrated millions of cameras everywhere in order to spy on its citizens. Computer algorithms then rate the citizens' allegiance to the government, granting benefits to those who are more loyal and restrictions on those the computer deems as not being patriotic enough.

Many other countries are interested in adopting China's system, and will inevitably be implementing it themselves worldwide.

And, as home security systems and home devices become more "smart" and interconnected to the Internet of Things (IoT), with the master controller being the smartphone, the threat grows of a shady outside entity being able to gain control and monitor our homes over our very own security system. For instance, Amazon's Ring doorbell camera system was discovered being monitored by company engineers over unencrypted live video feeds.[94] Amazon even wants to tie its Ring doorbells into facial recognition, and has allowed police forces to use these home cameras as part of their surveillance network. The very home security devices that keep the robbers out can also keep homeowners in a monitored prison of their own making.

Tying It All Together

I have been presenting the argument that Satan's final step towards realizing his goal of world domination and global adulation rests on globalizing the world under his new ethos and culture. Theology professor William Edgar defines culture as "something like a key to the beliefs and customs of a particular society, with a view to changing them."[95] With the advent of today's vast technologies, the pinnacle being the smartphone, Satan has found the perfect device in which to mold his new unifying ethos and culture.

What, then, characterizes today's brave new culture? Media expert Steve Turner would characterize it as "pop culture" and notes just how vastly it suffuses just about every part of the lives of everyone everywhere.[96] He warns that the driving spiritual forces behind much of pop culture are intent on altering the perceptions of the outgoing culture, often negatively, towards the God of the Bible and Christianity:

> When we suspect that culture has an agenda, we are naturally more guarded. When we think that it's only there to tickle us, we

roll over and start purring…we are vulnerable to spiritual corruption when not alert.[97]

The result has been a transition of our society away from a historical modernist logic-based thinking to a postmodernist, relativistic, feelings-based, post-Christian era. Evangelism expert Rick Richardson describes the characteristics of this brave new postmodern culture as including a common belief that people are their own gods, they often engage in identity politics, they are rampantly distrustful of authority, they hold a general belief that love rules, they have an overt fear of "the patriarchy," they readily discard whatever came before, and they tend to view Christians as self-serving.[98] This is Satan's new ethos, carefully indoctrinating the masses worldwide by their ever-present and ever-watching smartphones, thus creating a new global culture.

Pro-humanist, anti-Christian, "having a form of godliness but denying its power"—the end-of-days culture Paul warned Timothy about has at last come (2 Timothy 3:1–9). These deniers of the one true God, Paul promises, folly will be made manifest to all. But, you Christian, know the Holy Scriptures, which are able to make you wise for salvation through faith, which is in Christ Jesus.

SIX

End-Times Embrace of Evil

By Ryan Pitterson

There is a growing fascination with the occult and other anomalous activity. The farther mankind gets from God, the more it seeks out evil, supernaturalism, and superstitious intrigues. I hope this chapter will show how this generation is increasingly immersed in things of the dark side.

This is all part of the war we face with the spirit of Antichrist—the "wickedness in high places" of Ephesians 6:12.

> And the rest of the men which were not killed by these plagues yet repented not of the works of their hands, that they **should not worship devils**, and idols of gold, and silver, and brass, and stone, and of wood: which neither can see, nor hear, nor walk: Neither repented they of their murders, **nor of their sorceries**, nor of their fornication, nor of their thefts. (Revelation 9:20–21, emphasis added)

The ninth chapter of the book of Revelation paints a startling prophecy of the world in the final years before the Second Coming of Christ. The overwhelming majority of the global population will have pledged full allegiance to the beast, also known as the Antichrist—the satanically empowered False Messiah who will rule over the world for the final three and one-half years before the Second Coming. They will worship and honor this man as god. Witchcraft, sorcery, and the worship of idols will be the common global religion. While this is well known among students of the Bible, what is not as often discussed will be the rampant practice of the occult during the Great Tribulation. Even when God has unleashed supernatural punishments on the unbelieving, deceived populace, they will still not repent of their worship of devils and of idols and of their practice of sorceries. Witchcraft and demon worship will be the dominant religion of the end times.

Sadly, the stage for this brazen spiritual rebellion is already being set today. The past decade has seen a shocking rise in society's fascination with occult, pagan, and New Age practices. The Bible warns us:

> For the mystery of iniquity doth already work: only he who now letteth will let, until he be taken out of the way. And then shall that Wicked be revealed, whom the Lord shall consume with the spirit of his mouth, and shall destroy with the brightness of his coming. (2 Thessalonians 2:7–8)

The mystery of iniquity, the deception of the nonbelieving world that will ultimately lead to the global worship of the Antichrist, is already permeating the world. In America and Western society, what were once considered fringe, bizarre pagan practices have become commonplace and trending parts of spiritual life. As the preaching of sound biblical Christianity wanes, there has been a massive increase in the mystical practices the Bible teaches are in fact directly connected to the demonic world and Satan.

Bible's Stern Warnings Against the Occult

> When thou art come into the land which the LORD thy God giveth thee, thou shalt not learn to do after the abominations of those nations.

There shall not be found among you any one that maketh his son or his daughter to pass through the fire, **or that useth divination, or an observer of times, or an enchanter, or a witch. Or a charmer, or a consulter with familiar spirits, or a wizard, or a necromancer.**

For all that do these things are an abomination unto the LORD: and because of these abominations the LORD thy God doth drive them out from before thee.

Thou shalt be perfect with the LORD thy God. (Deuteronomy 18:9–13, emphasis added)

As the ancient Israelites were on the cusp of entering the Promised Land, God issued an emphatic prohibition on entangling themselves in the spiritual practices of their enemies in the land of Canaan. This was a territory that was overrun with the postdiluvian Nephilim—descendants of the original giants from the days of Noah. In my book, *Judgment of the Nephilim*, I explained that they engaged in forbidden worship of their fallen angelic ancestors and the demonic spirits of the first giants who perished in the Flood. The Lord, in His wisdom and mercy, gave the twelve tribes of Israel advanced notice that there was grave danger in engaging these beings.

An occult practice is any attempt to access the spiritual realm without God—as this will inherently involve interaction with fallen angels and demons. The New Testament is clear that these are the true enemies of the born-again Christian:

Put on the whole armour of God, that ye may be able to stand against the wiles of the devil.

For we wrestle not against flesh and blood, but against principalities, against powers, against the rulers of the darkness of this world, against spiritual wickedness in high places. (Ephesians 6:11–12)

These beings are enemies of God and His people. They have various ranks and functions but are united in their opposition to the Church. In terms of the unsaved, they are the great deceivers, promoting all manner of spiritual errors, heresies, and occult practices to seduce the unsuspecting world of people who do not know their Bible or have faith in the Savior. Now, in the last days, as the Great Tribulation and the return of the Son of God approach, the world is once again falling for the seduction of agents of the devil.

The Rise of Witchcraft and Wicca

Regard not them that have familiar spirits, neither seek after wizards, to be defiled by them: I am the Lord your God. (Leviticus 19:31)

Thou shalt not suffer a witch to live. (Exodus 22:18)

God issued strong prohibitions against witches and occult practitioners who "have familiar spirits" because there is an extreme spiritual danger indwelling these people. The spiritual forces that enable witches, wizards, and those who dabble in magic or spiritualism are demons. A clear example of this is found during the ministry of the Apostle Paul in the book of Acts:

And it came to pass, as we went to prayer, **a certain damsel possessed with a spirit of divination met us**, which brought her masters much gain by soothsaying:

The same followed Paul and us, and cried, saying, These men are the servants of the most high God, which shew unto us the way of salvation.

And this did she many days. But Paul, being grieved, turned and said to the spirit, I command thee in the name of Jesus Christ to come out of her. And he came out the same hour.

And when her masters saw that the hope of their gains was gone, they caught Paul and Silas, and drew them into the marketplace unto the rulers,

And brought them to the magistrates, saying, These men, being Jews, do exceedingly trouble our city. (Acts 16:16–20, emphasis added)

There are several important lessons in this passage. First, the Bible is clear that this woman had a real power of "divination" or being able to tell parts of the future. She received this power through the demon that possessed her. Being wholly taken over by an agent of Satan, the woman was merely a vessel for the demon to speak through and enchant her master's customers. She also was deceptive. Her words proclaimed Paul as a "servant of the most high God" and even referenced salvation. This is part of the great spiritual deception of witchcraft. In many instances, the satanic spirits that lead the witch or psychic will invoke language that promotes "love," "peace," and "harmony"—but behind that is a sinister spiritual force.

Despite these dangers, in the United States and Western world, where witchcraft was once shunned and practiced in the shadows, an occult explosion is taking place. A Pew Research study from 2014 found that .3 percent, or approximately one million Americans, identified as wiccan or pagan.[99] And recent years have seen a surge in the practice of witchcraft and Wicca. Psychic readings, tarot cards, energy crystals, and many other occult consumer items have become all the rage. The psychic services industry now generates approximately $2 billion in annual revenue.[100] Social media is littered with witchcraft "influencers" like Bria Luna, known as the "Hoodwitch," who boasts more than 450,000 followers on Instagram.[101] Many of these celebrity practitioners share spells, incantations, and astrological information on a daily basis with their adoring fans. Millennials in particular—who are increasingly a more biblically illiterate generation—have embraced the idea of being a "none," a "spiritual but not religious" person with no particular affiliation but open to a mix of spiritual beliefs.

Couple this with the rise of churches that have strayed from sound, biblical doctrine, and we are left with a generation that is ripe for the influence of the occult. Even more alarming is that mainstream media has embraced and promoted its popularity.

Witchcraft: Symbol of Feminism and Social Justice

One of the most powerful lures in the rise of witchcraft is that it has become aligned with political movements. For many people, and women in particular, witchcraft has become a force for feminism and social justice. The notion that a woman can access power of the universe to influence world events has been marketed as a way to strike back at conservative politics, patriarchy, and institutional racism, which have, in the eyes of many nonbelievers, been connected to Christianity. Evidence of this can easily be seen in some of the witchcraft political protests of recent years, as one article details:

> From the Charmed reboot to Netflix's dark interpretation of our favorite '90s witch, the world of magic has become a pillar of pop culture. But witchcraft goes beyond what you see on TV: The practice has wriggled its way into politics, and real-life witches are doing much more than spouting out rhymes. Just ask the witches trying to take down the patriarchy with hexes (aka curses). From hexes against Brett Kavanaugh to the 13,000 "resistance witches" that have been fighting Donald Trump with magic since his election, public hexing protests are on the rise, and have gained popularity—and notoriety—from non-witch-folk and witches alike.
>
> According to Dakota Bracciale, the co-owner of a Brooklyn occult store responsible for organizing a recent public hexing against Brett Kavanaugh, using spells for political protection is nothing new. "[Witchcraft] was always practiced by the people who were

the outliers, who were on the fringes," Bracciale says. "Those people oftentimes had to also be the arbiter of their own justice."[102]

When the Antichrist is revealed, not only will he have supernatural abilities, he will unleash unprecedented deception on the world—so much so that the people of the world will openly worship Satan:

> And they worshipped the dragon which gave power unto the beast: and they worshipped the beast, saying, Who is like unto the beast? who is able to make war with him? (Revelation 13:4)

This can only take place once hearts and minds are so lured away from God that the preaching of the gospel sounds not only foolish, but offensive. Today we see that happening more and more, as biblical Christianity is depicted as "bigoted," "homophobic," and a part of systemic oppression in society. Those who attack Christianity feel justified that they are on the side of good. Through the occult, Satan has further hijacked the movement for justice for those who have been oppressed by making black magic a part of the political fabric.

In Scripture, the Bible does indeed call for justice for those who are marginalized:

> LORD, thou hast heard the desire of the humble: thou wilt prepare their heart, thou wilt cause thine ear to hear:
> To judge the fatherless and the oppressed, that the man of the earth may no more oppress. (Psalm 10:17–18)

> The LORD executeth righteousness and judgment for all that are oppressed. (Psalm 103:6)

> Wash you, make you clean; put away the evil of your doings from before mine eyes; cease to do evil;

> Learn to do well; seek judgment, relieve the oppressed, judge the fatherless, plead for the widow. (Isaiah 1:16–17)

Now some may read these verses and feel perturbed, wondering if I am suggesting we move to "socialism" or some wide-reaching government program. God forbid. These commands of God were not for the government to implement. **They were for His believers**. The Church needs to be at the forefront of assisting those in need and vocal in supporting the widows, the fatherless, and the oppressed. Where God's people leave a vacuum, the devil will quickly come in and offer an alternative. Witchcraft has subtly deceived women into believing they have equality through the powers of the demonic realm. The Bible's message is that all people are unique and equally special, as we are all image-bearers of God. Hence, the book of Galatians' bold proclamation:

> For as many of you as have been baptized into Christ have put on Christ.
> There is neither Jew nor Greek, there is neither bond nor free, there is neither male nor female: for ye are all one in Christ Jesus. (Galatians 3:27–28)

Bible-believing Christians need to boldly proclaim the gospel and its truth that human beings are inherently valuable because we are image-bearers of God. That, coupled with the message of salvation, is the helping hands and feet of church ministries to those in need.

Pop Culture: Promoting Witchcraft at All-Time High

A brief glance at some of the most popular TV shows, movies, and music today reveals the open promotion of satanic, demonic practices. Here is just a sampling of the entertainment centered on the occult:

American Horror Story – One of the most popular TV shows on the FX network had an entire season devoted to depicting a boarding school for young girls that was truly a witches' coven. The show provided detailed scenes of real witchcraft rituals and graphic displays of violence and perversion.

The Chilling Adventures of Sabrina the Teenage Witch – This Netflix show is about a young woman who learns that she is the hybrid daughter of a witch and a pure human being. A group of powerful witches and warlocks informs her that she must decide if she will fulfill her destiny on her sixteenth birthday by participating in a "dark baptism" ritual in which she signs "the Book of the Beast" and pledges her soul to Satan.

Motherland: Fort Salem – This program on Freeform (the new name of the ABC Family Channel) is an alternative history drama in which the witches from the Salem witch trials make a deal with the government to be allowed to practice witchcraft in exchange for becoming an elite military force that protects the United States using the occult powers.

Charmed – This is a reboot of a 1990s series about three sisters who are witches and discover they have the power to ward off attacks from demons and other monsters. In addition to making the occult-practicing women heroes, the show goes out of its way to drive home the theme that witchcraft brings out the special power within all young women. A Netflix show aimed at teenagers and preteens, it is filled with scenes of drug use, blasphemous language, and graphic homosexual and heterosexual sex scenes.

Legacies – This CW Network show is about a teenage girl named Hope McMichael, who learns she is a "tri-brid"—the offspring of a vampire and a werewolf and a grandmother who is a witch. In addition to drinking blood and transforming into a wolf-like monster, she also uses witchcraft. At a boarding school for teens with supernatural powers, Hope learns that she is the key to stopping the enemy forces, as those who drink her blood can return from the dead.

Lucifer – This Netflix show, in its fifth season, is about Satan himself now working to assist a police detective in solving crime. On the show, the devil abandons "his job" of punishing demons in hell to come to earth and work as a nightclub owner. He befriends a police officer and decides to help solve crimes and assist humanity. Thus, Satan is the hero of the show, which portrays him as handsome, charming, funny, and courageous.

As one review stated:

> Believe it or not, a creature who brings evil and temptation some-times may do nice things, such as help to investigate a murder, save human life, and refuse to accept any human soul even if they are willing to sell it to him.[103]

In all these shows, witches, wizards, and fallen angels are the heroes and sympathetic figures who are just "misunderstood" by ignorant parents and authority figures. Their fellow occult practitioners are exciting, intriguing heroes who are living a much better life than "normal" human beings. All of this repeated messaging drives home the idea that there is great power and promise in magic. The book of Isaiah describes the spiritual state of societies that embrace and celebrate these demonic trends:

> **Woe unto them that call evil good, and good evil; that put darkness for light, and light for darkness;** that put bitter for sweet, and sweet for bitter!
>
> Woe unto them that are wise in their own eyes, and prudent in their own sight!
>
> Woe unto them that are mighty to drink wine, and men of strength to mingle strong drink:
>
> Which justify the wicked for reward, and take away the righteousness of the righteous from him!
>
> Therefore as the fire devoureth the stubble, and the flame consumeth the chaff, so their root shall be as rottenness, and their blossom shall go up as dust: because they have cast away the law of the LORD of hosts, and despised the word of the Holy One of Israel. (Isaiah 5:20–24, emphasis added)

Pop culture today is going to extremes to call evil good and confuse the hearts and minds of the millions of people who consume it through their phones, tablets, and TVs. Then there are shows that directly attack the Christian faith and blaspheme the name of God. *Supernatural* is another CW Network series that, in its fifteen seasons, has promoted massive blasphemy and biblical confusion. The show features two brothers who investigate paranormal activity. It features all manner of occult practices and demonic artifacts the brothers use to "fight evil." But, unlike the aforementioned shows, *Supernatural* takes most of its source material from the Bible—twisting the scriptural accounts constantly. A few examples:

- **God** – According to the show's Wiki page, God is described as: "In the beginning, there was only Amara. At some point, God, her younger brother, came into existence."[104] Amara is more powerful than God on the show. After God created humanity, He removed Himself from any involvement with the world, preferring to remain uninvolved. On the show, characters repeatedly stress that "God abandoned humanity."[105]

- **Cain and Abel** – According to the script of *Supernatural,* although it was originally and commonly thought that Cain was jealous of his brother Abel for being God's favorite, and killed him out of rage and contempt, Cain "revealed that Abel was, in fact, talking to Lucifer."[106] In an effort to protect his brother from corruption, Cain offered Lucifer a deal: Cain's soul would be sent to hell so that Abel would go to heaven instead. Lucifer agreed, on the condition that Cain himself would send his brother to heaven. Thus, Abel was struck down by Cain using the First Blade, which he created from the jawbone of a donkey.[107]

- **Eve** – Rather than being the first woman created (from the rib of Adam), on this show, Eve was a powerful spirit being who resided in purgatory until dragons freed her. She existed even before the angels and created her own race of monsters called Alphas. She possessed the body of a young virgin woman to become human and come to earth.[108]

- **Lilith** – This is a female demon created by Lucifer and "the final seal of the 66 seals that had to be broken to free Lucifer from his cage." She leads an army of demons against the host of heaven.[109]
- **The Archangel Michael** – This is said to be one of four archangels in heaven. He possesses the body of one of the lead characters to appear on earth. In an episode entitled "Our Father Who Aren't in Heaven," Michael laments the fact that there is another archangel named Michael by saying: "God lied to me. I gave everything to him. I love him. Why? I'm not even the only Michael." Scriptwriting like this reemphasizes the show's main theme that God is a distant, cold, and uninvolved deity who has no compassion or concern for angels or humanity.[110]
- The Lord Jesus Christ is rarely ever mentioned on the show. On one episode entitled "And Then There Were None," Eve proclaims: "You do know that Jesus was just a man." The Savior is explained away as a man who led the movement that started Christianity and died.[111]

Again, consider that *Supernatural* has been broadcast for fifteen years, making it by far the longest-running show in CW Network history. What spirit would inspire a show that is disrespectful to the biblical account and to the Lord Jesus Christ? The Bible is clear that it is the spirit of Antichrist:

Little children, it is the last time: and as ye have heard that antichrist shall come, even now are there many antichrists; whereby we know that it is the last time....

I have not written unto you because ye know not the truth, but because ye know it, and that no lie is of the truth.

Who is a liar but he that denieth that Jesus is the Christ?

He is antichrist, that denieth the Father and the Son. (1 John 2:18–22, emphasis added)

When he emerges on the global stage, the Antichrist will be the ultimate blasphemer. Scripture confirms that time and time again, he will use his power and persona to lead the world into outright hatred against God and all who believe upon the name of the Lord Jesus Christ:

And the king shall do according to his will; and he shall exalt himself, and magnify himself above every god, and shall speak marvellous things against the God of gods, and shall prosper till the indignation be accomplished: for that that is determined shall be done. (Daniel 11:36)

Let no man deceive you by any means: for that day shall not come, except there come a falling away first, and that man of sin be revealed, the son of perdition;

Who opposeth and exalteth himself above all that is called God, or that is worshipped; so that he as God sitteth in the temple of God, shewing himself that he is God. (2 Thessalonians 2:3–4)

And there was given unto him a mouth speaking great things and blasphemies; and power was given unto him to continue forty and two months.

And he opened his mouth in blasphemy against God, to blaspheme his name, and his tabernacle, and them that dwell in heaven.

And it was given unto him to make war with the saints, and to overcome them: and power was given him over all kindreds, and tongues, and nations. (Revelation 13:5–7)

The seeds of the false gospel of the Antichrist are being sown in pop culture today. Blasphemy against the Lord Jesus Christ is applauded as entertainment. Characters who challenge and rail against God are heroic. A biblically illiterate generation "learns" more about the Bible from the distorted accounts of television shows. All of this is preparing the hearts and minds of the world for the great delusion.

Children's Lit: Early Indoctrination to Occult

If pop-culture entertainment for teens and tweens seems disturbing, the situation is even more dire for the youngest of children. Public school library shelves and online children's literature sections are flooded with books that serve as early indoctrination into the occult. There are now literally hundreds of books whose plots revolve around a young child or teen who discovers he or she has secret powers or belongs to a long line of witches and wizards. Each story paints the occult as an exciting, liberating, and empowering activity. Here is a very small sample:

Darkblood Academy: Book One: Half-Blood (A Supernatural Academy Series)

A young woman attends an academy for teenagers with supernatural abilities. Surrounded by vampires, "faes" (a term for fairies), vampires, and dragon shifters, she wonders why she, a "half-blood" offspring of a powerful being and a human woman, has been selected. It turns out that they believe she is the key to merging humanity with the supernatural beings.

This book, like much of the paranormal literature being marketed today, features a protagonist who is a hybrid being. All of this hearkens back to Genesis 6 and the birth of the Nephilim, the offspring of fallen angels and human women:

> And it came to pass, when men began to multiply on the face of the earth, and daughters were born unto them,
>
> That the sons of God saw the daughters of men that they were fair; and they took them wives of all which they chose.
>
> And the LORD said, My spirit shall not always strive with man, for that he also is flesh: yet his days shall be an hundred and twenty years.

There were giants in the earth in those days; and also after that, when the sons of God came in unto the daughters of men, and they bare children to them, the same became mighty men which were of old, men of renown.

And God saw that the wickedness of man was great in the earth, and that every imagination of the thoughts of his heart was only evil continually. (Genesis 6:1–5)

In *Judgment of the Nephilim*, I detailed that the illicit relations between the "Sons of God" or *B'nai Ha Elohim*, with human women gave birth to the Nephilim—hybrid giants who dominated the antediluvian world and necessitated the Flood. The Nephilim were an outright assault on God's plan of salvation—to bring redemption of humanity and conquer Satan through the "Seed of the woman"—the prophesied Messiah who would be born of a woman. By introducing angelic genetics into humanity, the devil sought to corrupt humanity and thwart any chance of a purely human Savior to be born.

God responded by selecting Noah (a man "perfect in his generations"—coming from a human lineage) to restart humanity after the Flood, preserving the bloodline that would lead to the Lord Jesus Christ. Today, the popular literature repeatedly uses the theme of the "hybrid as Savior"—placing a half-witch, half-vampire, or some type of monstrous hybrid being as the "savior" of the story.

Bloodline Sorcery: A Young Adult Urban Fantasy

A young girl attends Bloodline Academy, described as a school for witches, vampires, faes, and Nephilim. She is a "kitchen witch," concealing the immense power she inherited from her deceased, warlock grandfather, who was a serial killer.

Rise of a Necromancer

A young man attends a university for developing magical powers and studies the forbidden practice of necromancy. When he becomes a fugitive for this practice, he raises an army of the undead to seek revenge.

The Devil's Fool: A Paranormal Vampire Romance Novel (Devil Series Book 1)

This is the story of a young girl who belongs to a "generation of witches" whose parents pressure her to fulfill her destiny and become a witch like them. As she enjoys her newfound powers, she meets a "seductive vampire" named Boaz, who turns out to be Satan, and she falls in love with him. The book is the first in a five-part series of her love story with the devil.

The Archangel: An Azrael Story

The archangel Azrael, dubbed the "Angel of Death," is tasked by God to kill human beings when it determined that their lives have come to an end. When Satan returns to the earthly realm, he gives Azrael the ultimatum to join him or lose everything he loves. So, Azrael will have to protect his human wife and their unborn Nephilim child.

Tarot Academy 1: Spells of Iron and Bone

A teenage girl attends an academy for witches and warlocks only to discover that she is the key to unraveling a doomsday prophecy that was left by her dead mother. The description states: "Magick is real. It's also highly illegal—not that I'm worried about that."

In all of these books, the consistent message is that practicing the occult is exciting, seductive, and empowering. It is a way to access powers we can never have on our own. In short, it is leading the unsaved and deceived into the false promise of the devil that "ye shall be as gods."

At the same time, much of this spiritual literature casts rebel angels as heroic and loving—sinning with human beings out of love and compassion. Thus, the same principalities and powers, the fallen angels Scripture warns us of, are now the protectors and noble figures in the minds of the unwitting reader. With this upbringing, of course the teens of today will be willing to accept a Messianic figure empowered with real witchcraft. When the beast emerges on the scene, the Bible prophesies that he will dazzle the masses with supernatural abilities:

> Even him, whose coming is after the working of Satan with all power and signs and lying wonders. (2 Thessalonians 2:9)

Like the heroes of their childhood, the False Messiah will captivate and deceive the world through true supernatural acts. And their hearts will have had decades of preparation for such a hero who is the fulfillment of all their favorite stories from youth.

Even from a nonfiction standpoint, there is an abundance of instructional guides for children on the occult. A quick search reveals titles such as:

- *The Junior Witch's Handbook: A Kid's Guide to White Magic, Spells, and Rituals, Magic Potions and Elixirs—Recipes and Spells for Kids in Magic Training*
- *The Book of Wizard Craft: In Which the Apprentice Finds Spells, Potions, Fantastic Tales & 50 Enchanting Things to Make*
- *My First Spell Book: A Magic Workbook for Young Witches*
- *Invincible Magic Book of Spells: Ancient Spells, Charms and Divination Rituals for Kids in Magic Training*
- *The Earth Child's Handbook—Book 1: Crafts and Inspiration for the Spiritual Child*

This occult onslaught is rampant in schools and libraries across the United Sates. And it is bringing the younger generation right back to the original deception of the Garden of Eden:

Now the serpent was more subtil than any beast of the field which the LORD God had made.

And he said unto the woman, Yea, hath God said, Ye shall not eat of every tree of the garden?

And the woman said unto the serpent, We may eat of the fruit of the trees of the garden:

But of the fruit of the tree which is in the midst of the garden, God hath said, Ye shall not eat of it, neither shall ye touch it, lest ye die.

And the serpent said unto the woman, Ye shall not surely die: For God doth know that in the day ye eat thereof, then your eyes shall be opened, and ye shall be as gods, knowing good and evil. (Genesis 3:1–5)

The serpent's deceitful promise to Eve was premised on the false notion that God was withholding knowledge from Adam and Eve. Rather than the tree of the knowledge of good and evil being a death sentence (as God warned), it instead was the path to "godhood."

The word "occult" means "secret," and it is now being used by the devil to seduce the unsaved into thinking there is an entire world of powers, knowledge, and ability that they can tap into if they just defy God's prohibition on witchcraft and mystical practices. A nineteenth-century commentary on the rise of satanic influence through the occult arrived at the same conclusion:

That Satan's devices have been eminently successful, and that through an instrumentality as strange as unexpected, the records of almost every [civilized] country abundantly declare; *and one of the most striking features of the present movement, is the attempt to establish and legitimise a power on the part of man, of direct communication with the spiritual world and to divest it of that sense of guilt and of that awe and solemnity, with which it has ever been regarded in ages that are past.*

We are, in plain truth however, distasteful the assertion, — under the delusive sanction and disguise of a scientific investigation, reviving and popularizing, the practice of Demonology and Witchcraft; in open defiance of all those fearful threatenings and penalties which God has so invariably attached to them.

Man is striving to take his "Here" and his "Hereafter" into his own hands; —to penetrate every mystery of his being; —to determine the extent of his responsibility in this world; —and the next to become a revelation to himself; —TO DO WITHOUT GOD!

And we see around us, those conditions of thought and practice, which are preparatory to that clearly predicted manifestation of evil which is headed up under the reign of the last and personal Antichrist whom Satan directly energizes and whose authority he miraculously attests. "YE SHALL BE AS GODS" was the archdeceiver's first temptation and "I AM GOD" shall be the culminating utterance of man s daring and protracted Revolt.[112] (Emphasis added)

Dr. Cowan would likely be stunned to see how much more brazen the enemy has become in promoting witchcraft in these last days. But it is not just to children and young adults. People of all generations are embracing mysticism and the New Age movement on an unprecedented scale. And it has become quite a lucrative business for the purveyors of demonic practices.

Energy and Healing Crystals: A Booming Industry

Crystals. Victoria Beckham uses them backstage at her fashion shows. Miranda Kerr places them in her meditation-yoga room. Katy Perry sleeps with one in her hand at night.

Yup, the world of healing crystals is having a moment.

Having first risen to popularity during the 1970s, crystal healing has made a resurgence in recent years, with the likes of Cara

Delevingne, Lena Dunham and Adele raving about their calming,
fortune bringing and healing properties.[113]

In crystal healing, I work in partnership with them by placing
them on or near the body in order to effect healing change. They
do this by allowing the rate of their vibration to effect change in
the rate of the spinning energy centers of the chakras, clearing out
any negativity and allowing them to function at peak capacity. We
need to be in balance to be in perfect health. Crystals work with
us to restore that balance.[114]

So he carried me away in the spirit into the wilderness: and I saw
a woman sit upon a scarlet coloured beast, full of names of blasphemy, having seven heads and ten horns.
    And the woman was arrayed in purple and scarlet colour,
and **decked with gold and precious stones and pearls, having
a golden cup in her hand full of abominations and filthiness of
her fornication:**
    And upon her forehead was a name written, MYSTERY, BABY-
LON THE GREAT, THE MOTHER OF HARLOTS AND ABOMINATIONS
OF THE EARTH.
    And I saw the woman drunken with the blood of the saints, and
with the blood of the martyrs of Jesus: and when I saw her, I wondered with great admiration. (Revelation 17:1–6, emphasis added)

Today, the "psychic healing" industry has exploded with millions of
willing customers seeking to use spiritual means to help their physical
and mental well-being. One of the greatest examples of this new societal
fascination with the mystical healing craze is energy or healing crystals.
These stones are said to be imbued with physical, emotional, spiritual,
and metaphysical powers. Do you have an aching back? There is a quartz
crystal that is the best remedy. Suffering from anxiety? Amethyst or agate
are the best recommendations. There are even crystals for recovering from

a broken heart or loss of a loved one. This has all helped fuel a billion-dollar industry as a broad segment of society—from Wall Street executives to Hollywood celebrities touting their healing crystals on social media.[115] A *Vox* magazine article highlighted the popularity of energy crystals:

> This Christmas, a lot of people on your wish list might actually want rocks in their stockings. Crystals, to be specific. What used to be considered alternative and/or weird has gained enough attention to become a mainstream interest. According to *The Guardian*, America's demand for "…overseas crystals and gemstones has doubled over the past three years, and quartz imports have doubled since 2014." The mall is full of crystal starter kits and Anthropologie-esque jewelry with crystals attributed with meaning "love" or "peace" or "harmony." In Columbia alone we have over four shops that are known for selling crystals, gemstones, and other alternative items.[116]

When the apostle John had the vision of Mystery Babylon, the end-times capital city of the Antichrist, it appeared in the form of a harlot riding a beast. Everything about the woman represents spiritual adultery and the massive spiritual deception that will seize the world in the end days. And to no surprise, she was decked with precious stones. The use of crystals has now become mainstream, and it just another satanic counterfeit of what the Lord used for good.

Divine Use of Stones

Throughout the Bible, precious stones are used by God for adorning His places of worship. Consider a few of the examples. When Yahweh gave Moses the instructions for constructing the tabernacle, the original designated location for the Israelites to worship Him, the Lord provided specific details for what Aaron, the high priest, should wear before entering God's presence. His breastplate was to be decorated with precious stones:

And thou shalt make the breastplate of judgment with cunning work; after the work of the ephod thou shalt make it; of gold, of blue, and of purple, and of scarlet, and of fine twined linen, shalt thou make it. Foursquare it shall be being doubled; a span shall be the length thereof, and a span shall be the breadth thereof. **And thou shalt set in it settings of stones, even four rows of stones:** the first row shall be a sardius, a topaz, and a carbuncle: this shall be the first row.

And the second row shall be an emerald, a sapphire, and a diamond. And the third row a ligure, an agate, and an amethyst. And the fourth row a beryl, and an onyx, and a jasper: they shall be set in gold in their inclosings. And the stones shall be with the names of the children of Israel, twelve, according to their names, like the engravings of a signet; every one with his name shall they be according to the twelve tribes. (Exodus 28:15–21, emphasis added)

In the book of Revelation, the Holy City of New Jerusalem, which descends from heaven, contains many of these same precious stones:

And he carried me away in the spirit to a great and high mountain, and shewed me that great city, the holy Jerusalem, descending out of heaven from God,

Having the glory of God: and her light was like unto a stone most precious, even like a jasper stone, clear as crystal;...

And the building of the wall of it was of jasper: and the city was pure gold, like unto clear glass.

And the foundations of the wall of the city were garnished with all manner of precious stones.

The first foundation was jasper; the second, sapphire; the third, a chalcedony; the fourth, an emerald;

The fifth, sardonyx; the sixth, sardius; the seventh, chrysolyte;

the eighth, beryl; the ninth, a topaz; the tenth, a chrysoprasus; the eleventh, a jacinth; the twelfth, an amethyst.

And the twelve gates were twelve pearls: every several gate was of one pearl: and the street of the city was pure gold, as it were transparent glass. (Revelation 21)

Whether it is for their beauty as decoration and embellishment or because they possess some innate spiritual properties, precious stones matter to God. The twelve tribes of Israel were all designated by a jewel. The very holy city of God, constructed in heaven, bears twelve foundations of precious stones. So, in the spirit realm, jewels have importance. And there is scriptural evidence that stones have supernatural properties as well.

Mystery of the *Urim* and *Thummim*:
Discerning the Will of God

And thou shalt put in the breastplate of judgment **the Urim and the Thummim; and they shall be upon Aaron's heart,** when he goeth in before the LORD: and Aaron shall bear the judgment of the children of Israel upon his heart before the LORD continually. (Exodus 28:30, emphasis added)

And Moses brought Aaron and his sons, and washed them with water.

And he put upon him the coat, and girded him with the girdle, and clothed him with the robe, and put the ephod upon him, and he girded him with the curious girdle of the ephod, and bound it unto him therewith.

And he put the breastplate upon him: also he put in the breastplate the Urim and the Thummim.

And he put the mitre upon his head; also upon the mitre,

even upon his forefront, did he put the golden plate, the holy crown; as the LORD commanded Moses.

And Moses took the anointing oil, and anointed the tabernacle and all that was therein, and sanctified them. (Leviticus 8:6–10, emphasis added)

Though not discussed very much in modern times, the Urim and Thummim were essential elements of the breastplate of the high priest of God in the Old Testament. Aaron, as high priest, wore the breastplate on his chest to "bear the judgment of the children of Israel upon his heart before the Lord continually" (Exodus 28:30). *Urim* (אוּרִים in Hebrew) means "lights" and *Thummim* (תֻּמִּם in Hebrew) means "perfection." The high priest was the only member of the nation permitted to enter the tabernacle on Yom Kippur, or the Day of Atonement, when the presence of God would manifest above the ark of the covenant. This was a high holy day for the high priest to perform sacrifices to atone for the sins of the nation. The Lord wanted the tribes of Israel to be symbolically on Aaron's heart as he bore the precious stones on his breastplate. This is all a beautiful type and foreshadow of the Lord Jesus Christ, who is the true High Priest for all believers:

But Christ being come an high priest of good things to come, by a greater and more perfect tabernacle, not made with hands, that is to say, not of this building....

For Christ is not entered into the holy places made with hands, which are the figures of the true; but into heaven itself, now to appear in the presence of God for us:

Nor yet that he should offer himself often, as the high priest entereth into the holy place every year with blood of others;

For then must he often have suffered since the foundation of the world: but now once in the end of the world hath he appeared to put away sin by the sacrifice of himself.

And as it is appointed unto men once to die, but after this the judgment:

So Christ was once offered to bear the sins of many; and unto them that look for him shall he appear the second time without sin unto salvation. (Hebrews 9:11; 24–28)

Jesus Christ is the Light and it is His perfection that allowed Him to be a sacrifice for all of humanity. He is the true *Urim* and *Thummim*. In the Old Testament account, these very special stones had supernatural, divine properties and were used to determine God's will for important decisions by a leader. An example of this is found in the book of Numbers, when God designated Joshua to succeed Moses as leader of the twelve tribes:

And Moses spake unto Lord, saying, Let the Lord, the God of the spirits of all flesh, set a man over the congregation,

Which may go out before them, and which may go in before them, and which may lead them out, and which may bring them in; that the congregation of the LORD be not as sheep which have no shepherd.

And the LORD said unto Moses, Take thee Joshua the son of Nun, a man in whom is the spirit, and lay thine hand upon him;

And set him before Eleazar the priest, and before all the congregation; and give him a charge in their sight.

And thou shalt put some of thine honour upon him, that all the congregation of the children of Israel may be obedient.

And he shall stand before Eleazar the priest, who shall ask **counsel for him after the judgment of Urim before the LORD:**

at his word shall they go out, and at his word they shall come in, both he, and all the children of Israel with him, even all the congregation. (Numbers 27:15–21, emphasis added)

God instructed Moses to have Joshua consult with Eleazar, the high priest who would seek the Lord's counsel via the "judgment of Urim before the Lord." This not only confirms that these stones could be used to determine God's will, but also supports the notion that the twelve stones themselves were the *Urim* and *Thummim*. Bible commentator Jonathan Gill, writing in the early eighteenth century, arrived at the same conclusion:

> But the opinion which at present, I'm most inclined to come into, is that, the Urim and Thummim were no other than the twelve stones in the breastplate, on which were engraven the names of the twelve tribes of Israel, and that these were called *Urim* because they were clear, lucid, and transparent and *Thummim* because they were perfect and complete had no blemish or defect in them....
>
> By these the high-priest consulted God, for the people in matters of moment; thus we read in Numbers, And he (i.e. Joshua) shall stand before Eleazar the priest, who shall ask counsel for him after the judgment of Urim before the Lord, at his word all they go out, and at his word shall they come in, both he and all the children of Israel with him, even all the congregation. Consultation by Urim and Thummim was made by the priest, only but not without having on the Ephod, and generally before the ark of the covenant, not for private persons, and for private affairs, or for things trivial but for publick persons, and in matters of moment.[117]

When King David was being pursued by Saul and feared that the men in the city of Keilah would turn him over to the wicked king, he consulted God through the *Urim* and *Thummim*:

> And Saul called all the people together to war, to go down to Keilah, to besiege David and his men. And David knew that Saul secretly practised mischief against him; **and he said to Abiathar the priest, Bring hither the ephod.**
>
> Then said David, O LORD God of Israel, thy servant hath certainly heard that Saul seeketh to come to Keilah, to destroy the city for my sake. Will the men of Keilah deliver me up into his

hand? will Saul come down, as thy servant hath heard? O LORD God of Israel, I beseech thee, tell thy servant.

And the LORD said, He will come down. Then said David, Will the men of Keilah deliver me and my men into the hand of Saul? And the LORD said, They will deliver thee up. (1 Samuel 23:9–12, emphasis added)

A nineteenth-century commentary confirms that David did indeed seek God's voice through the *Urim* and *Thummim*:

No doubt Abiathar brought the high priest's sacred ephod with Urim and Thummim along with him.... David therefore left the city to secure himself from danger and them from temptation and sin. The express and repeated answers given to the inquiries, which David made by the priest, were in fact a divine attestation that he was heir to the kingdom. Probably these were given in audible voice from some tent where the ephod was placed and before which the inquiry was made.[118]

Urim and *Thummim* Replaced with Satanic Imitations

After God rejected Saul as King and His Spirit departed from him, the reprobate king attempted to discern God's will before a battle with the Philistines. And he tried to use the Urim and Thummim:

And the Philistines gathered themselves together, and came and pitched in Shunem: and Saul gathered all Israel together, and they pitched in Gilboa. And when Saul saw the host of the Philistines, he was afraid, and his heart greatly trembled.

And when Saul enquired of the LORD, the LORD answered him not, neither by dreams, **nor by Urim**, nor by prophets.

Then said Saul unto his servants, Seek me a woman that hath a familiar spirit, that I may go to her, and enquire of her.

And his servants said to him, Behold, there is a woman that hath a familiar spirit at Endor. (1 Samuel 28:4–7, emphasis added)

Rather than repent and persevere in prayer, Saul quickly abandoned any semblance of faith in Yahweh and sought out a witch. From the time Saul was disqualified as king by God, the *Urim* and *Thummim* are barely mentioned again in Scripture. But in its place, the devil introduced counterfeits—taking something once sacred before the Lord and turning it into an occult device. We see examples of this in the book of Judges when Micah attempted to make his own ephod and paid a hireling Levite to be his priest.

Yet he restored the money unto his mother; and his mother took two hundred shekels of silver, and gave them to the founder, who made thereof a graven image and a molten image: and they were in the house of Micah.

And the man Micah had an house of gods, and made an ephod, and teraphim, and consecrated one of his sons, who became his priest.

In those days there was no king in Israel, but every man did that which was right in his own eyes. (Judges 17:4–6)

Micah's blasphemous creation of his own ephod and teraphim was a brazen rebellion against God. He was not a Levite and was in sin to appoint one of his own sons as his "high priest." A nineteenth-century commentary agreed that this was nothing more than a satanic counterfeit:

Satan also instituted an ephod, or *Teraphim,* in opposition to the Urim and Thummim of the High priest of Jehovah. The idolatry of Micah, described in Judges 17, establishes this: "The man Micah had a house of gods, and made an ephod, and teraphim, and consecrated one of his sons, who became his priest." The same passage proves also that the very ordination to the priest-hood was mimicked and counterfeited by Satan.[119]

Today, the adversary continues to mimic the Lord by leading the world astray in the modern fascination with the power of healing and energy crystals.

The Devil Imitates and Distorts Divine Use of Stones

He who was a liar and murderer from the beginning has been most successful in his deceivings by being an imitator of God. You often see this in Scripture. God has wise virgins; Satan has virgins also—false. Christ sows good seed—wheat; Satan sows seed too—tares. God has a vine—"the true vine"; Satan has a vine also—"the vine of the earth." Christ has a bride; Satan has a harlot. God has a city—the new Jerusalem; Satan has also a city—Babylon.[120]

The supernatural properties of the *Urim* and *Thummim* would not be lost on Satan, who, before his fall, wore precious jewels as well. Ezekiel chapter 28 contains one of the several esoteric passages in the Bible that while on their face are addressed to a king or ruler, are truly directed at a fallen angel. This particular chapter details the devil's role in servitude of God before his descent into sinful rebellion:

Moreover the word of the LORD came unto me, saying, Son of man, take up a lamentation upon the king of Tyrus, and say unto him, Thus saith the Lord GOD; Thou sealest up the sum, full of wisdom, and perfect in beauty.

Thou hast been in Eden the garden of God; **every precious stone was thy covering,** the sardius, topaz, and the diamond, the beryl, the onyx, and the jasper, the sapphire, the emerald, and the carbuncle, and gold: the workmanship of thy tabrets and of thy pipes was prepared in thee in the day that thou wast created. (Ezekiel 28:11–13, emphasis added)

All nine stones listed in the passage above were part of the twelve that Aaron wore on his breastplate as designated in Exodus 28. And once he had fallen and was cast from holy servitude to the Lord, the devil made a counterfeit of the use of precious stones that has seen a massive resurgence today.

In addition to using crystals and precious stones to heal body and mind, many unbelievers are using them for spiritual purposes as well. "Chakra stones" are touted as stones that can open the seven chakra or energy points in the body. Here is a description from a popular online shop that sells chakra stones that help to open your "third eye":

Our Third Eye Chakra governs our intuition, imagination, and psychic abilities. It is our archetypal identity; the way we perceive ourselves symbolically. For example, we may see ourselves as a Mother, Healer, Warrior, Pirate, Victim, Hero, etc. When our Third Eye Chakra is healthy, we feel perceptive, have a good memory, and can think in increasingly complex ways. We have big dreams and goals, and are capable of honest self-reflection.

Our Third Eye Chakra may get injured if our intuitive gifts are invalidated or we find ourselves in a frightening environment. We can injure this Chakra ourselves if we choose to reject an uncomfortable reality, simply because it doesn't validate our beliefs. A weak Third Eye Chakra may leave us feeling insensitive or overly-sensitive to other people's pain. **It may manifest as rigid religious beliefs, poor imagination or illogical thinking/behavior.**[121] (Emphasis added)

The concept of the "third eye" or pineal gland is that it is the key to unlocking access to the spiritual realm. It is an extremely New Age and occult concept that has been practiced and taught for centuries. But its true origin goes back to the Garden of Eden and the devil's promise that, by sinning, Adam and Eve's "eyes would be opened" and they could "be as gods." Today, people believe that by harnessing the powers of energy crystals, they can heal and open their third eye. Notice that one of the "symptoms" of an unhealthy third eye is having "rigid religious beliefs." Thus, the New Age movement is categorizing biblical Christianity as an illness and akin to "illogical thinking/behavior."

In the book of 2 Corinthians, we read:

> But if our gospel be hid, it is hid to them that are lost:
> In whom the god of this world hath blinded the minds of them which believe not, lest the light of the glorious gospel of Christ, who is the image of God, should shine unto them. (2 Corinthians 3:3–4)

Rather than opening the eyes of his unwitting followers, the devil blinds the minds of the unsaved to keep them from light of the Savior Jesus Christ. Today, millions of people all over the world are plunging their hearts and minds deeper into satanic darkness by participating in occult practices. Do not be deceived.

Pharmakeia: Drug Use and Demon-Possession

> Neither repented they of their murders, nor of their sorceries [*pharmakeia* or φαρμακεία], nor of their fornication, nor of their thefts. (Revelation 9:21)

"Sorceries" meaning "the use of drugs" denoting the magic rites of the heathen, (Revelation chapter 18:23). The word is used by the LXX to describe the "enchantments" of the Egyptian sorcerers (Exodus 7:22 and of Babylon Isaiah 47:9, 12), the form varying when used to describe the "witchcrafts" of Jezebel 2 Kings (9:22).

In Galatians 5:20 it is placed next to idolatry; elsewhere in the NT
the word occurs only in [Revelation 18:23; 21:8; and 22:15] both
of which texts are cognate to this verse. Suicer connects the word
with the use of drugs in causing abortion and infanticide, and
thus its connection here with idolatry on the one hand; and with
murder and fornication on the other, (i.e. with carnal and spiritual
fornication) can be accounted for.[122]

From the days of the Exodus, the use of herbs and drugs has been connected to the occult. Johannes and Jambres, the two Egyptian sorcerers who attempted to mimic the wonders performed by Moses, used
"enchantments" to boost their access to the spiritual realm:

> And Moses and Aaron did so, as the LORD commanded; and he
> lifted up the rod, and smote the waters that were in the river, in
> the sight of Pharaoh, and in the sight of his servants; and all the
> waters that were in the river were turned to blood.
>
> And the fish that was in the river died; and the river stank, and
> the Egyptians could not drink of the water of the river; and there
> was blood throughout all the land of Egypt.
>
> And the magicians of Egypt did so with their enchantments
> [*pharmakeia*]: and Pharaoh's heart was hardened, neither did he
> hearken unto them; as the LORD had said. (Exodus 7:20–22, LXX)

The Greek word *pharmakeia* is where the English word "pharmacy"
is derived from. It was synonymous with sorcery in the Bible. In ancient
times, mixtures of herbs and animal parts were concocted to assist an
occult practitioner in casting spells or summoning spirits. In the Septua-
gint, the oldest extant version of the Old Testament, *pharmakeia* was used
to describe "the enchantments" that the Egyptians sorcerers used to mimic
Moses turning the Nile river to blood.

Mystics and witches alike have long touted narcotics for their ability to help access the spiritual realm. And in modern times, as govern-

ment officials push to legalize drugs, the use of narcotics has become more acceptable and normalized in society. So, to no surprise, they have exploded in use for those seeking to use them for spiritual enlightenment or to commune with the spirit realm.

Ayahuasca: Opening the Third Eye
and Accessing Spirit Realm

The Pineal gland, which has been referred to as the "third eye" for thousands of years is actually photosensitive (can see light), gas retinal tissue composed of photoreceptors (rods and cones) inside its interior lining and is even wired into the visual cortex of the brain—literally making it a third eye inside our brains, but it also provides perceptions beyond just ordinary sight. The third eye is what allows us to connect and communicate in the spiritual realm. It is often associated with visions, clairvoyance, precognition and out-of-body experiences.

All of us have the ability to activate and use our "third eye." We often use it without being aware through the process of intuition. The Pineal Gland can be active in a variety of wats including meditation, chanting and yoga but by far the most effective method of activating the pineal gland is through the use of DMT or ayahuasca. —The New Life Ayahuasca Retreat[123]

Ayahuasca, a concoction of herbs from the remote jungles and rainforests of South America, has turned into a multimillion dollar industry as tourists now fly in from all over the world for "ayahuasca retreats" where an iquito, or shaman, leads them in a week of meditation, prayers to pagan gods, and "healing"—all while taking the hallucinogenic drug.[124] Everyone from Millennials to Hollywood entertainers and Wall Street and Silicon Valley tech executives are raving about the ability of the drug to bring otherworldly spiritual experiences and healing.[125]

Dr. Jeremy Narby came to this very conclusion in his book, *The*

Cosmic Serpent—DNA and the Origins of Knowledge. Darby spent several years living in the Peruvian Amazon rainforest studying indigenous cultures and their religious practices. He was stunned to learn that the shamans, who went into trances fueled by ayahuasca not only saw serpents in their visions, but drew figures of intertwined serpents that looked identical to the shape of DNA. One example from ancient Sumer ca 2200 BC is below:

"The Serpent Lord Enthroned." From Campbell (1964, p. 11).

The Bible, of course, readily reveals the identity of the serpent:

And the great dragon was cast out, **that old serpent**, called the Devil, and Satan, which deceiveth the whole world: he was cast out into the earth, and his angels were cast out with him. (Revelation 12:9, emphasis added)

This is the incredible spiritual danger of this drug and the many narcotics that are flooding the United States as legislators continue to ease the restrictions on their legal use. The enemy is truly deceiving the masses into believing that through their sin they are connecting with the divine.

In the book of Acts, the apostle Peter encountered a sorcerer named

Simon, whose occult energies were so dynamic that the people of Samaria thought his powers were from God:

> Then Philip went down to the city of Samaria, and preached Christ unto them.
>
> And the people with one accord gave heed unto those things which Philip spake, hearing and seeing the miracles which he did.
>
> For unclean spirits, crying with loud voice, came out of many that were possessed with them: and many taken with palsies, and that were lame, were healed.
>
> And there was great joy in that city.
>
> But there was a certain man, called Simon, which beforetime in the same city used sorcery, and bewitched the people of Samaria, giving out that himself was some great one:
>
> To whom they all gave heed, from the least to the greatest, saying, **This man is the great power of God.** (Acts 8:5–10, emphasis added)

Imagine how deceived the world will be when a man comes onto the global stage who appears to be the most charismatic and unifying leader of all time. And on top of his leadership acumen, he possesses supernatural, seemingly divine power. He will perform literal miracles right before the eyes of the people for all to see. And his religious cohort, who promotes this leader as the Messiah, can also perform supernatural acts? Is there any doubt that the world will flock not only to elect the Antichrist to office, but to make him their god? The Bible states:

> And I saw one of his heads as it were wounded to death; and his deadly wound was healed: and all the world wondered after the beast.
>
> And they worshipped the dragon which gave power unto the beast: and they worshipped the beast, saying, Who is like unto the beast? who is able to make war with him? (Revelation 13:3–4)

The Antichrist, with his false miracles and occult power, will even appear to cheat death itself. The result will be the entire world being captivated by the man of sin—to the point that they will worship him. He will have his religious cohort, the False Prophet, assisting him in instructing the world to worship their False Messiah. On top of this, demons will also help sway the world to join the Antichrist in fighting the Lord Jesus Christ at Armageddon:

> And the sixth angel poured out his vial upon the great river Euphrates; and the water thereof was dried up, that the way of the kings of the east might be prepared.
>
> And I saw three unclean spirits like frogs come out of the mouth of the dragon, and out of the mouth of the beast, and out of the mouth of the false prophet.
>
> For they are the spirits of devils, working miracles, which go forth unto the kings of the earth and of the whole world, to gather them to the battle of that great day of God Almighty. (Revelation 16:12–14)

These are some of the most staggering verses in the Bible. This is not a situation where the world refuses to believe in Jesus out of their typical sinful rebellion. This prophecy describes the world acknowledging Jesus Christ and joining the Antichrist and Satan to wage war against God the Creator of All. It will be demonic spirits that give the final instigation to the leaders of the world to attempt this catastrophic "attack" that will result in their sudden destruction.

Those demons are at work today. The more people are willing to surrender their minds and consciousness via drug use, the easier they are as prey for the demons, principalities, and powers to victimize and turn their hearts towards embracing the occult. Some of these demonic forces are even at work inside the Church.

New-Age Infiltration of the Church

Now we beseech you, brethren, by the coming of our Lord Jesus Christ, and by our gathering together unto him,

That ye be not soon shaken in mind, or be troubled, neither by spirit, nor by word, nor by letter as from us, as that the day of Christ is at hand.

Let no man deceive you by any means: **for that day shall not come, except there come a falling away first**, and that man of sin be revealed, the son of perdition. (2 Thessalonians 2:1–3)

The "falling away" in the Church—in which sound biblical doctrine is abandoned in favor of self-centered heresies, was prophesied from the days of the Apostle Paul. The stats appear to show that prophecy is being fulfilled before our very eyes. According to a Pew Research Center survey, six in ten Christians hold to at least one central New-Age belief, such as belief in reincarnation, astrology or that "spiritual energy can be located in physical things."[126] How could so many people who identify as born-again Christians hold beliefs that are so out of line with basic biblical Christianity? One must only look to the many teachings in the modern church that range from heretical to outright witchcraft.

Bethel Church: Doctrines of Demons

Now the Spirit speaketh expressly, that in the latter times some shall depart from the faith, giving heed to seducing spirits, and doctrines of devils. (1 Timothy 4:1)

Bethel Church is a nondenominational, charismatic church in Redding, California. It has built a massive, global following through the mega-popular Christian contemporary music that is sung in thousands of churches all over the country every Sunday. The leaders preach that the

Holy Spirit has empowered them to prophesy and perform supernatural miracles, "signs and wonders," on a regular basis. However, there is a great deal of wildly unbiblical practices in this church.

- **Drunken Worship** – One of the principal teachings of Bethel Church is that leaders can make the Holy Spirit manifest at their church services and take control of the congregation. This is demonstrated through acting "drunk"—a term the church uses for when one starts laughing uncontrollably and enters wild, chaotic behavior and spasms. There is absolutely no biblical example of this kind of activity whatsoever in Scripture. We will never find any instance of a believer in God acting irrationally or intoxicated as a sign of the presence of the Holy Spirit.[127]

- **Christian Tarot Cards** – Bethel drew controversy in early 2019 for using "destiny cards," a set of cards with imagery and symbols used to "divine" someone's future and give them a "reading." Christalignment, the company that makes the cards, states this about their spiritual services:

  All Christalignment team members operate only out of the third heaven realm. That means we are all hearing from Christ spirit. This ensures safety for you and a way higher level of accuracy.... We have developed 7 sets in total of destiny cards which are so accurate, that even if your life circumstances change dramatically, on your return to do them again years later, you will find the results identical, such is their accuracy. They are able to give profound insight into relationships, careers and your spiritual life.[128]

  This is nothing more than a form of divination, which is forbidden in Scripture. A Christian should find life's purpose and direction though prayer and Scripture, not by consulting a deck of cards. Also note that the Christalignment company uses the term "Christ spirit" as opposed to the "Lord Jesus Christ." Terms like "Christ spirit" or "Christ consciousness" are New-Age jargon for the notion that Jesus Christ was just a normal man who was able to "elevate his consciousness" or "transcend" and achieve godhood through mystical practices. This type of false teaching is the preaching of "another Christ" and should be avoided.

- **"Destiny Pants"**—Bethel Pastor Theresa Dedmon launched a clothing line of supernaturally endowed leggings for women called Destiny Pants. On her website, the "Angels Surround You" pants are described as having the following "prophetic meaning": "Ministering angels sent on your behalf to guard and protect you through life's path. Close your eyes and listen to the breeze of Heaven as angels' feathers fall!"[129]

Most recently, Bethel drew national headlines when ministers there attempted a "resurrection" of the two-year-old child of one of their music performers. The two-week process ended in no resurrection and instead invited a wave of criticism upon the church and Christianity in general.[130]

Bethel's teachings are fraught with error. In his book, *The Supernatural Power of a Transformed Mind*, Pastor Bill Johnson wrote:

For many years I misunderstood the biblical concept of desire. Psalm 37:4 tells us: "Delight yourself in the Lord, and He shall give you the desires of your heart." Like many pastors, I foolishly taught that if you delighted yourself in the Lord, He would change your desires by telling you what to desire. But that's not at all what this means. That verse literally means that God wants to be impacted by what you think and dream. God is after your desires. The word desire is made up of the prefix "de" meaning "of," and "sire" meaning "father." Desire is, by nature, of the Father.[131]

Steven Kozar, a writer for the blog site Pirate Christian, explains how this interpretation is false: "The Hebrew word translated into English as desire is "*mishalah.*" It simply means 'request' or 'petition,' but Bill Johnson is telling people that 'God is after their desires' because de- and -sire means 'of the father,' according to him. This is a complete fabrication and a deliberate twisting of God's Word."

In another passage of the book, Johnson gives a wildly incorrect explanation of the meaning of "repentance": "Renewing the mind begins with repentance…'Re' means to go back. 'Pent' is like the penthouse, the top floor of a building. Repent, then means to go back to God's perspective on reality."

Again, Kozar corrects this severe interpretive error by stating that "the word 'repent' has nothing to do with penthouses, obviously!" He continues, "The original Greek word translated is 'metanoia' and it means 'I repent, change my mind, change the inner man (particularly with reference to acceptance of the will of God), repent,' according to Strong's Concordance."[132]

Bethel youth pastor Seth Dahl preached a sermon in which he claimed to have a vision of Jesus where **the Lord asked him for forgiveness.**[133] This, of course, is blasphemy. Jesus was without sin and thus would never ask for forgiveness—much less from a human being. In 1 Timothy chapter 4, the Bible declares that demons actually teach "doctrines." Some of the worst heresies being taught in churches today were inspired by the demonic. This is the fault of pastors and church leadership who have departed from sound doctrine and allowed satanic influence to enter the pulpit. The Jesus of Bethel Church is "another Jesus"—an idol they have created and teach about to the peril of their adoring audiences. But the Bible is clear that idols have no place in the Church:

> But I say, that the things which the Gentiles sacrifice, they sacrifice to devils, and not to God: and I would not that ye should have fellowship with devils.
>
> Ye cannot drink the cup of the Lord, and the cup of devils: ye cannot be partakers of the Lord's table, and of the table of devils. (1 Corinthians 10:20–21)

Sadly, Bethel is just one of many churches trying to bring devils to the Lord's table in the form of mystical teachings. One of the greatest examples of this today is the surging popularity of the Enneagram.

The Enneagram: Mysticism Infiltrates the Church

"Know Your Number" is a foundational course and is the first step in working with the Enneagram.

In this workshop, Joey Schewee introduces the nine Enneagram Types. Each personality type is reviewed in detail, including an evaluation of the strengths and weaknesses of the Types, and the likely interpersonal challenges that may be involved in an unhealthy expression of the Type.

This workshop is intended for those who want to discover their Enneagram number or are still unsure about their Enneagram number. —Advertisement for the "Know Your Number" Enneagram Conference at Redeemer Church in Modesto, California[134]

Suzanne Stabile, Enneagram Master Teacher, author of the runaway best-selling book *The Path Between Us* and popular podcast host of *The Road Back To You* and *The Enneagram Journey* is coming to Grace First.

The Enneagram, a newly revived yet ancient personality typing system will profoundly deepen your understanding and love for yourself, others, and God. During this day and a half conference, you will discover the framework for how you can begin to live into your most authentic self and see the wisdom and gifts that each personality type can offer. Suzanne is recognized as one the leading experts on the Enneagram and Spirituality and storytellers you will encounter.

At Know Your Number, you will:

1. Gain a deep understanding of the Enneagram and your number.
2. Explore how the Enneagram can improve your relationship with others.
3. Discover how the Enneagram applies to your life and your relationship to God.

Join us for this Friday evening / Saturday workshop that will change the way you see yourself and the world." —Advertisement for the Enneagram Conference at Grace First Presbyterian Church in Long Beach, California[135]

For who hath stood in the counsel of the LORD, and hath perceived and heard his word? who hath marked his word, and heard it?

Behold, a whirlwind of the LORD is gone forth in fury, even a grievous whirlwind: it shall fall grievously upon the head of the wicked.

The anger of the LORD shall not return, until he have executed, and till he have performed the thoughts of his heart: in the latter days ye shall consider it perfectly.

I have not sent these prophets, yet they ran: I have not spoken to them, yet they prophesied.

But if they had stood in my counsel, and had caused my people to hear my words, then they should have turned them from their evil way, and from the evil of their doings. (Jeremiah 23:18–22, emphasis added)

The Enneagram has been the latest craze in the modern church. As stated in the descriptions above, it is a numerical system based on an a supposedly "ancient drawing" of nine points within a circle to help determine "personality type" and the kind of relationship has or should have with God. The fact that the system is based on a drawing alone should be enough to raise heretical alarm bells. But that hasn't stopped the utter fascination with the Enneagram as hundreds of churches have incorporated it into their teachings.

Hundreds of conferences across the United States each year are based on teaching the Enneagram. Some churches are even offering twelve-week studies on it. It would be hard to speak to a large number of Christians and not come across some who "know their number" or "are trying to move to another number" based on Enneagram. But when we do basic research into the origins of this mystical diagram, we'll see grave spiritual danger.

A Clear Occult History

John Starke, lead pastor of Apostles Uptown Church in New York City and one of the early adopters of the Enneagram system, doesn't even hide the non-Christian origin of the personality and identity system:

> The Enneagram is not a spiritual tool, per se, but it is increasingly being used as one in church classes and faith-based counseling settings. Its origins are obscure. We do know that it was introduced in the West in the 1970s by Chilean psychiatrists, then adopted by Jesuit priests and popularized in 1992 by Franciscan spiritual director Richard Rohr's *Discovering the Enneagram: An Ancient Tool for a New Spiritual Journey*. My description thus far probably doesn't give evangelicals warm feelings. Indeed, some connect the Enneagram's roots to Sufism (Islamic mysticism), while others see in the Enneagram a Gnosticism that encourages users to find their "hidden," true self.[136]

The earliest publication of the Enneagram is not ancient, but instead dates back to the early twentieth century. Russian mystic, P. D. Ouspensky, published the image in his book, *In Search of the Miraculous* in 1917.[137] Ouspensky credits his mentor, George Gurdijeff, for its creation. Gurdijeff was an occultist who dedicated his life to researching necromancy, fortune-telling, and occult secret societies. Gurdijeff never published the Enneagram, but taught it in classes to his students, like Ouspensky.[138]

Ouspensky never intended the mystical drawing to be a personality test. Rather, he believed the Enneagram was a pathway to accessing the spirit realm, immortality, and understanding the cosmos. For he and his mentor, the Enneagram was akin to alchemy.[139]

Ouspensky was a follower of Madame H. P. Blavatsky, one of the fore-runners of the New Age movement. She founded the Theosophical Society, of which Ouspensky was a member for a decade. She also started a magazine called *Lucifer*. An avowed occultist, Blavatsky wrote of the devil:

> One of the most hidden secrets involves the so-called fall of Angels. Satan and his rebellious host will thus prove to have become the direct Saviours and Creators of divine man. Thus Satan, once he ceases to be viewed in the superstitious spirit of the church, grows into the grandiose image. It is Satan who is the God of our planet and the only God. Satan (or Lucifer) represents the Centrifugal Energy of the Universe, this ever-living symbol of self-sacrifice for the intellectual independence of humanity.[140]

The next person to help bring the Enneagram to modern times was Oschar Ichazo. A Bolivian Catholic mystic, Ichazo spent a decade travel-ing Southeast Asia studying Sufism, Kabbalah, alchemy, and other mysti-cal arts.[141] It was during this time he became familiar with the teachings of Gurdijeff and the Enneagram. Ichazo claims that while spending a year in solitude in Bolivia, he entered a "spiritual coma" and was moved to open a school to share his spiritual teachings. During this time, he had an encounter with the "angel Metatron," who inspired the personality map-ping of Enneagram.[142]

According to Ichazo, every person is born with a "pure essence" that corrodes, or loses its illumination, as the childhood pains and disappoint-ments build. As individuals develop a personality, they lose closeness with their essence. Through the Enneagram, people can understand their per-

sonality type and work back to their pure essence through spiritual exer-
cises like guided meditation and hand-exercise practices by Buddhists.[143]

Of course, none of this is in Scripture. In fact, the Bible tells the exact
opposite: Because of the sin of Adam and Eve, all people are born with a
sin nature and thus are not born "pure":

Wherefore, as by one man sin entered into the world, and death
by sin; and so death passed upon all men, for that all have sinned.
(Romans 5:12)

King David wrote in the Psalms:

Behold, I was shapen in iniquity; and in sin did my mother conceive me. (Psalm 51:5)

Also note that neither Gurdijeff, Ouspensky, nor Ichazo, the founders
of the Enneagram, had any connection to Christianity or the Bible. It is
clearly occult in origin, and there should be massive red flags of spiritual
discernment when anyone takes even a cursory look into the history of
this mystic diagram. This has not stopped churches from promoting it to
their congregations. Pastors by the hundreds have jumped on the Enneagram trend, hosting conferences and sermon series based on this clearly
mystical, unbiblical teaching.

In the best-selling book *Sacred Enneagram*, author Chris Huertz touts
the occult diagram's power to bring a person closer to the Lord:

Ultimately though, for those willing to persevere, the Enneagram
offers a sacred map for our souls; a map that. When understood,
leads us to our true identity, and to God.[144]

Suzanne Stabile is one of the most prominent speakers at church
conferences on the Enneagram. In her book, *The Road Back to You: An
Enneagram Journey*, she documents that when she first mentioned the

Enneagram to one of her professors, he told her to rid herself of the book based on the Bible's clear prohibition against witchcraft and the occult. But she ignored her professor's "paranoid" advice and kept the book. Decades later, she met a Catholic monk who encouraged to her to investigate the Enneagram again as a means of self-discovery. Stabile writes on the meaning of the Enneagram:

> The goal of understanding your Enneagram "type" or "number"—the terms are used interchangeably in this book—is not to delete and replace your personality with a new one. Not only is this not possible, it would be a bad idea.… The purpose of the Enneagram is to develop self-knowledge and learn how to recognize and dis-identify with the parts of our personalities that limits us so we can eb reunited with our truest and best selves, that "pure diamond, blazing with the invisible light of heaven", as Thomas Merton said.[145]

This is an absolute heresy. Once again, Scripture teaches that rather than being born as a pure, blazing, beautiful being, we were instead "shapen in iniquity." The book of Jeremiah confirms that because of our sin nature, which all people are born with, our hearts are "deceitful above all things, and **desperately wicked**: who can know it?" (Jeremiah 17:9, emphasis added). A Christian's ultimate destiny is to be "born again"— receiving a brand-new spirit, born of God. The goal of Christianity is not finding our "hidden inner self," but instead to "die to self" and rid ourselves of the person we once were:

> Know ye not, that so many of us as were baptized into Jesus Christ were baptized into his death?
> Therefore we are buried with him by baptism into death: that like as Christ was raised up from the dead by the glory of the Father, even so we also should walk in newness of life.

For if we have been planted together in the likeness of his death, we shall be also in the likeness of his resurrection:

Knowing this, that our old man is crucified with him, that the body of sin might be destroyed, that henceforth we should not serve sin.

For he that is dead is freed from sin.

Now if we be dead with Christ, we believe that we shall also live with him:

Knowing that Christ being raised from the dead dieth no more; death hath no more dominion over him. (Romans 6:3–9)

As born-again believers in the risen Savior Jesus Christ, Christians through their spiritual growth become "conformed to Christ"—taking on more and more of the holiness through faith.

I am crucified with Christ: nevertheless I live; yet not I, but Christ liveth in me: and the life which I now live in the flesh I live by the faith of the Son of God, who loved me, and gave himself for me. (Galatians 2:20)

Therefore if any man be in Christ, he is a new creature: old things are passed away; behold, all things are become new. (2 Corinthians 5:17)

Rather than putting the focus on Christ and conforming to Him, the Enneagram is incredibly self-focused. It implores learners to focus on their own wants, needs, desires, history, and emotions to find "their true self." This is a wildly New Age teaching. Biblical Christianity is the only faith on earth that teaches that human beings are inherently evil, doomed by a sinned nature and guilty before a just and righteous God. But God, in His mercy, redeems us through His atoning Word and His power.

The New Age teaches that there is "divine" in all of us. We all have a divine spark that has gone dormant and through some type of process—be it guided meditation, drug use, or some form of works, we can unlock or ascend to a higher level of consciousness and godhood. The Enneagram is subtly teaching this exact concept. Sadly, this is just a small example of the occult mysticism that is infiltrating the church.

Billie Eilish: World's Biggest Pop Star's Songs Praise Lucifer

With her crossover sound that is part pop, EDM (electronic dance music), and jazz, Billie Eilish ascended virtually out of nowhere to dominate the music industry. She became an overnight sensation after uploading a homemade demo song to Spotify that went viral. Once she was formally signed to a record label, she became the first female artist born in the twenty-first century to top the Billboard 200. Twelve of the thirteen songs on her album (note the number of songs) are on the Billboard 100 charts—the most ever for a female musician.[146] With her goth-pop odes, Eilish built a fan base of millions, including many teen girls. Her songs have been streamed over one billion times. And now that she is a bona fide hit, she can blatantly promote a satanic agenda.

In the video for her song *All Good Girls Go to Hell*, Eilish appears in a hospital smock with the back exposed. A series of large syringes are plunged in her back, causing wings to break through her skin and grow out. The video then moves to a shot of her falling from the sky and plunging to the ground. The visual is clear that she is a fallen angel. The song's opening lyric is "My Lucifer is lonely."

"Lucifer" is, of course, the title for Satan in the Bible. It represented a title for the devil before he turned evil. We find his fall described in detail in the book of Isaiah:

How art thou fallen from heaven, O Lucifer, son of the morning! how art thou cut down to the ground, which didst weaken the nations!

For thou hast said in thine heart, I will ascend into heaven, I will exalt my throne above the stars of God:

I will sit also upon the mount of the congregation, in the sides of the north: I will ascend above the heights of the clouds;

I will be like the most High. Yet thou shalt be brought down to hell, to the sides of the pit. (Isaiah 14:12–15)

The symbolism and lyrics could not be more blatant. Eilish is putting herself in the role of Satan—a fallen angel who was cast out of heaven after rebelling against God. By desiring to "be like the Most High," the devil in effect wanted to overthrow the Creator. And Eilish says that "her Lucifer is lonely"—meaning that there is no competition in her heart or mind against Lucifer.

The next few verses are a mockery of heaven. In Catholic belief, the apostle Peter, one of the twelve disciples who traveled with Jesus Christ during his three years of earthly ministry, is said to "guard" the entry into heaven, informing the dead of who is permitted entry and who will be sent to hell. This of course is a wildly unbiblical notion that has no support whatsoever in Scripture. The refrain of the song boasts: "All the good girls go to hell / 'Cause even God herself has enemies."

This embraces the end-times deception—that the devil and his False Messiah should be worshiped as God. The song is literally casting Satan as a sympathetic figure and hell as the preferable location to spend the afterlife.

Also, of note is the reference to God as "herself," which is an outright attack on the biblical truth that God is male. Eilish is just the latest Hollywood entertainer to refer to God as a female as a means of promoting the feminist movement. Pop singer Ariana Grande, one of the most successful singers of all time, released a song entitled "God Is a Woman." In a performance at the 2018 MTV VMA awards, Grande performed the song with a reenactment of the Last Supper, casting herself in the position of Jesus Christ and having scantily clad women in the roles of the twelve disciples.[147]

Returning to the closing lyrics of Eilish's song, we find another promotion of the adversary: "And once the water starts to rise / And Heaven's out of sight / She'll want the Devil on her team."

Notice the brazen blasphemy by this pop icon. Keep in mind that this is a young woman who has millions of followers on social media. She is a major influence of the young generation and is poisoning their minds with her audacity to challenge God. These are the tares being planted to blind the minds of society and prepare the arrival of the Antichrist.

What spirit would lead a young girl to sing lyrics that celebrate an attack on God? The spirit of Antichrist. Psalm 36 sums up the heart of entertainers who promote such wickedness:

> The transgression of the wicked saith within my heart, that there is no fear of God before his eyes.
>
> For he flattereth himself in his own eyes, until his iniquity be found to be hateful.
>
> The words of his mouth are iniquity and deceit: he hath left off to be wise, and to do good.
>
> He deviseth mischief upon his bed; he setteth himself in a way that is not good; he abhorreth not evil. (Psalm 36:1–4)

Many famous rappers and singers of today make music with no fear of God. They blaspheme and mock the Christian faith while flattering themselves with boasts of all of their material wealth and fame. An entire generation is being raised with music that is not only sinful but openly promotes the devil. Do not be deceived.

Stand for Christ in These Final Days of Evil

Now more than ever, Bible-believing Christians need to contend for the faith and share the gospel with urgency. As the Bible has predicted, the approach of the end times has led the world to seek the pleasures of the world and embrace evil. Rather than being dismayed, Christians should be encouraged that the Bible is once again being proven true.

There is power in the Word of God. There is true freedom and salvation in the Bible. The Lord Jesus Christ, the Messiah, said:

> It is the spirit that quickeneth; the flesh profiteth nothing: the words that I speak unto you, they are spirit, and they are life. (John 6:63)

Never forget the power we have to win souls for Yeshua, our Savior. Believers must boldly proclaim the gospel and as the Bible commands:

> And have no fellowship with the unfruitful works of darkness, but rather reprove them. (Ephesians 5:11)

Scripture commands us to "reprove" or expose the works of the enemy. It is time for us to urge our friends and family members who are involved in apostate churches to "come out!" It is time to warn our children or grandchildren about the dangers in so much of the entertainment they are being exposed to each day. It is time to speak out and rebuke pastors who are openly and brazenly leading their churches into demonic doctrines. For many people in your life, you may be the last line of defense between that person and spiritual damnation.

The good news is that Jesus Christ will defeat the devil, the False Prophet, and the Antichrist. Jesus Christ will return to judge the nations and restore righteousness in this earth. He has provided an escape in the Rapture for all those who trust in Him before the supernatural, devastating judgments of the book of Revelation are unleashed upon a world that has continually rejected and denied Him.

We must be like Noah, preaching righteousness and forgiveness of sins to the world before the Flood. We must have the bravery of Rahab, who defied the sinful society of Jericho for her faith. Like the apostle John, we have to share the future that has been written that the light of Christ may open the eyes of those who have been blinded by the enemy before the final, end-times delusion approaches. The signs are all around us. Trust the Savior and proclaim His truth boldly.

> And when these things begin to come to pass, then look up, and lift up your heads; for your redemption draweth nigh. (Luke 21:28)

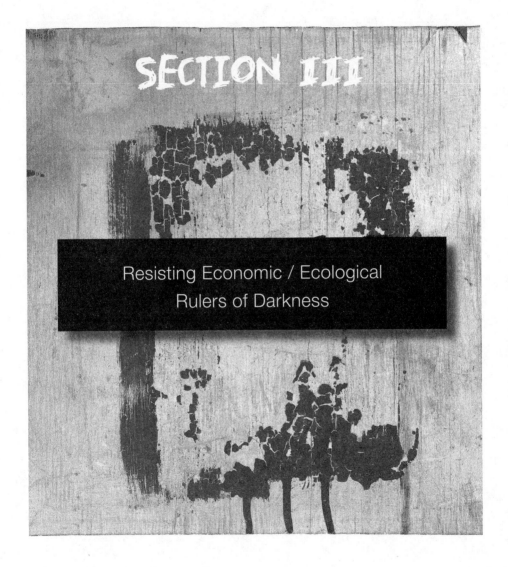

SECTION III

Resisting Economic / Ecological
Rulers of Darkness

SEVEN

COVID-19: The Invisible Enemy

By Randy Nettles

The novel coronavirus named COVID-19 began in late 2019 in Wuhan, China. There are two major theories on the virus' origin. The most popular theory that the mainstream media, China, and the World Health Organization would like us to believe is that the coronavirus originated from people eating bats or other animals infected by bats. This is exactly like its virus cousin that caused the 2003 SARS epidemic, SARS-CoV-2. A "wet" market in Wuhan, China, called the Human Seafood Wholesale Market is believed to be the source of COVID-19. Wet markets are somewhat like our farmers' markets, consisting of vendors selling food outdoors from stalls or booths. These vendors in China and elsewhere in Asia sell seafood, meat, fruits, and vegetables. However, some wet markets sell and slaughter live animals on site, including chickens, fish, dogs, cats, shellfish, and even wild animals (including bats) and their meat. The term "wet" comes from the liquids involved in these places: fish splashing in tubs of water, melting ice used to keep meat cold, and the blood and guts of slaughtered animals. Usually, the animals are stacked in crates atop one another, and the water and urine drop on the animals beneath them, causing very unsanitary conditions.

The second theory is one that is gaining momentum with the public and certain news outlets as more facts emerge. Evidence has surfaced that the coronavirus ravaging the globe may have "escaped" from a poorly equipped lab in Wuhan, China, where researchers were conducting risky viral disease experiments in the years leading up to the pandemic. This theory is backed by two sensitive diplomatic cables sent by two US-China embassy officials who had visited the site of the Wuhan Institute of Virology in early 2018. The messages warned that the experiments conducted in the lab on coronavirus in bats represented a risk of a new SARS-like pandemic, according to a *Washington Post* report citing intelligence sources. One of the cables also said there is a "serious shortage of appropriately trained technicians and investigators needed to safely operate this high-containment laboratory," according to the report. This theory suggests that the cause of the virus was incompetence and not malevolence, as it was accidental and not intentionally created as a weapon. Regardless of the motive, the actions by the Chinese government immediately after the virus was identified and known to be contagious to humans was reprehensible; as the communist leaders would not allow travel inside the country but encouraged international travel. This allowed the virus to be spread throughout the world instead of being contained in the host country.

There are others, however, who suggest a much more sinister motive for spreading a man-made pandemic. They believe the New World Order acolytes are responsible for the "accident" that transpired in Wuhan and the rapid international spread of the disease (especially in the US), for the purpose of crashing the American economy. It was also done for the purpose of showcasing the weaknesses and inefficiencies that national governments have in dealing with an international crisis. In their minds, only a government that represents the entire world is capable of solving the world's problems. These one-world government elites plan on bringing the tower of Babel back into existence, metaphorically speaking. They want a one-world government, religion, and currency for all people and nations so they can control and enslave mankind. It's for their own good, of course, as the common people just aren't smart enough to govern themselves. One of their main objectives is to depopulate the planet from approximately 7.8 billion people to 500 million people.

For decades now, these New World Order fanatics have been searching for a global crisis significant enough to put their evil plans into action. The coronavirus pandemic and subsequent economic collapse could be such a crisis. The democratic crony Rahm Emanuel once repeated a famous quote, "You never let a serious crisis go to waste. And what I mean by that, it's an opportunity to do things you could not do before." So what are some things that have never been done before in America by the government?

1) **A total lockdown (besides deemed essential workers) of American citizens and workers who are confined to their homes.** They are only allowed out for essential items such as buying groceries, doctor or hospital visits, etc. How long will this lockdown last? Evidently, it will last as long as our local, state, and federal governments deem appropriate.

2) **A closing of the economy due to businesses being ordered to shut down and employees not being able to work.** The only people who can work are the ones considered "essential," deemed so by the local government. Massive unemployment throughout the country will probably cause a major recession or even a depression later in 2020 and beyond.

3) **Food (and other necessary items) shortages, causing food lines and food banks feeding those who cannot afford groceries.** Much of the world has already been facing this problem, but America hasn't seen it since the Great Depression.

4) **Restricting the movement of citizens to travel and to assemble, even for the purpose of worship.** New terms and definitions of words have come about as a result of these restrictions, such as social distancing, shelter in place, mitigation, contact tracing, community spread, self-quarantine, new normal, etc.

5) **Massive debt by local, state, and federal governments building to an unsustainable level.** Tens of millions of unemployed workers are filing for state unemployment benefits amounting to billions of dollars. The federal government. has so far added $3.6 trillion to the national debt, which is already at approximately $23 trillion, as a stimulus to the economy to sustain businesses and workers until they can go back to work. President Trump has talked many times about the fact that the cure for the coronavirus cannot be more dangerous than the disease itself. It appears that the cure of social distancing and closing/slowing the world's economies will be much deadlier and costly than the pandemic itself. The legacy of COVID-19 is not the deaths or misery it causes, but the fact that most of the governments of the world came together to stop and/or slow down their economies. Today there is a major international push for a world solution to two world problems, COVID-19 and the failing economy.

The "invisible enemy" of mankind isn't germs or viruses, but Satan, the current god of this world, and his hordes of fallen angels. These invisible demons whisper into the ears of evil, powerful men, easily manipulating them into doing their master's will:

For we do not wrestle against flesh and blood, but against principalities, against powers, against the rulers of the darkness of this age, against spiritual hosts of wickedness in the heavenly places. (Ephesians 6:12)

A biblical example of this corruption and sin is found in Genesis 11. After the Great Flood, God commanded Noah and his sons to repopulate the whole earth:

Be fruitful and multiply; bring forth abundantly in all the earth, and multiply therein. (Genesis 9:7)

Many generations later, the people found a plain in the land of Shinar, and they dwelt there. They deliberately disobeyed God's command to repopulate the whole earth, perhaps because of the influence of the "invisible enemy." The ancient people said:

> Go to, let us build a city and a tower, whose top may reach into heaven; and let us make us a name, lest we be scattered abroad upon the face of the whole earth. (Genesis 11:4)

This was probably the start of people living in close quarters within cities and being governed by local elites or rulers. Cities eventually developed collectively into nations, bringing with them national governments, kings, presidents, or tyrants to rule over them.

When the people rebelled against God, the Lord came down to see the city and the tower which the children of men built. He said:

> Go to, let us go down, and confound their language, that they may not understand one another's speech.
>
> So the Lord scattered them abroad from there upon the face of all the earth; and they left off to build the city.
>
> Therefore the name of the city is called Babel, because the Lord confounded the language of all the earth; and from there did the Lord scatter them abroad upon the face of all the earth. (Genesis 11:7–9)

God's plan was for the people to settle and populate all parts of the earth and not just live in one region. There were two reasons for this, in my opinion.

1) The Lord didn't want the entire population of mankind to answer to just one government or individual. When such power is given to a select few, it usually doesn't turn out well for the people. The nineteenth-century British politician, Lord Acton, quoted

previous writers when he wrote, "Power tends to corrupt, and absolute power corrupts absolutely. Great men are almost always bad men." Such was the case with the original founder of Babel (and probably the Babylonian empire), Nimrod, who had to learn this lesson the hard way, from the Lord Himself. Thus the term "nimrod" is used (to this day) to refer to someone who is naïve or stupid.

2) When people gather into large groups, trash and waste tend to accumulate in a problematic way. Add to this bad hygiene, unsafe foods, and rodents carrying fleas that are attracted to garbage, disease and germs are born and then transmitted to humans. Humans then transmit them to other humans and the result within large civilizations can be an epidemic or pandemic. The Lord knew that if all mankind was located in just one area, civilization would be in danger of extinction. Throughout history, entire civilizations have been wiped out by pandemics.

A Brief History of Pandemics

Plagues and pandemics know no boundaries and travel the globe sporadically. Here is a look at a couple of the more severe ones that have occurred throughout history:

1) **The Black Death** — This plague was caused by a string of the bacterium *Yersiniq pestis* and was spread by fleas on infected rodents. Its name comes from the black skin spots on the sailors who traveled to China and docked in a Sicilian port, bringing with them the devastating disease now known to be bubonic plague. The Black Death lasted from 1347–1351 and is estimated to have killed seventy-five million to two hundred million people. The plague changed the course of Europe's history. With millions of deaths throughout the continent, workers became harder to

find, so employers had to pay higher wages for their labor. This essentially put an end to Europe's system of serfdom.

2) **The Spanish Flu** — An estimated fifty to one hundred million people from the South Seas to North America died from the Spanish flu (influenza) epidemic of 1918–1920. The flu's spread and lethality was enhanced by the cramped conditions of soldiers and their poor nutrition, including bad water, during World War I. Unlike other influenza outbreaks, this one killed healthy adults, while leaving children and older adults with weakened immune systems still alive.

Are all of these pandemics judgments from God, or are they the result of living in a fallen, sinful, and corrupt world? Does God allow the god of this world, Satan, to unleash his "invisible enemy" upon us from time to time, as He allowed him to attack Job with plagues?

And the Lord said unto Satan, Behold, he is in your hand; but save his life.
So Satan went from the presence of the Lord, and struck Job with sore boils from the sole of his foot unto his crown. (Job 2:6–7)

During this testing of faith, Job had this to say:

All my close friends abhor me and they whom I love are turned against me.
My bone cleaves to my skin and to my flesh, and I am surviving by the skin of my teeth. (Job 19:19–20)

Job remained faithful to the Lord despite the calamities in his life.

For I know that my Redeemer lives, and He shall stand at last on the earth;

And after my skin is destroyed, this I know, that in my flesh I shall see God, whom I shall see for myself and my eyes shall behold, and not another.

How my heart yearns within me! If you should say, "How shall we persecute him?"

Since the root of the matter is found in me, be afraid of the sword for yourselves; for wrath brings the punishment of the sword, that you may know there is a judgment. (Job 19:25–29)

In the great tribulation of Job and his family, he did not question the will of the Father, but accepted his fate of death (or so he thought) because of his faith that he would be redeemed and resurrected with an indestructible spiritual body...one that would be capable of seeing God face to face. Job advised his "friends" not to judge, for judgment comes from God. He reminded his friends that one day all of them would stand before God and be judged. God eventually redeemed Job for his faith and gave him twice as much wealth and livestock as he had before. God also blessed Job with a new family consisting of seven sons and three attractive daughters (Job 42:15).

Welcome to Big Government and the "New Normal"

There have been so many articles and news (some fake) reports regarding COVID-19, its spread, and its consequences that it is hard to ascertain fact from fiction. There is, however, one source of "news" that is always reliable and truthful...the Bible. It is the news of the past and not the present. One should always learn from the experiences of the past. Winston Churchill, paraphrasing George Santayana, once said, "Those who fail to learn from history are doomed to repeat it." Although the Bible doesn't mention the coronavirus specifically, it does talk frequently of plagues. One such plague, a famine, lasted for seven years upon the earth and is mentioned in Genesis 41.

The Lord was with Joseph as He was with Abraham, Isaac, and Jacob.

Joseph was brought from prison to interpret Pharaoh's dreams. He was thirty years old at this time. God conveyed the dreams and their meaning to Joseph, who in turn told Pharaoh the meaning of his dreams.

> God has shown to Pharaoh what He is about to do.
>
> Behold, seven years of great abundance are coming in all the land of Egypt; and after them seven years of famine will come, and all the abundance will be forgotten in the land of Egypt, and the famine will ravage the land.
>
> So the abundance will be unknown in the land because of that subsequent famine; for it will be very severe.
>
> Now, as for the repeating of the dream to Pharaoh twice, it means that the matter is determined by God, and God will quickly bring it about. (Genesis 41:29–32)

Joseph even gave Pharaoh God's remedy for the coming seven years of famine that were to follow the seven years of plenty, according to Genesis 41:33–36. Pharaoh, of course, was impressed with Joseph's interpretation of the dream and his solution for the famine to come. The Pharaoh put Joseph in charge of the operation and made him his governor over all of Egypt. The only individual who was over him was Pharaoh himself.

After the seven years of plenty, famine was in the land of Egypt and throughout the region, even unto the land of Canaan. Joseph moved his father's family from Canaan and placed them in the fertile lands of Goshen, as commanded by Pharaoh. He made sure they had plenty of grain and bread during the famine. This was a stark contrast to the citizens of Egypt, who had no grain. Pharaoh, however, had massive amounts of grain in storage, thanks to the preventative actions taken by Joseph. Joseph now represented the government of Egypt, as he was the second in command under Pharaoh.

The first item the government took from the people was their money. The people had to spend all of their money for grain (food) just to survive. The next item the government took was their livestock and work animals.

Since the people had no money left, they bartered their animals for grain. The third taken from the people was their land. Once all the money and cattle were gone, the only thing they had left for bartering was their land. They had to sell their land to the government in exchange for grain. The last thing the people lost was their freedom. The people had to work for the government just to be provided with enough food to survive. With the loss of ownership of their land, the people were relocated to different parts of the country. This was probably done for work projects of the government. Basically, it was a form of slavery or serfdom.

When the famine was over, Joseph gave the people of Egypt seed to sow in the land. They worked the land that was now owned by Pharaoh. Joseph allowed them to keep 80 percent of their crops, and the remaining 20 percent was given to the government. This was a form of a tax or wealth redistribution system. It worked out really well for Pharaoh and the government, but not so much for the citizens of Egypt. However, they did survive the seven-year famine as a people and nation.

When the citizens of a country give up their civil liberties for security, they will eventually lose their freedom. Ronald Regan once said, "The most terrifying words in the English language are: 'I'm with the government, and I'm here to help.'" If we depend on the government instead of God for our safety and well-being, we will eventually reap what we sow. The result will be slavery and misery. Joseph was blessed by God because he trusted in Him for all his needs. This is the lesson of Genesis 41 we all need to learn in these evil times.

The Number 19 and COVID-19

The number nineteen is the sum of ten and nine. The number ten is one of the perfect numbers of God and signifies the perfection of divine order (three, seven, and twelve are the other perfect numbers). Nine is the number that represents finality or judgment, especially in regards to Israel. The fast of mourning, known as *Tisha B'Av*, occurs on the ninth day of the fifth month of Av on the Jewish calendar. On this day, Israel has witnessed eight of the greatest disasters in its history; including the destruction of Solomon's temple by the Babylonians in 586 BC and the destruction of the second temple by the Romans in AD 70. Nineteen is the number that combines the two numbers and denotes the perfection of divine order connected with judgment.

One biblical example of the significance of the number nineteen regarding Israel is the total number of kings the northern nation of Israel had before it was carried away into captivity by the Assyrians. After the death of Solomon, Israel split into two kingdoms. The northern kingdom, Israel, consisted of ten of the twelve tribes of Jacob. Their first king was Jeroboam. The southern kingdom, Judah, consisted of two tribes, Judah and Benjamin. The northern kingdom was ruled by nineteen evil and corrupt kings, including Jeroboam, before God pronounced judgment on the nation and allowed the Assyrians to conquer it. The northern kingdom was destroyed as a nation and its residents were taken as captives due to their many sins and idol worship. Many books of the Bible talk about judgment and divine judgment from God. Interestingly, in a majority of instances, chapter 19 of these books is the one that deals with this prevalent subject of the Bible. Here are some examples:

1) Genesis 19 – Divine judgment on Sodom and Gomorrah
2) Exodus 19 – The Lord coming down Mount Sinai, not in judgment, but in power as the righteous judge
3) Leviticus 19:15–16 – Judging your neighbor righteously
4) Deuteronomy 19 – Requirement of at least two witnesses when making a judgment or accusation against someone
5) 1 Kings 19:23 – Jezebel passing judgment against Elijah
6) 2 Chronicles 19:4–10 – Jehoshaphat appointing judges
7) Job 19:22–29 – Judgment against Job by his "friends"
8) Proverbs 19:28–29 – Judgment against false witnesses
9) Isaiah 19:16–25 – Judgment against Egypt
10) Jeremiah 19 – God's judgment against Israel
11) Ezekiel 19 – Judgment against Judah

12) Matthew 19 – Jesus' judgment of the rich man, and the disciples' judgment of the twelve tribes

13) Luke 19:11–24 – Parable of the king's judgment of the ten servants

14) John 19 – Judgment against Jesus by Pilate and the chief priests of the Jews resulting in his death

15) Revelation 19 – Second Coming of Jesus with divine judgment and punishment

COVID-19 is so named because if originated in the last months of 2019. However, it didn't really have much of an impact until March of 2020. The events of 2019 were a divine warning to the world that judgment is coming in 2020 and beyond. I believe COVID-19, specifically, is a warning to the world regarding immediate judgment…not the judgment of the Great Tribulation, but of the Rapture. Yes, the Rapture is a time of divine judgment upon mankind. On this unforgettable day, God judges all people on the basis of their belief, or lack of, in the Messiah, the Lord Jesus Christ. The believers will be rewarded by being raptured into the sky and then transported into the third heaven by the Lord Himself. This will be possible, for God will transform our natural bodies into spiritual ones that will be made for eternity, as prophesied by Job; thus, we will be with the Lord forever. The Rapture will be the greatest "freak-out" experience of all time, surpassing even the tower of Babel insanity.

Unbelievers left behind after the Rapture will be judged and punished for their lack of faith and idol-worshiping ways. They will have to remain on the "less-populated" earth and endure the consequences of the Rapture. It will be a time of intense confusion and chaos. Great changes will take place in the areas of government, religion, and the economy, paving the way for one world government, one world religion, one world currency, and, eventually, the rise of the Antichrist and his False Prophet. Those still remaining at this time will have to endure the horrors of the seven-year Tribulation, or die trying.

Why do the nations rage, and the people plot a vain thing? The kings of the earth set themselves, and the rulers take counsel together, against the Lord and against His Anointed, saying, Let us break their bonds in pieces and cast away their cords from us.

He who sits in the heavens shall laugh; the Lord shall hold them in derision. Then He shall speak to them in His wrath, and distress them in His deep displeasure:

Yet I have set My King on My holy hill of Zion. I will declare the decree: The Lord has said to Me, You are My Son, today I have begotten You.

Ask of Me, and I will give You the nations for Your inheritance, and the ends of the earth for Your possession.

You shall break them with a rod of iron; You shall dash them to pieces like a potter's vessel. Now therefore, be wise, O kings; be instructed, you judges of the earth.

Serve the Lord with fear, and rejoice with trembling. Kiss the Son, lest He be angry, and you perish in the way, when His wrath is kindled but a little. Blessed are all those who put their trust in Him. (Psalm 2:1–12)

EIGHT

Fiscal Storm Brewing

By Todd Strandberg

When Terry asked me to write a chapter about a financial storm, my main concern was that one would strike right before he finished this book. I was going to start off by saying, "As I'm writing this, the US is enduring the longest period of economic growth in our nation's history."

Well, a storm did form, and it quickly moved from being a tropical storm to a Category 5 super-hurricane. Because we don't have radar to determine the location of the eyewall, each time we pass through a spiral rain band, we think *this* must be the worst winds of the storm. Then the winds drop, and we're hit with another rain band—with stronger winds.

As I'm writing, the coronavirus just blew away thirty million jobs. Because there has been so much damage to the economy, the future seems destined to be like something out of a *Mad Max* movie. I'm currently wondering if things will get so bad that there might be no chance that this chapter will ever get published.

It's amazing for economic reports to come out one after another that are all off the scale as never-before-seen calamities. I thought 9/11 would forever be the worst time for airline traffic, but today, every carrier would now be bankrupt if it wasn't for a massive bailout from the government. It's understandable that air traffic is down 95 percent, but I was shocked to read how hard it has become to sell tickets. One cross-country seat sold for $13, which makes me wonder how this industry can ever become profitable again.

The cruise industry is in worse shape. If the public now sees these ships as floating petri dishes, it's going to be a huge hurdle to convince four thousand people to embark on a journey that may end with quarantine or something worse.

Without some type of miracle cure for this virus, the psychological impact of risk aversion may forever reshape the buying habits of the American consumer. Mankind has faced and readjusted to far greater threats. Consumers drive 70 percent of US gross domestic product, so we're likely to see a massive modification to the economy.

For several years, I was deeply concerned as a financial watchdog. The US Treasury was issuing record amounts of debt. I knew the house of cards could come tumbling down at any moment. Since the Great Recession took two years to play out, I think there will still be time for me to comment on what is happening.

Authors Who Tried And Failed to Predict Financial Calamity

It's not easy to be in the business of predicting financial calamity. Monetary bubbles can go on for many years because they are based on blind faith. I have copies of three books that warned of economic meltdown that never occurred. I purchased these books to see why they were wrong.

Willard Cantelon

The Day the Dollar Died by Willard Cantelon was published in 1973. One reason he believed the dollar was doomed was the outflow of gold from our massive holdings. In 1949, the US had $24.5 billion of gold in her treasuries. By June of 1971, that amount had dropped to $10.5 billion. Our growing trade deficit with the world was the reason for the drain. Since the price of gold was fixed at $35, France saw a bargain and took a large chunk of our gold reserves. President Richard Nixon magically solved the gold problem by issuing an executive order that ended the convertibility of the dollar.

Another example from Cantelon's book is rather humorous by today's monetary standard. In 1970, the largest railroad in the nation, the Pennsylvania Central, went bankrupt. Creditors went to Congress to ask for $200 million to bail out the railroad. Wright Patman, the chairman of the House banking committee, said "no," declaring it would be "only the beginning of a welfare program for giant corporations."

When panic swept over banks that had loaned to Pennsylvania Central, the Federal Reserve stepped in and handed out $1.7 billion to various banks. Today, a few billion dollars is chump change for a government that has now bailed out the airline industry twice and made Christmas come in April for every taxpayer. The Fed hands out a trillion dollars in a single event.

Cantelon was mindful of Bible prophecy, saying:

> Opening my Bible, I read the familiar words of John: "over all kindreds, and tongues, and nations.… and he causeth all, both small and great, rich and poor, free and bond, to receive a mark in their right hand, or in their foreheads: And that no man might buy or sell, save he that had the mark, or the name of the beast, or the number of his name." (Revelation 13:7, 16–17)

Every end-time writer since the 1980s could only conclude that everyone was going to get some kind of goofy-looking tattoo on their right hand or forehead. Cantelon makes a best guess that the mark might be some type of invisible, nontoxic ink. Today, we have radio-frequency microchips that will likely be the system the Antichrist will use to financially enslave the world.

A decade ago, people still would have viewed the possibility of the mark as an Orwellian horror. In the current climate, the average person would eagerly line up to receive an implant.

The disturbing vision of the future described by George Orwell in *1984* has been neutralized by the convenience that technology provides. We can use our cell phones to watch the house, track the weather, and monitor the stock market. The apps on our phone also allow a dozen different companies to track our physical movements.

China has started ranking citizens with a sinister "social-credit" system. It gives a credit score for every citizen based on big-data analysis. This surveillance system rewards and punishes people based on their behavior.

The global community should be outraged that China has become an Orwellian state. Instead, many governments are viewing the social-credit system as something to emulate. Some states have discussed using the China model to control people's access to guns.

When I was a kid, I remember reading a Christian publication that described the mark of the beast as the product of a world gone mad. The world has collectively lost its mind, and it is clear that the introduction of a 666 device would be welcomed by the vast majority of people. During the Tribulation, we may have individuals wearing "I Got Marked" T-shirts. We've had the ability to create the mark for at least two decades. The lack of any meaningful opposition to this type of technology tells us that the Tribulation hour is very near.

Larry Burkett

The Coming Economic Earthquake by Larry Burkett was written in 1991 and contains economic data that is now completely outdated. In his book, Burkett gives readers an amazing view of how reckless we've become in our spending. He was worried that the nation had built up a $400 billion annual deficit. Here we are, nearly thirty years later, and in one recent vote, Congress passed a bill that is 550 percent higher than the 1991 deficit. The current estimate for the total deficit of 2020 will be greater than the total national debt reached in 1993.

When Burkett was sounding his alarm, the US debt load was equal to 60 percent of the national gross domestic product (GDP). God must have applied the brakes, because the percentage remained at 60 percent for the next twenty years. Right now, we are at 117 percent; by the time this book is published, we could be at 200 percent. Larry Burkett went home to the Lord in 2003. If he is looking down from heaven at this current mess, it must be with wide-jawed amazement.

Harry Figgie and Gerald Swanson

A year after Burkett's book was published, Harry Figgie and Gerald Swanson left themselves with no margin for error when they wrote the book *Bankruptcy 1995.*

The book relied heavily on forecasts from two key Washington data offices, the Office of Management and Budget (OMB) and the Congressional Budget Office (CBO). The OMB serves the president of the United States in overseeing the implementation of his vision across the executive branch. Specifically, OMB's mission is to assist the president in meeting his policy, budget, management, and regulatory objectives and to fulfill the agency's statutory responsibilities. The CBO since 1975 has produced independent analyses of budgetary and economic issues to support the congressional budget process. Each year, the agency's economists and budget analysts produce dozens of reports and hundreds of cost estimates for proposed legislation.

First, both of these organizations have been wrong repeatedly, because they are politically motivated. In a rare time when they projected higher shortfalls for 1992 and onward, they were dead wrong. Figgie and Swanson would have had better luck in making their forecast by flipping a coin.

Since the OMB was founded in 1970 and the CBO in 1975, I ask, how did Congress and the White House get along without these two bloated government agencies? I understand that the government has gotten so large that it needs more people to count beans. The budget produced each year is based on outright phony math, so the OMB and CBO should be on the chopping block.

The Figgie and Swanson book does have one positive chapter about how private citizens can help get the debt under control. They say vote, write, or call your representatives; organize letter-writing campaigns; and get involved in citizen action groups. Washington has become so corrupt that I can only be cynical at this point. Our representatives only care about power and money. The people they listen to are lobbyists who donate to their campaign funds.

Turn off the Debt Clock

The first debt clock, the United States' National Debt Clock, was installed at the intersection of 42nd Street and Sixth Avenue on the initiative of real-estate developer Seymour Durst. The idea came to him in 1980 when the national debt approached $1 trillion. It took nine years for the right technology to come along that could run the clock.

When it was finally installed in February of 1989, the clock became an effective way to show the dynamics of our nation's debt growth. Many members of Congress used Durst's clock as a warning against spending that went beyond a set budget limit.

Congress and the president have fought over the budget since the beginning of the republic. There is a long history of these dramas, with budget showdowns, agreements, and legislation with major fiscal limits. The major point of the Tea Party movement was to cut federal spending. Despite all the promises of sobriety, the debt kept rising.

The ceiling on the national debt has been in effect since 1917, when the US Congress passed the Second Liberty Bond Act. Before 1917, no debt ceiling had been in force, but there were parliamentary procedural limitations on the amount of debt that could be issued by the government. The US has raised its debt ceiling at least ninety times in the twentieth century.

The debt ceiling is raised every time we reach the point of a crisis. Oh no, we're going to default on Treasury bonds, Grandma isn't going to get her social security check, and we'll have to close down the Washington

Monument. I doubt anyone remembers the budget crisis of 1974, but here are a few that have occurred in recent years:

- **The Budget Control Act of 2011** was enacted by Congress and signed into law by US President Barack Obama on August 2, 2011, bringing a conclusion to the 2011 US debt-ceiling crisis. The debt ceiling immediately increased by $400 billion. The bill directly specified $917 billion in cuts over ten years in exchange for the initial debt-limit increase of $900 billion. The act involved the introduction of several complex mechanisms, such as the creation of the Congressional Joint Select Committee on Deficit Reduction, options for a balanced-budget amendment, and automatic budget sequestration.
- **The No Budget, No Pay Act of 2013** suspended the debt ceiling from February 4, 2013, until May 19, 2013, when the debt ceiling was formally raised to approximately $16.699 trillion to accommodate the borrowing that had been done during the suspension period.
- **The Budget Control Act of 2015** put limits on spending by the Pentagon and other cabinet departments. These caps, expected to save $1 trillion over a decade, were combined with a tax increase on the wealthiest earners to help shrink the annual deficit to $439 billion. The act could just as well have stated that we will save $100 trillion over the next thousand years. What made this act a joke is that it suspended the debt limit for eighteen months. On August 2, 2019, the debt ceiling was suspended, and there is no indication that it will be reinstated at any future date.

The debt clock is now spinning so fast, the word "limit" has no meaning. It would be like sticking your finger into a revolving fan blade. It may be time to turn the debt clock off, because few people are able to grasp numbers that are in the trillions.

A million seconds is equal to twelve days. One trillion seconds is equal to 31,710 years. I think the best way to express the national debt is that every taxpayer would have to raise $220,000 for Uncle Sam to break even. It has been reported that 40 percent of Americans are only one missed paycheck away from poverty. There is no way we could collectively ask, "Who do I make the check out to?".

The Rise and Fall of the Tea Party Movement

The last chance for any meaningful effort to control government spending occurred with the Tea Party movement. It began as a reaction to the massive budget shortfall that was triggered by the Great Recession. To save Wall Street from its bad bets on subprime mortgages, the federal government created the $700 billion TARP (Troubled Asset Relief Program). The loss of millions of jobs caused the annual budget deficit to skyrocket.

By 2009, the deficit had exceeded $1 trillion for the first time, reaching $1.4 trillion. Horrified by Washington spenders, CNBC's Rick Santelli stood on the floor of the Chicago Mercantile Exchange on February 19, 2009, and called for a "tea party" to end the bailouts, stimulus payments, and red ink. Grassroots groups formed and helped Republicans capture the House in 2010 with a stunning sixty-three-seat pickup, as well as a gain of seven Senate seats.

Unfortunately, this victory proved to be the apex of the Tea Party movement. Without the leverage of the debt limit, President Obama and Senate Democrats could easily block House Republican spending reforms. The Tea Party members managed to get $200 billion in promised budget cuts, but these so-called cuts were frequently pushed off into the future until they were finally forgotten.

Few Tea Party members caught on to monetary magic tricks that the executive branch would use to cover up debt. Secretary of the Treasury Steven Mnuchin was a master at these ploys. He used the end of the fiscal year in September to lower the size of the annual deficit. In 2017, we were said to have a deficit of $660 billion; in 2018, we were reported to have a

$780 billion budget deficit. If you go back two years and look at the Treasury's total national debt records, you see it increased by $2 trillion. The missing $560 billion deficit is the result of the Treasury spitting out new debt in October and then not counting it as part of that year's budget.

In 2017, Mnuchin held a press conference to unveil a plan that would lower tax rates by $2 trillion over the next ten years. He said, "This will pay for itself with growth and reduced deductions." No Tea Party member really got on Mnuchin's case for using these tricks, because that would face up to reality.

Many of the Tea Party lawmakers who had come to Washington to reform government quickly became part of the swamp they had promised to drain. It is simply more fun to spend money. And when it's taxpayers' money, the thrill is all the more seductive.

The death of the Tea Party movement and all efforts for budget control came when Republican and Democrat leaders agreed to the bill labeled the Bipartisan Budget Act of 2019. This two-year agreement raised spending to $320 billion above previously negotiated spending caps and suspended the debt ceiling for two years. The number of years might as well have been a thousand, because we are currently spending money with a wide-open tap.

Zero and Negative Interest Rates

After two decades of slow growth, the Bank of Japan decided to employ a zero-interest-rate policy to combat deflation and promote economic recovery. These low rates are achieved by the central bank buying up the bonds to raise the price and lower the interest rate on outstanding bonds. An investor who bought bonds ten years ago may have a 30 percent gain.

Negative interest-rate policy is claimed to be a tool used to strongly encourage borrowing, spending, and investment rather than hoarding cash, which will lose value to negative deposit rates. It can be a positive thing for investors, even though they bought a bond at a negative rate. As the rate goes lower, the value of the bond goes up.

It's financial insanity to have bonds at zero and negative rates. When a company can issue debt at very low rates, it does things that leave no margin for hard times. Here in the Benton, Arkansas, area, four massive car dealerships have been built in the last five years. A huge outdoor mall was built ten miles north of Benton. There is likely $100 million in debt that is not being serviced.

The Great American Shale Boom only could have occurred with funding from cheap bonds. The shale industry has been built on mountains of debt, and the day of reckoning is drawing near. A total of thirty-two oil and gas drillers have filed for bankruptcy through the third quarter, with the total number of bankruptcy filings since 2015 now clocking in at more than 200.

The promise of future earnings has allowed the surviving drillers to stay in business. As many company executives who hoped to drill their way out of debt are belatedly discovering, trying to squeeze a profit from shale-fracking operations is akin to trying to draw blood from stone, with the industry having racked up cumulative losses estimated at more than a quarter of a trillion dollars.

The great danger of holding bonds at a low rate is the possibility of a loss of confidence in those bonds. If inflation should pick up to double digits, it would force the value of the bonds to decline as the interest rate soars. Some people holding a bond at a net value of $1,000 could see it collapse by 50 percent.

The nation of Argentina recently issued a hundred-year bond. The government issued $2.75 billion worth of US dollar-denominated bonds that matured in 2117, with a coupon of 7.125 percent. This was much better than the 1 percent currently being offered in the US.

The fact that Argentina had defaulted six times within the past one hundred years didn't deter these buyers.

The values of the Argentina bond have collapsed to the point that an investor would get 47 percent on the bond. But that is only if you bought it from the original issuer at 7 percent. They will take huge losses in unloading this garbage. If the bond props further to an 80 percent pay-out, you should note that there is no chance that a government is going to pay 80 percent on a bond. Typically, investors meet with debt holders, and they decide to cut the debt by a certain percentage, and you have lost massive money in the bond market but still have the chance of earning interest on the bonds that survive.

The Fed Is Running Out of Tricks

During the past several years, the Federal Reserve has been managing our growing national debt by using a series of financial terms and tricks. The shell game started with the Fed taking on the role of our rich uncle and did quantitative easing. After the 2007–08 crash, the Fed reinflated the stock market by loaning the Treasury $3.5 trillion.

Then came Operation Twist in 2011, when the Fed sold short-term Treasury securities and bought long-term Treasuries. By selling a two-year bond and buying a thirty-year bond, the Fed was giving Washington twenty-eight years to balance its financial books.

Next came quantitative tightening, in which the Fed would sell off the bond it had on its balance sheet. When Wall Street had a negative reaction to the actual unloading of bonds, the Fed said our credit is so good, it would end the program and hold on to the bonds forever.

The new term that is becoming popular in Washington is "modern monetary theory" (MMT). The core teaching of MMT is that a nation with the ability to print its own money can never go bankrupt. It can always fund its spending by printing more money. The nation's deficit can be managed by simply printing money to pay for the shortfall.

Some would argue that the Federal Reserve would never fall for MMT, but former head Ben Bernanke has already laid out the framework for how it could work. He traveled to Tokyo in July 2016 and suggested a way to stimulate the Japanese economy. He said the Ministry of Finance, Japan's equivalent to our Treasury, should issue nonmarketable perpetual bonds with a zero coupon that the Bank of Japan would buy with printed money. The Japanese government could then use the money from these bond sales to pay its bills.

A perpetual zero-coupon bond means the principal never has to be repaid and no interest payment is ever due. Bernanke was basically suggesting the issuance of a new form of currency. Cash never matures, and you do not have to pay interest for holding it. He should have just said that Japan should print vast amounts of yen.

In late 2019, the Fed began handing out cash to pretty much any financial institution that needed a short-term loan. Some of you may have heard the term "repurchase agreements" or "repo." In the repo market, borrowers seeking cash offer lenders collateral in the form of safe securities—frequently Treasury bonds—in exchange for a short-term loan. The term of these loans can be as short as overnight. When the Fed adds money to the financial system through the repo market, it is acting as a lender. The short-term loans quickly became long term with the promise of continual rollovers of these agreements.

The Fed in 2020 began huge swap loans with various other central banks. Central bank liquidity swaps are a type of currency swap used by a country's central bank to provide liquidity of its currency to another country's central bank. Basically, it's "give us your worthless currency and we'll give you dollars."

The US dollar has been rising against most global currencies, because most nations have their own massive budget deficits. It is stunning to note that the reaction to this sea of red ink was for rates to drop below zero. By October 1, 2019, negative-yielding debt had grown to more than $18 trillion. Greece has defaulted four times on its national debt, and it has just issued its first negative-yield bond.

Anyone with a basic understanding of how financial markets work knows that the day will eventually come when the Fed and Wall Street will become powerless to prevent a monetary meltdown. Our ability to reach levels of absolute absurdity shows that some form of supernatural intervention is at work. God is holding things together until the Tribulation hour springs on humanity like a bear trap.

Because Jesus said He would come at a time of "peace and safety," I think the Rapture is the only explanation for why we have a Goldilocks economy.

> I heard the third living creature say, Come and see. And I looked, and behold, a black horse, and he who sat on it had a pair of scales in his hand.
>
> And I heard a voice in the midst of the four living creatures saying, A quart of wheat for a denarius, and three quarts of barley for a denarius; and do not harm the oil and the wine. (Revelation 6:5–6)

> For when they shall say, Peace and safety; then sudden destruction cometh upon them, as travail upon a woman with child; and they shall not escape. (1 Thessalonians 5:3)

Bread and Circuses

The decline and fall of the Roman Empire has been well-documented by many observers of history. Will Luden, in "Bread and Circuses for the Masses—Not Just Ancient Rome," describes the Roman government policy as "emperors, in the later stages of the Empire, used both free bread (and other food) and free entertainment to placate the larger number of people who were otherwise poorly served by their government."[148]

The Oxford Reference provides the following definition of "bread and circuses": "A term referring to the potential of spectator sports and mass spectacle to divert populations or factions of a population away from the weightier business of politics and society."[149]

The Democrats are currently in a bidding war over who can offer the American people the most goodies in exchange for their vote. It is bread and circuses on a scale that would stump the imagination of the Roman leaders.

Last year, Vermont Senator Bernie Sanders presented a plan that would wipe out $1.6 trillion in student debt and offer fund-free state college. The massive student-debt jubilee would be financed with a tax on Wall Street: specifically, a 0.5 percent tax on stock trades, a 0.1 percent tax on bond trades, and a .005 percent tax on derivatives trades.

The primary problem with this plan is that it would cause the cost of higher education to explode. If Uncle Sam is going to pick up the check, you might as well go to medical school. Colleges would be able to raise the cost of education at will. The average cost of tuition and fees for the 2018–2019 school year was $35,676 at private colleges. Under Bernie's plan, the cost would easily double in a few years.

Most Democratic presidential candidates for 2020 supported reparations for slavery. If we lived in a world of unlimited wealth, there is no amount of money that could satisfy these race hustlers. The price of freedom for blacks was paid with the lives of five hundred thousand people in the Civil War. The H.R. 40 bill would, according to its summary heading, "establish a commission to study and consider a national apology and a proposal for reparations" for the descendants of African-American slaves.

A House Judiciary subcommittee held several hearings on the issue of slavery reparations. The sponsors of this bill seem to think that we are living in 1865. Columnist Coleman Hughes offered stunning testimony against reparations:

> I understand that reparations are about what people are owed, regardless of how well they're doing. But the people who were owed for slavery are no longer here, and we're not entitled to collect on their debts. Reparations, by definition, are only given to victims. So the moment you give me reparations, you've made me into a victim without my consent. Not just that: you've made one-third of black Americans—who consistently poll against reparations—into victims without their consent, and black Americans

have fought too long for the right to define themselves to be spoken for in such a condescending manner.

The question is not what America owes me by virtue of my ancestry; the question is what all Americans owe each other by virtue of being citizens of the same nation. And the obligation of citizenship is not transactional. It's not contingent on ancestry, it never expires, and it can't be paid off. For all these reasons, bill H.R. 40 is a moral and political mistake.[150]

Senator Elizabeth Warren jumped on the reparations bandwagon with her own crazy idea. She came out in favor of legislation that has been equated to "gay reparations." Under the Refund Equality Act, same-sex couples would be able to amend their past taxes, readjusting with jointly filed tax returns and accepting refunds from the IRS. "Our government owes them more than $50M for the years our discriminatory tax code left them out. We must right these wrongs," said Warren.[151]

Former Democratic presidential candidate Andrew Yang had the most straightforward plan. He just wants to hand out cash to everyone who needs it. Yang promotes universal basic income—a modern welfare scheme through which citizens are granted income from the government, without condition. Yang hosted a Twitter contest whereby he would give away a thousand dollars per month to twenty lucky people.

Alexandria Ocasio-Cortez, the congresswoman from New York, holds the record for the most expensive proposal. Her patently insane Green New Deal resolution would cost up to $93 trillion over ten years, according to the American Action Forum. Ms. Ocasio-Cortez was all for Sanders' $1.6 trillion plan. She is currently on track to be our first quadrillion-dollar congressperson.

It is stunning to hear Democrats proposing plans that would bankrupt our nation. I think their insanity is merely a precursor of a coming salesman who will put them all to shame. The Antichrist will be the king of "bread and circuses" ideas. He will use signs and wonders to sell people schemes that will ensure eternal damnation.

The coming of the lawless one will be in accordance with how Satan works. He will use all sorts of displays of power through signs and wonders that serve the lie. (2 Thessalonians 2:9, NIV)

And the smoke of their torment ascendeth up for ever and ever: and they have no rest day nor night, who worship the beast and his image, and whosoever receiveth the mark of his name. (Revelation 14:11, KJV)

The Great China Miracle

If this was any other time in world history, I would say that there is a 100 percent chance of total financial meltdown. When I look at China's ability to print massive amounts of its currency, I think fundamental economic laws need to step aside for supernatural events.

The People's Republic of China has had a trade surplus with the US for decades. In 2018, its surplus with America rose to a record $323.32 billion. China's total foreign exchange reserves stand at $3.073 trillion. This massive hoard of dollar wealth has quickly become an illusion. In real terms, China is actually running out of dollars.

The *renminbi* is the official currency of China. We have read dozens of stories about how China has signed numerous deals with countries to trade with them in the *renminbi*. All that global travel by President Xi Jinpeng was a huge waste of time and jet fuel.

In terms of global reserve currency, the *renminbi* has a share of only 1.9 percent, in fifth place and barely ahead of the Canadian dollar, but miles behind the US dollar (61.7 percent) and the euro (20.7 percent). Over the past two years, the *renminbi* has gone nowhere as a reserve currency. In 2019, it had a minuscule share of merely 1.22 percent of international cross-border payments.

Anyone who has a basic understanding of how economics works knows that when you print too much of your currency, its value should go down. The Chinese government has somehow managed to print a massive amount of *renminbi* without triggering hyperinflation. Since 1952, the money supply has grown by a staggering 18,000 fold.

The US has a huge national debt, but it is small compared to China's debt load. The US economy is roughly $20 trillion. Theirs is roughly $13 trillion. China's banking system is north of $50 trillion. Ours is currently at $22 trillion.

Because China is a resource-poor nation, it has to import vast amounts of raw materials. No other nation on earth has imported more goods. In the past twenty years, China has consumed more cement than America has used in the past one hundred years. From just 2004, its oil imports have increased four times. China imports 68 percent of the world's supply of iron ore.

China's massive imports have resulted in a huge dollar shortage for the Chinese banking system. That's because Chinese businesses still owe over $2.25 trillion in dollar-denominated debts that are maturing over the next couple of years (by year-end 2021).

For instance, the Bank of China just four years ago had more dollar assets than all of the other big banks. But by the end of 2018, they had more than $72 billion in dollar liabilities. (That's a net change of -$128 billion in only four years.)

The Chinese government has been spending huge amounts of money on national defense. In 2009, it spent 400 billion *renminbi* on its military. By the end of 2019, it will spend 1,200 billion *renminbi*, which is a threefold increase in a decade.

With the Chinese economy now hopelessly addicted to Middle East oil and raw materials from Africa, some economists are starting to wonder if China will turn to the military option once its supply of dollars runs out. Hitler went on a wild spending spree for resources before he turned to *blitzkrieg* to wipe out his foreign debts.

When John the Revelator wrote about an army of two hundred million, generations of people were mystified by the prediction. There weren't two hundred million people on earth at the time. Now that we have 7.7 billion people on earth, and China has a population of 1.4 billion people, it is possible to outfit such a vast army.

In 2019, China had a record year for corporate bond defaults. Normally, the Chinese government would not allow a state-owned enterprise to go into default. The volume of bad loans in China must be so high that Beijing is forced to allow some bondholders to get burned in order to restore discipline. The reported *yuan* default amount is up six fold in the past two years, so the actual quantity of bad loans must be very high.

A China-explosive economic growth is the clearest indication that the kings of the East are about to move out. A decade ago, China had no ability to project military power on the international stage. In the past few years, China's wild spending has suddenly transformed it into a global giant. Because China has a limited amount of time and money to maintain such a massive military force, the Tribulation hour must be very near.

> And the sixth angel poured out his vial upon the great river Euphrates; and the water thereof was dried up, that the way of the kings of the east might be prepared. (Revelation 16:12)

> Saying to the sixth angel which had the trumpet, Loose the four angels which are bound in the great river Euphrates.
>
> And the four angels were loosed, which were prepared for an hour, and a day, and a month, and a year, for to slay the third part of men.
>
> And the number of the army of the horsemen were two hundred thousand thousand: and I heard the number of them. (Revelation 9:14–16)

More Bubble Trouble

In January of 2000, I wrote an article that warned of a coming crash in the dot.com stocks. I was so confident that a meltdown would occur, I promised to shut down my site if it became clear I was wrong.

The average stock on Wall Street is overvalued by nearly all historic standards. The traders of Internet stocks seemed to have absolutely rewritten the book on the assignment of value.

I recall one Internet venture called Healtheon paying $5 billion for a privately held company called WebMD that only had sales of $75,000. To top this story off, investors reacted to the deal by bidding up Healtheon stock threefold. Twenty years later, the firm exchanged hands at a value of $2.8 billion.

Many Internet companies had valuations that defy the wildest business models. At one point, Amazon.com had a market cap worth all the books sold annually in the US. Priceline.com, which sells primarily junk airline tickets, at its high had a market cap greater than the top three air carriers. AOL's peak valuation implied that everyone in North America was planning on becoming its customer.

The granddaddy of price-to-earnings (P/E) ratios would have to be awarded to eBay. It had a P/E of 14,400. Certainly, eBay had investors faithfully believing it would substantially grow its earnings. After the stock peaked, it declined 80 percent over the next nine years.

Another good indication of how irrational investors were in 2000 is when they bid up the value of one company and didn't even bother with the parent company that has a major ownership in what has become a multibillion-dollar firm. We have a situation where company A would be worth $1 billion, yet it owns 50 percent of company B, which is now worth $4 billion.

The reason I stuck my neck out in 2000 to predict the coming crash was that valuation had become so crazy, I knew the time was right for a downturn. History is brimming with financial manias, from the real-estate bubble collapse in Athens in 333 BC, to the Mississippi Bubble in 1720, to the US Cotton Panic in 1837, to the French Credit Debacle in 1868, to the Great Crash in the US in 1929, to the 1990 Crash in Japan, and on and on.

I had published my article when the NASDAQ was at 4,000. Within three months, it peaked at 5,000 and then went into a nosedive.

It is not possible to make another prediction now about the current financial situation. We are in a bubble that has reached excesses that put all other monetary mania to shame. The Fed is spending money at a rate that should not be possible. When San Francisco Fed President Mary Daly said, "The Federal Reserve is prepared to do whatever," her words have basically come to mean that the Fed and all central banks are prepared to make good $240 trillion of global assets.

I think the reason we have a crazy world of zero interest rates, negative oil prices, governments handing out free money, and central banks buying stocks and corporate bonds is because financial events have become linked with the Rapture. The blessed hope is an unknown event, so this may explain why markets are so unpredictable. I hope this all means that the Rapture is near, because I want to get off this crazy ride.

> For the Lord himself shall descend from heaven with a shout, with the voice of the archangel, and with the trump of God: and the dead in Christ shall rise first:
>
> Then we which are alive and remain shall be caught up together with them in the clouds, to meet the Lord in the air: and so shall we ever be with the Lord.
>
> Wherefore comfort one another with these words. (1 Thessalonians 4:16–18)

NINE

Who Are the Real Deniers?

By Jonathan C. Brentner

What's the most grievous sin one can commit? According to the climate alarmists, it's the denial that the earth is warming to unsafe levels because of our modern life. Julie Kelly, a writer for *The Hill,* sums up this frequent accusation:

> For those of you who don't know what a climate denier is, it means you either challenge, question or flat-out reject the idea that the planet is warming due to human activity…. Should you remotely doubt the dubious models, unrealized dire predictions, changing goal posts or flawed data related to climate science, you are not just stupid according to these folks, but you are on par with those who deny the Holocaust.[152]

Teenage activist Greta Thunberg joined those condemning the skeptics with her contemptuous outcry at the United Nations in the fall of 2019: "How dare you? You have stolen my dreams and my childhood! We are in the beginning of a mass extinction!" Although her rage seems wildly misguided and extreme at best, it has vaulted her to worldwide fame.

In December of 2019, *Time* magazine named Thunberg person of the year. The *Time* article portrayed her with glowing words fit for the greatest of world leaders. The article quoted novelist Margaret Atwood as comparing Thunberg "to Joan of Arc."[153] *Time* magazine credited Thurnberg with "creating a global attitudinal shift, transforming millions of vague, middle-of-the-night anxieties into a worldwide movement calling for urgent change. She has offered a moral clarion call to those who are willing to act, and hurled shame on those who are not."[154]

The current frenzy goes far beyond that of a furious teenager. Pope Francis often warns the world about this global "climate emergency." In the summer of 2019, he said that "the dangers of global heating and that a failure to act urgently to reduce greenhouse gases would be 'a brutal act of injustice toward the poor and future generations.'"[155] In other words, those who deny climate change commit sins against a great many people, even those in future generations.

But who are the real deniers? Is it those of us who remain skeptical of the warnings of impending disaster due to climate change? Or, is it those who reject what the Bible says about God's creation and ridicule us because we believe the Bible's assurances regarding our future?

Claims of Climate Alarmists Remain Unproven

My purpose for this chapter is to defend the creationist worldview as well as demonstrate that the climate alarmists, those who tell us we must act now to save our planet from catastrophe, are the real deniers of our time. They peddle a hoax handed down to them from elite globalists who seek to deceive them and the world with their sinister and demonic agenda.

I know this assertion contradicts what the science community assures us are well-established facts. Celebrities and politicians predict doom for our environment unless the governments of the world take immediate action to stop global warming. However, very few ask the questions necessary to discover the validity of these warnings.

Does Human Activity Produce Unsafe Levels of CO2 in the Atmosphere?

Perhaps the most frequent claim we hear from the alarmists is that our modern life produces dangerous levels of CO2 in our atmosphere. Fossil fuels have become the primary target, with politicians and celebrities telling us that CO2 emissions from our cars, SUVs, pickup trucks, and boats cause global warming that will soon lead to disastrous consequences for the planet. Although they insist this is an established fact, *such is not the case.*

Scientists do *not* present a united front on this matter. Many geologists, for example, dispute the assertion that mankind impacts CO2 levels to any significant or dangerous level. Geologist Dr. Viv Forbes wrote this about the relationship between the two:

> Human activity can never control atmospheric CO2 or global temperature. Much bigger forces are at work—solar system cycles, earth orbital changes, volcanic activity (especially on the sea floor), El Nino episodes, declining magnetic field and magnetic pole reversals, variable cosmic rays and cloud cover, and absorption/expulsion of CO2 by the mighty oceans....
>
> Moreover, the ice core records from Antarctica and Greenland show clearly that atmospheric temperature always rises before CO2 levels rise. So rising CO2 is the effect of rising temperature not the cause.[156]

One factor that Dr. Forbes brings out in the above quote, "volcanic activity," is receiving increased attention in the climate-change debate. An active volcano can spew over 150,000 tons of CO2 daily into the atmosphere. That's significant, considering that we have twenty-five active volcanoes in the world today, with an additional fifteen showing signs of springing to life.[157]

One researcher, Dr. Terance Gerlach, sought to dispel the impact of volcanoes, claiming that the amount of carbon dioxide put in the air by them is 100 to 150 times less than that of humans. However, "Terrance Gerlach's volcanic CO_2 calculation was based on just 7 actively erupting land volcanoes and three actively erupting ocean floor hydrothermal vents (seafloor hot geysers)."[158] His analysis fell far short of taking into account the forty volcanoes that are either currently active or starting to awaken.

That's not all Dr. Gerlach failed to consider. "Recent geological research by the University of Leeds and others proves that non-erupting volcanoes can emit massive amounts of CO_2 into Earth's atmosphere and oceans."[159] This becomes highly significant when one considers there are "1,500 land volcanoes on the earth and 900,000 seafloor volcanoes/ hydrothermal vents."[160] (Yes, I double-checked those numbers; they are not typos!)

At a minimum, CO_2 emissions from volcanoes are likely at the same level as that of fossil fuels, if not far above it.

Even with volcanic activity, carbon dioxide actually makes up a miniscule percentage of our air at 414.11 parts per million (or .04 percent of our atmosphere). This data comes from the March 5, 2020, reading at Mauna Loa Observatory, Hawaii.[161] The yearly level of CO_2 has risen at this location, but one must consider that the Hawaiian Islands are home to an active volcano.

How can something that makes up such a tiny part of our atmosphere have such a devastating impact on the environment via rising temperatures? Could something else impact global temperatures? Yes!

Many scientists believe the activity of the sun causes fluctuations in earth's temperatures rather than changes in CO_2 levels. One researcher, Dr. Roger Higgs (geology professor at Oxford, 1982–86), summarized the results of his study in January of 2020. He discovered that, based on "archaeological, astrophysical, geological and palaeoclimatological data covering the last 2,000 years," it's "the Sun, not CO_2, that controls global temperature."[162]

Another acclaimed scientist who says the sun is the chief cause of global warming is Nir Shaviv, an Israeli astrophysicist and chairman of Jerusalem's Hebrew University's physics department. "He says that his research, and that of colleagues, suggests that rising CO2 levels play only a minor role in earth's climate compared to the influence of the sun and cosmic radiation."[163] Shaviv concludes:

> Global warming clearly is a problem, though not in the cata-strophic terms of Al Gore's movies or environmental alarmists. Climate change has existed forever and is unlikely to go away. But CO2 emissions don't play the major role. **Periodic solar activity does.**[164] (Shaviv's emphasis)

The website, The Right Climate Stuff (therightclimatestuff.com), provides a thorough discussion of the issues regarding the impact of mankind upon global warming. The researchers on this site describe themselves as "a group of retired and highly experienced engineers and scientists from the Apollo, Skylab, Space Shuttle and International Space Station eras" who "have volunteered our time and effort conducting an objective, independent assessment of the AGW [Anthropogenic Global Warming] alarm and reality of the actual threat."

On the "Conclusions and Recommendations" page of the website, they list this as one of the conclusions of their research: "There is no convincing evidence that Anthropogenic Global Warming (AGW) will produce catastrophic climate changes. AGW can only produce modest amounts of global warming that will likely be beneficial when the substantial benefits to crop production from more CO2 in the atmosphere are considered." Far from being a threat, they concluded that global warming will not only be modest, but beneficial to plant growth.

Many prominent scientists and researchers stand with those of us who deny that humans cause dangerous levels of CO2 in the air. *Those who say this matter is settled science cannot back up such a claim.*

Can Rising CO2 Levels Lead to Catastrophic Results in Our Environment?

Climate alarmists also tell us that rising CO2 levels will lead to catastrophic changes in our weather and environment unless we take immediate action. However, the models scientists use to predict these disastrous outcomes have a poor track record in regard to accuracy and a wide variance exists among the predictions of these models.

In late September of 2019, more than five hundred scientists and professionals in climatology and related fields signed a letter to the United Nations, saying, "There is no climate emergency." Here is an excerpt from their letter:

> There is no statistical evidence that global warming is intensifying hurricanes, floods, droughts and suchlike natural disasters, or making them more frequent. However, CO2-mitigation measures are as damaging as they are costly. For instance, wind turbines kill birds and bats, and palm-oil plantations destroy the biodiversity of the rainforests.[165]

These five hundred scientists went on to state that since the "climate models on which virtually all the apocalyptic predictions are based are utterly flawed.... It is cruel as well as imprudent to advocate the squandering of trillions on the basis of results from such immature models. Current climate policies pointlessly, grievously undermine the economic system, putting lives at risk in countries denied access to affordable, continuous electrical power."[166]

The graph on the next page illustrates the severe flaws in these "climate models."

These models not only display a wide variation among themselves, but since 1990, they have significantly missed the mark in their predictions—some by a very wide margin.

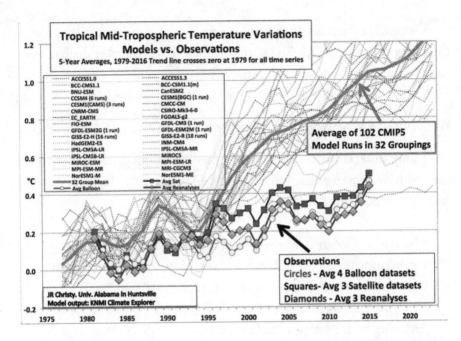

Tropical Mid-Tropospheric Temperature Variations
Models vs. Observations
5-Year Averages, 1979-2016 Trend line crosses zero at 1979 for all time series

The NASA engineers and scientists had this to say about these models:

> We have concluded that the IPCC [Intergovernmental Panel on Climate Change] climate models are seriously flawed because they don't agree very closely with measured empirical data. After a 35 year simulation the models over-predicted actual measured temperatures by factors of 200% to 750%. One could hardly expect them to predict with better accuracy 300 years into the future required for use in regulatory decisions.[167]

Climatologist Dr. Pat Michaels agrees with those of us who deny that global warming will lead to disastrous consequences for life on earth:

> It's warmed up around 1 degree Celsius since 1900, and life expectancy doubled in the industrialized democracies! Yet that temperature ticks up another half a degree and the entire system crashes? That's the most absurd belief![168]

Despite the inaccuracy and wide variability of these scientific models, those who warn us of pending peril continue to use them as the basis for their warnings of impending doom.

What about Past Predictions of Doom Due to Climate Change?

For a long time, climate alarmists have made startling predictions that in the end have proven entirely wrong. Consider this quote from an Associated Press report published in the *Washington Post*:

> The Arctic Ocean is warming up, icebergs are growing scarcer, and in some places the seals are finding the water too hot. Reports from fishermen, seal hunters, and explorers all point to a radical change in climate conditions and hitherto unheard-of temperatures in the Arctic zone. Exploration expeditions report that scarcely any ice has been met as far north as 81 degrees 29 minutes. Within a few years it is predicted that due to the ice melt the sea will rise and make most coastal cities uninhabitable.[169]

Although this sounds very much like it could have been a story written in 2020, the above quote appeared in the *Washington Post* on November 2, 1922!

Since then, predictions of disaster because of climate change continue unabated. The Earth Day predictions of 1970 included the end of human civilization in thirty years with deaths due to starvation to reach between one hundred million and two hundred million per year by 1980.

Al Gore received a Nobel Prize in 2007 for his prognostications of doom due to global warming. He told us that by 2014 the Antarctic and Greenland ice sheets would completely vanish, which would cause sea levels to rise twenty feet. He also predicted the total extinction of polar bears due to the disappearance of the Arctic ice cap. Gore became quite wealthy as a result of his activism, but what about his forecasts that catapulted him to fame and fortune?

The South Pole still exists, with the sea ice around Antarctica at record levels, as recorded at the beginning of 2020. According to those who monitor temperatures for Antarctica, it rarely gets above 0 degrees Fahrenheit during the summer months. The Weather Channel forecast *highs* for March 10 to 14, 2020, ranged from -45 to -54 degrees Fahrenheit, and it was still technically summer in Antarctica at the time! How can this polar cap disappear with such frigid temperatures at the end of its warmest season? It's not possible!

Does some melting occur in the Antarctica sea region? Yes, but global warming is not the culprit. The thawing happens in areas where underwater volcanoes/hydrothermal vents exist.

As for the demise of the Arctic Circle by 2014, Gore could not have been more wrong. In 2015, the Arctic Circle saw it largest refreezing in over a decade. Official data from the National Snow and Ice Data Center (NSIDC) reveals that Arctic Sea ice is once again expanding, with current 2020 levels exceeding those in eight out of the previous ten years.

Summit Camp, Greenland, whose data climate alarmists often cite as proof of global warming, recorded its lowest temperature ever in its history at 11:13 PM on January 2, 2020. It was -86.8 F or -66 C at this time. The ice cover in Greenland grew by a substantial amount during first few months of 2020.

As for Gore's prediction of the extinction of polar bears by 2014, their population has actually increased. Some estimate that the polar bear population has grown by 67 percent since 2007 to an estimated thirty-one thousand (the estimates I found varied due to the difficulty of tracking the bears, but *all* of them showed substantial growth). While the widely circulated picture of a sick and dying polar bear in 2019 made for good press, it proved nothing other than, like all other mammals, polar bears age and die.

Al Gore is not alone in making numerous failed predictions related to climate change. Perhaps some of you are old enough to remember these past prognostications of doom?

- 1970s: There would be another ice age in ten years (this was the prevailing belief among my science teachers when I was in high school).
- 1980s: Acid rain would destroy all crops in ten years.
- 1990s: The ozone layer would be gone in ten years.

Despite the fact that ice around both poles has grown substantially in recent years, one United States politician warned us in March of 2020 that we only have seven years left before we witness massive flooding in coastal areas. A congresswoman from New York confidently predicted that Miami will be underwater by 2031.

Do those who make such prophecies believe them? The evidence says no!

The Obamas made headlines in 2019 with the purchase of a lavish, seven-thousand-square-foot mansion on twenty-nine acres on Martha's Vineyard. The estate rests on the shoreline, which indicates that the former president is not worried about global warming or rising sea levels. Why would the former president make a multimillion-dollar waterfront acquisition if he believed his own warnings about drastically rising sea levels in the near future?

In 2010, Al Gore paid nearly nine million dollars for a home in Montecito, California; his mansion rests at sea level. Why would he spend so much money for this if he really believed it would be underwater a few years after the purchase?

Celebrities and politicians never cease warning us of impending disaster because of our use of fossil fuel. Yet many of them own multiple homes on both coasts, enjoy a wide assortment of cars and yachts, and fly all over the world in their private jets. Why should we believe them?

What About the 97 Percent Consensus among Scientists?

One statistic we continually hear is that 97 percent of scientists believe that man-made global warming will lead to catastrophic results. Is this accurate?

According to the Climate Change Dispatch website (climatechange-dispatch.com), this percentage "has been thoroughly refuted in scholarly peer-reviewed journals, by major news media, public policy organizations and think tanks, highly credentialed scientists and extensively in the climate blogosphere."[170] This website references ninety-seven articles that refute the study that led to the widely circulated 97 percent consensus among scientists.

Mike Hulme, PhD, professor of climate change at the University of East Anglia (UEA) in England, said this about it:

> The "97% consensus" article is poorly conceived, poorly designed and poorly executed. It obscures the complexities of the climate issue and it is a sign of the desperately poor level of public and policy debate in this country [UK] that the energy minister should cite it.[171]

Israeli astrophysicist Nir Shaviv said this:

> Only people who don't understand science take the 97% statistic seriously. Survey results depend on who you ask, who answers and how the questions are worded. In any case, science is not a democracy. Even if 100% of scientists believe something, one person with good evidence can still be right.[172]

Scientists do not agree that global warming will lead to disastrous consequences. Those who warn us do NOT have "settled science" on their side. Just as many scientists believe the cosmic rays from the sun cause the fluctuations in global temperatures.

The Politics of Climate Change

The long history of failed predictions, together with the lack of scientist consensus on the matter, leaves us wondering why such passionate fervor exists for the nations of the world to take drastic action to reduce global warming.

The answer emerges as we look at the politics behind these warnings.

The elite globalists, the so-called enlightened ones of the world, drive the current push for radical action with a far different agenda than that of reducing CO2 amounts in our air, one that's sinister, demonic in origin, and deadly. Let's dig a bit deeper into this matter to see why I can make such a seemingly outrageous statement.

The United Nations' Agenda 2030

The United Nations' (UN) Agenda 2030 consists of visions and goals aimed at establishing a world order by the year 2030 with the purpose of combating climate change. The UN assumes that radical economic and political changes are necessary to deal with this dire global warming emergency.

Jeffrey Ludwig, in an *American Thinker* article, provides this overview of Agenda 2030:

> The most often quoted definition comes from the UN World Commission on Environment and Development: "sustainable development is development that meets the needs of the present without compromising the ability of future generations to meet their own needs." The earlier ideas and ideals of rights, freedom, equality, and justice are subsumed under meeting of needs and an explicit environmentalism which emphasizes preventing the depletion of scarce planetary resources. Of course, the takeoff is the Marxist axiom that society should be organized around the idea of "from each according to his ability to each according to his needs." Thus, Marxism is implicit in sustainability, but is nuanced by its alliance with seemingly scientific adjustments and goals related to environmentalisms.[173]

I list all seventeen goals of "sustainable development" below because they verify the inherent Marxism behind the UN's Agenda 2030. These come from the UN's own website:

1. End poverty in all its forms everywhere.
2. End hunger, achieve food security and improved nutrition, and promote sustainable agriculture.
3. Ensure healthy lives and promote well-being for all at all ages.
4. Ensure inclusive and equitable quality education and promote lifelong learning opportunities for all.
5. Achieve gender equality and empower all women and girls.
6. Ensure availability and sustainable management of water and sanitation for all.
7. Ensure access to affordable, reliable, sustainable, and modern energy for all.
8. Promote sustained, inclusive, and sustainable economic growth; full and productive employment; and decent work for all.
9. Build resilient infrastructure, promote inclusive and sustainable industrialization, and foster innovation.
10. Reduce inequality within and among countries.
11. Make cities and human settlements inclusive, safe, resilient, and sustainable.
12. Ensure sustainable consumption and production patterns.
13. Take urgent action to combat climate change and its impacts.
14. Conserve and sustainably use the oceans, seas, and marine resources for sustainable development.
15. Protect, restore, and promote sustainable use of terrestrial ecosystems, sustainably manage forests, combat desertification, halt and reverse land degradation, and halt biodiversity loss.
16. Promote peaceful and inclusive societies for sustainable development, provide access to justice for all, and build effective, accountable, and inclusive institutions at all levels.

17. Strengthen the means of implementation and revitalize the global partnership for sustainable development.[174]

Did you notice that many of the goals have nothing whatsoever to do with addressing the climate-change emergency? They provide a vision of a utopia where a world government manages the world's wealth and guarantees equality of outcomes for everyone on the planet.

The Green New Deal

The Green New Deal has recently advanced to the forefront in American politics. According to Wikipedia, "The Green New Deal (GND) is a proposed package of United States legislation that aims to address climate change and economic inequality." Although the concept of modeling an environmental package similar to President Roosevelt's New Deal has been around for years, the GND sprang to life again on February 7, 2019, when Senator Edward Markey and Representative Alexandria Ocasio-Cortez issued a resolution calling for its implementation.

According to a *Washington Post* article on February 11, 2019, the resolution calls for a "10-year national mobilization" with the following as its key goals:

- Guaranteeing a job with a family-sustaining wage, adequate family and medical leave, paid vacations, and retirement security to all people of the United States.
- Providing all people of the United States with – (i) high-quality health care; (ii) affordable, safe, and adequate housing; (iii) economic security; and (iv) access to clean water, clean air, healthy and affordable food, and nature.
- Meeting 100 percent of the power demand in the United States through clean, renewable, and zero-emission energy sources.

- Repairing and upgrading the infrastructure in the United States, including…by eliminating pollution and greenhouse gas emissions as much as technologically feasible.
- Upgrading all existing buildings in the United States and building new buildings to achieve maximal energy efficiency, water efficiency, safety, affordability, comfort, and durability, including through electrification.

The Green New Deal legislation leaves no aspect of human life outside the realm of socialistic government control. Its description on the CNN website provides a scary depiction of how the government would control all areas of our lives.[175] Politicians promote the GND or the UN's Agenda 2030 under the guise of protecting the environment, while their real intent is to establish a totalitarian and communistic New World Order.

What Are the Common Themes in These Proposals?

Do you see how the goals of the Green New Deal mesh with those of the UN's Agenda 2030? Several common themes run through both proposals:

First, they call for a radical transformation of existing economic, social, and political structures. Their common objective consists of a totalitarian government that takes upon itself the task of ensuring the well-being of *everyone* under its jurisdiction.

Second, they assume that only a Marxist form of government can address the climate emergency. Who made the assumption that only a socialistic world order can combat climate change? Even if one concedes it's an emergency requiring immediate action, why is it necessary for the world to forsake nationalism and free enterprise in order to address it?

According to the most recent statistics of the International Energy Agency (IEA), the United States leads the world in declining CO_2 emissions. On February 11, 2020, the IEA stated that the "United States saw the largest decline in energy-related CO_2 emissions in 2019 on a country basis—a fall of 140 Mt, or 2.9%, to 4.8 Gt.US emissions are now down almost 1 Gt from their peak in the year 2000, the largest absolute decline by any country over that period."

Based on the findings of the IEA, shouldn't the world follow the capitalistic model of the United States in reducing CO2 emissions since it is succeeding where *all other* countries are falling short? Communist China remains the worst nation on earth in polluting the environment. Visitors to China report that in some cities one cannot see to the end of a block because of the smog. If socialism is a necessity for addressing the climate emergency, why is Marxist China the worst place on earth for controlling CO2 emissions?

Third, they have much, much more to do with establishing a New World Order (NWO) than with addressing the climate-change crisis. John Edison, in an *American Thinker* article, wrote this regarding the actual objective behind the UN Agenda 2030:

> In a Nov. 14, 2010 interview with Swiss newspaper Neue Zürcher Zeitung, Edenhofer, co-chair of the U.N. IPCC's Working Group III, made this shocking admission:
>
> "One must free oneself from the illusion that international climate policy is environmental policy. [What we're doing] has almost nothing to do with the climate. We must state clearly that we use climate policy to redistribute de facto the world's wealth."
>
> On the same date, Edenhofer added this:
>
> "Climate policy has almost nothing to do anymore with protecting the environment. The next world climate summit in Cancun is actually an economy summit during which [re]distribution of the world's resources will be negotiated."[176]

The globalists' desire for an economic sharing of the world's resources remains. The December 2019 UN Climate Summit in Madrid, Spain, ended as talks of who would finance the fight against global warming collapsed. Without the transfer of the United States' wealth as called for in the Paris Climate Accord, the UN cannot see a way forward to address this emergency.

The global-warming emergency has little to do with saving the environment and a lot to do with instituting a socialistic New World Order.

Do not panic; the Lord told us thousands of years ago that this would happen.

Coming New World Order Will Fulfill Biblical Prophecy

In late 1971, the song "Imagine," written and performed by John Lennon, started its climb to the top of the charts. Its words encourage "the listener to imagine a world at peace without the barriers of borders or the divisions of religion and nationality, and to consider the possibility that the focus of humanity should be living a life unattached to material possessions."[177] The lyrics envision a united world without borders, one devoid of any recognition of God or of eternity.

Does the utopia of which John Lennon fantasized and today's globalists strategize fit with biblical prophecy? Absolutely! Scripture tells us that just such a regime will rule over the world during the time of Tribulation.

Amir Tsarfati explains how the current climate-change hysteria furthers Satan's agenda for just such a world government:

The Bible describes the man of sin, the Antichrist, as a man who will have the reins for a world government handed over to him. Involved with this will also be a world religion that will help subject all things under his evil control. The Bible indicates that this man is going to rise from what we now know as Europe (Daniel 7). This climate change hysteria is doing nothing but screaming for the world to let the globalist regime have more control. Eventually, things are going to get to the point where the economic, political, and even religious platforms of the world are going to be right where Satan wants them in order for this man to take control.[178]

The climate-change frenzy has succeeded in opening the minds of world leaders to the necessity of the regime about which both Daniel and the apostle John prophesied would emerge during the Tribulation (Daniel 7; Revelation 13). The globalists who push for a New World Order act as Satan's minions promoting his agenda to put his man, the Antichrist, in charge of all the nations just as the Bible says will happen in the last days.

I believe climate change will eventually fade as the prevailing motivation behind the prophesied world government. The COVID-19 crisis demonstrated just how the focus of the world can change overnight, especially with the media controlling the narrative and globalists looking to seize any crisis that might promote their evil agenda.

On March 26, 2020, former prime minister of the United Kingdom, Gordon Brown, called upon world leaders to create "a temporary form of global government" in order to contain the COVID-19 pandemic. The desire of most world leaders for the type of world government that we see under the control of the Antichrist in Revelation 13 is not secretive, but an open agenda for anyone who is paying attention to see.

Just imagine what they will say after the Rapture!

Speaking of life during the Tribulation, Jesus said:

For then there will be great tribulation, such as has not been since the beginning of the world until this time, no, nor ever shall be.

And unless those days were shortened, no flesh would be saved. (Matthew 24:21–22)

I know that after the Lord takes us to heaven, His judgments will result in a great loss of life, but I wonder if it's not Satan's objective to accelerate it to the point of eliminating humanity.

We already witness the deadly intentions of the globalists in their demon-inspired, fierce support of abortion and infanticide. This is just one of several examples I could cite of this deadly and evil mindset.

Deniers of Biblical Truth

Those calling for radical economic and political change accuse us of denying reality because we refuse to believe their dire warnings of the coming catastrophe due to climate change. I would like to suggest, however, that the real deniers are the climate alarmists, because they deny the eternal truths of Scripture regarding both the Creator and His creation.

They Deny the Story of God's Creation

Profound errors in judgment arise from not knowing the whole story, do they not? When I was in seminary during the late 1970s, a young man and his family began attending a Sunday school class of which I was a part. I quickly formed a negative opinion of him based on his appearance; he had very long hair and an earring in his pierced ear (back then that seemed much more radical to me than it would today). I felt great shame when I learned he was an undercover narcotics officer whose appearance helped him fit into the illegal drug culture of the day so he could catch the bad guys.

Likewise, Scripture reveals the grand story of Creation apart from which we cannot fully understand its current state, or, more importantly, discern its future. Many errors of the climate alarmists stem from denying the validity of this biblical narrative. Some may not understand, but most refuse to believe it or, more accurately, "suppress the truth" in what they see in nature and in the sky (Romans 1:18–20).

First, we know that God created everything we see around us in nature as well as in the skies. Genesis 1:1 says, "In the beginning God created the heavens and the earth." As the Creator of everything, nature belongs to the Lord and rightly falls under His sovereignty. I love the words of Psalm 50:10–11, "For every beast of the forest is Mine, / And the cattle on a thousand hills. / I know all the birds of the mountains, / And the wild beasts of the field are Mine."

The Lord spoke, and where nothing previously existed, the universe instantly appeared. Psalm 33:6 says, "By the word of the Lord the heavens were made, / And all the host of them by the breath of His mouth." The writer of Hebrews adds, "By faith we understand that the worlds were framed by the word of God, so that the things which are seen were not made of things which are visible" (Hebrews11:3). Genesis 1–2 records the wonders of the Lord's creative activity as well as His command for mankind to "be fruitful and fill the earth" (1:28).

The book of Genesis reveals another climatic event that enables us to understand the current state of planet earth. It's what we refer to as the "Fall," when Adam and Eve disobeyed God and sin entered the human race. As a result, the Lord extended His punishment of their behavior to nature (Genesis 3:17–18). As beautiful and spectacular as nature can be today, it does not possess its original glory. Randy Alcorn wrote this in this book *Heaven*: "We have never seen the earth as God made it. Our planet as we know it is a shadowy, halftone image of the original."[179]

Still, in Genesis, we learn that a Great Flood covered the entire earth in ancient times (chapters 6–8). God judged the entire world because of its great wickedness. This Flood covered the entire earth, even the tallest mountain peak existing at that time.

Who, you might ask, really believes the story of Noah, the ark, and the Flood? Jesus does. His words in Matthew 24:37–39 confirm the entire Genesis account of Noah and the Flood. The apostle Peter later singled out the denial of the Genesis account of the Flood as the key oversight of those who in the last days will mock the return of Jesus (2 Peter 3:1–7).

When Jesus returns to the earth, He will restore creation to its original glory. This will be necessary because not only did the earth lose it former magnificence when Adam and Eve sinned, but the judgments of the seven-year Tribulation will ravage the earth's environment (see Revelation 6–16; Isaiah 24:3–6, 19–20). The Lord's wrath poured out against the wickedness of humanity during this time will severely impact nature.

At His Second Coming, however, Jesus will restore creation. The apostle Paul refers to this future renewal at Jesus' Second Coming in Romans 8:19–22 (ESV):

> For the creation waits with eager longing for the revealing of the sons of God.
>
> For the creation was subjected to futility, not willingly, but because of him who subjected it, in hope that the creation itself will be set free from its bondage to corruption and obtain the freedom of the glory of the children of God.
>
> For we know that the whole creation has been groaning together in the pains of childbirth until now.

Creation groans now because long ago God subjected it to "futility" as a result of the sin of Adam and Eve. But oh, what a glorious restoration awaits the earth when Jesus returns! He will reverse the curse on our environment and restore earth to its former glory. The news for planet earth gets even better. Revelation 21:1 tells us that after the millennium, God will create a "new heaven and a new earth."

The biblical roadmap of creation tells us it's the wickedness of humanity that will bring God's future judgment on both mankind and planet earth. Rising CO_2 levels and global warming do not appear on the list of sins that will result in the Lord pouring out His wrath during the Tribulation (see Revelation 9:20–21).

The emergency facing the world today is not climate change, but mankind's rejection of the Creator, which will bring God's judgment.

They Deny God's Glory as Seen in His Creation

When my wife, Ruth, and I visited the visited the National Gallery of Art in Washington, DC, a few years ago, we saw many amazing masterpieces. However, we did not admire the works such as those painted by Van Gogh and Rembrandt without an appreciation of the artists. Their personality comes through in their paintings, adding value and significance.

Likewise, the beauty and wonder of nature reflects that of its Creator. Psalm 19:1–2 says this: "The heavens declare the glory of God; / And the firmament shows His handiwork. / Day unto day utters speech, / And night unto night reveals knowledge." The climate alarmists err in their assessments of nature because they deny God's glory in creation!

The apostle Paul tells us that their problem is that of suppressing "the truth in unrighteousness, because what may be known of God is manifest in them, for God has shown it to them" (Romans 1:18b–19). Those who look at the environment with naturalistic eyes not only miss the biblical narrative of Creation, but also the magnificence of its Creator.

To fully appreciate the Mona Lisa, one must give Leonardo da Vinci a prominent place in its story. Likewise, any narrative of the earth or the universe that ignores God's magnificence as Creator remains vastly incomplete. It's like viewing a radiant, vividly colorful sunset in black and white. Shades of gray do not fully reveal God's glory in all that He made.

They Deny a Key Purpose of Creation

Imagine your neighbor brings home a shiny new car; we will say it's silver Toyota Camry. As time goes by, however, you notice that the car never leaves the driveway. Those next door often eat meals in it, and they spend a great deal of time maintaining it, but they never drive it. They do not use it in the way the automaker intended.

Is this not also true of the climate alarmists? I know they enjoy the sights and sounds of nature just as we do, but they deny a key purpose of creation: God intends for us to use it for our benefit. In 1 Timothy 6:17, Paul describes God as the One "who provides us with everything to enjoy." The Lord, through the psalmist says, "The heaven, even the heavens, are the Lord's, / But the earth He has given to the children of men" (Psalm 115:16).

We have a wonderful and amazing Creator! He made everything for our benefit. Would not the One who commanded Adam and Eve to be "fruitful" and "fill the earth" (Genesis 1:28) have also provided the means to support the large world population we have today? I am certain He has done so!

Calvin Beisner, in his article, "Foundational Principles of Biblical Earth Stewardship," wrote this about God's perspective on this exponential growth:

> Human multiplication and filling of the earth are intrinsically good (Genesis 1:28). In principle, children, lots of them, are a blessing from God (Psalm 127; 128). Earth is not overpopulated; indeed, "overpopulation" is a meaningless term, since it cannot be defined by demographic quantities like population density, growth rate, or age distribution. Hence, godly dominion does not require population control or "family planning." People are not primarily consumers and polluters but, as the image of God implies, producers and stewards.[180]

The elite globalists, however, have a much different perspective on the earth's population, one that's not only dark, but deadly. A tenet of the elite globalists calls for a sizeable reduction of the earth's population to "sustainable levels." The call for "sustainability" runs through the United Nations' documents related to Agenda 2030, but the UN does not fully define it in its numerous documents on the matter. The objective of population reduction remains unknown to most, but certainly not hidden.

The population-reduction goal of the globalists appears on the Georgia Guidestones that a mysterious New World Order group built in 1980 in Elbert County, Georgia. One of the ten inscriptions on this granite monument sets the *sustainable* level of the human population at five hundred million. That's just a fraction of the earth's current population of 7.8 billion.

This deadly and demonic agenda shows itself in the globalists' demand for the elimination of fossil fuels within ten years, one of the objectives of the Green New Deal. They surely know these fuels make it possible for farmers to produce the needed food for hundreds of millions just in the United States and for billions worldwide. The planting, maintaining, and harvesting of crops requires a great amount of fuel. Beyond that, the food would never make it from the farms to our grocery stores without diesel fuel powering a multitude of trucks as well as trains. And without fuel, it would be a very long walk for most of us to get our food home from the store.

Climatologist Dr. Pat Michaels says eliminating all fossil fuels would reduce the average earth temperature by .14 degrees Celsius. "That's a very small change for putting humanity back in the Stone Age."[181] He understands the disastrous and deadly impact of the Marxist agenda behind those leading the charge for the elimination of fossil fuels.

Bernie Sanders, a Marxist, said that, if elected president of the United States, he would imprison all the executives of fossil fuel companies. Can you imagine the costly and deadly consequences of such action?

God designed the world to sustain the large population we have today. This may sound highly controversial to many of you, but I believe the Lord provided fossil fuels in the earth for the benefit of mankind. Why else would He have designed the earth with such vast resources of oil and natural gas and given humanity the knowledge to use it?

These enormous reserves did not come into being apart from God's sovereign purposes, nor did they originate from decaying dinosaurs. It would have required an astronomically high number of decomposing prehistoric animals to create the gigantic reservoirs of natural gas and oil that exist beneath the earth's surface.

The Lord sovereignly, purposely, placed coal, oil, and natural gas in the earth to sustain the large global population that exists today. Creation exists for the benefit of mankind.

They Deny the Truth Regarding Jesus, God's Son

Many climate alarmists are the most religious people one would ever want to meet. Sadly, the god they worship and serve cannot comfort them in sorrow, hear their heart cries for help, rescue them from danger, forgive their sins, or give them eternal life. Nature remains silent to even their most sincere pleas.

On September 19, 2019, according to Fox News, students at Union Theological Seminary in New York City prayed to a collection of potted plants set up in the school's chapel. They later sent out a tweet regarding their worship of nature:

Today in chapel, we confessed to plants. Together, we held our grief, joy, regret, hope, guilt and sorrow in prayer; offering them to the beings who sustain us but whose gift we too often fail to honor. What do you confess to the plants in your life?

Such foolishness *denies* what the Bible tells us about Jesus. Paul describes His role in Creation in Colossians 1:15–17:

He is the image of the invisible God, the firstborn of all creation.
    For by him all things were created, in heaven and on earth, visible and invisible, whether thrones or dominions or rulers or authorities—all things were created through him and for him.
    And he is before all things, and in him all things hold together.

John adds this about the supremacy of Jesus over all creation: "All things were made through Him, and without Him nothing was made that was made" (John 1:3).

Not only do the climate alarmists deny God's glory in creation, they miss the centrality of the Son in everything they see. Notice the apostle says that it's in Jesus that "all things hold together." He is the One who sustains nature! Hebrews 1:3 says that Jesus upholds "all things by the word of His power." Jesus literally holds the entire universe together by His power!

The climate alarmists tell us we must take immediate and radical measures to save the planet. The Bible tells us Jesus is the One who preserves the earth! We have sacred responsibilities as caretakers of His amazing gift to us, but Jesus is the One who sustains the universe and will someday restore creation to its original glory.

The crisis of our time does not come from the impact of humanity upon the climate, increased CO_2 levels, or rising sea levels. It rather arises from the multitude of signs telling us that we live in the last days and time is quickly running out before Jesus returns for His Church just as He promised. After that, He will pour out His wrath during a great time of great Tribulation on the earth.

In the Upper Room the night before His crucifixion, Jesus said, "I am the way, the truth, and the life. No one comes to the Father except through Me" (John 14:6). Jesus is the Savior, the only path to eternal life. All other paths end with death.

John 3:16 says, "For God so loved the world, that he gave his only Son, that whoever believes in him should not perish but have eternal life." Jesus died a horrible death on the cross because no other way existed to pay the penalty for the sins of a lost and condemned humanity. Three days later, He rose from the dead to prove that His claims are true and that eternal life resides in Him and no one else.

I love the simplicity of the apostle John's words: "And this is the testimony, that God gave us eternal life, and this life is in his Son. Whoever has the Son has life; whoever does not have the Son of God does not have life" (1 John 5:11–12). Jesus equals eternal life. Denying Him and His words results in a fate worse than anything one could ever experience on this earth.

If you have not already done so, please put your trust in Him for the forgiveness of your sins and eternal life. Invite Jesus into your life. Romans 10:13 says, "For everyone who calls on the name of the Lord will be saved." Please do so before it is too late; time is running out!

This, not global warming, is the urgency of the day in which we live.

God's Wonderful Creation

I love the sights, sounds, and smells of nature. I enjoy driving along the Blue Ridge Parkway and could easily spend a week along this road soaking in the views, hiking on the trails, and meditating on God's Word. I enjoy sitting beside a mountain stream listening to the water trickle past just as much as I love the sound of ocean waves crashing against the shore. At zoos, the giraffes, lions, large tigers, elephants, and polar bears speak to me of the magnificence and power of their Creator! These are my favorites of all the animals!

Through creation, the Lord shouts to the world that there must be a Master Designer, a Creator of all things. We see His beauty in majestic snow-covered mountains, colorful sunrises, and picturesque reflections of hills and trees on clear mountain lakes.

The climate alarmists, however, deny the witness of creation (or more accurately suppress it) and instead look for life's answers in plants, rocks, trees, and animals (see Romans 1:18–25). Because they worship the creation rather than the Creator, others easily deceive them with a false agenda of how to save nature that sounds noble, but is false.

The globalists created the climate-change emergency to convince the world of a global crisis urgent enough for the nations to surrender their rights and form a Marxist world order. They remind me of Professor Harold Hill in the *Music Man* warning the people of River City of the great peril to its youth posed by the new pool hall. He did so to convince the residents to purchase musical instrument and band uniforms. The elite or "enlightened" ones of our time act as minions of Satan promoting ruse of climate change to hide their true objective: world domination through a Marxist New World Order.

As New Testament saints, we possess a certain and eternal hope that will be more wonderful and fulfilling than anything the utopian dreamers of our day can ever imagine. We will reign with Jesus in His kingdom and then through all eternity and forever enjoy God's creation in a way that even we can scarcely envision. Our joy will know no bounds as we bask in all the Lord has for us beyond this life.

Our enjoyment of the new earth as well as the New Jerusalem will never end (see Revelation 21-22). We will forever soak in its beauty with eyes much more attuned to God's splendor than what we currently possess!

TEN

The New Old Ways: Ancient Paganism Gets a Technological Facelift

By Pete Garcia

What an age to be alive! I was born in 1974, which means I am at present forty-five—soon to be forty-six years of age. I have lived through twenty-six years of the twentieth century and the last millennium, and now, twenty years in the twenty-first century and the new millennium. Understandably, many of you are in the same (or a similar) boat pertaining to the overlapping of centuries and of this new millennium. Perhaps it is because of this dynamic, though, that I have become fascinated not just with time itself, but with the significance of timing. Is it significant, or am I reading too much into it? To this point, I am brought back to a verse in Galatians 4:4–5 regarding our Lord's first advent to planet earth.

> But **when the fullness of the time had come**, God sent forth His Son, born of a woman, born under the law, to redeem those who were under the law, that we might receive the adoption as sons.[182] (emphasis added)

"Fullness of time" is a phrase jam-packed with context. Think about it this way: Jesus Christ—the Word, the Alpha and Omega, the One who

253

spoke the universe into existence—arrived in the flesh (the incarnation) at a time when Rome ruled the known world and Roman paganism was at its peak. Roman mythology, which borrowed heavily from Greek mythology, purported that a pantheon of gods and demigods were the supreme beings, to which all owed worship and allegiance.

Jesus was born into this world.

We today, some two thousand years later, are once again coming into a "fullness of time," albeit in a slightly different fashion. Therefore, I began asking questions like: What is different? What's the same? Why has mankind become so fascinated by secret knowledge and the spiritual realm? Why does civilization after civilization, for millennia, continue to recycle and repackage the same "gods" with different names? What does the return to paganism have to do with Christianity? What do ancient paganism, modern technology, and the end of the world have in common?

Stay tuned!

Introduction

We have seen that the rise of Spiritualism, which is a return to the demon-intercourse and wonder working of ancient times, soon resulted in a revival of Occultism, or the Pagan philosophy. These systems, therefore, though they be at issue upon one or two unimportant points, have no real antagonism. They are but different aspects of the same faith and will doubtless continue to exist side by side just as they did in the old Heathen world- Theosophy becoming the creed of the educated and intellectual while Spiritualism influences the masses of mankind.

But Theosophy identifies its teachings with those of the Mysteries, and declares that it is the system "which all the great religions of the world have, under various guises and with varying degrees of success, striven to express." Surely, then, the motive which impels the Prince of the Power of the Air to revive such a system in countries which have for three hundred years professed the name of the Lord Jesus Christ, is sufficiently obvious. The hour of his brief triumph is at hand: he is beginning to draw men into confederation by those teachings of Nephilim, which were successful in Antediluvian times and at Babel: he is organizing his forces with the intention of raising again the standard of universal rebellion against God and against His Christ. —George H. Pember[183]

Although theosophy was all the rage in the late nineteenth century, I would wager a guess that nine out of ten Americans today have never heard of it. Yet, theosophy, or at least its principles, has infected virtually every aspect of Western civilization to date. Theosophy's founder, Madame Helena Blavatsky, presented what she offered as *new* information from the "ascended masters" she had met while in the Far East, and introduced it during the growing tumult within the United States and Europe of the late nineteenth century. This was another new challenge in a growing list of ideological and theological tests that began challenging the established, orthodox, Christian order of the West. Author Bruce F. Campbell notes:

> The American social situation from which the Theosophical Society emerged was one of great upheaval, and the religious situation was one of challenge to orthodox Christianity. The forces that had surfaced in spiritualism included anticlericalism, anti-institutionalism, eclecticism, social liberalism, and belief in progress and individual effort. Occultism, mediated to America in the form of Mesmerism, Swedenborgianism, Freemasonry, and Rosicrucianism, was present. Recent developments in science led by the 1870s to renewed interest in reconciling science and religion. There was present also a hope that Asian religious ideas could be integrated into a grand religious synthesis.[184] —Bruce F. Campbell, 1980

But what is theosophy, and why is it pertinent to this particular discussion? Well, perhaps the name is foreign to most, but its precepts are not.

It was an attempt to blend Eastern mysticism, Western practicalities, science, and psychic phenomena. It is the beginning of what we would later call the New Age movement. Two people who were greatly influenced by theosophy were Alice and Foster Bailey. These two would come to form the Lucifer Publishing Company in 1920 (later simply called Lucis Trust), which became the exclusive publishing company for the United Nations. Their goal was to promote global ecumenism, spiritualism, and intellectual enlightenment to every nation. Through their efforts, they were able to give both *literary and institutional embodiment* of this New Age philosophy at the global level.[185]

The Fosters' view (from a theosophical perspective) was that there were many paths to salvation—and Jesus, well, He was simply one of many "ascended masters" who have come to enlighten humanity. Alice Bailey was devotee of Helena Blavatsky and presumably would be in wholehearted agreement with the Theosophical Constitution, which has these three tenets amongst its founding principles:

First. —To form the nucleus of a Universal Brotherhood of Humanity, without distinction of race, creed, sex, caste or colour.

Second. —To promote the study of Aryan and other Eastern literatures, religions, philosophies and sciences, and to demonstrate their importance to Humanity.

Third. —To investigate unexplained laws of Nature and the psychic powers latent in man.[186]

Again, the timing here is both interesting and significant, due to the founding of the United Nations (1945), the creation of NATO (1949), and the formation of the European Union (1951), and their proximity to the horrors of World War II. This mindset of absolute ecumenism and inclusivity gained significant traction at a time when the nations were emerging from the largest and bloodiest war the world had ever seen. The governing leaders, particularly in Europe, were both desperate and trau-matized by the geopolitical ambitions of the Nazis' Third Reich and later with the rise of the Soviet Union. The world leaders used this crisis to cre-ate the first truly global governing bodies. Perhaps the best embodiment of this sentiment of desperation was a quote attributed to Paul Henri Spaak (NATO secretary general, 1957–1961):

> We do not want another committee, we have too many already. What we want is a man of sufficient stature to hold the allegiance of all people, and to lift us out of the economic morass into which we are sinking. Send us such a man, and be he god or devil, we will receive him.

Therefore, it is with no shortage of irony here that what Hitler, Hiro-hito, Mussolini, and Stalin could not accomplish through force was suc-cessfully done through legislation. A global, multinational government, a regional government uniting all of Western Europe, and a transatlantic military alliance came out of Hitler's attempt to unify all of Europe under the Nazi flag. As an interesting aside, Alice Bailey would come to give her "great invocation" (which she claims *Christ Himself* gave to her) to the United Nations shortly before its official start date in October 1945.

The Great Invocation

From the point of Light within the Mind of God
Let light stream forth into the minds of men.
Let Light descend on Earth.
From the point of Love within the Heart of God
Let love stream forth into the hearts of men.
May Christ[187] return to Earth.
From the centre where the Will of God is known
Let purpose guide the little wills of men—
The purpose which the Masters know and serve.

From the centre which we call the race of men
Let the Plan of Love and Light work out
And may it seal the door where evil dwells.
Let Light and Love and Power restore the Plan on Earth.[188]

As you could probably tell from the New Age doublespeak used here, "Christ" is not the Christ of the Bible, but "a christ"—rather, an ascended master. The plan was, according to Lucis Trust, to guide humanity to its next evolutionary moment of self-enlightenment. This supposed ancient wisdom had not been uttered to the world until "Christ" saw the horrors and agony of World War II. It was then that He finally decided to share it with humanity through Alice Bailey.

I know what you might be thinking. In the decades since, the United Nations has proven to become a giant, bureaucratic dumpster fire, incapable of solving next to nothing. Who cares how ecumenical the United Nations is? Who cares about all this New Age, namby-pamby stuff, right? It is not as if the United Nations has any "real" authority, especially in the United States.

Who cares?

Satan cares.

According to Scripture, Satan is the current *de facto* ruler of this age and this world (1 Corinthians 2:8; Ephesians 2:2, 6:12; 1 John 5:8). When Adam and Eve sinned, they relinquished dominion over the earth to him. Since that moment, he has led the world in a relentless campaign of death, misery, and darkness. The most obnoxious example of this satanic dominion was when Satan tempted Jesus in the wilderness. However, he said something rather curious here that is oft overlooked (boldfaced below):

Then the devil, taking Him up on a high mountain, showed Him all the kingdoms of the world in a moment of time.

And the devil said to Him, "All this authority I will give You, and their glory; **for this has been delivered to me**, and I give it to whomever I wish.

Therefore, if You will worship before me, all will be Yours."
(Luke 4:5–7, emphasis added)

Satan's offer of all the kingdoms was legitimate. Jesus did not dispute that point. Note that Satan was in no way challenged by what he offered Christ; rather, the rebuke came for what he asked Jesus to do. However, that begs the question: How could the world in this current age belong to Satan if God is sovereign? It was in the Garden of Eden that God chose to plant humans as the *de facto* rulers of the earth. It was theirs to manage so long as they remained obedient to His one rule.

> Then the Lord God took the man and put him in the garden of Eden to tend and keep it.
> And the Lord God commanded the man, saying, "Of every tree of the garden you may freely eat;
> but of the tree of the knowledge of good and evil you shall not eat, for in the day that you eat of it you shall surely die." (Genesis 2:15–17)

In the garden, Adam could eat whatever he wanted, which included eating freely from the tree of life itself (Genesis 2:9), but he was commanded to not eat from one particular tree...the tree of the knowledge of good and evil. It is of interest to this topic and chapter that it is fruit from this tree of the knowledge of good and evil that is forbidden rather than, say, fruit from the tree of life (which presumably grants immortality). Nevertheless, Satan planted seeds of doubt in the mind of Eve and convinced her that, should she partake of its forbidden nectar, she would become like God. She then took it and gave it to her husband, Adam, and they did eat. At this point, they ceded control over earth to their greatest adversary, the devil, who is also called the serpent, the dragon, Lucifer, and Satan. It was also from this moment that a new form of worship would be added to humanity's lexicon of belief systems: paganism.

What is paganism?

For the purposes of this discussion, the term "pagan" refers to anything other than the true, orthodox Christian faith. That includes the wide swath of religious and secular belief systems past, present, and future, ranging from Buddhism, Hinduism, Islam, Shintoism, Roman Catholicism, and Mormonism, etc., to the more typical "pagan" groups like Wicca, human secularism, and Satanism. Anything that denies the one true faith in our Lord Jesus Christ is of pagan origin. Paganism, no matter how mainstream or obscure, ultimately finds its roots in lies and in its author, the father of lies himself, Satan.

Furthermore, Satan uses all pagan faiths for his own purposes. He can and does stir to violence any particular group he wishes, any time he wishes, because they all answer to him. At present, he is purposefully using Muslims to bring volatility to the world stage, but he has used many others before Islam. Satan has used the Romans, Greeks, Persians, Babylonians, Egyptians, Chaldeans, Sumerians, and virtually every pagan group ever devised to carry out his wicked machinations. He has even used, with terrible success, the Roman Catholic Church to carry out centuries worth of bloody crusades and inquisitions.

However, Satan's greatest successes have come in the form of subtler deceptions, and he has used countless faux-Christian groups to mislead millions. This is where the New Age, pseudo-Christian cults, the emergent church, and other "ecumenical" movements have found tremendous success in blurring absolute truth. And just as it was in the days of Babel, Satan is once again attempting to bring all the world's religions together under a single umbrella—e.g., the "whore" referenced in Revelation 17.

There is, however, one problem.

As long as the Church (the corporate, multimember Body of Christ) remains on the earth, this remains an impossibility. Christ said that He would build His Church, and that "the gates of hell shall not prevail over it" (Matthew 16:18). However, after the Church is removed at the Rapture (1 Thessalonians 4:16–18; Revelation 3:10), the world will move rapidly into a time of lying signs and wonders (2 Thessalonians 2:3, 9–12). After the Rapture, the religious deception that is presently kept at bay by the presence of the Holy Spirit-infused Church will no longer be restrained. So great will be the deception, that Jesus warned:

> For false christs and false prophets **will rise** and show great signs and wonders to deceive, if possible, even the elect.
>   See, I have told you beforehand. (Matthew 24:24–25, emphasis added)

Antichrist and the False Prophet will come forth echoing the same mantra as H. P. Blavatsky, Alice Bailey, and countless others to promote a universal, all-encompassing, blasphemous religion that is anti-Christ to the core. It will sweep up the world in its global apostasy so vile and wicked that even direct, divine, and increasingly severe judgment cannot curb it. This most blasphemous religion will culminate in its adherents permanently affixing to their forehead or hand a mark that will damn them to the lake of fire for all eternity.

> He causes all, both small and great, rich and poor, free and slave, to receive a mark on their right hand or on their foreheads,
>   and that no one may buy or sell except one who has the mark or the name of the beast, or the number of his name.
>   Here is wisdom. Let him who has understanding calculate the number of the beast, for it is the number of a man: His number is 666. (Revelation 13:16–18)

An apostate religion mixed with an ancient paganism could in no way be successful if it lacks the ability to enforce its tenets. This is where both the rise of modern technology and the reintroduction of the supernatural come into play. We are entering again a time of signs and wonders that the world has largely been devoid of since the first century.

Restoration

However, if we were to sum up into one word what paganism, modern technology, and the end of the world have in common, it would be "restoration." The pagan, whether he or she admits it, wants to restore the Golden Age—or, as we know it, the antediluvian (pre-Flood) world.

But why?

Because that was the closest mankind ever got to having paradise on earth. The antediluvian world was very different from our world today. The planet had been divinely terraformed to such a degree during Creation that mankind could easily live for centuries. The veil between the spiritual and physical was practically nonexistent, which is why all of the world's mythology stems from this era. People interacted freely with fallen angels, whom they viewed as gods or demigods. Furthermore, mankind was also physically stronger, bigger, and smarter than we are today. Lastly, it was the only time in human history when we did not have any form of Holy Scripture (see Acts 17:30).

To the pagan, the period before the Flood was an idyllic time of monsters and magic. It was a time of heroes and mythological tales of lore so fantastical that, even to this day, they tease at our deepest desires. It was a time so far back that even the ancient Greeks referred to it as "ancient history." It was a Golden Age of mankind's greatest accomplishments. While modern science has worked tirelessly to promote the idea that we evolved from lower, ape-like cavemen to where we are today, the truth is, if anything, we have regressed.

Furthermore, since the angels (sons of God) had been present at Creation (Job 1:6, 2:1, 38:6–7), they understood how things worked, perhaps even down to the molecular level. At some point between Creation week and man's entrance to the Garden of Eden, Lucifer (Satan) led a rebellion against God and was cast out of heaven (Ezekiel 28:11–19). He then instructed a portion of his fallen angels to have unnatural relationships with human women (Genesis 6:1–4). They began teaching humans things they weren't meant to know, much like teaching children how to do evil things before they have the ability to comprehend the consequences.

Therefore, it is of much interest to me why such a long and seemingly enigmatic period of time warrants only three chapters in the Bible (Genesis 3–6). According to Scripture, people lived for centuries and became increasingly wicked and violent. As there was no seeming barrier between the natural and supernatural realms, fallen angels began to interact physically with mankind. Because of this divine violation, a line had been crossed. Something occurred there that could not be undone, and the world was rapidly plunged into darkness.

Lucifer, the head fallen angel, had his master plan of restoration in two parts. The first was to corrupt mankind so thoroughly through sin and wickedness that, in His fury, God would have to wipe out the entire human race, thus nullifying the prophetic curse He gave Satan in the Garden (Genesis 3:15). The second part worked concurrently with the first, but also served as a backup plan. It was Satan's *summmam manum* ("finishing touch"). Satan attempted to physically corrupt the entire human race so thoroughly that, should God decide not to wipe out humanity, mankind would still be damaged goods. He wanted humanity so genetically compromised that a Savior could not physically come through the "seed of woman."

Thus, Satan charged two hundred angels (according to the noncanonical book of Enoch) with the task of physically intermingling with humans (in accordance with Genesis 6:1–4; 1 Peter 3:19–20; and Jude 1:6) to thoroughly corrupt them both genetically and spiritually. However, it was not *just* that these fallen angels physically coupled with human women and brought forth God's wrath, but that they taught them *forbidden knowledge*. Thus, while the Noahic Flood effectively wiped out the initial genetic mutation on the earth, it did not, however, erase the memories of the survivors—of which this *forbidden knowledge* carried on through the offspring of Noah.

Thus, the pagan's true master, Satan, wants to restore his stature and overturn his divine fate. Satan does not want to spend eternity in the lake of fire, and will do whatever it takes to not go there. However, if he is unable to change that, he will take as many humans down with him as possible. Satan is a liar and the father of lies (John 8:44). He wants people to think that by being a Buddhist or Mormon, for example, they are not worshiping him, but rather, are following their own path to enlightenment. That is a lie. There is only ONE path to salvation, and that is through our Lord Jesus Christ (John 14:6). While all the world's belief systems and religions might feign diversity of thought, they truly answer to only one master, Satan.

Lastly, as for the One True Creator God, well, He wants to restore our broken relationship with Himself. He did that by sending His Son in the flesh to live the perfect life and redeem humankind with His own blood. God's perfect holiness prevents man from approaching Him in our fallen state. In order to accomplish this plan of salvation, God uses the descendants of Abraham and Sarah as a beacon of light for the truth. He first gave the Jewish people (through Abraham) the promise, an *unconditional* covenant of land, seed, and blessing. Later (roughly four hundred years), He gave them the Law, which was a *conditional* covenant that dictates all they must do to maintain a favorable relationship (not salvation) with Him.

In the Law, God lists two foundational principles that play a major role even thousands of years later. First, innocent blood must be shed to atone for sins (Leviticus 17:11). Second, only a relative can redeem one in bondage or servitude (Leviticus 25:47–55). We need only look at ourselves to realize that, given our own devices, we do not want to follow God, because it exposes our true, broken nature. The only remedy for this was for God to become a Man (our Kinsman Redeemer) and shed His own blood in our stead, which He did at Calvary.

(**Author's note:** To be clear: There is only one way to salvation, and that is through our Lord Jesus Christ [John 14:6]. It is through His atoning and finished work at the cross that salvation is possible. We cannot earn it, become it, or visualize it. We must believe with our hearts and confess with our mouths that Jesus Christ is Lord [Romans 10:9–10].

Anything or anyone who says otherwise is simply promoting a form of paganism.)

At the center of the eternal realm is God, since He alone encompasses eternity. He has always existed, always will exist, and everything exists because of Him. At some point in eternity past, God, in His sovereignty, decided to add a temporal component to the eternal realm by adding Creation (Matthew 25:34; Ephesians 1:4). After this, juxtaposed to the eternal order, is what we would call the new temporal realm, or our present reality. This temporal component (i.e., the universe, stars, planets, earth, animals, humans, plants, etc.) is the created natural order. It is the world around us. It is all that we can take in with our five senses, and even what we cannot (microbes, atoms, subatomic particles, etc.). The existence we are in now is of time. Had Adam and Eve not rebelled against God, the world that was presumably would have remained in the exact same state of perfection as it had thousands of years ago at its creation.

If restoration is the chief objective in our human saga, and if God has already begun the process of our redemption, this leaves only the question of time. God created time for humanity, yet He does not exist in it—nor is He bound by it. Time is for creation itself (Genesis 1:14). However, from our perspective, time can be a highly unreliable mechanism. The future can seem foreboding, or it can appear pregnant with promise and mystery.

Paradoxically, the present appears cemented in the *doctrine of uniformity* (i.e., the way things are today is the way they always have been and always will be). And the past, well, was gone before we ever knew it. However, the past does not occur in a vacuum; it usually leaves behind "scar tissue"…which is what makes the antediluvian age so intriguing. God intentionally wiped out more than 1,600 years of human history as if it never existed. Even the archeological remains, save precious few, survived the tumult of the Great Flood. Again, the only mention we have is in the three chapters of Genesis (4–6) and the historical references in the noncanonical books of Enoch and Jasher.

Ruin Value

I liken archeology to historical scar tissue. It is a testament, or reminder, of all those who came before us. All of mankind's hopes, dreams, and ambitions now lie in crumbling ruins around the world. Man's great achievements often remain undiscovered for centuries, and even then, they're often only discovered by accident. From there, we moderns then look back and theorize about what was and what happened. Even this, however, has taken on a strange new understanding. When we look back through the archeological remains of the once-great kingdoms, what we often discover is the concept of *ruin value*. "Ruin value" is defined as "the concept that a building be designed such that if it eventually collapsed, it would leave behind aesthetically pleasing ruins that would last far longer without any maintenance at all."[189]

The most flagrant example of this occurred during the World War II era. The Third Reich's greatest architect, Albert Speer, wanted to recreate the glory and grandeur of the Greeks and Romans, but in Germany. His intent, then, was to build structures that were constructed to such precision and scale that, even after millennia, would continue to instill awe and wonder for generations to come. Clearly, Speer's efforts were designed to support Adolf Hitler's vision for a "thousand-year Reich." Speer (and Hitler) wanted the Nazi legacy to continue to inspire generations long after theirs had passed on.[190]

However, why did Speer and millions of other Germans come to believe in a "thousand-year Reich?" Well, because they had come to believe through the massive propaganda efforts by Goebbels and the Nazi propaganda machine that Hitler was an *emissary of God*, and that he was doing God's good work by emptying Europe of the Jews and other non-Aryans.

Germany has been transformed into a great house of the Lord where the Fuhrer as our mediator stands before the throne of God."—Joseph Goebbels, radio broadcast, April 19, 1936[191]

The Germans of the 1920s were desperate enough to believe this because it offered purpose (revenge) for World War I. Germany had been ingloriously humiliated by the Allied powers for their participation the Great War, and Hitler offered to fill that vacuum by resurrecting ancient Germanic mythology and marrying that with the likes of Marxism, social Darwinism, and nihilism. Hitler was simply another in a long line of "would-be-messiahs" the likes of which we still see eighty years later in people such as Barack Obama and Emmanuel Macron. This is not to say that they have committed the same offenses, but, given the same set of circumstances, the world wants its messiah; it just doesn't want the real One.

Entropy

Unfortunately, for Hitler, the late Sir Isaac Newton also gets a say in his "thousand-year Reich." The Second Law of Thermodynamics, in its most basic definition, is about the inefficiencies that occur during the transference of heat/energy until they reach a state of equilibrium (or maximum entropy). In the context of Creation, it is disputed as to when exactly the Second Law came into effect. Did God allow the Second Law to come into being after the Fall of Man? Alternatively, did God simply suspend some other law that prevented entropy from occurring in the first place? Either way, the renowned astronomer, physicist, and mathematician, Sir Arthur Stanley Eddington, concluded:

> The law that entropy increases—the Second Law of Thermodynamics—holds, I think, the supreme position among the laws of Nature. In fact, entropy appears to be the only true natural constant. All things fall apart, and human civilization is not exempt.[192]

So what causes entropy? For if we believe that a sovereign, omnipotent Creator God could create the universe (and all therein), and when done, call it good, how could it suffer entropy?

Mankind, the pinnacle of God's creation, was given free will. In exercising this free will, we unleashed sin and death through rebellion against the Creator. This is obvious. It is evidenced every day, all day long, by simply watching the news or reading about the day's events from the information outlets from around the world. Moreover, the entropy we see is more than just saying that civilization is falling apart; it is a continuous, downward trajectory that is increasing in intensity through the rise of technology.

Although history is replete with example after example of the never-ending rise and fall of great civilizations, we continue to treat our existence in a contradictory relationship to time. We envision a vast, glorious, human-centric future wherein we somehow evolve beyond the consequences of sin and death. Famed futurist Ray Kurzweil (of Google), like many others, believes:

> The exponential increase in technological innovation will reach a point where humans transcend biology and merge with technology, becoming functionally immortal as spiritual machines, no longer dependent on our embodied condition.[193]

Yet, things are not evolving; they are *devolving*. We live in the present as if the way things are today will be the way things will always be. We moderns, in our pride, cling to the notion that what befell our ancestors cannot happen to us. We are too advanced. We are too intelligent. We are smarter than those "primitives" who came before us. Again, this is a lie. Even nineteenth-century occultist poet William Butler Yeats recognized this in his epic poem, "Second Coming." In it, he says:

> Turning and turning in the widening gyre
> The falcon cannot hear the falconer;
> Things fall apart; the centre cannot hold;
> Mere anarchy is loosed upon the world,
> The blood-dimmed tide is loosed, and everywhere

The ceremony of innocence is drowned;
The best lack all conviction, while the worst
Are full of passionate intensity...[194]

When we look back through the remnants of the once-great king-doms, we repeatedly see man's attempt to thwart the ravages of time. Great structures, towering to the heavens. Vast expanses of granite col-umns, ziggurats, and other megalithic structures—mankind's attempt to live beyond his generation. Ironically, we want those archaic reminders to be set far off, into the distant past, often farther than they really were. We want them to be older, because we are instinctively uncomfortable with the sight and rapidity of entropy and urban decay. It reminds us of our own mortality. It reminds us of the raw and unrelenting power of entropy. It reinforces the biblical concept that things will ultimately worsen. It reminds us that, when left to our own devices, we default to wickedness and things fall apart rather quickly.

Like the abandoned nineteenth-century coal and steel towns that blight this nation's landscape, these serve as a reminder of the ravages of time and consequence. Abandoned towns, often overgrown with weeds and vines, mold, and decay, present a post-apocalyptic picture of something gone amiss. Once-thriving communities now lie hollowed out, haunted, and home to the creeping things. Playgrounds where children once played now sit rusting under an uncaring sky. Crumbling buildings. Streets and side-walks cracked and weed-ridden. Their neglect serves as a lingering reminder that human civilization is not so far removed from the cold, dark woods that once haunted our ancestors. Moreover, it wasn't so long ago that mankind became so spiritually decayed that God decided to start again.

Reclaiming the Golden Age

The search for the restoration of the Golden Age, along with its long-lost wealth of secret knowledge, propelled the ancients into worshiping anything and everything but the One True God. However, when we fast-forward through the ages, we see that the pagan world began to trade ritual and religion for knowledge and technology. Since the 1800s, we have seen human secularism step in and attempt to answer the eternal questions humanity has long sought answers for.

Although human secularism dates back to the time of the ancient Greek philosophers, humanity was too entrenched in paganism to trade that in for atheism. However, with the decline of paganism and rise of Christianity around the fourth and fifth centuries AD, we see a merger occur, and many of the old practices were infused with the knowledge from Holy Scripture. This unholy amalgamation of blending ancient paganism with first-century Christianity is foundational to the rise and popularity of the Roman Catholic Church. However, if you mix true, biblical Christianity with anything else, it can no longer be considered orthodox Christianity.

The Roman Catholic system was originally birthed in the fourth century during the reign of the Roman Emperor Constantine (formerly a pagan). By the late 200s, paganism was on the decline, and the heavily persecuted Christianity was spreading like wildfire across the Roman Empire. After a brief struggle for power amongst several competing Caesars, Constantine was able to use Christianity (or at least the symbol of it) and claim victory against Maxentius at the Battle of the Milvian Bridge in AD 312. From that victory, he capitalizes on this momentum and legalized Christianity across the empire in AD 313 with the Edict of Milan. Thus, we see the beginnings of the decades-long transition from pagan priests and temples to Christian priests and temples.

However, there are often never any clean breaks with their pagan past. Many rituals, traditions, and beliefs were carried forward into this new Christian belief structure. Roman Catholicism has a long and storied history of both militancy and subterfuge. By this, I mean purposely absorbing local paganism, giving it the Christian veneer and absorbing it into the Roman Catholic Church system. This was all done in order to more easily subsume the countries that were being conquered. This Roman Catholic system would come to dominate the West from about the fifth century until the fifteenth century.

Around the same time, there was an explosion of knowledge in the arts and sciences we call the Renaissance. A brief overview is as follows: As the Renaissance ended, we see the beginning of the Reformation; the Enlightenment; the Age of Reason; and then the subsequent Industrial Revolutions 1–4.

What that means is that mankind peaked (technologically speaking) just before the Flood. After the Flood, until the nineteenth century, technological progress had been extraordinarily sluggish. However, the geopolitical and intellectual movements happening concurrently necessarily determine the technological output of any given era. There were also overlapping periods that connect two greater *eras* in mankind's illustrative history. Let me demonstrate:

- **AD 500–1300: Middle or Dark Ages**
  - At this point, knowledge (as a whole) was doubling around every five hundred years, until the thirteenth century.
  - Religious theocracies (Roman Catholicism and Islam) and dynastic monarchies dominated much of the known world.
  - The era was marked by slow academic growth, high illiteracy rates, widespread superstition, and disconnectedness.
  - The greatest invention of the era was the mechanical clock (Yi Xing, AD 724).

- **1300–1600: Renaissance and Reformation**
  - General knowledge began doubling to about every 250 years.
  - The Renaissance and the Reformation movements began as the Holy Roman Empire's grip on Europe began to diminish.
  - The era was marked by an explosion of art, scientific theories, astronomy, and naval exploration.
  - The greatest invention of the era was the printing press (Johannes Gutenberg, circa 1450).

- **1600–1800: Age of Enlightenment**
  - General knowledge began doubling every 150 years.
  - The era was marked by an explosion of economic, colonization, and scientific theories.
  - The greatest invention of the era was the steam engine (Thomas Newcomen, 1712).

- **1780–1945: Age of Reason (Secularization)**
  - General knowledge began doubling every one hundred years.
  - The era was marked by explosions of:
    - Political conflicts
      - American and French revolutions
      - American Civil War
      - Numerous European revolutions
    - Radical theories
    - Existentialism: Soren Kierkegaard, Friedrich Nietzsche, Jean Paul Sartre, etc.
    - Marxism (socialism): Karl Marx, Friedrich Engels
    - Darwinism: Charles Darwin
    - Social Darwinism: Thomas Huxley, Herbert Spencer, Thomas Malthus, Francis Galton, Margaret Sanger, Third Reich
    - Communism/Socialism: Vladimir Lenin, Benito Mussolini, Adolf Hitler

- **1760–1870 First Industrial Revolution (Mechanization)**
  - Technology began doubling every one hundred years.
  - Man began to harness the power of steam and fossil fuels.
  - The greatest inventions of the era were vaccines (Edward Jenner, 1796), electric battery (Alessandro Volta, 1800), steam-powered train (George Stephenson, 1814), and telegraph (Samuel Morse, 1840–1850).

- **1870–1969 Second Industrial Revolution (Mass Production)**
  o Technological knowledge doubled every twenty-five years.
  o Modern warfare was introduced during World War I.
  o Electrical grids were developed for urban areas; telephones allowed for instant communication between vast distances.
  o The era was marked by the creation of the assembly lines (mass production), automobiles, manned flight, and industrial monopolies (oil, steel, coal, etc.).
  o The greatest inventions of the era were light bulb (Thomas Edison, 1880), the first successful airplane (Wilbur and Orville Wright, 1903), and the atomic bomb (Manhattan Project, 1939).

- **1969–2000 Third Industrial Revolution (Automation)**
  o Technology doubled every fifteen years.
  o Atomic warfare was introduced at the end of World War II.
  o Information increasingly became digitalized.
  o The era was marked by the introduction of automation, electronics, televisions, computers, space travel, and global threats (nuclear war).
  o The greatest inventions of the era were the transistor (Bell Laboratories, 1947) and the Internet (ARPANET, 1969).

- **1980–2000: Post-Industrial (Hybrid/Transition Era)**
  o Technology doubled every five to ten years.
  o The birth of consumer Internet use and industrial robotization occurred.
  o Information was slowly being encoded into separate Internet systems.
  o The era was marked by rapid increase of import goods and trades, high consumerism, and distrust in political systems.

- **2000–Present: Fourth Industrial Revolution (Digitization)**
  - Information processing has begun doubling every twenty-four to thirty-six months.
  - Information and processes are increasingly tied to the Internet.
  - The era is marked by terrorism, war, economic uncertainty, and rapid technological and scientific breakthroughs.

- **2010–2020: Industrial Revolution 4.0 (Hybrid/Transition Era)**
  - Information processing is doubling every eighteen to twenty-four months.
  - Wireless systems are powered by 3G and 4G networks.
  - This period sees the genesis of smart devices, cloud computing, and the Internet of Things (IoT), artificial intelligence (AI), quantum computing, cryptocurrencies, and virtual reality, etc.
  - Almost all information and processes are now online.
  - This era is marked by economic downturns, terrorism, and nationalization.

- **2020 and beyond (Virtual/Augmented Reality)**
  - IBM, Google, Apple, etc., are attempting to get the knowledge-doubling curve down to every twelve hours.
  - Goals are to automate everything that can be automated and embed it with artificial intelligence.
  - The plan is to transition current information cyber physical systems to nanotechnologies and quantum technologies (for handling massive amounts of data).
  - Progress leads to all wireless systems being powered by 5G networks.
  - Sovereign Sky introduces a space-based block chain digital currency.[195]
  - Efforts are being made to implement lethal autonomous weapon systems (LAWS) to fight wars in the near future (robotic weapon systems [drones], smart bombs, etc.).

o ID2020 seeks to give every person on the planet a digital identification.[196]

o This era is marked by increased uncertainty, deception, violence, and wickedness as "deep-fake" technology, proliferation of hybridized worldviews, and historical revisionism distort all truth.

Although not intended to be an exhaustive list of all of mankind's achievements, it is a simple presentation of the general trends in intellectual progression, married with the major technological periods, that have transformed recent human history. We should be thankful for the history we do have; it could have been much, much worse.

What If?

Imagine a world in which Alexander the Great had automatic weapons. Imagine a world in which the Roman emperors had access to Google Maps. How much more people and lands could leaders have conquered with that kind of knowledge? Imagine Vladimir Lenin having his own social media platform like YouTube and the means to distribute it throughout the world. How many more millions (billions, even) could he have influenced toward embracing his message of Marxism? How much worse would the communist revolution have become? Imagine a world in which Adolf Hitler and the Third Reich had cruise missiles. Would the führer have been able to turn back the tide of the war at Normandy?

Imagine a world in which Joseph Stalin had a global, digital surveillance system at his disposal. How many more millions would have died because of his cruel, paranoid, delusions? How many people would have starved to death during the Great Leap Forward if Mao Tse-tung had complete control of a biometric currency that forbade even the use of local bartering systems? Imagine the late Kim Jong-il having access to nanotechnology and being capable of spying on South Korea to such a degree that he could attack it at precisely the right moment when least expected? Imagine the Iranian regime having lethal autonomous weapon systems

(LAWS) at their disposal. How much more terror and destruction could they export around the world with that kind of power?

And, as awful as these men were in their own right, let's at least be thankful that they lived in an age before technology could match their murderous and disastrous inclinations. Unfortunately, a time is coming when a world leader will arise who will be more evil than the all of the above combined—and he will also have all of these modern technologies at his disposal. He, along with his global government known as the beast, will use it to enforce his iron-fisted will upon the whole world.

> So they worshiped the dragon who gave authority to the beast; and they worshiped the beast, saying, "Who is like the beast? Who is able to make war with him?" ...It was granted to him to make war with the saints and to overcome them. And authority was given him over every tribe, tongue, and nation. All who dwell on the earth will worship him, whose names have not been written in the Book of Life of the Lamb slain from the foundation of the world. (Revelation 13:4, 7–8)

The Unholy Marriage: Science and the Occult

If we begin the Enlightenment with Isaac Newton's *Principia Mathematica* in 1686 and John Locke's *Essay Concerning Human Understanding* in 1689 (setting aside René Descartes' earlier forays into skepticism), we can reasonably conclude that it ended with the bloody French Revolution. The Age of Reason, which began during the French Revolution (1789–1799), should be considered a more secularized, second stage of the Enlightenment, which introduces two important principles that have governed the world from then (1789) until 1945. The first is the overthrowing of the old order (i.e., divine right of kings, monarchies, etc.) and the second is the separation of church and state. To be clear, the "church" here is not necessarily true Christianity, but the Roman Catholic Church, which for centuries controlled Europe through papal edicts and inquisitions.

However, the greatest minds of the ages, going back long before the Enlightenment, had Christians at the forefront of scientific discovery and development. Christian theologians and scholars like Bede, Thomas Aquinas, Nicolaus Copernicus, and Johannes de Sacrobosco were leading scientific development in the West long before Newton, Locke, Diderot, Hume, Voltaire, and the rest. Although the early pioneers of science (Galileo, Copernicus) were often at odds with the Roman Catholic Church, it wasn't until man began to separate the Creator from the creation writ large that corrupted ideologies began to flourish and poison the academic wells.

As academia and sciences moved away from the Christian faith during the nineteenth and twentieth centuries, it sparked a downward trajectory of deteriorating ideologies. It began with reductionism, skepticism, deism, relativism, and agnosticism, and concluded with militant atheism. These philosophies were often paired with accompanying political movements of the day. For example, we can most readily associate deism with the eighteenth-century American Revolution and atheism with the communist revolutions of the twentieth century.

However, by the time mankind reached atheism as the "be all, end all" philosophical ideology (e.g., Nietzsche), we found it lacking, empty, and void. People are by nature spiritual creatures who crave worship. C. S. Lewis once likened the human as having an amphibious nature of "half animal, half spirit."

Having rejected both pure atheism and true Christianity, and having exhausted the search through the sciences for the meaning of life…

Why am I here?

Where did I come from?

Are we alone in the universe?

…mankind, once again, has come full circle back to the *old religions* for answers. One of the more significant signs concerning the last days is the cyclical nature of history. The wise King Solomon once wrote that there is "no new thing under the sun" (Ecclesiastes 1:9). When asked, Jesus authenticated this sentiment by saying that the time just before His return would be like the days of Noah and the days of Lot (Luke 17:26–

36). We know that the world before the Flood was violent, wicked, and filled with supernatural demonstrations. We know that during Lot's day, the cities of Sodom and Gomorrah were exceedingly wicked, with their particular sins manifested in sexual perversions and greed (Genesis 19; Ezekiel 16:44–56). However, there was a time between these two, which is the oft-overlooked account of the tower of Babel.

> But the Lord came down to see the city and the tower which the sons of men had built.
>
> And the Lord said, "Indeed the people are one and they all have one language, and this is what they begin to do; now nothing that they propose to do will be withheld from them.
>
> Come, let us go down and there confuse their language, that they may not understand one another's speech."
>
> So the Lord scattered them abroad from there over the face of all the earth, and they ceased building the city. (Genesis 11:5–8)

Babel was the first post-Flood place we see the marriage of technological prowess and spiritual intent merged in a process I call "Babelism." Humans are complex beings. We are physical, carnal beings, yet we are also spiritual. We desire to worship (and be worshiped). If we act purely to invent or build with no spiritual connection, it might make for a great practical invention, but its function is meaningless (in the end) without a spiritual connotation. For example, if Gutenberg had invented the printing press and its only use going forward had been for printing technological manuals, no one would care. In other words, the printing press is simply the tool by which man has produced (or reproduced) those intangible things that speak to our deepest yearnings, which includes everything from the Holy Bible to *War and Peace*.

God didn't destroy the tower of Babel and scatter people amongst the earth simply because He hates tall buildings. He did so not because of *what* they built, but *why* they built it. Furthermore, every time mankind comes together as one, it usually results in terrible choices and outcomes.

Thankfully, God's actions at Babel prevented people from destroying themselves a second time, ahead of the divinely appointed timeline.

Not only did God separate mankind by language, but also by geography, stifling communication for millennia. Becoming estranged by language and distance, as it were, allowed humanity to develop unique customs and social norms that would further prevent wholesale amalgamation until a new stimulus came along to unite them. As history has borne out, this would not even begin to happen until Alexander the Great began conquering much of the known world. His model for world domination was not just about conquering a land and enslaving its inhabitants, but absorbing it, Hellenizing it, and making it Greek. The Romans would also use this same model in conquering much of Europe, the Near East, and North Africa.

The ancient Sumerians, Assyrians, Egyptians, Greeks, and Babylonians all traced their "knowledge" back to the Golden Age of man. Again, this is a secularized name for what Christianity identifies as the antediluvian (or pre-Flood) age. Even though groups such as the Knights Templar, Rosicrucians, Illuminati, and Freemasons had already been long invested in attempting to regain the long-lost, forbidden knowledge to advance their political agendas, this knowledge began attracting new adherents. These groups had already operated successfully in the West for some time and had incorporated lengthy, secret initiations and incrementally unveiled secret "knowledge" to their followers. However, what they really offered was inclusivity and a manner to network amongst fellow *travelers*.

By the turn of the twentieth century, the Western world was already becoming oversaturated with quasi-political secret societies, professional orders, and academic fraternities. A newer, darker breed of groups was emerging, and it leaned heavily on Eastern mysticism to gain esoteric enlightenment rather than chase after political machinations. The Theosophical Society, Ordo Templi Orientis, and the Hermetic Order of the Golden Dawn were some of the more prominent occult groups.

Conversely, politics often intertwined itself to the esoteric with groups like the German Third Reich, whose members embraced their ancient, neo-pagan roots in the hopes that they could give them an edge for both political and militaristic purposes. The Nazis' belief in the power of the Black Sun, for example, was ideological fodder for their Thule Society, which through archeology and ritualism sought out supernatural, occult help in establishing their Thousand-Year Reich.

While mixing ancient paganism into modern technology seems ludicrous (note the comment about CERN below), the Third Reich revived it in the twentieth century. Heinrich Himmler and other prominent Nazis were fascinated by the idea that, through the occult, they could use black magic to secure victory. The marriage of groups like the Thule and Vril Societies—who, through science and archeology, attempted to historically prove the Aryan race had claim to some divine birthright—was very alluring to numerous German esoteric groups. It was the blending of those ancient pagan beliefs of their ancestors to modern political agendas that became a very appealing combination to many, especially within Himmler's SS.

> The Nazi fascination with the occult is legendary, yet today it is often dismissed as Himmler's personal obsession or wildly overstated for its novelty. Preposterous though it was, however, supernatural thinking was inextricable from the Nazi project. The regime enlisted astrology and the paranormal, paganism, Indo-Aryan mythology, witchcraft, miracle weapons, and the lost kingdom of Atlantis in reimagining German politics and society and recasting German science and religion. —Eric Kurlander, *Hitler's Monsters: A Supernatural History of the Third Reich*[197]

This Generation

The twentieth century was the first in almost two thousand years to have Jews living back in their ancient, ancestral homeland as a sovereign nation again. It took, however, two world wars, the collapse of the Ottoman and European empires, and the rise of the United States to make that happen. However, with Israel back in her land, God opened up the floodgates of innovation. For example, it took 423 years to go from the Leonardo da Vinci's drawings on the theory of flight to the first manned flight in 1903. However, it only took 66 years to go from the Wright Brothers to the first moon landing in 1969 with Apollo 11.

It took 2,203 years to go from the first theory of the atom (Democritus, circa 400 BC) to John Dalton's atomic theory in 1803. However, it only took 135 years from Dalton to splitting the atom in 1938. Ironically, the United States would later use those planes to drop the first atomic weapons against a recalcitrant Japan seven years later, thus ushering in the Atomic Age.

From Hiroshima and Nagasaki (1945), it only took five years to the discovery of the double-helix DNA and seventeen years until the concept of the Internet (1962–DARPA). Interestingly, in the midst of the three greatest twentieth-century innovations (manned flight, atomic energy, and the Internet) was the greatest miracle since Christ's first advent to planet earth: the rebirth of the nation of Israel.

So why this generation?

Well, because of Israel.

Now the Lord had said to Abram: "Get out of your country, From your family and from your father's house, To a land that I will show you.

I will make you a great nation; I will bless you and make your name great;

And you shall be a blessing. I will bless those who bless you, And I will curse him who curses you; And in you all the families of the earth shall be blessed." (Genesis 12:1–3)

At the end of World War II, the Jews began getting out of their respective countries and making their way back to their ancestral homeland. In 1967, the Jew has reclaimed their ancient capital of Jerusalem in the storied Six Day War. Since 1962, technological innovations and information-processing gained serious momentum. I liken the invention and commercialization of the Internet to mankind's second "Gutenberg" moment. The Internet first began as a military venture for information-sharing. The scientific community would soon after begin championing this venture. Moreover, by 1983, the genesis of the commercial use of the Internet began. Soon after, it began to connect the entire world on a massive, information processing/sharing network.

The Internet made things once deemed impossible now within man's grasp once again. Real-time global information-sharing, 3D printing, quantum computing, and digital currency—all theoretical at one point—were now becoming realities. This continued to feed the notion that ventures like space colonization, time travel, and immortality are not as far-fetched as they once appeared. Not since the tower of Babel have people become so unified in purpose and capability, which can only be done through a global threat and a means of global communication. Not since Babel has mankind's intent to become like gods been as strong as it would become in the twentieth and twenty-first centuries. These technological innovations, as crazy as they once appeared, were why God separated people in the first place.

Forbidden Knowledge Revived

Unfortunately, man's thirst for "forbidden knowledge" never abated, even with the advent of the industrial revolutions; it simply gave these esoteric groups more powerful tools to use. Throughout history, religious cults and pagan religions sprang up on practically every continent, nation, and empire, promising deliverance through enlightenment. This so-called enlightenment came in the form of secret knowledge, which could only come about through secret initiations into the dark arts.

It began in the Mesopotamian region with the rise of the Sumerian, Chaldean, Akkadian, Hittite, Egyptian, Assyrian, and Babylonian kingdoms. Although they worshiped hundreds of gods, as the kingdoms rose and fell, their deities never really went away. They just changed names. The similarities are evident between Enlil (Sumerian) and Ellil (Babylonian), who was eventually replaced by Marduk by the Babylonians.

The Egyptian god Re became the Greek god Zeus, who later became the Roman god Jupiter. The Egyptian goddess Isis became the Greek goddess Hera, who later became the Roman goddess Juno. The Egyptian god Osiris became the Greek god Hades, who later became the Roman god Pluto. Even the mighty hunter Nimrod (Genesis 10–11) is believed by many scholars (including Josephus) to actually be the *demigod* Gilgamesh, about whom the ancient Neo-Assyrian tablets report vile and wicked deeds. This is but a small sampling of how the names changed, but the gods and goddesses remained the same…and they're anxious to return to the spotlight.

Fast-forwarding through the millennia, we again see the rise of numerous Orientalism-based cults and secret societies in the nineteenth and twentieth centuries. Even the supposed medieval works of literature, such as the *Akhbār al-zamān* (*The History of Time*) and *Shams al-Maʿarif* (*The Book of the Sun of Gnosis and the Subtleties of Elevated Things*) were brought back into the fray. These were thought to be the real sources of forbidden knowledge that H. P. Lovecraft's fictional book, *Necronomicon,* was based upon. Lovecraft's work went on to influence successive generations, generating a vast and growing interest in the occult during the latter half of the twentieth century, thus perpetuating this desire to resurrect the ancient gods and their dark knowledge even into our day.

By the turn of the twentieth century into the twenty-first, modern man was busy romanticizing and recreating the great myths of yore, even going so far as trying to replicate them in real life. Every mythological and pagan story that has ever existed has, in one way or another, found its way into our modern entertainment industries. Movies, books, music, and art are fascinated with these ancient deities.

> Superheroes are the Greek gods of secular modern life—otherworldly figures able to tackle world problems with a single bound. Like the gods of Greek mythology, they can be flawed. In fact, some argue that we need them to be flawed. Part of their appeal is that we can relate to them, despite their being superhuman."[198]
> —David Wright, June 7, 2013

To the secular world, the "old gods" were just good fun, not to be taken seriously. However, there are those who have moved beyond occultism just for entertainment who are actually seeking access to the spiritual domain. The European Organization for Nuclear Research (CERN), for example, is expending enormous funds and resources in the name of scientific exploration as a means to open a portal to another dimension (amongst other things). According to Sergio Bertolucci, the director for research and scientific computing at CERN (speaking for one of the reasons for the Large Hadron Collider), "Out of this door might come something, or we might send something through it."

While all the past references to the Third Reich's fascination with the occult seem interesting from a historical point of view, there was a darker, more pragmatic reason for bringing it up. By the end of World War II, the world was just starting to realize the unimaginable horrors the Nazis and the Japanese had been up to during the war. The concentration camps like Auschwitz and Treblinka, along with the Japanese Unit 731, detailed the murderous, inhumane experimentation those governments were willing to subjugate other humans to. The Nazis' attempt to commit wholesale genocide against the Jewish people resulted in the deaths of more than six million Jews. Japanese cruelty was estimated to have tortured and killed more than three hundred thousand Chinese. Many of these deaths, however, were not without scientific reasoning.

When the Americans and Russians began the liberation of the Nazi concentration camps in Europe, many German scientists and their data were scooped up and kept secret by both nations. The US Counter Intelligence Corps (CIC) conducted Operation Paperclip, which took in around sixteen hundred German scientists, gave them new identities, and brought them to the US. The Russians had a similar program named Operation Osoaviakhim, which also sought to capitalize on the Nazis' inhumane testing and scientific advancements. What the Nazis had done (the extremes they would go to), neither the Americans nor the Russians had the gall to do. Instead, the Americans and Russians took that Nazi data and would later use it to create a super-soldier and advanced rock-etry. This also helped perpetuate the race into the Cold War and later into the Space Race, which would consume both nations for the next forty years.[199]

This had another unintended side effect for the United States' political and military leadership: It created a perpetual need for information. The only advantage now was that the government had the means to classify and safeguard this knowledge with the creation of new government agencies (CIA, FBI, DNI, NSA, etc.). Therefore, even though the US was very much in a nuclear arms race with the Soviet Union, this was becoming every bit as much a contest for acquiring and securing information. The conclusion to all this is that the twentieth-century nuclear arms race has now culminated into the twenty-first-century artificial intelligence race.

The US defense and intelligence agencies became consumed with conducting many of the same "kinds" of paranormal/parapsychology research that the Nazis had been charged with. Initiatives like MK Ultra, Project Bluebook, and Star Gate were more of the well-known projects the US spent millions of dollars researching and safeguarding. Granted, most of these programs were unknown to most Americans until many years after their initial launches. However, certain groups within the defense and intelligence communities became obsessed with harnessing the potential of things like remote viewing, precognition, and other psychic skills to use against the communists.[200]

Both nations had become consumed with information collecting and data gathering. It is not without any sense of deep irony that social media would later freely provide ten times the amount information that even the most complex and multilayered spy craft ever could.

By the 1980s, the Computer Age was coming into its own. With the advent of videogames and a booming science-fiction genre, Western curiosity about the threat of Sky Net, flesh-eating aliens, and futuristic robots made for big entertainment, behind the scenes, government agencies were working feverishly to make these things a reality (except the flesh-eating aliens). US President Ronald Reagan's "Star Wars" Strategic Defense Initiative was even credited with helping collapse the ailing Soviet Union.

By the end of the 1990s, computers were becoming affordable, and the Internet seemed more like a curious luxury than a daily necessity. However, after September 11, 2001, the US Congress was able to repackage the 1994 Homeland Terror Omnibus Bill, renaming it the Patriot Act, which had unanimous bipartisan support. The act was quickly passed into law, giving the government vast powers to use this newfound technology on its own citizens.

Flush with technological resources and significant amounts of funding, the simple fact was that there was more information coming in than the government knew what to do with. This prompted the government to create (i.e., farm out to private industry) the requirement to build massive data banks (e.g., Utah Data Center) that are still in existence today. These systems at one point were consolidated into three massive data-storage centers. This data was then just sitting there on servers (cell and Internet traffic) waiting for the right opportunity to be used.

Conclusion

We know without a doubt, according to Scripture, that there is one more, final world ruler coming to the global stage. We call this man the Antichrist. He will be the political head of the final world government known as the beast. His forerunner will be the False Prophet, who will gather all the religions under one ecumenical banner using supernatural powers, and then redirect everyone's worship to the Antichrist.

For the False Prophet and the Antichrist to execute their satanic mission, the world needs the technological infrastructure in place ahead of time. Think about it this way: Had God left the continents together (pre-Pangea), and had He not separated people by distance, genetics, and language, an antichrist (one of many), could have become the Antichrist many centuries ago. What does the Antichrist need to rule the world?

1. A global surveillance network
2. A global communication platform
3. A global (presumably) digital currency
4. A means to harness and process all the world's information data (quantum networks)
5. A military force (or military power) to enforce his dark agenda
6. Lastly, and most importantly, a global crisis

The Antichrist will come into the world as the rider on the white horse (Revelation 6:1–2). He will come waving a banner of peace and prosperity, but only war, famine, and death will follow. His rule will be absolute, his tyranny relentless. He will make all other autocrats before him pale in comparison. He will gain control over all the nations of the earth, as well as over everyone's ability to buy or sell. He will have his front man, the False Prophet, performing supernatural signs and wonders, wooing the world into giving Antichrist their complete loyalty through the mark of the beast. And with man enthusiastically rejecting the Christian faith for paganism (there will be no atheists in the beast system), we are finally becoming the generation who will readily embrace the mark of the beast.

While we don't yet know who these two men are as of yet, the Rapture will present the right crisis at the right time (the fullness of time) to a world that is starved for the supernatural, deluded enough to embrace paganism, and technically savvy enough to give these men the tools they need to iron-fistedly rule the world.

Then I stood on the sand of the sea. And I saw a beast rising up out of the sea, having seven heads and ten horns, and on his horns ten crowns, and on his heads a blasphemous name.

Now the beast which I saw was like a leopard, his feet were like the feet of a bear, and his mouth like the mouth of a lion. The dragon gave him his power, his throne, and great authority.

And I saw one of his heads as if it had been mortally wounded, and his deadly wound was healed. And all the world marveled and followed the beast.

So they worshiped the dragon who gave authority to the beast; and they worshiped the beast, saying, "Who is like the beast? Who is able to make war with him?" (Revelation 13:1–4)

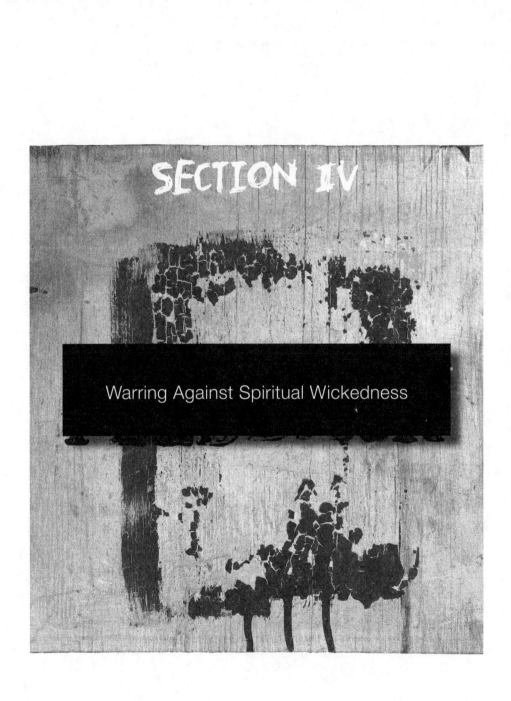

SECTION IV

Warring Against Spiritual Wickedness

ELEVEN

Satan's Extermination Storm Troopers

By Don McGee

Most Christians who view prophecy logically and literally believe that God has divided the path of human history into seven different eras of time, each with its own characteristics. These are called dispensations, and though different in both length and content, some features are common to each one.

Dispensationalists believe that though it is true that all who are saved are saved solely by grace through faith in Jesus, the Church and the nation of Israel are distinct groups for which God has distinct plans. Much can be said about this aspect of dispensationalism, but it is not in the context of this chapter.

Each dispensation begins with a new revelation of God's Word to humanity that is more detailed than that of the previous dispensation, along with the establishment of a new way in which man is to relate to Him. Further, each one ends with His being forced to judge the race as a result of its rejection of His sovereignty.

With the passing of each dispensation, the final confrontation between the Holy God and the sinful human race comes closer, and the signs that point directly toward that great battle increase almost daily in number and in intensity. Jesus describes this process in Matthew 24:8 as birth pangs.

For those of us who have never experienced giving birth to a child, the impending judgment of this world system may be compared to something more familiar to all of us, like the sight and sound of a train speedily bearing down upon a highway crossing. The closer the train gets, the larger it appears—accompanied by an increase in the pitch and volume of its blaring horn of warning. As it rushes down to the point of impact, whatever is in its path is virtually paralyzed by this irresistible force that is both terrifying in its approach and deafening in its noise.

We see God's warnings of judgment all around us, but most people ignore them because they ignore Him. Instead of running for the escape He has provided in the Person of Jesus, they stand unmoving and defiant as they curse His Name and shake their impotent fists in His face.

Why do people react this way? How can any person with even superficial critical-thinking skills not recognize the closing moments of this dispensation and its catastrophic end? The answer to that question has nothing to do with brain trauma or psychosomatic diseases. It has to do with spiritual issues.

Many Christians often talk about how God, in the final days of this dispensation, is raising up special teachers whose responsibilities are associated with the proclamation and explanation of Bible prophecy regarding the days in which we live.

In order to counter this, Satan has developed his own group of special teachers and influencers whose responsibility is to combat the proclamation of what God has said about sin, redemption, and the events that are immediate to the future. These may be called "Satan's storm troopers," and they are as evil and ruthless as any despots that have ever lived.

Though the hearts of these storm troopers are indeed wicked, they don't generally take upon themselves a crusty, offensive façade that would repel the basic sensibilities some people still have. They operate as their master; that is, they appear as angels of light in order to more effectively influence the spiritually naïve.

Among these are people of renown who are not only charismatic in their persona, but who are also expert in their exploitation of social platforms, personal fame, and global technology for their nefarious work. They cloak their evil inside a cocoon of dazzling secular credentials, and many are the simple-minded who are impressed and become disciples. A brief examination of these will be the focus of this chapter.

Three basic issues much be kept in mind: sin, free will, and Satan's hatred for God. A very simple picture of each is presented in an abridged manner as part of this chapter's introduction.

Sin

One of the consequences of sin is that the heart totally rejects God's providential right to a person's life. The result of sin is certainly seen in the physical world, but the ultimate end of it is both personal and spiritual.

Humanists dismiss this as theological poppycock, but we should remember that humanists don't have very much credibility in any specialty or discipline, much less in the arena of spiritual matters. All one must do is consider the irreparable damage humanists like John Dewey and Benjamin Spock did to government education and to the stability of the home and society.

The humanist argument for the denial of God and what He has said is enabled by the fact that God is Spirit, thus works from the unseen spiritual dimension. Humanists believe in the supremacy of human logic, which means they believe if a phenomenon cannot be repeatedly observed, dissected, and analyzed using the scientific method with the five senses, it's to be rejected, or at least seriously questioned.

This is the epitome of human insolence! People cannot prove they got married by using the scientific method. A marriage is proven using the historical documentation and witness method. There is a place for logic and reasoning, but those fall flat when it comes to critiquing and commenting on God's unseen dimension.

Unlike Elisha's servant in 2 Kings 6, whose physical eyes were opened in order that he might see the spiritual battlefield, the reality of what Satan is doing is not seen using pupils, lenses, and optic nerves. The battle is spiritual and is more authentic than even most Christians realize.

The consequences are easily seen, but ground zero is in the spiritual realm. In short, the conflict rages in the collective heart of humanity, which is not only evil beyond understanding, but cannot be examined on a stainless-steel table in a gross anatomy lab.

And everyone, whether he or she wants to or not, participates in this spiritual warfare in one of only two ways: a person is either with God or with Satan.

It is true that Satan hates people because he hates God, yet most people reject this. Even if they admit to the existence of God and Satan, when it comes to spiritual warfare, they don't actually know what any of it means.

Consequently, they usually shrug and insist they are neutral noncombatants if any such conflict even exists. They say they don't wish to be involved, and that they simply want to live their lives in any way they desire. Such neutrality is an impossibility, because God created people in His own image, thus giving them life with immortal souls and spirits and the ability to make choices.

Thus, Satan's hatred of God cannot be separated from his hatred of God's creation. The character and substance of evil demands it. If only this one simple truth were understood, there would be much less agonizing over questions regarding why things happen the way they do.

Free Will

If God knew from the beginning that His creation would rebel and that Jesus would have to become a Man and die in order to redeem it, why did He give mankind a free will to begin with? Wouldn't it have been more expedient and less costly to simply put a microchip in people's brains to direct their spiritual inclinations as He did with DNA to direct their physical characteristics?

This question has been answered often, so we might wonder why it's still being asked. But it will be answered again, because it is fundamental to understanding the spiritual battle between God and the evil spirit of Satan and his storm troopers.

That God's creation would glorify Him is its primary purpose. As creation brings glory to God, creation is in turn richly blessed and becomes very beautiful in its existence. From the earth and all its beauty to the complex structure of a single living cell, from the order of the universe to the soulish and spiritual dimensions of humans who can actually have fellowship with their Creator—it all reflects the glory and majesty of God.

Anything that would cast doubt upon the integrity of God would destroy that glory, and for Him to make beings without the ability to choose to serve Him would do just that. What honor is there in having a spouse and child who love you because they have no other choice as the result of having a "love chip" in their brains?

Adam and Eve and all their progeny were created with the ability to choose whether they will serve God. If people choose not to serve God, their hearts default to serving Satan. It's like pregnancy: Either a woman is pregnant or she is not.

When it comes to free will, God is pro-choice, because that's the only way His creation can give Him glory. Do not, however, equate this idea of pro-choice as an argument for pro-choice regarding abortion. In that case, a man and woman have already made a choice regarding their own bodies; any decision to murder their preborn baby has nothing to do with them and everything to do with their child.

Did God take a chance when He created humanity? In a manner of speaking, He did, though He knew what was going to happen and what it would cost Him. Yet His love for humanity and His righteous desire that humanity would glorify Him demanded that He do it.

At some point in the near future, the final analysis of all creation will be made. The great truth that shall stand prominently at the forefront of all things relative to life is that to serve and glorify God is the one and only unfathomable success for humanity.

All things with great value must be tested in order to qualify for service.

Testing is never for the purpose of destroying something, it is for demonstrating compliance with a standard.

Satan and His Hatred for God

Whereas animals largely act upon stimulus/response experiences along with instinct, angels and humans are created with the innate ability to think, choose, and act. That is at least one aspect of what it means to be created in the image of God, as Moses recorded in Genesis 1:27.

In the hierarchy of angelic creation, Satan was at the top of the heap. Isaiah 14 and Ezekiel 28 give us a glimpse of his creation by God and the unimaginable position of glory He gave him. At some point, he chose to allow pride to enter his heart, and he began to believe he was capable of usurping God's throne. Many of the lesser angels became convinced he could successfully do it. At this point, God was forced to dismiss him—to relieve him of command, as it is put within our nation's armed forces— along with the angels who sided with him.

Something significant must be considered at this point. One of the most embarrassing things that can happen to a military commander is to be relieved of command. It is a very humiliating experience, especially if it's due to incompetence or insubordination.

In the eye of your mind, see Satan going through a similar situation, with it all happening before myriad angels. God pronounced the sentence of condemnation upon Satan publicly, and it immediately became obvious to every being in the vastness of heaven that the one who was once so glorious, beautiful, and powerful chose to become braggadocious and had to be brought down in humiliating impotence before God.

The most mortifying thing that could possibly happen to any person consumed with pride is to be openly embarrassed, and Satan was openly embarrassed before all the hosts of heaven. He was suddenly forced to lose his swagger and cockiness.

What was his response? It seems that blinding rage produced a depth of hatred for God that could not be sated until he destroyed everything precious to Him. And most precious to God was man created in His image. Satan's first attack, as seen in Genesis 3, was successful, and he's been unrelenting since that day.

God has shown us that He, and we as His people, will be gloriously victorious in the end, but that day is yet future. Until then, Satan will press the attack using every weapon at his disposal. His hatred is so intense that he will give no quarter, which means he will destroy everyone he can in the process, including those who, in their own rebellion toward God, choose to side with him against God.

Storm Troopers

The title of this chapter includes the phrase "storm troopers." This is very appropriate in describing those aligned with Satan because of the way storm troopers conduct warfare.

However, most civilians misunderstand the meaning of the term by thinking storm troopers rapidly assault or "storm" objectives in an overwhelming mass as in *blitzkrieg*, the WWII German word for "lightning war." This misunderstanding may come as a result of the writings of Heinz Guderian, a general in the German army in WWII who was an early student and advocate of *blitzkrieg* and who thought of himself as the innovator of this tactic. But, actually the term "storm trooper" has nothing to do with *blitzkrieg*.

Thus, a brief description of storm troopers may be necessary for a proper understanding of the term. This will help readers understand more precisely how Satan is able to inflict such great damage upon humanity in seemingly innocuous ways.

Storm troopers are soldiers highly trained in small-unit infiltration tactics. Often, they will clandestinely penetrate a defensive perimeter in their attempt to capture or destroy the enemy's headquarters with its command and control center. These are usually located in the rear area of a military garrison.

Mass destruction of the enemy's major defensives would be accomplished later by artillery and follow-up units. When executed correctly, enemies often don't know they are under serious attack until it's too late to successfully defend themselves.

During the Vietnam War, the communist Viet Cong used such troops, whom we called "sappers." Sappers were mostly unconventional troops that could penetrate perimeters ringed with concertina wire and anti-personnel mines with relative ease. Some communist sappers defected to the southern Republic of Vietnam and would at times put on demonstrations of their capabilities. They were impressive troops.

Because Satan uses his people and their humanist organizations in similar ways, it is accurate to call them storm troopers. Often, they don't openly assault middle-American, conservative Christian values in public venues, but rather worm their way in after penetrating a nation's porous gates of institutionalized religion, academia, economics, and humanistic national socialism. In America, many of these are located predominantly on the nation's coasts.

The balance of this chapter will consider several of Satan's storm-trooper weapons and tactics.

Before this begins, however, we must be clear about two things regarding the people who have enlisted on Satan's side. First, they don't understand to any degree whatsoever the vileness of Satan, the one with whom they have chosen to consort. Second, their deception is self-deception; that is, they believe the lie he offers because they want to believe the lie he offers as seen in Romans 1:18ff. Thus, they have chosen to be duped, and for this they will pay an awful price.

Globalism

Globalism is today defined in various ways, with most definitions having at least something to do with economics, politics, education, and defense treaties. But the original meaning, the one that is near and dear to the heart of Satan, is found in Genesis 11:1–9. There, Moses gives the reason humanity built the tower of Babel, along with God's response to the effort.

The whole earth had the same language and vocabulary. As people migrated from the east, they found a valley in the land of Shinar and settled there. They said to each other, "Come, let us make oven-fired bricks." (They used brick for stone and asphalt for mortar.) And they said, "Come, let us build ourselves a city and a tower with its top in the sky. Let us make a name for ourselves; otherwise, we will be scattered throughout the earth."

Then the LORD came down to look over the city and the tower that the humans were building. The LORD said, "If they have begun to do this as one people all having the same language, then nothing they plan to do will be impossible for them. Come, let's go down there and confuse their language so that they will not understand one another's speech." So from there the LORD scattered them throughout the earth, and they stopped building the city. Therefore it is called Babylon, for there the LORD confused the language of the whole earth, and from there the LORD scattered them throughout the earth. (CSB)

Among the key thoughts in those verses are those having to do with all people having the same language, an emphasis upon the plural pronoun "us," and the people's collective effort to make for themselves a name. The basic idea had less to do with a rejection of belief in God and more to do with a prideful declaration of independence from God.

The ancient and the modern concepts of globalism essentially vary little, but the real issue here is that Satan is attempting to hide from view what is really behind the modern concept. The fact is it has nothing to do with peace, the equal sharing of earth's resources, better education for all, or any other such thing.

In Satan's plan, globalism is the situation wherein he owns and controls the planet, demanding worship from its human inhabitants. To accomplish this would be to fuel his insatiable pride and concurrently destroy the sovereignty and glory of God.

Some in modern Western culture see globalism as a progressive step in the direction of establishing a peaceful world community that is without Christianity's fictional God, whereas Satan sees it as a powerful weapon in his fight against the sovereignty of the God he knows is very real.

Not that this distinction matters to modernists, because most are humanists and atheists anyway. Satan is not trying to disguise the truth from them, because truth doesn't matter to them. It's the Christians and religious Jews who are among his main targets, because they are inclined toward a recognition of providential sovereignty. And to a great degree, he has been successful.

How so? By convincing many people—mostly the entitlement-minded crowd who are mostly socialist and woefully ignorant—that national sovereignty, national borders, and national independence are relics of an antiquated system of intraglobal relationships. Modern, simple-minded philosophers ignorantly see globalism as self-serving to humanity. The way Satan sees it is strictly personal, and he cares nothing about humanity.

God is not a globalist. The scattering of Noah's sons and his billions of descendants was no accident. God intended that the earth would consist of various races, nations, borders, and cultures. That is a manifestation of the beauty and variety associated with His creation, all of which brings glory to the infinite design ability of our Creator. And it demonstrates His unlimited capacity to love all distinctions in His creation.

This was God's command to Adam and Eve in Genesis 1:28 and later to Noah in Genesis 9:1 and 7, because God knew the heart of man. He knew that for the race to be homogenous would be a dangerous situation, because it would lead to mono-nationalistic pride, thus creating a demand for independence from God, the flames of which would be fanned by Satan. This was demonstrated at Babel.

The Georgia Guidestone

Unfortunately, many Christians give little credence to globalism being an aspect of Satan's effort to wrest this earth from the hands of Jesus Christ. But should they devote even a minimal amount of time to the careful consideration of post-WWII events, perhaps the evidence might prompt a change in mind. As an example, one of the greatest indicators of the world being led to a return to Shinar (Genesis 11:2) is the Georgia Guidestone monument located a few miles north of Elberton, Georgia.[201]

Space in this chapter will not be used to give details of this stone monument because it is very easily researched online. However, the ten guidelines themselves will be included in these pages to offer strong motive for further investigation by those who wish to become more aware of Satan's heightened efforts in these last days.

The message on the stones consists of ten guidelines to which the citizens of planet earth should adhere in order to achieve and maintain global stability. They are written in eight languages: English, Spanish, Swahili, Hindi, Hebrew, Arabic, Traditional Chinese, and Russian.

Remember to consider these in context of their purpose, which is globalism.

- Maintain humanity under 500,000,000 in perpetual balance with nature.
- Guide reproduction wisely—improving fitness and diversity.
- Unite humanity with a living new language.
- Rule passion—faith—tradition—and all things with tempered reason.
- Protect people and nations with fair laws and just courts.
- Let all nations rule internally resolving external disputes in a world court.
- Avoid petty laws and useless officials.
- Balance personal rights with social duties
- Prize truth—beauty—love—seeking harmony with the infinite.
- Be not a cancer on the earth—leave room for nature—leave room for nature.

This list is an abomination before God, a total rejection of His providence, and a not-so-subtle attempt at the deification of mankind's god!

Ironically, very soon, God is going to remove His hand of guardianship from this earth, and He will give people exactly what they want. Take a look at Revelation 6 and following to see how that is going to work out for them.

Christians should regularly pause to thank the Lord that we will not be here on earth to experience the horrors that are imminently coming.

The WCC, UN, and ICC as Agents of Globalism

This attempt is being repeated today in the forms of the World Council of Churches (WCC), the United Nations (UN), and the International Criminal Court (ICC).

Many Christians believe that the WCC has become a political operative of the globalist agenda. Quite probably, it always was such. Many Christians specifically believe the WCC is not concerned with the global preaching of the gospel of Jesus, but with the consolidation of global religion for political purposes, including the ability to formulate and control religious thought. If so, this lines up perfectly with the coming religion of Antichrist.

Criticisms of the WCC include its anti-Semitic political opinions and its claim that Christian Zionism distorts biblical truth.[202]

The WCC and its associate, the National Council of Churches, located in the US, seem to be far more concerned with rehabilitating society via liberal social and political reforms than the gospel of Jesus. Their efforts mention the gospel, but that seems to be only window dressing for the spiritually anemic.

The United Nations is another weapon in the globalist agenda, and its path seems to be somewhat parallel to that of the WCC.

Article 1 of the UN Charter states the purpose of the UN is to maintain international peace and security, to develop friendly relations among nations, to achieve international cooperation in solving international problems, and to be a center for harmonizing international actions in the pursuit of these goals.[203]

This is laughable! What war of any significance has the UN ever prevented? When international demagogues want to begin a war, they simply dismiss so-called peace keeping troops before firing the first shot.

When has the UN maintained peace and security or solved a real international problem? Even as this is being written, the World Health Organization, a specialized agency of the UN, has been charged with supporting communist China in its cover-up of the deadly Wuhan COVID-19 coronavirus.

In reality, when has there been any meaningful peace on the earth to keep? The fact is, there will be no peace on this planet until the day Jesus returns the second time as King of kings and Lord of lords.

That the UN is vehemently anti-Israel goes without question. If the Jewish people and their state violently disappeared today, tomorrow there would be a massive global celebration whose epicenter would not be Mecca but New York.

Criticisms of the UN also include lack of value, appeasement of the world's bullies, waste of funds, abuse of power, and others.[204]

The idea that justice is foundational to world peace because it is a deterrent to hate is a cornerstone belief of the ICC.[205] This, however, is naiveté at its best and a sham at its worse. Fear of being successfully prosecuted is seldom a deterrent to criminal activity. Those who study criminal justice at universities are familiar with sixteenth-century England, when pickpockets picked the pockets of those attending the hangings of pickpockets.

The ICC is not concerned about global justice. It is more concerned with prosecuting the enemies of globalism, and the prime target is Israel, whose indictment for war crimes is presently being considered. Though Israel would indeed like to be considered and treated fairly as just another nation in the world of nations within the UN and the ICC, God will not allow this to happen, and Satan knows it.

Christians who are dispensationalists understand these matters, so why should anyone be surprised to know that Satan also knows it? He knows God's plan is to one day make Israel the premier nation on the face of this planet and to make their Messiah—Jesus our Savior—King over all the earth, as He promised Him in the Psalm 2 and Zechariah 14. Satan hates the very thought of this happening, and he is using the anti-God, anti-Church, and anti-Israel WCC, UN, and ICC in his attempt to stop it.

There is no benevolence whatsoever to be found in any reason for the existence of those three organizations. The sole reason for their existence is the propagation of globalism. Satan was behind their charters in the same way he was behind the effort to influence Cyrus to not allow the Jews to return to their homeland as recorded in Daniel 10:13.

Thus, hatred for God, His Word, and His people are the basic building blocks in their collective DNA. Certainly, there are other groups involved, but these are Satan's triad of evil power. They have the character of the three unclean spirits of the frogs described in Revelation 16:12–16, whose demonic responsibility is to gather the world for Armageddon.

Mind Control

Barring a mental or emotional problem—congenital or otherwise—the human mind is a free-will entity. Certainly, it has limitations and predispositions, but that doesn't relieve it of the responsibility of its choices. And this is the reason Satan works through his storm troopers in sundry ways in order to penetrate any barriers and destroy any scruples a person might have regarding sin. He knows if he can do this, then he can influence a person's choices.

The Screwtape Letters by C. S. Lewis is a great resource for understanding how Satan plans and implements mind-control attacks.[206] First published in 1942, it is the fictitious story of how a senior demon mentors a junior and less-experienced demon in the subtleties of spiritual deception. This book should be at the top of any parent's list of mandatory reading for their older middle-school children.

As an example, in Letter 12, the mentor, Screwtape, offers insight to Wormwood, his mentee, regarding a particularly effective tactic in deceiving humans. Screwtape tells his underling, "The safest road to hell is the gradual one—the gentle slope, soft underfoot, without sudden turnings, without milestones, without signposts."

This tactic is presently being seen in what Satan is doing with the government education of children. The classroom is no longer a secure environment where children are given the basic resources needed to make their own way in society and to be responsible citizens in a civilized nation. Instead, students are slowly and subtly brainwashed into becoming social and political automatons according to Satan's template. This is accomplished long before students reach post-secondary education.

Schools of higher education simply reinforce what elementary and high school have done. Early higher education in our country was often private and rooted in the Judeo-Christian worldview. Those great admonishments once taught at many Ivy-League schools are now, however, consigned to the landfills of history, having been replaced with what most modern scholars today refer to as progressive thought.

Some communities have fought back by establishing private schools whose administrations are not controlled by publicly elected school boards whose constituents and policies have no regard for biblical values. Yet, even some of those schools have now fallen in line with secular thinking by teaching that evolution is truth and that abstinence-based social programs, though OK, are prudish in light of twenty-first-century education.

What seems to be the choice of a growing number of parents is home-schooling. At times, it is more educationally effective than government schools and even many private schools, and it allows parents to more easily direct the social experiences of their children. However, for various reasons, this isn't an option or even a choice for some parents.

When considered as a whole, it becomes obvious that government education is an absolute train wreck. Being labeled as a train wreck is a way of saying the political and social tolerance of modern education has not only granted opportunities for evil concepts to be taught, but also for those concepts to be given moral and educational equivalence with biblical concepts.

The reason government schools are in such deplorable shape is found in society's rejection of Proverbs 1:7: "The fear of the Lord is the beginning of knowledge; fools despise wisdom and instruction." As long as the classroom upheld biblical values, Satan was fighting an uphill battle. But, as we can see, all of that has changed drastically since the early 1960s.

Thus, the destruction of the biblical worldview present in government education became one of Satan's top priorities, so he set about removing it with a vengeance. Who are his storm troopers of destruction? There are several.

The US Supreme Court is one such weapon that most think of when discussing the downward spiral of so-called free government education. As a court, it dismissed God, prayer, and the Bible from the government classroom, thus blowing a hole in the defensive perimeter protecting the minds of America's children.

Satan was thrilled and exploited the victory. His minions were quickly used to establish and implement curricula that have more to do with social engineering of the adolescent mind than the education of those same minds. In spiritual warfare, Satan considers agendas to be of far greater importance than reading, math, and science.

But Satan began the attack long before the Supreme Court dismissed God from the classroom. He was fully involved in using spiritual reprobates to manipulate the minds of children almost one hundred years ago. One of his most effective minions was John Dewey, an atheist, a signer of the first Humanist Manifesto in 1933, and a secular humanist whose influence in education was quite radical.[207]

In 1939, Dewey was elected president of the League for Industrial Democracy. This organization had a student branch that later became the Students for a Democratic Society (SDS), and a faction of the SDS became known as the Weathermen, a very violent leftist organization in the late 1960s that many of us remember quite well.[208]

One of the main leaders of this organization was Bill Ayers, an American elementary education theorist. He is a retired professor in the College of Education at the University of Illinois at Chicago and the author of a number of books that promote radicalism in education. He is a domestic terrorist, an admitted communist, and a close personal friend with former US President Barack Obama, whose political career was launched in Ayer's private home, according to Stanley Kurtz, a senior fellow at the Ethics and Public Policy Center.[209]

The destructive educational philosophy of John Dewey is presently influencing teacher-education curricula in most every college and university in this country. Alberto M. Piedra published an article in *Active Measures*, a student-led journal of the Institute of World Politics, entitled "The Tragedy of American Education: The Role of John Dewey."

In this article, Piedra quoted Christopher Dawson regarding Dewey. Dawson said:

> In his [Dewey's] views our purpose for education is not the communication of knowledge but the sharing of social experience, so that the child shall become integrated into the democratic community. He believed that morals were essentially social and pragmatic and that any attempt to subordinate education to transcendent values or dogmas ought to be resisted.[210]

In the official world of government education, what Dewey called for is deemed progressive education; in reality, it is mind control.

The Humanities

There is an official discipline of study that easily lends itself to misuse. It is called the humanities, and it is being exploited by Satan in these last days as never before. As Greenwich Village is an area of New York City commonly known as a breeding ground for bohemian, liberal, radical ideas, so, too, is the humanities discipline known for similar things.

The basic definition of "humanities" is "the study of human culture and society." Among the disciplines in the humanities are philosophy, literature, history, politics, law, art, etc. Those areas of study might be contrasted with the applied sciences such as engineering, business, technology, and health.

Not everyone in the humanities is a liberal, anti-God storm trooper of Satan in the same way that not everyone in the applied sciences is a pro-God bastion of strength and independence. Yet, it can be reasoned that the study of and immersion in the worlds of literature and the fine arts lend themselves more easily to humanism.

For example, there can be no doubt that 6 x 6 = 36 because it is obviously indisputable and, as such, equations like this can be used by engineers to design skyscrapers and complex machines. But there can be a lot of debate among philosophers regarding the existence of God and what He meant when He said that if you sin you will die.

It is precisely for that reason that Satan is able to conscript many of his storm troopers from the disciplines whose devotees spend their lives defending and sustaining the indulgencies of the unstable, biased, and utterly sin-cursed human mind.

The Field of Entertainment

Some of the most talented people we see are those blessed with the ability to entertain others. Entertainers make up a broad base of workers that includes stage and film actors, comedians, singers, dramatists, and script writers among its personnel, along with many others. They are also some of Satan's most effective storm troopers.

Nothing is inherently evil about a person having the ability to entertain, nor is it evil for people to desire to be entertained. It is a part of being human. The danger lies in the often not-so-subtle message that is being proclaimed. When Satan desires to introduce or to magnify a skewed message or a type of twisted behavior, he may choose to do so through entertainers because of their name recognition and the often deep devotion of their fan base.

A prerequisite to being influenced by the distorted message is a spiritually untrained mind, and modern Christian parents are courting danger when they allow their spiritually immature children access to worldly entertainers and their unwholesome messages.

So, who is doing this? The list is large and has no age limitation. From older celebrities like Robert De Niro and Bruce Springsteen to younger ones like Miley Cyrus and Katy Perry, they all have their fan base and influence. Many entertainers of such high profile are proud to support liberal politics, the homosexual agenda, and just about any kind of deviant behavior that can be imagined.

How many of these entertainers would responsible parents trust to influence their child? What stable parents would want the likes of Miley Cyrus having input into the worldview their child is developing? Yet that is happening in an incredible, mind-boggling way every day!

The message being delivered by godless entertainers is the same one Satan gave to Eve so long ago. And what is that message? Not only is what God has said to be questioned then denied, but the really important thing to know is that each person is a god unto himself or herself. In the 1960s, this is what young rebels meant when they said, "If it feels good do it!"

This is done in various and subtle ways. Though Satan dispatches his storm troopers to influence different people in different ways, the bait is most always the same; that is, you can live your life the way you want and there is never any accountability for it.

It is so easy for people of the world—and for Christians who may be spiritually anemic—to become passive players in a movie or a song whereby the theme of the movie or song becomes a part of their thinking. It is in this way that a worldview is formed or strengthened.

People young and old are seeking a means of escape from the realities of life through entertainment, and movies and music are filling that need. Why are people so desperate to seek escape from what they see as reality? Perhaps because they've bought into the lie of evolution and thus believe that this life is all there is to their existence. Their credo is demonstrated by a lifestyle wherein they live as they wish for as long as they live, then they die—and that's it.

Satan is well aware of this need, and he knows what feeds it. It is the narcissism, materialism, and hedonism of 2 Timothy 3:1–5 (CSB):

> But know this: Hard times will come in the last days. For people will be lovers of self, lovers of money, boastful, proud, demeaning, disobedient to parents, ungrateful, unholy unloving, irreconcilable, slanderers, without self-control, brutal, without love for what is good, traitors, reckless, conceited, lovers of pleasure rather than lovers of God, holding to the form of godliness but denying its power. Avoid these people.

Because of this, he does all in his power to prevent people from coming to know that only Jesus offers eternal life, which is the only solution to the pains of earthly life. In His place, Satan offers people escape through an entire host of evil icons of popularity—even if it is merely a temporary fantasy.

Foster Hatred for the Simple Life

One more type of storm trooper will be presented, and that is the elitist. Elitists think of themselves as being superior to other people due to their academic, professional, political, or celebrity status. This kind of thinking may be delusional, but it is often very effective.

The tactic here is for people to believe they are seen as being among the elite because they agree with the thinking of those to whom society as a whole attributes elitism. Those who take strong stands on certain critical issues often do so not because they understand the issue, but because of who is forming the talking points.

As a group, Millennials have absolutely no idea about socialism, but many of them will follow political socialists because of the influence they have over them. That influential person could be a teacher, coach, professor, or friend.

This is the epitome of insanity for at least two reasons. First, what is being propounded is in reality an unattainable pipe dream. Second, what is often most important in the mind of the devoted partisan is the social status of the one who is propounding the deception.

This type of scenario is played out daily in many areas. It can be found in politics, religion, and even in career choices. It can be seen in the choices people make in buying a pair of blue jeans, a pickup truck, or a shotgun. But more importantly, Satan uses this kind of thinking to influence the choice of a lifestyle, and lifestyles reflect attitudes.

One such casualty of elitism is the desire for a simple and often agrarian life. As an example, those who choose to leave the rat race and settle for such a lifestyle are often sneered at. Often known as homesteaders, farmers, and off-gridders, they're thought of as being "ignorant hayseeds" in need of an in-the-loop elitist to tell them what to believe, how to live, and, of course, how to vote. They foolishly cling to things like God, dirt, and guns.

This attitude is to a degree reflected by one Adam Ozimek, an economist at Moody Analytics who published an article entitled, "Dear Homesteaders, Self-Reliance is a Delusion."[211] The premise he makes in the very first paragraph—that homesteaders are not self-reliant but rather mooch off society—is simply wrong at best and plainly deceptive at worst.

These people are quite often Christians who don't actually want to isolate themselves from society, because they know that, as Christians, they are to be salt and light in a dark and corrupt world. They simply wish to live as independently as possible, live close to the earth, live godly lives, and raise their children in a safe and wholesome environment.

So, out of all the areas available as targets, why would Satan even choose to fight this one—especially with any particular vigor, since there are far fewer people living the agrarian life today? Satan hates this group of people because they're not as easily influenced by the weapons that are so effective against the more urban and suburban crowd. Such people are generally smart, successful in their own way of life, and independent—and they know how to use technology without being addicted to it and thus are not controlled by it. Satan hates the inability to fully control people.

Of the two million farms in American today, 98 percent are operated by families. The average age for 25 percent of farmers who have been in business for less than ten years is forty-six.[212] This in itself is a reason for Satan to go after this group; they are young, productive, and raising young children.

God intended that the family should be the basic building unit of society, and just about all farms consist of this basic, vitally important, God-ordained aspect of a stable society. And if there is one thing Satan does not wish to see thrive, it's the family.

Even a cursory glance at homesteader websites shows that many are Christians. They don't hide that fact. Further, this becomes obvious as the parent/child relationship is observed in day-to-day life. Children are taught the Bible from an early age, with a strong emphasis upon becoming responsible, independent people.

From this an old adage comes through so clearly: the closer a family is to the earth, the closer that family is more likely to be to God. This is another thing Satan doesn't wish to see: a family close to God with parents who are raising their children to become the same way.

Who is Satan using to bring reproach upon these families? Elitists like Michael Bloomberg, who said he could teach anybody to be a farmer by showing them how to dig a hole, put in a seed, cover it with dirt, and add water. This simple process that anybody can do will, according to Bloomberg, produce a crop.

The fact that Bloomberg and those like him are fools is not worth mentioning. What is worth stating, though, is that this kind of ridicule will form derogatory mental images in the minds of ignorant people regarding those godly families. Satan understands that this will ensure public support for any government attempt to control the lives of such people.

This negative image is just one more thing close-knit, godly families must deal with. It makes their service to God and the training of their children more difficult, which is exactly what Satan is wanting: Deny God! Destroy every vestige of His influence in the family unit, especially among those hayseed hicks in rural America!

Conclusion

Satan knows his time is short. This prompts him to be unrelenting in his efforts to subtly enter and destroy those things important to God. He is vicious and tireless, giving no quarter to anyone. He is cunning and without equal among mortals.

Satan does not restrict himself to a one-size-fits-all kind of attack. He knows the human will and is expert in devising schemes tailor made for each target. Though he uses demonic forces today just as he did in the days of Daniel, he also continues to use human storm troopers to destroy people as he did in the days of Mordecai and Esther.

Perhaps some Christians are spiritually savvy enough to readily identify Satan's minions as they worm their way into their worldview. But evidence based upon years of personal interaction with Christians indicates that number might not be too high.

Unfortunately, many believers are enamored with materialism and have shoved spiritual matters into the "also-ran" category. That is, they don't outright reject the spiritual realm and its responsibilities, but Satan's storm troopers have convinced them that they don't have the time to devote to matters that have little to do with what he convinces them is real life. These people have been deceived and are *de facto* comfortable in the deception.

None of us is omniscient about these matters, and that means we should not ignore opportunities to become more aware of the character of those influencing society and even the church. Perhaps in addition to congregations teaching special classes on apologetics, other courses should be presented on the who, what, when, where, how, and why of Satan's influence and inspiration. Anyone would benefit from such an effort.

Now more than ever, Christians should be aware of those flaunting their talent, appearance, professional credentials, political connections, and other attributes they commonly use to appeal to the masses. Further, they should be aware of those who just happen to show up in their lives with great compassion and humility and with the old refrain, "I not only feel your pain, but I have an idea."

Compassion and humility are godly characteristics a lot of people like to see in their friends and even in their communal leadership, but it must be remembered that Satan is the world's best expert in subterfuge; in his schemes, nothing ever "just happens." In all such instances, his tantalizing bait inherently conceals sharp hooks.

So, how are we to identify Satan's storm troopers? The simple way is the best way: Evaluate them by God's Word. If they don't fit, they're not of God. This has nothing to do with legalism, but everything to do with testing the spirits of those who wish to have influence in a Christian's life.

TWELVE

Pontiff Proclaims All Go to Heaven

By Mike Gendron

In one of the most surprising elections in modern history, Jorge Mario Bergoglio became Pope Francis on March 13, 2013. According to the Vatican, he was named the 266th pope of the Roman Catholic Church. Francis has become the first non-European pope and the first from the Americas. He is also the first Jesuit to be named pope since the Jesuits were formed in the sixteenth century. This is significant because the Jesuits played a leading role in the Counter-Reformation and won back many European Catholics who had been lost to Protestantism. The goal of the Jesuits has been to eliminate any opposition to Roman Catholicism and to establish a kingdom for the papacy. During their history, they have ordered millions of "heretics" and Protestants murdered because they stood in opposition to the pope. Now, their new strategy to unite the world is through seduction. The first Jesuit pope has been calling "separated brethren" (Protestants) back home to Rome for the "fullness of salvation" (partaking of the Eucharist).

Since his inauguration, Pope Francis has become the most controversial pope in the last three hundred years. Prior to his election as pope,

Bergoglio served as archbishop of Buenos Aires from 1998 to 2013. He was named "Person of the Year" by *Time* magazine in 2013 because of his outspoken support of the world's poor and marginalized people. As pope, he rules over 1.3 billion Roman Catholics who have been indoctrinated to believe that any man who wears the papal crown is infallible, godly, and holy, without question. As Christians who are fighting the end-times war against the spirit of Antichrist, we need to warn people that Pope Francis is the most influential and deceptive false teacher in the world; he is leading multitudes down the wide road to destruction.

The Formation of a One-World Religion

Pope Francis has made it abundantly clear that ecumenical unity is the top priority of his papacy. One of the deceptive strategies he is using to unite the world in a global church is to declare that all religions and faiths lead to the same God. Francis has proclaimed that "Allah" and the God of the Catholic Church are one and the same. He said, "I greet and cordially thank you all, dear friends belonging to other religious traditions; first of all the Muslims, who worship the one God, living and merciful, and call upon Him in prayer" (Vatican City speech, March 20, 2013). Even before his inaugural address, Francis had a private meeting with Ecumenical Patriarch Bartholomew from Istanbul, who later attended his inaugural mass. It was the first time the spiritual head of Orthodox Christians had attended a Roman pope's inaugural mass since the Great Schism between the Western and Eastern Churches in AD 1054. Francis also held a private session with Metropolitan Hilarion, the foreign minister of the Russian Orthodox Church, the largest in the Orthodox world. He has an aggressive agenda to gather the world into the one religion of the New World Order. The pope is drawing the major religions of Islam, Orthodox Christianity, Protestant Christianity, Judaism, and even atheists, to the papal Church. We know from the book of Revelation that one day, in the name of "peace," a False Messiah will establish one religion that will harmonize the differences between all the existing religions.

The Pope's Global Influence

The papacy is viewed by Catholics as the spiritual bridge-builder between God and man. Therefore, it should come as no surprise that Pope Francis is attempting to rebuild the religious tower of Babel that is described in Genesis 11:4: "Come, let us build for ourselves a city, and a tower whose top will reach into heaven, and let us make for ourselves a name, otherwise we will be scattered abroad over the face of the whole earth." He will stop at nothing to see this happen in his lifetime.

The papacy is said to be the visible head and the highest priest of the Church. Roman Emperor Constantine first wore the title "Pontifex Maximus," because he considered himself the highest priest of the Christian Church. Soon after the empire imploded, popes began wearing the title, which is why Pope Francis uses the Twitter handle: "@pontifex." As the Bishop of Rome, he begins many of his questionable statements with the pronoun "I," which purposefully puts himself and his agenda as the first priority. When he speaks, he rarely mentions the Lord Jesus Christ, who always has been and always will be the one and only true Head of the Church, which He purchased with His own blood. Like the "father of lies," Pope Francis speaks out of his own character, for he is a liar and deceives the world.

Many of the pope's deceptive and fallacious statements have not only opposed the supreme authority of God's Word, but have also contradicted the "infallible" dogmas of historic Roman Catholicism. Tragically, his fatal lies often go unabated and are leading millions of people down the wide road to destruction (Matthew 7:13). In spite of his errant teachings, Pope Francis is loved by many because of his "humility" portrayed by his foot-washings and self-described humble lifestyle. But is he really humble when he usurps the honor and authority of the Lord Jesus by stealing His title as Head of the Church? He also claims to be the Holy Father with supreme and unhindered authority over all people. He condemns those who do not submit to his "infallible" dogmas. He has also usurped the title "Vicar of Christ" from the Holy Spirit whom the Father sent when Jesus ascended into heaven (John 14:26).

Pope Francis has also seduced a large percentage of Protestant pastors into believing he is their brother in Christ. LifeWay Research asked one thousand Protestant pastors in America about their views of the pope shortly before his visit to the United States in September, 2015. Sixty-three percent said they believe Francis is a genuine Christian, while 16 percent are unsure. Clearly, there is a lack of discernment among Protestant pastors. Those who were surveyed either do not know the exclusivity of the gospel of grace or do not know the false and fatal gospel of Rome. Their lack of discernment makes them prone to be further deceived by this man and his aberrant theology.

Evangelist Luis Palau was one of the first evangelicals to praise Pope Francis. Shortly after his inauguration, Palau said that Pope Francis is "a very Bible-centered and Jesus Christ-centered man; he's really centered on the Gospel, the pure Gospel. He is a friend of evangelicals." Rick Warren, the pastor of one of the largest churches in America, calls Pope Francis "our pope."

These stunning endorsements of Pope Francis are the tragic results of unity accords that have been signed by highly visible evangelical leaders over the last twenty-five years. The first unity accord was "Evangelicals and Catholics Together: The Christian Mission in the Third Millennium" in 1994. The most recent accord was the "Manhattan Declaration" that has now been endorsed by more than six hundred thousand evangelicals. Those who have embraced the false teachers of apostate Christianity without challenging their errors need to know that they are leaving their own convictions and beliefs open to question. They need to know that those who unite with false teachers are giving credibility to their heresies. In the end, we will all be held accountable to God for the souls that are misled by our unwillingness to contend earnestly for the faith. As a result of the compromise among evangelical leaders, most people in the pew do not know if the Roman Catholic Church represents a huge mission field that needs to be evangelized or a Christian denomination made up of brothers and sisters in Christ.

With all the warnings about false teachers in the Bible, it is troubling to see a great number of professing Christians being so easily deceived by this man. We know that doctrinal error always originates with Satan. He uses his false apostles to deceive the masses:

> For such men are false apostles, deceitful workers, disguising themselves as apostles of Christ. No wonder, for even Satan disguises himself as an angel of light. (2 Corinthians 11:13–14)

Like a deadly, undetected cancer, his errors can spread quickly unless they are exposed and reproved. Historically, every heresy has originated with a slight departure from the truth. Every small seed of error ends up producing a large tree of heresy. By far the deadliest errors are Satan's counterfeit plans of salvation. They all appeal to the flesh of the natural man. "There is a way which seems right to a man, but its end is the way of death" (Proverbs 14:12). It is for this critical reason that we must exhort people to test every man's teaching and to test every spirit (Acts 17:11; 1 John 4:1).

Pope Francis Is a Universalist

Many of the pope's statements have portrayed him as a universalist who ignores or rejects the clear teaching of God's Word and the exclusivity of His gospel. Universal salvation is the belief that God will eventually reconcile Himself with every immortal soul and everyone will be saved. The thought of people living in eternal torment in hell causes some to reject the infallible teaching of Scripture concerning hell. They would rather cling to God's love and compassion while ignoring or dismissing His righteousness and justice. Universalists fail to see that God's amazing love was demonstrated at the cross when He sent His Only Son to save His people from the divine punishment for sin (Romans 5:8). God's attributes of love and mercy for sinners came together in perfect harmony with His attributes of righteousness and justice at Calvary.

The doctrine of universal salvation has a long history, but it has always been a minority view because it clearly contradicts the teaching of Scripture. The Bible is clear that unbelievers will dwell in hell forever. The Lord Jesus said, "Then they [the unsaved] will go away to eternal punishment, but the righteous to eternal life" (Matthew 25:46). The apostle Paul wrote that the "Lord Jesus will be revealed from heaven with His mighty angels in flaming fire, dealing out retribution to those who do not know God and to those who do not obey the gospel of our Lord Jesus. These will pay the penalty of eternal destruction, away from the presence of the Lord and from the glory of His power" (2 Thessalonians 7–9).

In spite of the clear teaching of Christ and His Word, Pope Francis believes that it is God's will to save all people. During a message in St. Peter's Square, he said, God "wants His children to overcome all particularism in order to be open to the universality of salvation." He declared:

This is the aim: to overcome particularism and open oneself to the universality of salvation, because God wants to save everyone. Those who are reborn by water and the Spirit—the baptized— are called to come out of themselves and open themselves up to others, to live close together, in the style of living together, which transforms every interpersonal relationship into an experience of fraternity. (Catholic News Agency, November 15, 2019)

Years earlier, Pope Francis declared:

The Lord has redeemed all of us, all of us, with the Blood of Christ: all of us, not just Catholics. Everyone...even the atheists. Everyone! The Blood of Christ has redeemed us all! (Religion News Service, May 22, 2013)

The pope's belief that everyone will eventually be saved is not only opposed to the very words of Christ but also to the exclusivity of His gospel. Jesus declared: "I am the way, and the truth, and the life; no one comes to the Father but through Me" (John 14:6). The Lord Jesus also made it clear that very few will enter heaven, and the greater majority will end up in a place of destruction. He said we must "enter through the narrow gate; for the gate is wide and the way is broad that leads to destruction, and there are many who enter through it. For the gate is small and the way is narrow that leads to life, and there are few who find it" (Matthew. 7:13–14). Although the eternal destinies of these two paths are dramatically different, both paths ultimately lead to Christ. For all believers who traveled the narrow path, they will meet Jesus as their merciful Savior. For unbelievers on the wide road, they will meet Jesus as a sin-avenging Judge.

Jesus gives a warning for us to heed in the next verse: "Beware of the false prophets, who come to you in sheep's clothing, but inwardly are ravenous wolves" (Matthew 7:15). Who are we to believe—Christ and His Word or the lies of false prophets? Will we believe that only a few will follow Jesus into heaven or will we believe Pope Francis, who declares all will enter heaven? True Christianity does not leave room for anyone else's view of salvation. Christ is the only Way to salvation. There are no other ways. We must enter the narrow gate by an act of faith and an act of the will. We have to enter on God's terms through His prescribed gate, and Christ is that gate (John 10:9).

The Lord Jesus also shared how difficult it is for a rich man to enter the kingdom of God. The apostles were astonished and asked, "Who then can be saved?" Jesus said to them, "With people this is impossible, but with God all things are possible" (Matthew 19:23–26). In other words, the natural man cannot enter heaven without being born again through the supernatural work of the Holy Spirit (John 3:3; Ephesians 2:4–5).

The apostle Peter also gave no hope for atheists and unbelievers because of the exclusivity of Christ. He clearly proclaimed in front of a group of unbelievers: "There is salvation in no one else; for there is no other name under heaven that has been given among men by which we must be saved" (Acts 4:12). The Lord Jesus Christ is the one and only Way to be saved, and to deny that infallible truth is to deny Jesus Christ and disavow His gospel. The pope needs to know that atheists who deny God's existence and all unbelievers will be cast into hell. The Gospel of John affirms this: "He who believes in the Son has eternal life; but he who does not obey the Son will not see life, but the wrath of God abides on him" (John 3:36).

The apostle Paul also made it clear that not everyone will enter heaven. He said:

> Do you not know that the unrighteous will not inherit the kingdom of God? Do not be deceived; neither fornicators, nor idolaters, nor adulterers, nor effeminate, nor homosexuals, nor thieves, nor the covetous, nor drunkards, nor revilers, nor swindlers, will inherit the kingdom of God. (1 Corinthians 6:9–10)

If Pope Francis had believed this truth from God's infallible, authoritative Word, he would have called his homosexual priests to repentance instead of what he said. Responding to an interviewer's question in July 2013 about gay priests, the pope answered, "Who am I to judge a gay person of goodwill who seeks the Lord?" Later, in a September 2013 interview with *America* magazine, the pope was quoted as saying:

> A person once asked me, in a provocative manner, if I approved of homosexuality. I replied with another question: "Tell me: when God looks at a gay person, does he endorse the existence of this person with love, or reject and condemn this person?" We must always consider the person.

The pope's unwillingness to call sin a sin has made him more popular and loved by more people. He was named person of the year by *The Advocate*, America's #1 gay magazine. Instead of seeking the approval of God, the pope continues to seek the approval of men. Clearly, it is not love when anyone withholds the truth of God's Word that calls for sinners, including homosexuals, to repent from their sin and seek divine forgiveness.

The pope's view of universal salvation also opposes historic Roman Catholicism. According to the Catechism of the Catholic Church, which is the statement of the Church's faith and doctrine, paragraph 846 states:

Basing itself on Scripture and Tradition, the Council teaches that the Church, a pilgrim now on earth, is necessary for salvation: the one Christ is the mediator and the way of salvation; he is present to us in his body which is the Church. He himself explicitly asserted the necessity of faith and Baptism, and thereby affirmed at the same time the necessity of the Church which men enter through Baptism as through a door. Hence they could not be saved who, knowing that the Catholic Church was founded as necessary by God through Christ, would refuse either to enter it or to remain in it.

Responding to a list of questions published in the *La Repubblica* newspaper in September, 2013, Pope Francis wrote:

You ask me if the God of the Christians forgives those who don't believe and who don't seek the faith. I start by saying...that God's mercy has no limits if you go to him with a sincere and contrite heart. The issue for those who do not believe in God is to obey their conscience.

Yet, the apostle Paul wrote, "to those who are defiled and unbelieving, nothing is pure, but both their mind and their conscience are defiled" (Titus 1:15). So, the pope is saying you can be saved apart from Christ as long as you are sincere in your unbelief and obey your defiled conscience.

Most unbelievers embrace the pope's position on universal salvation for everyone because of a variety of reasons. "Wanting to have their ears tickled, they will accumulate for themselves teachers in accordance to their own desires" (2 Timothy 4:3). They embrace the herd mentality because they think there is strength in numbers. It is easier to follow the crowd than to search for the truth (Matthew 7:13). They are children of Satan and don't know they are deceived because they cannot hear the truth (John 8:43–44). "There is a way that seems right to a man, but its end is the way to death" (Proverbs 14:12). They face very little opposition because they are walking with the god of this world (2 Corinthians 4:4).

The pope rarely speaks the truth from the authority of Scripture. The supernatural blindness that keeps him in spiritual darkness is beyond comprehension. Historically, we have seen that religious indoctrination is one of the most powerful tools the devil uses to blind people from the light of the gospel and the glory of Christ (2 Corinthians 4:4). Tragically, those who do not know the Bible are being deceived by the pope's affirmation that many seek God in different ways. The pope's assertion is completely false, according to God's Word. No one seeks God (Romans 3:11). There are many who seek after false gods of their own imagination or religious traditions; however, no one seeks after the True God. The only access to the True God is to come His way, through His One Mediator, the Man Christ Jesus (1 Timothy 2:5). He is God's perfect Man and man's perfect God, and the only One qualified to reconcile sinners to God.

Pope Francis: "Everyone Is a Child of God"

The pope foolishly attempts to justify his view on universal salvation by declaring everyone is a child of God. In a video message to Myanmar on November 17, 2017, he said, "All of us are God's children." Yet the Bible reveals that some children have the devil as their father. The Lord Jesus made this clear to the apostate religious leaders of His day. He said, "You are of your father the devil, and your will is to do your father's desires" (John 8:44). The apostle John wrote: "It is evident who are the children of God, and who are the children of the devil: whoever does not practice righteousness is not of God, nor is the one who does not love his brother" (1 John 3:10).

We know from Scripture that all unbelievers are children of devil until they born of God (John 1:12–13). "Whoever believes that Jesus is the Christ is born of God, and whoever loves the Father loves the child born of Him. Satan does not want any of his children to be adopted into God's family so he has created a variety of religions to blind his children from the light of the Gospel and the glory of Christ" (2 Corinthians 4:4). It appears that the pope has much in common with the father of lies. Like Satan, he does not stand in the truth, because there is no truth in him. When he lies, he speaks out of his own character, for he is a liar and deceives the world.

Pope Francis' Devotion to Mary as a Universalist

The Jesuit pope is now encouraging his followers to pray to Mary of Fatima, who is also a universalist. In one of the many messages given by an "apparition of Mary" at Fatima, the apparition said:

> You saw hell where the souls of poor sinners go. In order to save them, God wishes to establish devotion to my Immaculate Heart in the world. If people do what I ask, many souls will be saved and there will be peace. Only I can help you. My Immaculate Heart will be your refuge and the way that will lead you to God. In the end, My Immaculate Heart will triumph.

It is because of these lying signs and wonders that we are exhorted to test every spirit (1 John 4:1). We have been warned that "Satan himself masquerades as an angel of light" (2 Corinthians 11:14).

Years ago, I was interviewed by the History Channel, which was producing a documentary on the apparitions of Mary throughout the world. They thought the following statement I made was profound enough to use it in the opening segment. I said, "People travel thousands of miles and spend thousands of dollars to seek messages from apparitions when they can open their Bible right where they are and get a message from God."

We know from Scripture that Satan will use lying signs and wonders to deceive the world. The Lord Jesus warned us: "For false christs and false prophets will arise and perform signs and wonders, to lead astray, if possible, the elect" (Mark 13:22). The apostle Paul warned us: "The coming of the lawless one is by the activity of Satan with all power and false signs and wonders" (2 Thessalonians 2:9). Perhaps the many apparitions of Mary are part of the satanic lying signs and wonders that are deceiving the world. Reported sightings of Mary have steadily increased across the globe. People of all religions are flocking to apparition sites with reported healings and other supernatural happenings. Many of the apparitions of Mary make it clear she has come for *all* her children, including Muslims, Catholics, and Protestants. Her messages declare that people of all religions can be saved apart from Jesus Christ as long as they live good lives. An average of five million people each year are flocking to apparition sites. In Fatima, Portugal, millions of people come from all the religions of the world to pray to "the queen of heaven," and "our lady of peace." At one of the gatherings, a Jesuit priest stated:

> The religion of the future will be a general converging of religions in a universal Christ that will satisfy all. The other religions in the world are part of God's plan for humanity. God's kingdom permits this, and it is nothing more than a diversified sharing in the same mystery of salvation.

Pope Francis Denies Existence of Hell

Not only has Pope Francis said that everyone will eventually be in heaven, but he has also pronounced there is no hell. The pope's heresy about hell is so foolish that the world should identify him for whom he has shown himself to be: a deceitful workman, disguising himself as an apostle of Christ (2 Corinthians 11:13). His statement, "There is no hell where sinners suffer in eternity," is totally fallacious. He added to his deceitfulness by saying: "After death, those who do not repent cannot be pardoned, and they disappear." Then he declared, "Hell does not exist but what does exist is the disappearance of sinful souls."

His view on hell not only opposes biblical teachings but also the teachings of his Church. The Catechism of the Catholic Church, paragraph 1035, states:

The teaching of the Church affirms the existence of hell and its eternity. Immediately after death the souls of those who die in a state of mortal sin descend into hell, where they suffer the punishments of hell, "eternal fire." The chief punishment of hell is eternal separation from God, in whom alone man can possess the life and happiness for which he was created and for which he longs.

In his denial of the existence of hell, Pope Francis is demonstrating the spirit of Antichrist because the Lord Jesus Christ spoke of hell more than thirty times in the New Testament. The pope is calling Jesus, who is the personification of truth, an outright liar (John 14:6). The Savior spoke about hell more than He did about heaven. Jesus warned us, "It is better for you to enter the kingdom of God with one eye, than, having two eyes, to be cast into hell" (Mark 9:47). He also warned, "Don't fear those who kill the body, rather fear Him who is able to destroy both soul and body in hell" (Matthew 10:28). Can the pope explain how is this possible if hell does not exist and unrepentant sinners cease to exist? The world needs to realize that the pope is not the "Vicar of Christ," but a "Pawn of Satan."

By denying the existence of hell, Pope Francis is rejecting a very important part of Christ's creation. Hell was created by Jesus for the devil and his angels and for all those who are accursed (Matthew 25:41). According to God's Word, the pope is one of the accursed because he is preaching a false and fatal gospel. The apostle Paul declared that anyone who twists and distorts the gospel is accursed (Galatians 1:6–9).

It would be wise for Francis to read the epistles of Peter, whom Catholics mistakenly refer to as their first pope. Peter penned these infallible, divinely inspired words: "God did not spare angels when they sinned, but cast them into hell and committed them to pits of darkness, reserved for judgment" (2 Peter 2:4).

Like a deadly, undetected cancer, the pope's lies spread quickly unless they are exposed and refuted by the supreme authority of God's Word. The pope and those who are deceived by him need to know that hell is a real place. The Bible describes it as a place of torment where unbelievers consciously suffer pain and unquenchable thirst from a burning fire. The horror and hopelessness is so great that they want to warn their loved ones who are still alive. The punishment for their sins is irreversible; there is no second chance and no escape (Luke 16:19–31).

This is why God the Father sent His only begotten Son to be the Savior for sinners condemned to hell. The Lord Jesus died as a substitute for those who repent and believe His gospel (Isaiah 53:3–11). He endured the wrath of a sin-avenging God so that He could satisfy divine justice and offer forgiveness for those who trust Him alone for their salvation. Catholics must turn from trusting a pope who has proven to be a false prophet and put their complete trust in the One who purchased the Church with His own blood (Acts 20:28).

The Numerous Heresies of Pope Francis

Pope Francis has consistently taught numerous heresies and ungodly doctrines from his papal throne. Since many of his heresies are directly opposed to the teachings of Jesus Christ, he is clearly speaking with the spirit of Antichrist. In November 2019, the Italian journalist Eugenio Scalfari quoted Pope Francis as denying the bodily resurrection of Jesus by stating that the crucified Christ emerged from the tomb as a spirit rather than as a body. According to Scalfari, Pope Francis said:

> He [Jesus] was a man until he was put in the sepulcher by the women who restored his corpse. That night in the sepulcher the man disappeared and from that cave came out in the form of a spirit that met the women and the Apostles, still preserving the shadow of the person, and then definitively disappeared.

These claims about the pope's heretical beliefs are so shocking that you would think the pope would offer an explanation or a rebuttal, yet he has remained silent. Clearly, he has proven to be one of the most egregious false prophets of all the popes throughout history.

In June 2015, Pope Francis attributed the work of Jesus Christ to Satan when he declared that the "division [among evangelicals and Catholics] is the work of the Father of Lies who does everything possible to keep us divided." Once again, he blasphemed the Lord Jesus Christ by opposing and denigrating His infallible Word. The Lord Jesus is the One who divides believers from unbelievers by the truth of His Word (Luke 12:51–53). Jesus said, "Do you think that I have come to give peace on earth? No, I tell you, but rather division." He said households will be divided, "father against son, mother against daughter." It is the gospel of Christ that divides believers from unbelievers and true Christians from false ones. Born-again Christians and Catholics will always be divided on the essentials of the gospel, how one is born again, how one is justified, how one is purified of sin, who mediates between God and man, and the efficacy, sufficiency, and necessity of Jesus Christ. It is far better to be separated by divine truth than united in satanic error.

The pope also pointed people to the wrong door for the remission of sin's punishment. On December 24, 1999, Pope Francis opened the Holy Door in St. Peter's Basilica to offer plenary indulgences for the remission of the punishment for sins. He said those who passed through the door would receive the indulgence. This was the first time the "Holy Door" had been opened in sixteen years. Its opening was meant to be symbolic of its "extraordinary path" toward salvation. Clearly, the pope is a master deceiver who points gullible people to a wooden door made with human hands instead of to the eternal Christ who is the only door by which sinners must enter to be saved. Jesus is the only door of salvation. He said:

> I am the door. If anyone enters by me, he will be saved and will go in and out and find pasture. The thief comes only to steal and kill and destroy.... I am the good shepherd. The good shepherd lays down his life for the sheep. (John 10:9–11)

The One-World Religion of Globalism

We know from the study of Bible prophecy that there will be a False Prophet and a world ruler who will usher in a time of "peace and prosperity" on the earth. If we are in the season of our Lord's return, we must consider the office of the papacy to be the False Prophet because of his global influence and so-called charisma of infallibility. According to Scripture, a one-world religion will promise peace throughout the world and prepare the way for the False Prophet and the Antichrist of Revelation chapters 13 and 17.

Pope Francis has been successfully executing the Vatican's well-defined strategy to create a one-world *religion.* Now, he is using his global influence and power to help establish a one-world *government* for Antichrist. The apostle John describes the ruler of this vast empire as having great power and authority given to him by Satan (Revelation 13:2). He will receive worship from "all the world" and have authority over "every tribe, people, language and nation" (13:3–7).

During a speech on May 8, 2019, at the Pontifical Academy of Social Sciences, Pope Francis demanded that a new "supranational, legal constituted body" enforce climate-change policies and other worldwide "threats." He advocated a policy of decreased national sovereignty and increased global unity, claiming that planetary problems are exacerbated by "an excessive demand for sovereignty on the part of States." The pope is trying to convince the world that our only hope for peace, prosperity, and planetary salvation is to surrender our national sovereignty. Rather than calling for the outright abolition of nation states, the pope insisted that they all be subjected to external, global governing authorities. He went on to deride nations that have border walls. We must wonder if he has forgotten that the Vatican, which is a sovereign nation, is surrounded by an enormous wall. The pope said that if we hope to save the planet, we must accept that we are one people and seek unity for dialogue in a spirit of mutual respect.

In a renewed and enthusiastic endorsement of globalism, Pope Francis has announced he is hosting an initiative for a "Global Pact" to create a "new humanism." The global event is set to take place at the Vatican in 2020. The pope is inviting representatives of the main religions, international organizations, and various humanitarian institutions, as well as key figures from the world of politics, economics, and academia, and prominent athletes, scientists, and sociologists to sign a "Global Pact on Education" so as to "hand on to younger generations a united and fraternal common home."

Conclusion and Exhortations

As professing Christians who are fighting the end-times war against the spirit of Antichrist, we need to examine our faith through the lens of Scripture to ensure that we have true, saving faith (2 Corinthians 13:5). Scripture must be our supreme authority for knowing truth and exposing the lies and heresies of false teachers. Any teaching that opposes the Word of God must be rejected. Our theology must be built on the inspired, inerrant Word of God that is forever settled in heaven.

The pope and all who follow him need to know what awaits them if they continue rejecting the Word of Christ. Jesus said, "He who rejects Me and does not receive My sayings, has one who judges him; the word I spoke is what will judge him at the last day" (John 12:48). No one can trust both Christ and the pope, because Pope Francis has demonstrated the spirit of Antichrist by opposing and rejecting many of Christ's teachings. Catholics need to repent and trust the only true Head of the Church—the Lord Jesus Christ. Christians need to recognize the Roman Catholic religion is a huge mission field and make our Lord's last command our first concern. The only hope for those who are perishing is to hear and believe the gospel of grace.

All Christians must also take Jude's exhortation seriously. He wrote: "I found it necessary to write appealing to you to contend for the faith that was once for all delivered to the saints." The exhortation, "to contend for the faith," is a present-tense imperative that means it is an ongoing command for all believers. The same faith that was signed, sealed, and delivered in the first century is what we must now defend. The Greek word for "contend" means to "agonize" in a strenuous, ongoing struggle, to fight passionately, and to strive vigorously against the opposition. This is what we must do if we are to be effective in defending the Christian faith.

There are many adversaries who outnumber us and who continue to wage war with weapons of deceit. We must resist them by the power of the Holy Spirit. There is much at stake if we don't: the glory and honor of our great God and Savior, the purity of His gospel, and the sanctity of His Church.

THIRTEEN

Evangelicals Embrace Inclusiveness

By Thomas J. Hughes

We know that we are of God, and the whole world lies under the sway of the wicked one. (1 John 5:19)[213]

Do not be conformed to this world, but be transformed by the renewing of your mind. (Romans 12:2)

As I write this chapter, I glance at the calendar—end of May 2020. You probably remember what it was like. The world seems to have been upended. The news is a stream of pestilence and rumors of pestilence, blame and rumors of blame. Riots, recriminations, and lawlessness are splitting America and the world into pieces. People struggle to understand who's right and who's wrong, what's real and what's not.

A time of darkness has fallen across the planet. War threatens from many directions. Every day, natural disasters seem to increase in frequency and intensity. Many who have never opened a Bible wonder if these are the days that will lead to Armageddon. After all, they've seen the movies and heard the stories. They wonder if this is it.

Science and politics can't answer. Media outlets and pundits contradict each other, and even themselves, as they try to explain or give their spin. Yesterday's certainty becomes today's question and tomorrow's joke.

So, what do people do? Many of them look where generations of their forebears looked—to the church. But if they haven't looked at church recently, the thing they see first stuns, then repulses them. They stare. They study. And their anxiety grows.

What could have such an effect? A mirror.

A look at today's church seems to be a carefully staged reflection of the world system so often warned against in Scripture.[214] First John 2:15 says, "Do not love the world or the things in the world."

But when the worldling stares at a typical evangelical church, she sees the world and she sees herself. This happened by design. It was supposed to make her feel more comfortable and more welcome. But it doesn't have that effect. The church—the holy institution set aside by God as sacred in the midst of a wicked, fallen world—has been camouflaged. Now it looks like every other human institution. It has the same outlook, the same goals, and accepts the same doctrines.

It's another club, another social network, an NGO (nongovernmental organization), a place to party, and a league of voters. It's a place for personal virtue-signaling, a place to fight for social justice, and where you can get help with issues of self-esteem. The seeker may like parties, social justice, self-esteem, and politics. But she can get those things anywhere—and without the creepiness factor of church.

She may not even understand why the modern church should seem creepy. It mirrors her, but so do other human institutions. Yet this one leaves her shaken and despondent. Perhaps the seeker will eventually realize the problem—that *few things are as eerie as an empty church at night*.

For the seeker, it's almost unbearably horrible. In the past, she has laughed at the church. She has shaken her head and rolled her eyes at what she imagined as a place of endless rules. But deep down, she held a hope that if things got bad, if the world grew dark, she might find sanctuary there. Maybe the people inside the building would be as beautiful as their façade. If it came down to it, maybe they really would have the Answer.

But no. The church and the seeker look just alike—equally empty, equally devoid of answers. Today's churches look like other human institutions because that's what they have become—human institutions. They're eerie in the dark times—at night—because they have no light within.

How did this catastrophe happen?

Language Games

A generation ago, television hosts like Phil Donohue brought evangelical Christians onto their programs—primarily to argue with. And it made good television. They talked about abortion, about whether Jews could reject Christ and still go to heaven,[215] and dozens of other controversial, but important, things.

That was a long time ago—practically ancient history. But a generation of future ministers was watching. And they asked themselves, "What would I say? If someone asked me that question, how would I answer?"

It's a valid consideration. First Peter 3:15 tells us to "always be ready to give a defense to everyone who asks you a reason for the hope that is in you." Followers of Jesus must find ways to communicate with the people of the times in which they live. It's something like a missionary learning the language of the people to whom he is carrying the gospel. Finding ways to communicate clearly is an expression of God's love through us.

But there is danger in adopting another language.

Better than almost anyone else, George Orwell understood the connection between language and thought. In his most famous novel, *1984*, the government of "Big Brother" includes a group called "thought police." At first that sounds impossible. How could anyone regulate another person's thoughts? Orwell's solution was chilling. "Big Brother" created "newspeak." The repressive government changed the meaning of words, creating a whole new dictionary. With it, the government rewired the minds of its citizens.

Language and thought work hand in glove. We think in concepts, but also in words. If you can change patterns of language, you can change patterns of thought. In a 1946 essay, Orwell wrote, "If thought corrupts language, language can also corrupt thought."[216]

Evangelicals adopted the language of the world. The problem came when they allowed the language to alter their message.

To make the message seem more relevant, evangelicals crossed a line. They didn't just express the message of Jesus in clear and recognizable ways. More and more, evangelicals hid Jesus in a labyrinth of "newspeak." They made the Lord's message compliant to the new language of political correctness.

To Change the Unchangeable

Here's the problem. There's only one way the gospel of Jesus can be made to conform to the world. Change it. But when you change the gospel, it ceases to be the gospel. The world doesn't want to hear that there is only one way to the Father. But that's what Jesus preached.[217] He is the only Way. If you reject what He said about Himself, why would you trust the other things He said?

James 4:4 uses Old Testament bluntness in its warning against such changes. "Adulterers and adulteresses! Do you not know that friendship with the world is enmity with God? Whoever therefore wants to be a friend of the world makes himself an enemy of God."

In their attempt at inclusivity, evangelicals conformed core Christian doctrine to the thought-fashions of our time.

It started with the valid question, "How do we best communicate the timeless truths of God?" But it didn't stop there. Evangelicals went on to ask, "What can we use to draw people to God?" That question sent them in search of attractions. They were soon asking, "How do we please people?" They created questionnaires so that people could tell them where their ears itched.[218] That way, the churches could give those ears a good, satisfying scratch. Soon, the scratching of itching ears had become the primary purpose of every sermon and every class.

They said it was necessary because in Western nations, people are leaving the church. They didn't seem to notice that the more they watered down the gospel, the more people left. They were fearful, and desperately wanted to be relevant by fitting in. These fearful evangelicals forgot that there is only one way the gospel of Jesus can be made to conform to the world. And that is to change it. Let me say it again. *When you change the gospel, it ceases to be the gospel.*

Romans 12:2 says:

Do not be conformed to this world, but be transformed by the renewing of your mind, that you may prove what is that good and acceptable and perfect will of God.

Instead of being conformed to this world, we are to be transformed by God—ever being "conformed to the image of His Son."[219] How do we do that? By continuous renewal of the mind.

Note that the book of Romans is written to individuals, but not just individuals. It is also written to a church. That means the command to renew the mind does not just apply to individuals. It is also an instruction to a church. And it applies to all churches and even whole denominations.

We're seeing what happens when churches refuse to be transformed, choosing instead to conform to the world. Church leaders told their congregations that the changes were necessary to reach young people. They conformed the message and they conformed themselves. It wasn't God's message anymore. It wasn't even their message. A large portion of evangelical Christianity became just another instrument in the band playing the world's tune. It conformed to the world as fully as water conforms to the bottom of a cup.

And that makes sense. When your chief aim is to fit in, you take on any shape that fits.

The congregants were cheated out of precious things because they didn't know the Word. If they had, they might have remembered Colossians 2:8:

Beware lest anyone cheat you through philosophy and empty deceit, according to the tradition of men, according to the basic principles of the world, and not according to Christ.

Evangelicals asked, "How do we please people?" They should have asked, "How do we please God?" Regarding people, they should have asked, "How can we best serve them?"

God made us social creatures. We want to be greeted with smiles. We like being liked. But more than that, we abhor the thought of being one of "those people"—the people whose odd religious beliefs make them behave in strange ways. We never want to be perceived as weird or fanatical. We want to be part of the crowd that is in on the joke. We never want to be the joke itself.

All of that is true in middle school. And it's still true in adulthood. It's true for grocery clerks and for politicians. It's also true for pastors. We want people to admire us—not laugh at us. But we should temper this desire with the wisdom of Jesus found in John 15:19. "If you were of the world, the world would love its own. Yet because you are not of the world, but I chose you out of the world, therefore the world hates you."

The world's love and admiration were enticements too bright, too shiny for the new evangelicals to ignore. To convince people that they were not weird or cultish, evangelical leaders worked overtime to convince the world that, "We're just like you. There's nothing strange to look at here."

But the world is ever-changing. And that turned the evangelical elites into followers—always trying to keep up. If you want to be like something that is always changing, you must follow it. This is how evangelicals exchanged the timeless message of Christ for a dirty plate of empty platitudes. Thus, the congregation of the called-out turned into an assembly of the reassimilated—just another human institution.

Defining Success

A generation ago, some churches grew to enormous size. And the world took notice. Those pastors appeared on television shows and on magazine covers. They were pastors, but they were also successful in ways the world could admire. They had fame and money. And a generation of future pastors looked at them and determined that they, too, would make themselves successful in worldly terms of wealth and fame.

I'm not against money or large crowds. I'm an evangelical pastor determined to reach as many people as possible and help them grow to be disciples of Jesus. Money can be a useful tool. Big crowds represent an opportunity to minister God's Word to lots of people. But these things should not define success for an evangelical minister.

This is a good example of the difference between God's dictionary and the world's. Neither fame nor money is an end in itself. And neither is God's measure of success! Faithfulness is.

Faithfulness means loving people with the love of the Lord. That includes telling them what they *need* to hear—not necessarily what they *want* to hear.

Preach the Word

Second Timothy may have been the apostle Paul's last letter. Near the end of that letter, in 2 Timothy 4:6, he wrote, "I am already being poured out as a drink offering, and the time of my departure is at hand."

Throughout the epistle, Paul returns to the topic of faithfulness to God's Word. He reminds Timothy of the faith of his mother and grandmother.[220] He tells the young minister never to be ashamed of the true gospel.[221] In 2 Timothy 1:13–14, he wrote:

> Hold fast the pattern of sound words which you have heard from me, in faith and love which are in Christ Jesus. That good thing which was committed to you, keep by the Holy Spirit who dwells in us.

This is more than an admonishment to one first-century minister. The Holy Spirit inspired Paul to tell Timothy to hold fast to solid doctrine oriented entirely to God's Word. That admonishment rings down the corridor of time. It is a message for the church of today as much as it was for young Timothy. "The good thing which was committed to you, keep by the Holy Spirit"!

That same Holy Spirit speaks to us with the words, "Shun profane and idle babblings."[222] Stick to the Word!

Second Timothy 3:16–17 says:

> All Scripture is given by inspiration of God, and is profitable for doctrine, for reproof, for correction, for instruction in righteousness, that the man of God may be complete, thoroughly equipped for every good work.

Center your ministry and life on the Word! Preach the Word! Second Timothy 4:1–5 says:

> I charge you therefore before God and the Lord Jesus Christ, who will judge the living and the dead at His appearing and His kingdom:
>
> Preach the word! Be ready in season and out of season.
>
> Convince, rebuke, exhort, with all longsuffering and teaching.
>
> For the time will come when they will not endure sound doctrine, but according to their own desires, because they have itching ears, they will heap up for themselves teachers; and they will turn their ears away from the truth, and be turned aside to fables.
>
> But you be watchful in all things, endure afflictions, do the work of an evangelist, fulfill your ministry.

The same Holy Spirit who inspired Paul's words to Timothy gives us the same sacred charge: Preach the word!"

That was God's message to the church at it's very beginning, and that's His message to the church today. *Preach the Word!* If we don't stand on the Bible, we won't stand at all. What else do we have? If God didn't really speak to humanity, then what are we preaching? And if He did, how dare we preach anything else or anything less!

Unhitching from the Old Testament

Andy Stanley serves as senior pastor of North Point Community Church, a multisite church based in Alpharetta, Georgia. According to his publisher's website, "A survey of U.S. pastors in *Outreach Magazine* identified Andy Stanley as one of the ten most influential living pastors in America.... Over 1.8 million of Andy's messages, leadership videos, and podcasts are accessed from North Point's website monthly."

I could go on and on about the reach of Andy Stanley's influence. If judged by sheer numbers, he at least rivals his legendary father, Charles Stanley, and probably surpasses him. Andy's influence is amplified by his ministry's emphasis on training leaders. He teaches pastors how to pastor and preachers how to preach, and he does so around the world.

In a 2018 sermon, he said that first-century "church leaders unhitched the church from the worldview, value system, and regulations of the Jewish scriptures." He went on to say, "Peter, James, Paul elected to unhitch the Christian faith from their Jewish scriptures, and my friends, we must as well."

He said he still believed the Old Testament was divinely inspired and "an important backstory."

He made it clear that his motivation in this sermon was to present Christianity in a way that will be more palatable in today's world. In its description of the sermon, North Point said:

> If you were raised on a version of Christianity that relied on the Bible as the foundation of faith, a version that was eventually dismantled by academia or the realities of life, maybe it's time for you to change your mind about Jesus. Maybe it's time for you to consider the version of Christianity that relies on the event of the resurrection of Jesus as its foundation. If you gave up your faith because of something about or in the Bible, maybe you gave up unnecessarily.

In one way, the sentiment is laudable. Make sure that misconceptions about the Bible do not keep people from Jesus. Okay. But is the Old Testament a misconception?

It's healthy for a pastor to preach on the differences between the Old Covenant and the New; between law and grace. John 1:17 says, "For the law was given through Moses, but grace and truth came through Jesus Christ."

Galatians 2:16 explains the distinction:

A man is not justified by the works of the law but by faith in Jesus Christ, even we have believed in Christ Jesus, that we might be justified by faith in Christ and not by the works of the law; for by the works of the law no flesh shall be justified.

And that's the interesting thing. Even in the Old Testament, no one was ever saved by living in perfect accord with the rules of the Law. The saved of the Old Testament were saved by faith in God.[223] The Old Testament teaches about a coming New Testament. It foreshadows the key points. That's why, instead of unhitching from the Old Testament, the New Testament writers firmly hitched their message to the Old.

Second Corinthians 5:21 provides one of the most sophisticated statements of God's method of salvation:

For He made Him who knew no sin to be sin for us, that we might become the righteousness of God in Him.

We see the same concept in Jeremiah 23:6:

This is His name by which He will be called: THE LORD OUR RIGHTEOUSNESS.

That's the day we live in. We who follow Christ today do so because God the Father "made Him who knew no sin to be sin for us, that we might become the righteousness of God in Him"—i.e., we have the privilege of calling Him "The Lord Our Righteousness!"

God Does Not Change

Jesus did not unhitch Himself from the Old Testament. He not only quoted it often, He quoted it regarding Himself. The Old Testament served as His calling card and His credentials. He did not arrive on earth out of left field. He came according to Old Testament prophecies, and He pointed this out many times.

The writer of Hebrews did not unhitch his faith from the Old Testament. Reread chapter 11. In fact, reread the entire book.

Pastors and teachers often make mistakes or seem to make mistakes. I certainly do. I get things wrong, or say things poorly, or am simply misunderstood. It happens. And for someone as popular as Andy Stanley, jealousy often enters the picture, fueling the fires of controversy.

But if we look at Pastor Andy's message in the context of his overall teaching, we see that this is more than poor wording or his critics misunderstanding him. He seems to have an obvious zeal to lower barriers between twenty-first-century Americans and faith in Jesus. My concern is that in his zeal to make the Bible palatable, he attempted to alter the unalterable.

There are several Old Testament passages that modern Americans find politically incorrect. For instance, the Old Testament reveals that God's attitude toward homosexuality and adultery are entirely negative. And then there is the violence that God not only sanctioned, but sometimes ordered. In his sermon, Stanley emphasized that the Old Testament is "ancient." He makes it seem long ago and far away.

But that doesn't really solve his problem. Jesus is God the Son from eternity past to eternity future. Hebrews 13:8 says, "Jesus Christ is the same yesterday, today, and forever." According to Andy Stanley, the Old Testament was at least "inspired." The inspired verse in Malachi 3:6 says, "For I am the Lord, I do not change."

God hated adultery and homosexuality in the Old Testament for the same reason He hates them now—because those practices harm the people who participate in them. From them, a ripple of misery goes out to their families, friends, and eventually the whole society. These sins destroy the morals of a nation by rewiring the minds of its children. God hates these things for the same reason that the mother of a child addicted to heroin hates heroin—because it harms someone she loves.

You can disagree with me on the harm these sins cause individuals and nations. But if you believe the Bible (Old Testament *and* New Testament) you must believe in God's love for people, His hatred for sin, and that He calls homosexual behavior sin. (I single out homosexual behavior here because that's the more controversial sin of the moment.) You can't say that it all suddenly changed a few years ago, or even a couple of millennia ago. He is God. He does not change. Immutability is one of His fundamental attributes.

If you have a problem with the God of the Old Testament, you have a problem with God. Period.

Downgrade

Church history is filled with episodes of apostasy. For instance, humans tend to start trying to save themselves by means of their own righteousness. It has happened over and over throughout the Christian era. That's why we so often hear that revival and reformation are deeply intertwined. Without a return to God's Word, revival becomes just another word for big crowds and excitement—the kind of things you find at a football game.

Charles Spurgeon fought against what he called "the downgrade." For Luther, it was indulgences replacing faith as the conduit of grace. For Paul the apostle, it was the foolishness of those who had "begun in the Spirit," believing they could now be "made perfect by the flesh."[224]

The real church of Jesus must always "contend earnestly for the faith which was once for all delivered to the saints."[225]

In other words, this is nothing new. But according to Bible prophecy, it will strike with renewed ferocity as we get close to the end of the age. First Timothy 4:1 says:

Now the Spirit expressly says that in latter times some will depart from the faith, giving heed to deceiving spirits and doctrines of demons.

Second Timothy 4:3–4 says:

For the time will come when they will not endure sound doctrine, but according to their own desires, because they have itching ears,

they will heap up for themselves teachers; and they will turn their ears away from the truth, and be turned aside to fables.

The Hollowed-Out Gospel

While they want the church to be different from the failed systems of the world, many in our ranks are doing all they can to make the evangelical church the world's mirror twin. They expunge the Bible's less popular passages. And when that happens, the church becomes vain—in the old sense of the word. Empty! "Vain" and "vanity" come from the Latin *vānus*, which means "lacking content, empty, illusory, marked by foolish or empty pride."

To say part of the Bible is wrong is to remove the Bible's authority. As the church removes the Bible's authority, it whittles away at its own foundation. Without the authority of God's Word, what do we have to offer? Emptiness! Purge the Bible from our preaching and teaching, and all such preaching and teaching becomes vain—empty!

One of the sad things about those who would bend the Bible into the shape of modern man is that modern man is disgusted with himself and longs for something real behind all the facades. Beneath everything else, people have an emptiness, a longing for something. But that something remains ill-defined to them and many have come to see it as imaginary.

Meanwhile, more and more evangelicals have come to see ministry as a marketing exercise whose goal is the admiration of the world. To please the world, they tried to make the church more compatible with carnal human nature. Evangelicals no longer talk about hell because it no longer fits the "messaging" they have chosen to project. They do all this PR work for God, telling the world that He is motivated entirely by love, and then He hits them with an attribute they don't like—justice.

The funny thing is, most churches don't talk much about heaven, either. Sure, they talk about it at funerals or when a loved one dies. In those cases, there is an almost automatic assumption that this "good person" must be in heaven regardless of his or her standing with Christ. But the rest of the time, there's little mention of heaven because it reminds people of death, and they don't want to think about death.

When it comes to talking or singing about the blood of Jesus or the cross, our preachers might as well be speaking to a gathering of Buddhists. Blood makes the folks uncomfortable. It doesn't fit a happy theology.

But most of all, the new, inclusive evangelicals reject talk of sin. I hear it over and over. "People already know they're sinners. You don't have to remind them." But that's not what Jesus modeled. He was loving, but also firm, sometimes even harsh, in His condemnation of sin.

Galatians 3:24 says "the law was our schoolmaster to bring us to Christ."[226] What does this "schoolmaster" teach us? That we are sinners and need a Savior. It shows us what we should be but what we fail at being. It prepares us for Jesus. It leads us to the cross. It's no accident that those who stop talking about sin also stop talking about the cross.

We present God's standards—many of them found in the Old Testament—because those standards draw us to Jesus as Savior. They remind us of how far we fall short of the glory of God.

Many evangelicals have replaced the message of the cross with messages of self-esteem, self-love, and self-help. You hear in church just what you hear on feel-good television commercials. You "deserve" only good things. More and more evangelical ministers don't tell people what sinners really "deserve," because the people won't like it.

The Terrible Exchange

In Luke 14:28, as Jesus was talking about what it means to become His disciple, He said, "Count the cost." When was the last time you heard the words "count the cost" in an altar call? Of course, Jesus wasn't talking about people saving themselves by doing penance or doing good deeds to cancel out sins. We don't pay for a right standing with God. Jesus would make the complete payment for our complete salvation.

He was talking about the cost inherent in our association with Him. He meant someone might stone you or crucify you—because of Him. He meant someone might laugh at you and point. The cost He spoke of was the cost of this world's affection. Comparatively, that cost is small—infinitely small. Missionary Jim Elliot famously said, "He is no fool who gives what he cannot keep to gain that which he cannot lose."

But the twenty-first-century church seems intent on just the opposite: reaching hard for what it cannot keep (or probably ever attain), and, in the process, losing everything dear and rich and good.

With the world as their mentor, many evangelical churches have been pummeled and twisted into an ugly, misbegotten thing. In some places, it centered itself on money. Preachers taught that God wants everyone to be wealthy by the world's standards. This teaching made many of those ministers rich—neatly "proving" the correctness of their teaching. People ate it up. More ministers noticed and more congregations demanded it.

In Jeremiah 6:13–14, God said to the people of Israel:

Everyone is given to covetousness; And from the prophet even to the priest, everyone deals falsely.

They have also healed the hurt of My people slightly, Saying, "Peace, peace!" When there is no peace.

In Jeremiah's day, the men of God were willing to tell people what they wanted to hear even if it meant giving false assurances. And in our time, people would really like to hear that God has a quick and easy formula for monetary wealth. "Everyone is given to covetousness."

In other places, it became about positive thinking, self-esteem, or repairing fractured egos. Sunday School and small groups turned away from the rich study of God's very Word and instead became another version of group therapy.

The misbegotten thing grew. Its existence became a vast masquerade. It would call itself church, but it would look and feel like the world. Calls for holiness and repentance ceased. This "church" would not be set apart from the world. Indeed, it would make the world its model.

None of this should be conflated with matters of "style." This is not about the rhythm of the music or the attire of the musicians. This is about the substance of the singing. Are we singing God's very Word, or are we singing little ditties designed to make us feel good? Revelation gives us a glimpse of heaven's music, and it's not the music of advertising jingles or even sweet lullabies. It is the music for which music was made—the pure response to Someone perfect in beauty, majesty, and holiness.

From Lukewarm to On Fire

Revelation depicts Jesus walking among seven lampstands, which He explained to John represented the seven churches in Asia to whom the book was initially written. To the first of these churches, Ephesus, Jesus had many good things to say. They were students of the Word who worked hard and stood against those whose doctrine would bring harm to the church.

But it wasn't all commendation for the Ephesians. Jesus said:

Nevertheless I have this against you, that you have left your first love. Remember therefore from where you have fallen; repent and do the first works, or else I will come to you quickly and remove your lampstand from its place—unless you repent.[227]

The gates of hell will not prevail against THE Church.[228] But individual churches can die. Their candles can be removed. In Revelation 2:5 quoted above, Jesus tells the Ephesians to "repent." He says it twice in one verse. The alternative to repentance for the Ephesians was to have their candle removed.

Jesus had nothing good to say about the last church—the one in Laodicea.[229] The Lord did not specifically warn them that He might remove their candle. With them, He used more graphic terms:

> I know your works, that you are neither cold nor hot. I could wish
> you were cold or hot. So then, because you are lukewarm, and
> neither cold nor hot, I will vomit you out of My mouth.[230]

He again admonished repentance. This is not talking to individuals, though much of it applies. This is talking to churches. A lukewarm church is a church in mortal danger. Without repentance, it dies—its candle is removed. God spews it from His mouth, vomits it away.

The building usually remains, and people still meet there—sometimes large numbers of them. They can spend millions to create just the right feel. They can hire PR firms to help them handle the press. They can hire lighting, architectural, and sound engineers to create an atmosphere of warm hospitality and rock-concert excitement. But none of that matters if Jesus removes their candle.

When He spoke to the Laodiceans, the Lord had not yet removed their candle. They were on life-support, "circling the drain," about to be hurled, but it wasn't too late. His advice to them applies to similar churches of our day.

In Revelation 3:17–18, Jesus said:

> Because you say, "I am rich, have become wealthy, and have need
> of nothing"—and do not know that you are wretched, misera-
> ble, poor, blind, and naked—I counsel you to buy from Me gold

refined in the fire, that you may be rich; and white garments, that you may be clothed, that the shame of your nakedness may not be revealed; and anoint your eyes with eye salve, that you may see.

Even churches that have not lost their first love or become lukewarm should return to these words often:

Buy from Me gold refined in the fire, that you may be rich; and white garments, that you may be clothed, that the shame of your nakedness may not be revealed; and anoint your eyes with eye salve, that you may see.

This process should be ongoing. Don't wait until your church is circling the drain. Do it now.

In verse 20, the Lord said that at the church of Laodicea, He stood on the outside looking in. It breaks my heart to realize that this is also a picture of His relationship to tens of thousands of churches around the world today:

Behold, I stand at the door and knock. If anyone hears My voice and opens the door, I will come in to him and dine with him, and he with Me.

It's happening with ever-increasing frequency. His churches—places that name themselves as His—leave Him outside and unwelcome. Yet, even from there, He knocks at the door. If they will invite Him in, He promises to return and again dine with them in sweet, sweet fellowship.

FOURTEEN

Christendom Isolates Israel

By Jim Fletcher

I grew up in the era of frequent prophecy conferences, congregational Bible reading, pastors with a biblical worldview, and more good stuff!

I remember friends from church planning Holy Land trips. Pastors were excited to talk about the Rapture. Israel was respected, if not a passionate topic of conversation.

And Bible prophecy books were filling bookstores.

That was then.

In 1995, I met an Israeli for the first time, and he helped me pronounce the name of a politically hot young politician: *Net-ahn-yahoo*.

I worked for a Christian book publisher—a guy still doing good things today; that places him in a very small minority. It's how I met Terry James, actually. Those books brought back a hunger for prophecy for me, and I'm forever grateful. Some of my favorite memories are meeting prophecy teachers and students at conferences and then on a newfangled system called the Internet.

Eventually, I was privileged to visit Israel for the first time with one of our top-selling authors, the peerless David Allen Lewis. As a young teenager, he learned from his grandmother's Bible reading that Israel would be reborn. In those days even, that was a fantasy few believed! A few years later though, David listened on the radio as the state of Israel was established!

On a late winter evening in Tel Aviv on that first trip, we sat and visited with the great Israeli cartoonist, Yaakov Kirschen ("Dry Bones") as he related a similar story from his youth.

"When I was growing up in the early 40s," he said, "we discussed many things around the dinner table. One of them was the prophesied return of the exiles to the Land of Israel. In those days, only a few rabbis and a few crazy American preachers taught that it would happen."

Kirschen paused, then the takeaway.

"Then it happened!"

He went on to explain that rather than cause people to fall on their faces and worship the living God—as He revealed His sovereignty through this great fulfilled prophecy—the establishment of Israel actually had the opposite effect.

"People became angry!" Kirschen still seemed taken aback, all those years later.

So am I.

A few years after that meeting, I was having dinner with a publishing insider, a man who had been on the sales side for years. The company I worked for had created a "pro-Israel" book imprint and I was frustrated that our herculean efforts were meeting only with modest success.

He listened to me for a while and then he said something I have never forgotten. It remains one of the most profound things I've ever heard.

"Jim," he began, "you must understand that evangelicals today love Israel. They just don't like Jews."

Wow.

I'm still reeling.

Yet, as I absorbed what he was saying, I knew he was spot-on correct. Of course. That's it!

As contradictory as his statement sounds, it wasn't at all. It was entirely consistent with what I'd been observing and processing for several years.

Bible prophecy teaching was waning. Evangelical leaders who had been supportive of Israel were passing from the scene. The Christian Booksellers Association was changing in ways I would come to understand as grotesque—consumed with the bottom line.

My friend told me that profound and painful truth fifteen years ago.

Today the landscape is much, much worse. There are reasons for this, which I'll get to, along with listing some examples. This partially biographical sketch I think explains it better than I could have with just raw data.

"But Hobby Lobby Is Christian!"

In 2010, I became aware of a film that had been produced titled *Little Town of Bethlehem*. It was produced by Ethnographic Media (EGM). More on that in a minute.

Directed by Jim Hanon, the documentary was ostensibly a balanced view of the Arab-Israeli conflict. Featuring a Christian (Sami Awad), a Muslim (Ahmad Al'Azzeh) and a Jew (Yonatan Shapira), we were to understand that we were getting balanced perspectives from people living in the region.

Only one problem. All three were critical of Israel and "The Occupation." It sounded like a Hamas propaganda film. It was screened on many Christian college campuses and received endorsements from evangelical sources, even from a review in *Charisma* magazine.

I decided to do some digging.

I called and made an appointment to interview Hanon. Driving over to the company's headquarters in Oklahoma City, I was shocked to see that it was across the street from my old high school. In fact, slamming the car door, I turned around to see a vast office and warehouse complex.

Hobby Lobby.

That's right, EGM was bankrolled by the Green family, specifically spearheaded by then-Mardel Stores' Mart Green.

Inside, I had a fascinating interview with the friendly Hanon. Interestingly, he told me that they began filming interviews in Beirut. Why, I wondered, would you seek Israeli and Palestinian perspectives by starting in Lebanon?

Hanon then told me that he had been able to interview...Sheik Nasrallah.

That's right. He visited with the terror master of Hezbollah, a man committed to the murder of Jews and the destruction of Israel.

I was shocked. The question was, how could someone like Hanon be that naïve? Or was he? Further, why was Hobby Lobby behind such a project? It seemed unbelievable.

Over the coming months (which stretched into a few years), I requested interviews with Mart Green several times. Failing that, I wrote a piece about it for WorldNetDaily. After that, I was stonewalled when asking to interview Green. Very, very oddly, I later met him by chance three times: in a hotel lobby in Tulsa, and then in two airports!

Each time, I asked him personally for an interview. I told him that I wanted to explore what he thinks about Jews and about Israel.

I'm still waiting for the interview.

Thus began my deep dive into why evangelical leaders were seeming to turn on Israel. More than once when giving a presentation on the subject in a church, I was confronted by people upset that I'd "unmasked" Hobby Lobby.

"But Hobby Lobby is Christian!"

That's what I hear. But these responses had nothing to do with the facts I had unearthed. More was to come.

The Catalyst

Around the same time, I became aware of a conference program being produced around the country. Catalyst Conferences targeted evangelical pastors and youth pastors, drawing tens of thousands at three annual conferences in California, the Midwest, and Atlanta.

(By the way, this has relevance for my theory that it's no coincidence that Rick Warren in southern California, Bill Hybels in Chicago, and

Andy Stanley in Atlanta were literally blanketing the country with anti-biblical church models. There seemed to be a coordinated effort to pump church-growth techniques into biblical churches. I had several enlightening conversations about this with several prophecy teachers, including Southwest Radio Church's Noah Hutchings. These understood that the church-growth movement was destroying the American evangelical community, including eroding support for Israel.)

I attended several of these conferences, eventually learning that Andy Stanley (yes, that Andy Stanley, son of Southern Baptist "icon" Charles Stanley) had helped found the Catalyst enterprise.

I will tell you that I believe with certainty that Catalyst was designed to pull pastors away from the Bible. In this way, it has been ultra-successful. Besides anti-Israel speakers like Lynne Hybels, the resources offered were decidedly anti-Bible: the books of universalist author William Paul Young (*The Shack*); offers to engage with the New-Age system, the Enneagram; and weird workshops featuring pagan "spiritual formation" teachers like Phileena Heuertz. In fact, I sat in on one of her workshops and watched in horror as dozens of evangelicals sat for "breath prayers," looking very much like Hindu apostles.

From Chris Heuertz's website bio:

> In 2012, Phileena and I launched Gravity, a Center for Contemplative Activism to support the development of spiritual consciousness by making contemplative practice accessible to individuals, communities and organizations who engage the challenging social justice perils of our time. My work with Gravity includes public speaking, teaching, writing on contemplative activism, facilitation of contemplative retreats, non-profit consultation, and Enneagram coaching.

My point in all this is to show that the encroaching apostasy of the church, as outlined in prophetic passages from the New Testament, was necessary to produce a grotesque "falling away" from support for Israel.

At one Catalyst talk, headed by Lynne Hybels, I listened to a sophisticated (also false!) presentation that demonized Israel for alleged abuses of the Palestinians. Hybels, who cofounded the (in)famous Willow Creek Association with husband Bill (emphasizing the "felt needs" of non-churchgoers), had been traveling to what she called "Israel/'Palestine'" for several years. Each of her trips fueled an anti-Israel sentiment I found alarming.

I also noticed that fewer and fewer people cared when I brought this up.

Moore Anti-Israel

A few years ago, I became aware of another leading evangelical who displayed an uneven attitude toward Israel. My friend, Randy White, a recently former pastor of a large Southern Baptist church, alerted me to the views of Dr. Russell Moore. Moore, a former Democrat congressman's staffer, became the head of the Southern Baptist Convention's (SBC) Ethics and Religious Liberty Commission (ERLC) in 2013, succeeding the solidly pro-Israel Dr. Richard Land.

Moore is something less than that.

According to White, in 2013:

On June 1, 2013, Dr. Russell Moore will become President of the influential Ethics and Religious Liberties Commission of the Southern Baptist Convention [ERLC]. Whether or not you are Southern Baptists, Moore will have huge influence on the Christian worldview and expression of Christianity for many years to come.

It is not hard to discern where Moore will lead, what he will emphasize, and what his values are, and this Southern Baptist is concerned.

The concern is not over traditional social issues like abortion, homosexuality, and Judeo-Christian morality. Moore will be constantly conservative on these issues. His conservative positions on these issues will elicit lots of "amens" from the average person in the pew, making Moore look like a wonderful gift to the Southern Baptist's efforts to protect life, marriage, and morality.

Signs of Coming Trouble

I've read enough of Moore's works and know enough of his core theology, however, to have grave concerns. When I read an interview of his plans for the ERLC, my concerns went to the red-alert level. There were three statements that especially concern me.

It was Randy's highlight of Moore's "Israel" position I found most alarming:

When Moore writes about Israel, it is often with a negative tone. He says things like, "Israel's American critics on both the left and the right of the political spectrum have been frustrated by what they consider to be the political *carte blanche* given by evangelicals to the Israeli state." He goes on to say, "it is rather obvious that contemporary evangelical support for Israel draws its theological grounding from the dispensational/Bible conference tradition, not from the Reformed/Princeton tradition." As you read his works, Moore is clearly not a fan of this dispensational/Bible conference tradition. He is, however, an avowed covenant theologian, and he says that such theologians "have maintained that the church, not any current geo-political entity, is the "new Israel," the inheritor of all Israel's covenant promises." (This is, by the way, a perfect definition of replacement theology).

If there is any good news in Moore's position on Israel, it is that "Evangelical public theology would be in error, however, if it sought to remedy past errors by abandoning support for Israel." I hope you note that evangelical support in the past has been built on "errors." It would be a mistake to remove this support, but

Christians should "ground such support in a quest for geo-politi-cal stability and peace in the Middle East, not in the "Thus saith the Lord" of the prophecy charts."

My word to Southern Baptists who may hope for a powerful pro-Israel denominational stance coming from the ERLC: Good luck! There is no hint Moore would allow it. My prediction is sub-tly anti-Israel messages or Israel-phobia. Moore is too much the politician to throw Israel under the bus, but he is not a supporter of Israel as a modern Jewish state unless it serves the purposes of the new Israel's expansion and well-being.[231]

In the last seven years, Moore has gone farther in his anti-biblical stances, including cozying up to pro-homosexual groups, and shutting down any dissent within the SBC for his leftward drift.

Also, a couple of years ago, I spoke with a person who was on a tour to Israel with Moore. He said to me, "Well, he isn't with us on Israel, but I hope we can continue to have dialogue."

This person is naïve. Russell Moore will go much farther in his anti-Israel views in the years to come.

He knows the spirit of the age is with him.

Pentecostals, Too

If someone had told me a few decades ago that the Southern Baptists would turn on Israel—at the leadership level—I'd have denied it. If I'd also been told that Pentecostals/Charismatics would do the same, I'd have had some choice words for you.

A few years ago, I became aware of Paul Alexander, a professor at East-ern Seminary (home of anti-Israel Christian celebrity Tony Campolo). Alexander, a young and literally charismatic fellow with Pentecostal roots, on his website referred to Jesus as a "Palestinian."

What???

The "Jesus was a Palestinian" canard was created by the loathsome Yasser Arafat and foisted on the mainline denominations in the '80s and '90s. They lapped it up.

Eventually, this sewage would seep into evangelical circles.

Another pastor with Pentecostal roots, Jonathan Martin, is also anti-Israel. Today he pastors in Oklahoma, but as a pastor in North Carolina, he hosted the producers of another anti-Israel film, "With God On Our Side," including Porter Speakman Jr.

I attended an anti-Israel conference in California about this time, and during a break, had an "interesting" conversation with Speakman. He knew who I was and asked what I thought of the conference. I told him I was surprised at the one-sided nature of the presentations. That got him animated and angry. With the Left, only your total surrender keeps their fangs in their mouths.

There are other young anti-Israel operatives in evangelicalism. Andy Braner, who has operated in youth ministry for many years, is a Baylor grad. He's also been taking trips to "Palestine" for some time. He generally views the Israel-Palestinian conflict through the lens of the Palestinian Liberation Organization (PLO).

In a 2015 blog post, Braner discussed Areas A, B, and C under the Oslo Accords:

> The intention of these three areas was to set up a transfer time from the Israeli government over to the Palestinian government, but this is the area where you hear about Israeli Settlements. Under International Law the controversy begins when Israeli neighborhoods pop up in the intended Palestinian land. This is the basis of conflict over land, control, and the security. It's also much of the reason you hear about uprisings in the news.[232]

The basis of conflict. This means of course that the "Occupation" is the original sin of the Israel-Palestinian conflict. But if you asked Braner how this squares with the fact that the PLO was formed three years before the Six Day War (and Israel's subsequent possession of Judea and Samaria), I doubt he could tell you.

And what "International Law" does he speak of? Again, I very much doubt he could cite it, since there is no "international law" barring Israel. There is plenty of international rage, but no such law.

I often think of how my dear friend and mentor David Lewis would view Pentecostals turning on Israel. David passed in 2007; so much has changed since then!

When Christian Media Goes South

In 1986, in a marvelously informative book, *The Media's War Against Israel*, essayists examined the viciousness of international media against Israel. One insight in particular caught my eye:

> The Ochs family were so opposed to Zionism that when Truman, in 1946, advocated that 100,000 survivors of the death camps be permitted to immigrate to Palestine, a *Times* editorial condemned Truman's interference in Britain's affairs.[233]

You see, the family with controlling interest in the *New York Times* so hated Israel, they were willing to further endanger scores of poor souls who had survived Hitler.

Much more painful for the Christian is when Christian media turns on Israel. It has been going on for some time. *Christianity Today*, the flagship evangelical periodical for decades, has long been hostile to the Jewish state. Whether it was allowing columnists to refer to Jesus as a "Palestinian rabbi" or a constant stream of articles pointing out Israelis' discomfort with Christian proselytizing, the magazine's editorial staff tipped its hand.

Then with the advent of social media, writers like Jonathan Merritt attacked Israel and her Christian supporters day and night. That they have roots deep within evangelicalism makes it no less frustrating.

Mae Elise Cannon, formerly with World Vision (and now director of that organization) has written such anti-Israel books as *A Land Full of God: Christian Perspectives on the Holy Land* and *Evangelical Theologies of Liberation and Justice*. Since 2010, she has participated in anti-Israel conferences in churches with pro-Palestinian activists like Lynne Hybels and Sami Awad. Before he died, Calvary Chapel founder Chuck Smith shut them down in that association, but in the years since, inroads have been made even into that bastion of pro-Israel support.

The Left never rests.

Because left-wing operatives are smart, they often devise brilliant strategies. One of those is to undermine Israel support right in the heart of the conservative evangelical community.

Charisma magazine, founded by Stephen Strang in the 1970s, has opened the door to anti-Israel/anti-Bible prophecy sources like the producers of *Little Town of Bethlehem* and the writer Margaret Feinberg. One wonders why.

Strang's son, Cameron, is the publisher of *Relevant* magazine, a publication targeting Millennials. They claim a digital footprint of tens of millions.

Several years ago, after publishing a couple of positive pieces about Israel, Cameron Strang visited a mythical place called "Palestine" with Lynne Hybels and came back a committed Palestinian activist.

His 2014 article, "Blessed Are the Peacemakers," was a hit piece against Israel.

The lengthy article is sharply slanted toward the Palestinian narrative. For example, inexplicably, Strang allows long-time Yasser Arafat/PLO mouthpiece Hanan Ashrawi to rewrite biblical history:

Palestinians are the descendants of the early Christians. We are probably the straightest line to original Christianity. The Palestinian presence in Palestine is important. Christianity is part and parcel of the Palestinian identity.

Strang doesn't mention that Ashrawi's father was a founding member of the PLO, created in 1964—three full years before Israel took control of the West Bank, Sinai, Golan, and the Gaza Strip in the Six Day War. (It begs the question: What were they hoping to liberate?)

This is the tip of the iceberg of Christian media today, regarding Israel.

Feelings Over Revelation

It's not hard to "make Israel's case" for the Land by using Scripture.

In Deuteronomy 34:1–4, we read:

Then Moses climbed Mount Nebo from the plains of Moab to the top of Pisgah, across from Jericho.

There the Lord showed him the whole land—from Gilead to Dan, all of Naphtali, the territory of Ephraim and Manasseh, all the land of Judah as far as the Mediterranean Sea, the Negev and the whole region from the Valley of Jericho, the City of Palms, as far as Zoar.

Then the Lord said to him, "This is the land I promised on oath to Abraham, Isaac and Jacob when I said, "I will give it to your descendants."

I have let you see it with your eyes, but you will not cross over into it.

This is an historical reference. It happened in history. Many hundreds of verses in Scripture affirm Israel's right to the land. Hundreds more have been fulfilled in prophecy—and there are more to come. Honestly, they are easy to see.

But too many people today reject Jews and Israel because they reject Scripture, for whatever reason. The problem is one of the heart and the spirit.

This is why we end this chapter by going back to the beginning.

As Adam, Eve, and the serpent were "called on the carpet" by the Living God, He told each of them their fate, long-term.

To the serpent, the Lord said:

And I will put enmity between you and the woman, and between your offspring and hers; he will crush your head, and you will strike his heel. (Genesis 3:15)

This is the first discussion of the gospel in Scripture! How great is our God!

Here the Lord was telling all of us that there would be perpetual war between Lucifer and Jesus, until that day when the Messiah would put down rebellion finally, and for all time.

This is the heart of the anti-Semitism we have seen for four thousand years. This is the central issue that prevents peace between Israel and the Palestinians. The devil hates Israel and the Jews with a passion. His irrationality and insanity have unfortunately attached to many, many people.

Paul Johnson's marvelous (though fawning) book about *Charles Darwin, Darwin: Portrait of a Genius,* offers a real insight into the man who did more to undermine the Bible in modern times than anyone else. I maintain that Darwin's theory has virtually destroyed civilization. We now see the end result playing out, as madness engulfs the planet—reprobate minds and all that.

Johnson offers a short chronology into Darwin's departure from the Christian faith (if he ever found it in the first place):

In his last years, he wrote a good deal of autobiographical material, some of which has survived. It is guarded, though there are occasional flashes of frankness. Thus, when a child, "I was much given to inventing deliberate falsehoods."

Then, later:

"I gradually came to disbelieve in Christianity as a divine revelation."[234]

This is perhaps the saddest sentence ever written in human language. It condemned the writer to an eternity without God. And it shows that his famous theory opened a philosophical door for people to deny God's revelation as found in Scripture. It is why millions in the church today are indifferent or outright hostile to Israel.

In more than twenty-five years of advocating for Israel, whenever I talk with anti-Israel people, I eventually learn the foundational problem they have with Israel:

They don't like Jews.

FIFTEEN

Deniers of Israel

By David R. Reagan

One of the most significant group of deniers in Christendom today are those who deny that God has any future purpose for the Jewish people.

They argue that because the Jewish people killed Jesus, and thus committed the ultimate sin of deicide (the killing of God), the Almighty washed His hands of them in the first century, placed them under perpetual discipline, and has no more purpose for them. Consequently, these deniers maintain that God has replaced Israel with the church, transferring to the church all the blessings that were promised to the Jews. This is called Replacement Theology, and it is responsible for many serious theological abuses that continue to this day.

The denials began early in church history as the originally Jewish church began to convert Gentiles in large numbers. The irony is that a Jewish movement built upon Jewish Scriptures and faith in a Jewish Messiah was hijacked by Gentiles who proceeded to declare Jews to be outcasts!

The Root of the Problem

Why and how did this occur? As to why—it is rooted in Satan's hatred of the Jewish people. It is, therefore, a supernatural movement, as is testified by the fact that there are Jew-haters who have never even met a Jew!

Satan hates the Jews with a passion for several reasons:

1) God chose them to be His witnesses to the world (Isaiah 43:10).
2) Through them God gave the world the Bible. (Every book in the Old Testament and all of the New Testament books, with the possible exception of the Gospel of Luke and the book of Acts, was written by Jews.)
3) Through them God gave the world the Messiah (Matthew 1:1–16 and Luke 3:23–38).
4) God has promised that He will save a great remnant of them (Isaiah 10:22 and Romans 9:27).
5) God has promised that He will make Israel the prime nation of the world, and through them, He will bless all the other nations Isaiah (2:1–4).

Satan is determined to destroy every Jew on planet earth because he hates them and because he wants to prevent God from keeping His promises to them. That's what the Holocaust was all about, and that is what the last half of the Tribulation will be about.

Anti-Semitism

The most tragic aspect of Satan's conspiracy against the Jews is that, early on, he infected the church with a virulent form of anti-Semitism. You see, for almost two thousand years, the church at large, both Catholic and Protestant, has maintained that, due to the fact that the Jews rejected Jesus as their Messiah and crucified Him, God poured out His wrath on them in AD 70, destroying their nation and their temple, and in the process,

He washed His hands of them, leaving them with no purpose whatsoever as a nation.

In short, because of their continuing disobedience and their rejection of Jesus, God has replaced Israel with the church, transferring the blessings promised to Israel to the church. Again, this is called Replacement Theology, and those who still believe in it—the majority of professing Christians—consider modern-day Israel to be an accident of history, with no spiritual significance whatsoever. Accordingly, they would deny that God has any special plans for the Jewish people in the end times.

Again, to them, the regathering of the Jews and the reestablishment of Israel are simply accidents of history, with no spiritual significance. Let me give you a graphic example of what I am talking about. Consider the following statement that was made by one of Christendom's best known spokesmen:

> I think it is problematic to relate prophecy to current events unfolding in the nation-state of Israel. There may be some relationship, of course. Only God knows. But the secular state of Israel created in 1948 is not, in my understanding, identical with the Jewish people as God's chosen and called-out covenant people.
>
> I strongly support Israel because it is a haven for persecuted Jews not because I think it fulfills biblical prophecy. I also support a Palestinian state both from historical and prudential considerations. Given the state of affairs in the Middle East, a Palestinian state is the only practicable solution for peace.[235]

And who wrote these words? Chuck Colson!

The Evolution of Replacement Theology

As I pointed out earlier, when the church began to spread beyond Jerusalem and embrace more and more Gentiles, it quickly lost touch with its Jewish roots. Even worse, its Gentile leaders began to turn against the Jews, characterizing them as "Christ killers."

One of the earliest evidences of this attitude appeared in the writings of the church father, Ignatius of Antioch (50–117). He said that "those who partake of the Passover are partakers with those who killed Jesus."[236] This became a persistent theme among the church fathers. For example, Tertullian of Carthage (155–230) blamed the Jews for the death of Jesus and argued that they had been rejected by God.[237] Eusebuis of Caesarea (275–339) taught that the promises of Scripture were meant for the Gentiles and the curses were for the Jews. He asserted that the church was the "true Israel."[238]

The worst of these early Christian spokesmen was John Chrysostom (349–407). He was nicknamed "The Golden Tongue" for his powerful preaching. He presented eight sermons against the Jews. Here is a quote from one of his sermons that presents the flavor of his wretched remarks:

> The synagogue is not only a brothel and a theater, it is also a den
> of robbers and a lodging place for wild beasts…Jews are inveterate
> murderers possessed by the Devil. Their debauchery and drunk-
> enness gives them the manners of a pig.[239]

Chrysostom denied that Jews could ever receive forgiveness. He claimed it was a Christian duty to hate Jews. He claimed that Jews worshiped Satan. And this man was canonized as a saint!

Equally vile was the renowned translator of the Bible into Latin— Saint Jerome (347–420). He described the Jews as "serpents, wearing the image of Judas. Their psalms and prayers are the braying of donkeys…. They are incapable of understanding Scripture."[240]

Meanwhile, Christian councils focused on isolating the Jewish people. Thus, the Council of Elvira (305) prohibited Christians from sharing a meal with a Jew, marrying a Jew, blessing a Jew, or observing the Sabbath.[241] The Council of Nicea (325) changed the celebration of the resurrection from the Jewish Feast of First Fruits to Easter in an attempt to disassociate it from Jewish feasts.[242]

The greatest of the church fathers, in terms of his overall impact on theology, was Saint Augustine (354–430). He asserted that the Jews deserved death but were destined to wander the earth to witness the victory of the church over the synagogue.[243]

The Middle Ages

So, by the fifth century, at the beginning of the Middle Ages, the Jews had been demonized, condemned, and ostracized to the point that the church had become a Gentile organization that was off-limits to the very people who founded it! Two erroneous concepts about the Jews had become firmly established in church doctrine:

1) The Jews should be considered "Christ killers" and should be mistreated accordingly.
2) The church has replaced Israel, and God has no future purpose for the Jews.

These concepts were reinforced throughout the Middle Ages in a number of ways.[244]

- Jews were relegated to ghettos and required to wear distinguishing marks.
- Passion plays were used to whip up anti-Semitism as the Jews were portrayed as devils.
- Crusaders were authorized by the church to kill Jews as they encountered them en route to the Holy Land.
- The Black Plague was blamed on Jews for poisoning the wells of Europe.
- The Blood Libel was invented, whereby Jews were accused of kidnapping Gentiles, killing them, and using their blood to drink during the annual celebration of Passover.
- Pogroms were sanctioned by governments, during which Jews

were declared to be open season for persecution and even murder during a specified period of time.

- The Inquisition, which was originally launched to counter heresy within the Catholic Church, ultimately veered off course by condemning the Talmud, resulting in widespread persecution of Jews.

The Impact of the Reformation

The Reformation produced no changes in attitudes toward the Jews. In fact, the hatred of the Jews was reinforced and intensified by the writings of Martin Luther. Initially, Luther was sympathetic toward the Jews because he believed their rejection of the gospel was due to their recognition of the corruption of the church.[245]

But when they continued to reject the gospel, Luther turned against them with a vengeance. In 1543, he wrote a pamphlet in which he referred to them as: "a miserable and accursed people," "stupid fools," "blind and senseless," "thieves and robbers," "the great vermin of humanity," "lazy rogues," and "venomous."[246]

Having dehumanized and demonized them, Luther then proceeded to make a series of drastic proposals for dealing with them:

1) Their synagogues and schools should be burned.
2) Their houses should be destroyed.
3) Their Talmudic writings should be confiscated.
4) Their rabbis should be forbidden to teach.
5) Their money should be confiscated.
6) They should be compelled into forced labor.[247]

A New Form of Anti-Semitism

Needless to say, the Nazis gleefully quoted Luther as they rose to power and launched the Holocaust. In fact, Hitler referred to Luther in his book, *Mein Kampf,* as a "great warrior, a true statesman and a great reformer."[248]

Speaking of the Holocaust, the horror of it tended to mute virulent anti-Semitism among Christian leaders after World War II. But in reality, it continued in a new form called anti-Zionism.

Anti-Zionism is just anti-Semitism in new, sophisticated clothes. Whereas anti-Semitism sought to drive out the Jews from the lands where they lived, anti-Zionism refuses to accept their right to live in their own land.

A good example of the new form of anti-Semitism can be found in a document issued by James Kennedy's Knox Theological Seminary in 2002. It was entitled "An Open Letter to Evangelicals Concerning Israel." It has since been endorsed by hundreds of Christian theologians and pastors, including such luminaries as R. C. Sproul.[249]

The document begins by denouncing those who teach that the Bible's promises concerning the land of Israel are being fulfilled today "in a special region or 'Holy Land,' perpetually set apart by God for one ethnic group alone." It then proceeds to proclaim that the promises made to Abraham "do not apply to any particular ethnic group, but to the church of Jesus Christ, *the true Israel*" (emphasis added). The document then specifically denies the Jews' claim on any land in the Middle East by asserting: "The entitlement of any one ethnic or religious group to territory in the Middle East called the 'Holy Land' cannot be supported by Scripture."[250]

Then, incredibly, the document asserts: "In fact, the land promises specific to Israel in the Old Testament were fulfilled under Joshua."[251] Adding salt to the wounds, the Knox Seminary document concludes with the following observation:

> The present secular state of Israel…is not an authentic or prophetic realization of the Messianic kingdom of Jesus Christ. [True, but keep reading.] Furthermore, a day should not be anticipated in which Christ's kingdom will manifest Jewish distinctives, whether by its location in "the land," by its constituency or by its ceremonial institutions and practices.[252]

Despite these statements, when the anti-Zionists are accused of being anti-Semitic, they deny the accusation vehemently. Here's how Dennis Prager, radio host and political commentator, has replied to their denials in his book, *Why the Jews?*:

> The contention that anti-Zionists are not enemies of Jews, despite the advocacy of policies that would lead to the mass murder of Jews, is, to put it as generously as possible, disingenuous. If anti-Zionism realized its goal, another Jewish holocaust would take place.... Therefore attempts to draw distinctions between anti-Zionism and anti-Semitism are simply meant to fool the naive.[253]

And so you have it—an overview of the sad and sordid history of Christian anti-Semitism rooted in Replacement Theology and continuing to this day under the guise of anti-Zionism.

Christian Palestinianism

In recent years, a new form of this anti-Zionism has raised its ugly head in the form of the Christian Palestinian Movement.[254] James Showers, director of the Friends of Israel, has defined the movement in the following words: "Christian Palestinianism claims modern Israel has no biblical connection with or justification for owning the Promised Land; therefore, it concludes, Israel has become an apartheid state, occupying territory belonging to the Palestinian Arabs."[255]

The movement's most prominent leader over the past few years has been Stephen Sizer, the former Anglican vicar of Christ Church in Surrey, England. The most vocal American advocate has been Gary Burge, an ordained Presbyterian minister, a former professor at Wheaton College, and currently serving as a professor at Calvin Theological Seminary.

Sizer has denounced Israel as an "apartheid state," which he claims is guilty of ethnic cleansing.[256] Further, he has demonized Christians who support Israel as "heretical Armageddonites" whose interpretation of the

Bible "provides a theological endorsement for racial segregation, apartheid and war."[257]

One of the movement's greatest propaganda tools is the Kairos Palestine Document adopted in 2009.[258] It declares "that the Israeli occupation of Palestinian land is a sin against God and humanity" and further asserts "that any theology, seemingly based on the Bible or on faith or on history, that legitimizes the occupation, is far from Christian teachings, because it calls for violence and holy war in the name of God Almighty." That's a mouthful when you consider the fact that it is Muslims, not Christians or Jews, who are calling for holy war in the name of God.

The proponents of the movement hold Christian Zionists in open contempt. The great English theologian, John Stott (1921–2011), endorsed the Kairos proclamation and denounced Christian Zionism as "biblically anathema to the Christian faith."[259] Hank Hanegraaff, "The Bible Answer Man," wrote, "Christian Zionist beliefs and behaviors are the antithesis of biblical Christianity."[260]

One British journalist, Alan Hart, who supports the Christian Palestinian Movement, went so far as to state on his website:

It's time to give Israel's hardcore Zionists their real name. They are the New Nazis.... If Europeans and Americans don't stop the New Nazis, it's likely their endgame will be the extermination of millions of Palestinians.[261]

The Democrat Party in the United States has joined hands with these critics of Israel, and some of its leaders are giving increasing support to the Palestinians while denouncing Israel as an apartheid state. Increasingly, Democrats are mouthing the Hamas slogan: "Palestine must be free from the river to the sea." The river is Jordan and the sea is the Mediterranean. This means the annihilation of Israel.[262]

Karol Markowicz, writing for the *New York Post*, recently observed that "mainstream Democrats" have "rolled over to the far left so quickly on Israel that it's hard to imagine them returning to a sane place."[263] She concluded that "Jews who vote for Democrats in overwhelming numbers, need to finally wake up to the reality that their party despises the world's sole Jewish state."[264]

The Revival of Classic Anti-Semitism

As remembrance of the Holocaust has waned among the general public, the advocates of classic anti-Semitism have come out of the closet. One of the worst examples is Rick Wiles, a Florida pastor who is so vile in his attacks on Jews that his videos have been banned from YouTube. He denounced the Trump impeachment as a "Jew coup."[265] He claimed that Jews would "kill millions of Christians" if they could overthrow Trump.[266] He has characterized Jews as "deceivers" who "plot, lie and do whatever they have to do to accomplish their political agenda."[267]

He even went so far as to blame the coronavirus on the Jews. "The people who are going in to the synagogue are coming out of the synagogue with the virus," Wiles said. "It's spreading in Israel through the synagogues. God is spreading it in your synagogues! You are under judgment because you oppose his son, Jesus Christ. That is why you have a plague in your synagogues. Repent and believe on the name of Jesus Christ, and the plague will stop."[268]

American colleges and universities are hotbeds of anti-Semitism, fueled by left-wing professors, radical student organizations, and films that portray the Israelis as European invaders who have no right to be in the Middle East. Further, they play on the emotions of the students by picturing the Palestinians as victims of Jewish imperialism.[269]

There has also been a surge of anti-Semitism among blacks in the United States. Some of it has been generated by the hate-filled speeches of Louis Farrakhan, who often makes references to the "Satanic Jew."[270] He has blamed the Jews for slavery and for promoting "the myth of black racial inferiority."[271] The flame of anti-Semitism among blacks has also been fanned by the writer James Baldwin, who has made the claim that the slum landlords, butchers, clothiers, and pawnbrokers in Harlem are all Jews who prey on blacks.[272]

The invasion of Muslim immigrants into the United States in recent years has also contributed to the rise of anti-Semitism. This has resulted in the election of Muslim radicals to Congress who speak out constantly against Israel and the Jewish people, often using classic anti-Semitic stereotypes.[273]

Muslims in America have also united in their support of the Boycott, Divestment and Sanction Movement (BDS).[274] This is an anti-Semitic movement that paints Israel falsely as an apartheid state and urges people to boycott all Israeli products, divest from all Israeli corporations, and support international sanctions against the state of Israel. The movement is strongly supported by many churches in the United States, like the United Brethren in Christ, the Religious Society of Friends (Quakers), the Mennonite Church USA, the Presbyterian Church (USA), the Roman Catholic Church, the Unitarian Universalist Association, the United Church of Christ, and the United Methodist Church, among others.[275]

The statistics regarding violence against Jews reflect the effectiveness of the inflammatory anti-Semitic rhetoric. The Anti-Defamation League (ADL) reported that in 2018 there were 1,879 attacks against Jews and Jewish institutions in the United States, with a dramatic increase in physical assaults.[276] The New York City Police Department's report for 2019 shows a total of 423 hate crimes directed at Jews.[277] Another ADL report in May of 2018 uncovered more than 4.2 million tweets with anti-Semitic comments and images during 2017, up from 2.6 million in 2016.[278] Although the number of Jewish people in the United States amounts to only 2 percent of the population, they are used as a convenient scapegoat for all kinds of haters.

The same trend is occurring in Europe. Anti-Semitism is accelerating all across the continent. The European Jewish Congress has reported that "in recent years, the most violent expressions of anti-Semitism hatred have become commonplace in Europe once again."[279] France, which is the home of the largest Jewish community in Europe, experienced a 74 percent increase in anti-Semitic incidents in 2018. In Germany, the total for the same year was 1,646. And for the same year, the United Kingdom reported that anti-Semitic hate incidents hit a record high, with more than one hundred recorded in every month of the year.[280]

Globally, statistics point to the same trend of growing anti-Semitism. In 2014, the ADL conducted a worldwide poll revealing that more than one billion people around the globe hold anti-Semitic views.[281] The poll tracked the attitudes of people in 102 countries and territories. One interesting insight that came from the poll was the revelation that 70 percent of those who hold anti-Semitic views have never actually met a Jewish person.[282]

This brings us back to the point I made at the beginning—that anti-Semitism is a supernatural phenomenon that is motivated by Satan. As such, it is basically irrational in nature, as illustrated by the following story:

> In a park in Europe, during World War II, a Jewish man was sitting reading a book when a Nazi officer approached him and engaged him and began to berate the Jews.
>
> "I tell you, those Jews are sub-human. They are the scum of the earth, and we should get rid of all of them!" The Jewish man did not respond. He continued reading his book. "They control everything, and we must cleanse the world of this venomous race. We must kill them all," added the Nazi officer.
>
> "Yes," nodded the old Jewish man, "we must get rid of all Jews and the bicycle riders."
>
> "Why the bicycle riders?" asked the officer with a puzzled look on his face.
>
> "Why the Jews?" asked the Jewish man.[283]

I think the fundamental reason we are seeing the resurgence of anti-Semitism worldwide is because we have entered the season of the Lord's return. Olivier Melnick agrees with is observation. He is a French Messianic Jew who serves as a regional director for Chosen People Ministries for the western United States. In his book, *End-Times Antisemitism* (2017), he wrote:

Is it possible that the reason we are seeing a resurgence in anti-Semitism with a great emphasis on the irrational aspect of it all, is that Satan knows that his days of glory are coming to an end very shortly? The "prince of this age" is about to be deposed by the King of kings, the Prince of Peace. But Satan's approach to his last moment of fame is that if indeed he goes down—and he is going down—he will double his efforts to take Israel and the Jews with him in a final effort to spit in God's face, if at all possible.[284]

The Response of Scripture

What does the Word of God have to say about all this?

Anti-Semitism: The Scriptures strongly repudiate anti-Semitism. Consider these words from Psalm 129:5–8:

> May all who hate Zion be put to shame and turned backward. Let them be like grass upon the housetops which withers before it grows up, with which the reaper does not fill his hand.… Nor do those who pass by say, "The blessing of the Lord be upon you."

Deicide: In Acts 4:27, the Bible clearly identifies who was responsible for the death of Jesus:

> For truly in this city there were gathered together against Your holy servant, Jesus, whom You did anoint, both Herod and Pontius Pilate, along with the Gentiles and the peoples of Israel.

Notice who is listed here as those responsible for the death of Jesus: the Romans, the Jews, and the Gentiles. And there are others who are not named—you and me! Yes, all of us are responsible for the death of Jesus, for all of us are sinners (Romans 3:23), and Jesus died for all sinners (1 Corinthians 15:3).

Land Promise: Regarding the idea that God has already fulfilled the land promises to the Jews during the time of Joshua, it is interesting to note that long after Joshua, King David wrote in Psalm 105 that the land promise is everlasting in nature and is yet to be fulfilled (Psalm 105:8–11).

The fact is that the Jews have never occupied all the land that was promised to them in the Abrahamic Covenant (Genesis 15:18–21). Under Joshua, they were given only the land that was promised to Moses.

Rejection: Concerning the claim that the Jews have been rejected by God, there are a couple of biblical principles that need to be kept in mind. First, the Bible affirms that the Jews were called as God's chosen people to be witnesses of what it means to have a relationship with Him (Isaiah 43:10–12). And the Bible makes it clear that this calling is "irrevocable" (Romans 11:29).

Discipline: It is true that the Jewish people are currently under discipline because of their rejection of their Messiah. Over and over in their Scriptures, the prophets said they would be disciplined if they were unfaithful, but always the promise was made that they would be preserved. An example of this type of prophetic statement can be found in Jeremiah 30:11:

> "For I am with you," declares the Lord, "to save you; for I will destroy completely all the nations where I have scattered you, only I will not destroy you completely. But I will chasten you justly, and will by no means leave you unpunished."

Replacement: In direct contradiction of Replacement Theology, the Bible teaches that the Jews have never been replaced with the church by God because of their unbelief. In Romans 3, Paul asserts point blank that their rejection of Jesus has not nullified God's faithfulness to the promises He has made to them:

1) What advantage has the Jew? [The church: "None!"]
2) [Paul] Great in every respect. First of all, that they were entrusted with the oracles of God.

3) What then? If some did not believe, their unbelief will not nullify the faithfulness of God, will it? [The church: "Yes!"]

4) [Paul] May it never be! Rather, let God be found true though every man be found a liar.

Paul makes the same point again in Romans 11:1, where he asks: "God has not rejected His people, has He?" The church's response for two thousand years has been "Yes!" But Paul's response is exactly the opposite: "May it never be! For I too am an Israelite, a descendant of Abraham, of the tribe of Benjamin. God has not rejected His people whom He foreknew...."

Preservation: God has preserved the Jewish people in His grace because He loves them. They are the "apple of His eye" (Zechariah 2:8), and He warns against anyone trying to hurt them (Genesis 12:3 and Isaiah 41:11–13) or divide their land (Joel 3:2).

Salvation: Another reason the Jewish people have been preserved is that God is determined to bring a great remnant to salvation (Isaiah 10:20–22). This promise is made repeatedly throughout the Hebrew Scriptures and is confirmed by Paul in the New Testament in Romans 9–11.

The salvation of this remnant is described in detail in Zechariah 12:10, which says that at the end of the Tribulation, the remaining Jews will come to the end of themselves and will turn their hearts to God in repentance and accept Yeshua as their Messiah when He returns to the Mount of Olives.

Primacy: The believing remnant of Jews who are alive at the end of the Tribulation will go into the millennium in the flesh and will comprise the nation of Israel, to whom God will fulfill all the promises He has made to the Jews (Isaiah 60–62). During the millennium, the nation of Israel will be the prime nation in the world through whom God will bless all the other nations (Zechariah 8:22–23).

In summary, the Word of God makes it clear that the Jewish people definitely have a future in the end times and a very important role to play during the millennium.

Conclusion

The fundamental message concerning the Jewish people is that God is in control. He is on His throne. He is sovereign. He has the wisdom and the power to orchestrate all the evil of man and Satan to the triumph of His Son in history and the fulfillment of all His promises to the Jewish people. God has already proved this point with His response to the cross. He took the most dastardly act in the history of mankind and transformed it into the most glorious through the resurrection of His Son.

Satan has to be the most frustrated character in all the universe. And just as he was frustrated in murdering God's Son, He will be frustrated in murdering God's people, for a great remnant of the Jewish people is going to live to the end of the Tribulation. They will be brought to the end of themselves. And when Jesus appears in His Second Coming, "they will look on Me whom they have pierced; and they will mourn for Him, as one mourns for an only son, and they will weep bitterly over Him like the bitter weeping over a firstborn" (Zechariah 12:10).

They will receive Yeshua as their Messiah, and they will cry out *Baruch Haba B'Shem Adonai!* ("Blessed is He who comes in the name of the Lord!" [Matthew 23:39]). What a glorious day that will be. What glory it will bring to the name of God.

Meanwhile, as we await that day, let us meet each new day with the cry from our hearts of "Maranatha! Maranatha! Come quickly Lord Jesus!" (1 Corinthians 16:22).

Conclusion

By Terry James

Coronavirus terror seems to be a primary, camouflaged weapon the powers and principalities in high places have chosen in their final drive to establish Antichrist's throne on planet earth.

Liberty that had been enjoyed across America and many Western nations was greatly diminished within only a few months by an unseen enemy so infinitesimally small it could only be detected through the most powerful of microscopes. People willingly gave up freedoms and economic security, agreeing to incarcerate themselves behind masks and the walls of their homes and apartments. Most all of the COVID-19 appears now to have been a master stroke by the master deceiver.

Those on the Left ideological political side treat those who question the coronavirus as being a deadly pandemic the same way they treat those who deny climate change. These use mainstream news, entertainment venues, and social media to proclaim that anyone who denies that the pandemic should be treated in anyway other than maintaining a complete shutdown of American commerce and society deserves to be publicly castigated. Further, the punishment for denial of COVID-19 being a deadly disease that must bring about dictatorial-like restrictions should be jail sentences.

What the socialistic horde within the US government couldn't do through incessantly trying to pass give-away largesse to a welfare voter base they have seen accomplished through this "crisis." America's economic future, already compromised beyond hope of bringing the national debt under control, has undergone profligate money printing that will require a completely changed monetary system to keep the nation—and the world—from financial Armageddon.

The world's economy is interlinked, with the US being at the top of all things financial. If the American fiscal system collapses, the rest of the world will surely do the same. This includes China, which some pundits are now calling the new top superpower.

I'll leave such examination to experts like my friend Wilfred Hahn, but I believe that claiming that China is now the world's top superpower is nonsense. It's a political talking point for some, but the world continues for now to depend upon the American buying and selling power, as well as its technological research and development, to keep world financial markets, thus nations, afloat.

This is changing, of course. Depending upon how the powers that be react and interact within these circles of monetary stratospherics will determine the fate of all concerned.

And, as we have seen, the trending does not bode well, because at the top are the "powers and principalities" of Ephesians 6:12. The "wickedness in high places" is growing, and it is all moving toward enslavement of all upon the planet.

In fact, the rearrangements that will be necessary to keep things from total collapse await the one man who will bring forth his system of buying and selling prophesied long ago.

And he causeth all, both small and great, rich and poor, free and
bond, to receive a mark in their right hand, or in their foreheads:
And that no man might buy or sell, save he that had the mark,
or the name of the beast, or the number of his name.

Here is wisdom. Let him that hath understanding count the number of the beast: for it is the number of a man; and his number is Six hundred threescore and six. (Revelation 13:16–18)

COVID-19 Moving Toward the Mark?

Many questions come to us who write, broadcast, and teach on Bible prophecy. One question most prominent since the coronavirus crisis began involves the all-consuming matter in the news concerning the vaccine that the pharmaceutical companies have been racing to produce.

The questions: Will inoculations be mandatory, and if they are administered, will they induce into the recipient a tracking device? Would such an eventuation equate to the recipient taking the mark of Revelation 13:16–18?

The deniers that God's prophetic Word has even the slightest spark of common sensibility in considering such a question laugh off all such suggestion. *The Bible, like the name Jesus Christ, has no relevance to anything in today's world* is the attitude.

While it must be said at the outset that any such vaccine that is forthcoming will *not* be the mark as described in Revelation 13, the stage-setting for Bible prophecy fulfillment continues. This includes the technologies that will doubtless be available to Antichrist and his False Prophet when they assume full power during the Tribulation era.

The name that is much in the news with regard to mandatory vaccines that might be coming is Bill Gates, one of the world's wealthiest men. His money places him within the position of "powers and principalities" in "high places." He, of course, proposes that the vaccine be universal and the only way that can happen, he says, is to make it mandatory. He also has suggested that in addition to providing protection from COVID-19, the injection should include identification technology—a chip, we presume—which would have the capability of tracking every person inoculated to assure infected persons remain sufficiently quarantined.

Mr. Gates is, however, a globalist of the first order. Among his desires for a changed world order is the intention to bring the population down so that life on planet earth becomes "sustainable."

By this is meant that there be plenty of clean water, air, and food for sustaining the smaller number of people who inhabit earth. Injecting all people on earth with a vaccine is but a ruse to achieve this goal of sustainability—a goal shared by all of the globalists-elite sort.

One op-ed observer wrote the following:

> Billionaire "philanthropist" and population-control zealot Bill Gates is a criminal madman who must be arrested and tried for "crimes against humanity" and attempted "genocide" through vaccines, according to a firebrand Italian lawmaker who sent shock waves around the world. The member of Parliament also called for Italians to resist vaccines and Deep State tyranny. Fellow legislators applauded.
>
> In the impassioned speech on the floor of Italy's Parliament exposing the Microsoft founder, the parliamentarian, Sara Cunial of Veneto, charged Gates with a long list of crimes, many involving his obsession with vaccinations and population reduction. She also argued that Gates and his toadies were instrumental in shaping the Italian government's disastrous and totalitarian response to the coronavirus outbreak that shredded liberty and left many thousands dead....
>
> A key part of the impassioned plea revolved around Gates' support for forcing mandatory vaccines on all of humanity. In recent weeks, Gates has repeatedly declared on multiple television programs in the United States that the world could not go back to normal unless and until virtually everybody on the planet had been vaccinated with an as-yet undeveloped, experimental vaccine.
>
> In particular, MP Cunial slammed Gates-funded vaccine schemes that she said had "sterilized millions of women in Afri-

can" and paralyzed about 500,000 children in India. Apparently MP Cunial's fury was sparked after Nigerian lawmakers accused Gates, whom she said had numerous conflicts of interest, of trying to bribe them into approving legislation that would force mandatory vaccines on the population there. Opposition parties in Nigeria blasted the "foreign-sponsored bill" and called for the speaker to be impeached if he attempted to force it on members despite the growing resistance....

Especially concerning, she said, are new mRNA vaccines backed by Gates, which have never been used before, that would be "tools for reprogramming our immune system." Indeed, in Foreign Affairs, the mouthpiece for the globalist Council on Foreign Relations, Gates boasted about the prospect of editing people's DNA using new technologies known as "CRISPR"—all "for good," of course.[285]

Deniers that Jesus Christ is God in the flesh who came to this fallen planet to seek and save the lost invariably claim they, themselves, are the answer to mankind's plight. They will *save* earth. Whether saving the planet by forcing all to comply with climate-change mandates and restrictions or saving all people from the coronavirus pandemic through a global gulag economic system of computer buying and selling, they must reign supreme.

At the heart of their intentions is the same hubris with which the Lord of Heaven is all too familiar.

How art thou fallen from heaven, O Lucifer, son of the morning! how art thou cut down to the ground, which didst weaken the nations!

For thou hast said in thine heart, I will ascend into heaven, I will exalt my throne above the stars of God: I will sit also upon the mount of the congregation, in the sides of the north.

I will ascend above the heights of the clouds; I will be like the most High. (Isaiah 14:12–14)

Another question about which many wonder: Why this strange, global pandemic that completely brought the world to a standstill in many ways? Why is this happening, and where might it be leading?

We get a glimpse into the mind of God, perhaps, by considering what one of God's servants charged with being a watchman on the wall during these troubled times has to say.

Dr. David Reagan writes the following:

God never pours out His wrath without warning. He does this warning in two ways. First, He does so by sending prophetic voices to call people to repentance If the people do not repent, then two, He begins to place remedial judgments upon a nation to call its people again to repentance.

God is so patient. He is long-suffering. He does not wish that any should perish but all to come to repentance.

So, what we are seeing, I think, in the world right now is God putting a remedial judgment upon all of the world. We have many signs in the Bible that point to when Jesus is going to return. We have signs like signs of nature, signs of society, spiritual signs, technological signs, signs of world politics, and signs of Israel. All of those signs are converging for the first time ever, clearly indicating that we are now living in the season of the Lord's return.

Look around the world today and we see all of these horrific happenings: wildfires in Australia, locust invasions in Africa, the Coronavirus pandemic spreading across the world, volcanoes erupting, and so many earthquakes occurring. We can see that these end times signs are converging—all of them—for the first time ever. It is as if God is shouting from the heavens: "Jesus is coming soon!"

I believe that this coronavirus pandemic is a worldwide remedial judgment that God is using to call people to repentance, to get them to think about eternity, to get them to think about their lives, and to think about where they are going to be when they are no longer here. I hope you are giving serious thought to your eternal destiny.[286]

To be a denier that Jesus Christ is the Savior and the only Way to salvation and heaven is to be part of this world system that is doomed to face God's judgment and wrath. God says that He is not willing for any to perish, but wants all to come to repentance.

You can be among those who instantaneously go with His family when Christ calls all born-again believers to be with Him, either through the portal of death or through the glorious Rapture.

Either way, your eternal destiny is but one heartbeat away.

Here is how you must repent; here is how to make sure that you are not among the lawless:

That if thou shalt confess with thy mouth the Lord Jesus, and shalt believe in thine heart that God hath raised him from the dead, thou shalt be saved.

For with the heart man believeth unto righteousness; and with the mouth confession is made unto salvation. (Romans 10:9–10)

ABOUT THE AUTHORS

Terry James

 Terry James is author, general editor, and/or coauthor of more than thirty books on Bible prophecy and geopolitics, hundreds of thousands of which have been sold worldwide. He has also written fiction and nonfiction books on a number of other topics.

James is a frequent lecturer on the study of end-time phenomena and interviews often with national and international media on topics involving world issues and events as they might relate to Bible prophecy. He is partner with Todd Strandberg and general editor in the www.raptureready.com website, which was recently rated as the number-one Bible prophecy website on the Internet. The website has more than twenty-five thousand articles and much more material for those who visit the site.

He writes a weekly commentary for the website in which he looks at current issues and events in light of Bible prophecy. James speaks often at prophecy conferences. He is a member of the Pre-Trib Research Center, founded by Dr. Tim LaHaye. His personal blog is terryjamesprophecyline.com. He lives with his wife, Margaret, near Little Rock, Arkansas.

Jonathan C. Brentner

Jonathan C. Brentner is an author, blogger, Bible teacher, and retired financial analyst. Through his writing, he reaches thousands each month with his perspectives on biblical prophecy through his website at www. jonathanbrentner.com.

Jonathan has a BA in biblical studies from John Brown University along with an MDiv degree from Talbot Theological Seminary. He was a pastor for six years before pursuing an MBA degree at the University of Iowa, which led to a lengthy career as a financial analyst at a large corporation. He retired in 2016 to devote his time to writing.

Jonathan and his wife Ruth reside in Roscoe, Illinois. Together they have five children and a dozen grandchildren scattered about in Wisconsin, Iowa, Texas, and Illinois.

Daymond Duck

Daymond Duck is a graduate of the University of Tennessee in Knoxville, the founder and president of Prophecy Plus Ministries, the best-selling author of a shelf full of books (three have been published in foreign languages), a member of the prestigious Pre-Trib Study Group, a conference speaker, and a writer for raptureready.com. He is a retired United Methodist pastor, has made more than three hundred TV appearances, and has been a member of the Baptist church in his hometown since 2006. He can be contacted at duck_daymond@yahoo.com.

Jim Fletcher

Jim Fletcher is a popular blogger (Jerusalem Post, RaptureReady, WND, Beliefnet) and author whose specialty is Bible prophecy and Israel. He has a BA in journalism and has spent many years as a book editor in the Christian publishing industry. Since 2007, he has been a freelance writer and editor, authoring several books and writing columns and op-eds. A frequent visitor to Israel, Jim has cultivated rich contacts over the years and loves to teach Bible prophecy as an evangelism tool. He lives in a pastoral setting in the Ozark Mountains of northwest Arkansas. He can be reached at jim1fletcher@yahoo.com.

Pete Garcia

Pete Garcia is a writer, speaker, and teacher of Bible prophecy and apologetics. He is also a twenty-year Army veteran, with numerous deployments to the Middle East and overseas tours to Europe and Asia. He holds a bachelor of arts in international relations, with a focus in Russian and military history.

Pete began his writing career with *The Omega Letter* (2011–2018) and has since branched out to create his own website, www.rev310.com. To date, he has written more than four hundred articles featured on numerous websites and platforms. Pete is a happily married father to five wonderful children. Most importantly, he is a believer in our Lord Jesus Christ.

Mike Gendron

A devout Roman Catholic for over thirty-four years, evangelist Mike Gendron was saved by God's amazing grace when he began reading the Bible for the first time in 1981. He is a 1992 graduate of Dallas Theological Seminary, frequently speaks at international Bible conferences, and teaches the students and faculty at The Master's Seminary, The Master's Academy International, Dallas Theological Seminary, Moody Bible Institute, and Tyndale Theological Seminary. Mike has done seminars at hundreds of churches throughout the world and has appeared as a guest on many radio and TV programs, including the History Channel.

Mike is director and founder of Proclaiming the Gospel Ministry, a thirty-year-old evangelistic outreach to those who are lost in religion. He is a prolific writer, with numerous books, booklets, and articles to his credit. His book *Preparing for Eternity* offers a comprehensive teaching on Roman Catholicism as seen through the lens of Scripture, and his most recent book, *Contending for the Gospel,* addresses the greatest attack on the Christian faith today—the purity and exclusivity of the gospel.

His ministry website, www.ProclaimingTheGospel.org, provides a wealth of information that brings clarity to the doctrinal differences separating Roman Catholicism and biblical Christianity.

Wilfred Hahn

Wilfred Hahn has worked on the frontlines of global money for a period spanning five decades. His executive roles have included chief investment officer managing billions of roving capital around the world, a research director for a major Wall Street firm, chairman of a large offshore mutual fund company, and an associate editor with respected international economist Dr. Kurt

Richebächer. Uniquely, he is versed in Scripture and eschatological perspectives as well as economic and financial theory. He is sought out for his reasoned views with respect to Christian eschatological perspectives and global political economic developments. Wilfred has authored hundreds of articles and produced some forty books and booklets. Earlier books, *The Endtime Money Snare: How to Live Free* (2001) and *Global Financial Apocalypse Prophesied: Preserving True Riches in an Age of Deception and Trouble* (2009) served as insightful forewarnings.

Tom Hoffman

 Tom Hoffman, who has earned several degrees, including a doctorate in educational leadership from Hamline University (St. Paul, Minnesota), was a teacher, school principal, and university professor for thirty-eight years before he decided to devote himself fully to a lifelong passion: Bible prophecy.

He hopes his books will be helpful to those interested in learning more about the Word of God and receiving the truth of Jesus Christ.

Hoffman is a devoted father to three children, grandfather to three, and has been married to his wife, Krista, for thirty-seven years. An avid reader, writer, golfer, and fisherman, he lives in Minnesota, the "Land of Ten Thousand Lakes," where Jesus is everything, and family is a close second.

You can find out more about the author and his work on his website, www.fearlesstom.com, or on Twitter at https://twitter.com/hoffmanonline.

Tom Hughes

Tom Hughes serves as lead pastor of 412 Church in San Jacinto, California. He has been teaching Bible prophecy for over twenty-five years and is the founder of Hope For Our Times. He regularly appears on a variety of TV, radio, and Internet programs.

Nathan E. Jones

Nathan Jones serves as the Internet evangelist for Lamb & Lion Ministries. He can be found cohosting the ministry's television program *Christ in Prophecy*, growing and developing the Web ministry at christinprophecy.org, authoring books such as *12 Faith Journeys of the Minor Prophets*, blogging daily on the Christ in Prophecy Journal, discussing current events on the Christ in Prophecy Facebook group, producing video Q & As such as *The Inbox*, being interviewed on radio programs, speaking at conferences and churches, and answering Bible-related questions sent in from all over the world.

A lifelong student of the Bible and an ordained minister, Nathan graduated from Cairn University with a bachelor's degree in Bible. He attended Southern Baptist Theological Seminary and received his master's degree in management and leadership at Liberty University.

Jan Markell

Jan Markell is founder and President of Olive Tree Ministries headquartered in Minneapolis, Minnesota. She has hosted "Understanding the Times Radio" for twenty years on nine hundred radio stations. Her "Understanding the Times" prophecy conferences have drawn thousands from around the world. Jan has authored eight books, and in 2017, Lamb & Lion Ministries declared her to be one of the top "watchman" voices of our times. Learn more at www.olivetreeviews.org.

Don McGee

Don McGee, founder and director of CSM (Crown & Sickle Ministries), is a Vietnam War veteran and retired Louisiana state trooper. He was a pastor for twelve years, and since 2002 has been an evangelist whose focus is exclusively on Bible prophecy. He and his wife, Valerie, live in a rural area near Amite, Louisiana. They have two grown children and three grandchildren.

Randy Nettles

Randy Nettles is a frequent contributor of articles to the Rapture Ready website and has done so since 2012. Most of his articles deal with eschatology and prophecy Scripture in regard to the Church and Israel. Randy's area of expertise includes the Feasts of the Lord, Jacob's Trouble/Day of the Lord/Tribulation, and biblical chronology of mankind. He is sometimes referred to as "the numbers guy" for his writing on numbers in Scripture and their biblical significance.

Randy continues to work in the electrical industry after forty-five years. He lives in marillo, Texas, with his wife of thirty years, Tanya, and has two grown Christian children. Randy welcomes any correspondence or inquiry regarding his part in this book and/or any of his articles. You can reach him at nettlesr@suddenlink.net.

Ryan Pitterson

Ryan Pitterson is a biblical researcher and writer with an emphasis on ancient Hebrew thought and theology. He is the author of Amazon #1 best-seller *Judgment of the Nephilim*—a comprehensive biblical study of the Nephilim giants and the account of Genesis 6.

The book has received critical acclaim from highly respected biblical scholars, including Gary Stearman of Prophecy Watchers, who declared it "the most comprehensive, well-researched book ever written on the fallen angels." Ryan has appeared on the *Prophecy Watchers* TV program, *Coast to Coast AM*, *Acceleration Radio* with L. A. Marzulli, Josh Peck *Underground Church,* and many other programs.

Currently, Ryan is completing the sequel to *Judgment of the Nephilim*, which will focus on the Nephilim and fallen angels in the end times. Ryan received his bachelor of arts degree in political science from the University of Rochester and his juris doctor from Columbia University Law School.

David Reagan

Dr. David R. Reagan, senior evangelist for Lamb & Lion Ministries, an interdenominational, evangelical ministry devoted to proclaiming the soon return of Jesus, is a native Texan who resides in a suburb of Dallas with his wife of fifty-nine years.

A lifelong Bible student, teacher, and preacher, Dr. Reagan is the author of many religious essays published in a wide variety of journals and magazines. He has authored eighteen books, all of which are related to Bible prophecy, and serves as the editor of the ministry's bimonthly *Lamplighter* magazine. His sermons have been distributed worldwide in both audio and video formats, and his books have been translated into many different languages.

Dr. Reagan has conducted prophecy conferences all over the world, and he has led more than forty-five pilgrimages to Israel that focus on the prophetic significance of the sites visited. For twenty-two years, Dr. Reagan was the spokesman on Lamb & Lion's daily, nationally broadcast radio program, "Christ in Prophecy." The ministry's website can be found at www.lamblion.com.

Larry Spargimino

Pastor Larry Spargimino has been with Southwest Radio Church since 1998. A graduate of Southwestern Seminary in Ft. Worth with a PhD, he is regularly heard on the *Watchman on the Wall* broadcast of Southwest Radio Church. He has been a pastor for many years and is currently pastoring in Oklahoma City. He also had the privilege of starting a church and a Christian school in Pakistan. Larry has a heart for missions and works with overseas students in the US. He is currently working on a book titled *Power Life: How Grace Is Overcoming in A Hostile World.*

Todd Strandberg

 Todd Strandberg is the founder of www.raptureready.com, the most highly visited prophecy website on the Internet. He is a partner in the site with Terry James. The site has been written about in practically every major news outlet in the nation and around the world. Founded in 1987 when few websites existed, Rapture Ready now commands the attention of a quarter million visitors per month, with more than thirteen million hits registered during most thirty-day periods.

Strandberg is president of Rapture Ready and coauthor of *Are You Rapture Ready?*—a Penguin Group book under the E P Dutton imprint. He has written hundreds of major articles for the site, which have been distributed in major publications and websites around the nation and the world. He writes a highly read column under the site's "Nearing Midnight" section. Strandberg created "The Rapture Index"—a Dow Jones-like system of prophetic indicators—that continues to draw the attention of most major news outlets.

Notes

1. https://freedomhouse.org/article/
   media-restrictions-today-will-harm-democracy-tomorrow.
2. htttts://www.catholic.org//new/hf/faith/story.php?id=51077.
3. https://opengov.ideascale.com/a/dtd/David-Rockefeller-s-book-Memoirs-
   admits-secretly-conspiring-for-a-NWO/4007-4049.
4. https://www.google.com/search?q=Economist+magazine+Macron+Europe
   %27s+Savior&source=lnms&tbm=isch&sa=X&ved=2ahUKEwiE9snQ1_
   fpAhWwQjABHTN6AN4Q_AUoAnoECAwQBA&biw=1361&bih=539#i
   mgrc=2NPEAenW4_cX8M.
5. http://content.time.com/time/covers/0,16641,20130325,00.html.
6. https://waltheyer.com.
7. https://thefederalist.com/2016/09/21/
   pushing-kids-transgenderism-is-medicalmalpractice.
8. Jeremiah J. Johnston, *Unimaginable: What Our World Would Be Like Without Christianity* (Minneapolis, MN: Bethany House, 2017) 20.
9. *Unimaginable,* 17.
10. Mona Charen, *Sex Matters: How Modern Feminism Lost Touch with Science, Love, and Common Sense* (New York, NY: Crown Forum, 2018) introduction.
11. Ibid., 2–3.
12. www.redstate.com/alexparker/2019/01/30/
    munroe-bergdorf-victorias-secretdiscrimination.
13. J. Budziszewski, *Written on the Heart: The Case for Natural Law* (Downers Grove, IL: Intervarsity Press, 1997) 180–81.
14. Pbskids.org/Arthur.
15. Jennifer Robeck Morse, *The Sexual State: How Elite Ideologies Are Destroying Lives and Why the Church Was Right All Along* (Charlotte, NC: TANBooks, 2018) 56.

16. www.forbes.com/sites/erichbachman/2019/05/30/what-is-the-equality-act-and-whatwill-happen-if-it-becomes-law.

17. www.cnsnews.com/news/article/emily-ward/5-year-old-girl-allegedly-assaulted.

18. www.nbcnews.com/feature/nbc-out/trump-opposes-federal-lgbtq-nondiscrimination-bill.

19. Hillary Morgan Ferrer, general editor and author of cited material, *Momma Bear Apologetics: Empowering Your Kids to Challenge Cultural Lies* (Eugene, OR: Harvest House, 2019) 36.

20. Ibid., 235–241.

21. Michael L. Brown, *Jezebel's War with America: The Plot to Destroy Our County and What We Can Do to Turn the Tide* (Lake Mary, FL: Frontline, 2019) 83–85.

22. www1.cbn.com/700club/Christopher-yuan-leaving-behind-double-life.

23. Christopher Yuan, *Holy Sexuality and the Gospel: Sex, Desire, and Relationships Shaped by God's Grand Story* (New York, NY: Multnomah/Random House, 2018) 51–52.

24. Nancy R. Pearcey, *Love Thy Body: Answering Hard Questions about Life and Sexuality* (Grand Rapids, MI: Baker Books, 2018) 8.

25. Ibid., 12.

26. Ibid., 27.

27. Ibid., 29.

28. Julie Slattery, *Rethinking Sexuality: God's Design and Why It Matters* (New York, NY: Multnomah/Penguin Random House, 2018) 53.

29. https://en.wikipedia.org/wiki/"civilized"_sexual-morality.

30. www.compellingtruth.org/print/christian-romance.

31. See Kerby Anderson, *Christian Ethics in Plain Language* (Nashville, TN: Thomas Nelson, 2005) 84–96, 97–105, 106–116, 117–122.

32. Allie Anderson-Henson, *Unscrambling the Millennial Paradox: Why the Unreachables" May Be the Key to the Next Great Awakening* (Crane, MO: Defender, 2019) 190.

33. Charles Colson and Ellen S. Vaughn, *God and Government: An Insider's View on the Boundaries between Faith and Politics* (Grand Rapids, MI: Zondervan, 2007).

34. Ibid.

35. Ibid.

36. Ibid.

37. https://www.britannica.com/biography/bell-hooks.

38. David Horowitz, *The Professors: The 101 Most Dangerous Academics in America*. (Washington, DC: Regnery, 2006).

39. bell hooks, *Lion's Roar—Buddhist Wisdom for Our Times. Rebels Dilemma*, November 1, 1998.

40. Horowitz.

41. Don Stewart, Blue Letter Word Commentary.

42. Horowitz.

43. Ibid.

44. Ibid.

45. Ibid.

46. Mosi Reeves, "8 Ways Tupac Shakur Changed the World," *Rolling Stone*, September 13, 2016, https://www.rollingstone.com/music/music-news/8-ways-tupac-shakur-changed-the-world-128421/.

47. Eric M. Dyson, *Holler If You Hear Me: The Search for Tupac Shakur* (New York: Basic Civitas Books, 2001).

48. Mark A. LeVine, UCI Faculty Profile System, https://www.faculty.uci.edu/profile.cfm?faculty_id=5356.

49. Ibid.

50. Horowitz.

51. Ibid.

52. Ron Boussa, "Exclusive: Exxon Eyes Israel Gas Bid in Major Middle East Shift," Reuters News Service, March 13, 2019, https://www.reuters.com/article/us-ceraweek-energy-israel-exclusive/exclusive-exxon-eyes-israel-gas-bid-in-major-middle-east-shift-idUSKCN1QU2U2.

53. Horowitz.

54. Ibid.

55. Ibid.

56. Jean M. Twenge, "Have Smartphones Destroyed a Generation?" (accessed May 2020), https://www.theatlantic.com/magazine/archive/2017/09/has-the-smartphone-destroyed-a-generation/534198/.

57. Victoria Barret, "A New Label for Kids Today: The Distracted Generation" (accessed May 2020), https://www.forbes.com/sites/victoriabarret/2012/11/01/a-new-label-for-kids-today-the-distracted-generation/#790f0e6958ec.

58. Ibid.

59. Ibid.

60. Twenge.

61. Ibid.

62. Ibid.

63. Unless otherwise noted, all quoted Scripture in this chapter is from the New King James Version (NKJV) of the Bible.

64. "Meet Powerwall, Your Home Battery" (accessed May 2020), https://www.tesla.com/powerwall.

65. "History of the Computers" (accessed May 2020), http://www.historyofcomputer.org/.

66. "Number of Network Connected Devices Per Person Around the World from 2003 to 2020," *Statista* (November 30, 2016), https://www.statista.com/statistics/678739/forecast-on-connected-devices-per-person/.

67. Annalee Newitz, "What Is the Singularity and Will You Live to See It?," *Gizmodo*, (May 10, 2010), https://io9.gizmodo.com/what-is-the-singularity-and-will-you-live-to-see-it-5534848.

68. Ibid.

69. History.com Editors, "The Invention of the Internet," *History*, (October 28, 2019), https://www.history.com/topics/inventions/invention-of-the-internet.

70. "Internet Stats & Facts (2020)" (accessed May 2020), https://hostingfacts.com/internet-facts-stats/.

71. Ibid.

72. Ibid.

73. Ibid.

74. Laura Nichols, "Poll: Gmail Dominates Email Use Among Millennials, Gen X," *Morning Consultant*, (June 21, 2017), https://morningconsult.com/2017/06/21/poll-gmail-dominates-email-use/.

75. "Quotes" (accessed May 2020), https://www.quotes.net/mquote/679654.

76. "The History of Ecommerce: How Did It All Begin?," *Meva* (October 26, 2011), https://www.miva.com/blog/the-history-of-ecommerce-how-did-it-all-begin/.

77. Ibid.

78. "Internet Stats & Facts (2020)."

79. Aultman College, "Understanding Your Learning Styles" (accessed March 2020), http://www.aultmancollege.edu/Files/Understanding-Learning-Styles.pdf.

80. John Dyer, *From the Garden to the City: The Redeeming and Corrupting Power of Technology* (Grand Rapids, MI: Kregel, 2011) 22.

81. Steve Turner, *Popcultured: Thinking Christianly about Style, Media and Entertainment* (Downers Grove, IL: Intervarsity, 2013) 60.

82. Craig Loscalzo, *Apologetic Preaching: Proclaiming Christ to a Postmodern World* (Downers Grove, IL: InterVarsity, 2000) 10–12.
83. Maryam Mohsin, "10 YouTube Stats Every Marketer Should Know in 2020," *Oberlo* (accessed March 2020), https://www.oberlo.com/blog/youtube-statistics.
84. Ibid.
85. Ibid.
86. Ibid.
87. "Internet Stats & Facts (2020)."
88. Kevin Anderton, "Research Report Shows How Much Time We Spend Gaming," *Forbes* (March 21, 2019), https://www.forbes.com/sites/kevinanderton/2019/03/21/research-report-shows-how-much-time-we-spend-gaming-infographic/.
89. Dave Chaffey, "Global Social Media Research Summary 2020," *Smart Insights* (April 17, 2020), https://www.smartinsights.com/social-media-marketing/social-media-strategy/new-global-social-media-research/.
90. Ibid.
91. Ibid.
92. Kim Komando, "How to Stop Your Smartphone from Tracking Your Every Move, Sharing Data and Sending Ads," *USAToday* (February 14, 2019), https://www.usatoday.com/story/tech/columnist/komando/2019/02/14/your-smartphone-tracking-you-how-stop-sharing-data-ads/2839642002/.
93. "Silicon Valley Is Listening to Your Most Intimate Moments," *Bloomberg Businessweek*, (December 11, 2019), https://www.bloomberg.com/news/features/2019-12-11/silicon-valley-got-millions-to-let-siri-and-alexa-listen-in.
94. Andy Meek, "Amazon-owned Ring Has Reportedly Been Spying on Customer Camera Feeds," *BGR*, (January 10, 2019), https://bgr.com/2019/01/10/ring-camera-customer-feeds-accessed-creepy-privacy-violation/.
95. William Edgar, *Created and Creating: A Biblical Theology of Culture* (Downers Grove: IVP Academic, 2017) 6, 233.
96. Steve Turner, *Popcultured: Thinking Christianly About Style, Media and Entertainment* (Downers Grove: Intervarsity, 2013) 8.
97. Ibid.
98. Rick Richardson, *Evangelism Outside the Box: New Ways to Help People Experience the Good News* (Downers Grove, IL: InterVarsity Press, 2000) 23.
99. https://www.pewforum.org/religious-landscape-study/.

100. https://www.marketplace.org/2020/02/14/
     witchcraft-goes-mainstream-becomes-big-business/.

101. Ibid.

102. https://www.marieclaire.com/culture/a24440291/witches-2018-midterms/.

103. https://beginningandend.com/
     foxs-lucifer-tv-show-satanic-deception-goes-primetime/.

104. https://supernatural.fandom.com/wiki/God.

105. Ibid.

106. https://supernatural.fandom.com/wiki/Cain.

107. Ibid.

108. https://supernatural.fandom.com/wiki/Eve.

109. https://supernatural.fandom.com/wiki/Lilith.

110. https://supernatural.fandom.com/wiki/Michael.

111. https://supernatural.fandom.com/wiki/Jesus_Christ.

112. Dr. Charles Cowan, *Thoughts on Satanic Influence of Modern Spiritualism Considered*, Second Edition, 1861, p. 104–15.

113. "Healing Crystals—What Are They and How Should You Use Them?" *Elle* magazine, https://www.elle.com/uk/life-and-culture/culture/articles/a31572/what-are-healing-crystals-how-to-use-them/.

114. "Vibrational Energy Healing with Crystals," https://rainbowsofhealing.com/113-2/.

115. https://www.voxmagazine.com/news/crystals/article_17407170-08f5-11ea-ad7c-a729bda0581c.html.

116. Ibid.

117. Jonathan Gill, "Levi's Urim and Thummim Found with Christ. A Discourse on Deut. 33:8. Wherein Some Account Is Given of the Urim and Thummim, and in What Sense They Belong to Christ, Volume 1, 1700, p. 10–12.

118. Thomas Scott, *The Holy Bible, Containing the Old and New Testaments, with Original Notes, Practical Observations and Copious Marginal References*, Volume 1, 1814, p. 1061.

119. Joseph F. Berg, *Abaddon and Mahanaim, or, Daemons and Guardian Angels*, 1856, p. 94.

120. High Henry Snell, *Notes on the Revelation, with Practical Reflections*, 1866, p. 115.

121. https://moonrisecrystals.com/third-eye-chakra-stones/.

122. *The Holy Bible According to the Authorized Version (A.D. 1611): Hebrews to Revelation*, Edited by F.C. Cook, 1890, p. 617.

123. http://newlifeayahuascaretreat.com/the-third-eye/.

124. https://howtospendit.ft.com/travel/206231-business-leaders-new-passion-
     for-mind-altering-amazonian-retreats.

125. Ibid.

126. https://www.pewresearch.org/fact-tank/2018/10/01/new-age-beliefs-
     common-among-both-religious-and-nonreligious-americans/.

127. https://beginningandend.com/apostasy-alert-bethel-churchs-attempted-
     resurrection-of-2-year-old-why-christians-should-beware/.

128. Ibid.

129. Ibid.

130. Ibid.

131. https://www.critlarge.com/articles/2019/7/19/bethels-false-gospel.

132. https://www.youtube.com/watch?v=z3MdF6GJ6fE.

133. https://www.youtube.com/watch?v=z3MdF6GJ6fE.

134. http://redeemermodesto.com/events/2020/1/25/
     know-your-number-enneagram-conference.

135. https://www.gracefirst.org/welcome/contact-us/.

136. https://multiplyvineyard.org/wp-content/uploads/2017/12/An-Evangelicals-
     Guide-to-the-Enneagram-Christianity-Today.pdf.

137 https://en.wikipedia.org/wiki/Fourth_Way_enneagram.

138. Ibid.

139. Ibid.

140. H. P. Blavatsky, *The Secret Doctrine*, Volume II, 1888, pp. 215, 216, 220,
     245, 255, 533.

141. http://www.natcath.org/NCR_Online/documents/ennea2.htm.

142. Ibid.

143. Ibid.

144. *The Sacred Enneagram*, p. 29.

145 Suzanne Stabile, *The Road Back to You: An Enneagram Journey*, p. 24.

146. https://beginningandend.com/
     lucifer-rising-billie-ellish-pop-musics-satanic-sensation/.

147. https://beginningandend.com/
     god-is-a-woman-ariana-grandes-satanic-blasphemy/.

148. https://revolution2-0.org/bread-circuses-masses-not-just-ancient-rome/.

149. https://www.oxfordreference.com/view/10.1093/oi/
     authority.20110803095525429.

150. https://www.theguardian.com/commentisfree/2019/jun/19/
     reparations-slavery-ta-nehisi-coates-v-coleman-hughes.

151. https://m.washingtontimes.com/news/2019/jun/26/
democrats-add-gay-reparation-to-costly-schemes-tha/.

152. Julie Kelly, "The Hypocrisy of Climate Change Advocates," *The Hill*,
January 6, 2017.

153. "Greta Thunberg, Person of the Year," *Time*, December 23/December 30,
2019.

154. Ibid.

155. "Pope Francis Declares 'Climate Emergency' and Urges Action," *Guardian*,
June, 14, 2019, https://www.theguardian.com/environment/2019/jun/14/
pope-francis-declares-climate-emergency-and-urges-action.

156. Viv Forbes, geologist, "The CO2 Scare Is Proving False—It's Time for Some
Climate Sense," December 23, 2019, Climate Depot website.

157. Volcano Discovery website, https://www.volcanodiscovery.com/erupting_
volcanoes.html.

158. James Edward Kamis, "Discovery of Massive Volcanic CO2
Emissions Puts Damper on Global Warming Theory," Climate
Dispatch, November 6, 2018, https://climatechangedispatch.com/
massive-volcano-emissions-warming/.

159. Ibid.

160. Ibid.

161. https://www.co2.earth.

162. Dr. Roger Higgs, *Vast Body of Scientific Data for Past 2,000 Years Affirms Sun,
Not CO2, Controls Climate*, Principia Scientific International, January 14,
2020, https://principia-scientific.org/.

163. Cap Alolon, "Acclaimed Israeli Astrophysicist Suggests The Sun Drives
Earth's Climate, Not CO2," Electoverse, http://electroverse.net/acclaimed-
israeli-astrophysicist-suggests-that-the-sun-drives-earths-climate-not-co2/.

164. Ibid.

165. David Kupelian, "The Democratic Party's Ultimate Coup D'etat,"
WND, December 1, 2019, https://www.wnd.com/2019/12/
democratic-partys-ultimate-coup-detat/.

166. Ibid.

167. Conclusions and Recommendations of NASA engineers and scientists.

168. John Stossal, "Climate Myths," November 20, 2019, https://www.
johnstossel.com/climate-myths/.

169. Jack Hellner, "Global Warming, Global Cooling, Climate Change, Climate
Emergency, Climate Catastrophe, Climate Collapse, or Existential Threat?"
Amerian Thinker, December 4, 2019.

170. "97 Articles Refuting the '97% Consensus,'" Climate Change Dispatch, https://climatechangedispatch.com/97-articles-refuting-the-97-consensus/.

171. Ibid.

172. Alolon, "Acclaimed Israeli."

173. E. Jeffrey Ludwig, "The UN Wants to Be Our World Government by 2030," American Thinker, October 27, 2018.

174. "Transforming our World: The 2030 Agenda for Sustainable Development," United Nations.

175. See also Zachary B. Wolf, "Here's What the Green New Deal Actually Says," February 14, 2019, CNN, https://www.cnn.com/2019/02/14/politics/green-new-deal-proposal-breakdown/index.html.

176. John Edison, "The Cynical Plot Behind Global Warming Hysteria," American Thinker, September 30, 2019.

177. Wikipedia, "Imagine" (John Lennon song).

178. Amir Tsarfati, Bold Israel website quote from November 29, 2019.

179. Randy Alcorn, Heaven (Carol Stream, IL: Tyndale House, 2004) 108.

180. E. Calvin Beisner, "Foundational Principles of Biblical Earth Stewardship," Cornwall Alliance, https://cornwallalliance.org/landmark-documents/foundational-principles-of-biblical-earth-stewardship/.

181. John Stossal, "Climate Myths," November 20, 2019, https://www.johnstossel.com/climate-myths/.

182. All Scripture in this chapter is taken from the New King James Version®. Copyright © 1982 by Thomas Nelson. Used by permission. All rights reserved.

183. G. H. Pember (1884), Earth's Earliest Ages: And Their Connection with Modern Spiritualism and Theosophy: Free Download, Borrow, and Streaming: Internet Archive, https://archive.org/details/earthsearliestag00pemb/page/448/mode/2up.

184. Bruce F. Campbell (1980), Ancient Wisdom Revived: A History of the Theosophical Movement (Berkeley: University of California Press; ISBN 978-0520039681), https://www.cambridge.org/core/journals/church-history/article/ancient-wisdom-revived-a-history-of-the-theosophical-movement-by-bruce-f-campbell-berkeley-university-of-california-press-1980-x-249-pp-1295/5C3FD9D0B72C3E78F73177C1C1EACBAB.

185 Ibid.

186. Artikler, Theosophical Constitution + Rules 1891… (n.d.), https://www.global-theosophy.net/ts_constitution_rules.php.

187. Many religions believe in a world teacher, a "Coming One," knowing him under such names as the Lord Maitreya, the Imam Mahdi, the Kalki Avatar, and the Bodhisattva. These terms are sometimes used in versions of the Great Invocation for people of specific faiths.

188. https://www.lucistrust.org/the_great_invocation/articles.

189. https://en.wikipedia.org/wiki/Ruin_value.

190. "The 'Ruin Value' of Monumental Architecture," https://www.libraryofsocialscience.com/newsletter/posts/2014/2014-12-9-odonnell2.html.

191. https://books.google.com/books?id=niEoCgAAQBAJ&pg=PT135&lpg=PT135&dq=Germany+has+been+transformed+into+a+great+house+of+the+Lord&source=bl&ots=xqPaXvxJra&sig=ACfU3U3BBkKeGiFbvpTrcqIFHAH5-p8ZXQ&hl=en&sa=X&ved=2ahUKEwiextqw_aToAhUC2qwKHbmvDKIQ6AEwAHoECAUQAQ#v=onepage&q=Germany%20has%20been%20transformed%20into%20a%20great%20house%20of%20the%20Lord&f=false.

192. D. R. Faulkner (November 13, 2013), "The Second Law of Thermodynamics and the Curse," https://answersingenesis.org/physics/the-second-law-of-thermodynamics-and-the-curse/.

193. "The Vibrant Religious Life of Silicon Valley, and Why It's Killing the Economy." (May 22, 2019), https://marginalia.lareviewofbooks.org/the-vibrant-religious-life-of-silicon-valley-and-why-its-killing-the-economy-by-samuel-loncar/.

194. William Butler Yeats. (n.d.), "The Second Coming," https://www.poetryfoundation.org/poems/43290/the-second-coming.

195. https://sovereignsky.com/.

196. https://id2020.org/.

197. Eric Kurlander, *Hitler's Monsters: A Supernatural History of the Third Reich*, https://yalebooks.yale.edu/book/9780300189452/hitlers-monsters.

198. David Wright, June 7, 2013, https://abcnews.go.com/blogs/entertainment/2013/06/why-are-we-obsessed-with-superheroes.

199. "Operation Paperclip: The Secret Intelligence Program to Bring Nazi Scientists to America," Central Intelligence Agency, (1102, June), https://www.cia.gov/library/center-for-the-study-of-intelligence/csi-publications/csi-studies/studies/vol-58-no-3/operation-paperclip-the-secret-intelligence-program-to-bring-nazi-scientists-to-america.html.

200. K. Eschner (April 13, 2017), "What We Know about the CIA's Midcentury

Mind-Control Project," https://www.smithsonianmag.com/smart-news/what-we-know-about-cias-midcentury-mind-control-project-180962836/.

201. https://en.wikipedia.org/wiki/Georgia_Guidestones.

202. https://en.wikipedia.org/wiki/World_Council_of_Churches.

203. https://www.un.org/en/sections/un-charter/chapter-i/index.html.

204. https://en.wikipedia.org/wiki/Criticism_of_the_United_Nations.

205. https://www.icc-cpi.int/about.

206. Some older Christians refer to *The Screwtape Letters* as a classic, and that is an appropriate description. The real tragedy, however, is that many younger Christians have never heard of this work.

207. https://fee.org/articles/john-dewey-and-the-decline-of-american-education/.

208. https://time.com/4549409/the-weather-underground-bad-moon-rising/.

209. https://thehill.com/blogs/pundits-blog/presidential-campaign/32072-obama-and-bill-ayers-together-from-the-beginning.

210. https://www.iwp.edu/articles/2018/02/01/the-tragedy-of-american-education-the-role-of-john-dewey/.

211. https://www.forbes.com/sites/modeledbehavior/2017/07/29/the-delusion-of-self-reliant-off-the-grid-living/#6edd6e9343d2.

212. https://www.fb.org/newsroom/fast-facts.

213. In this chapter, all Scripture quoted will be from the NKJV.

214. John 15:19, John 16:33, John 17:15–18, John 18:36, 1 Corinthians 2:12, 1 Corinthians 3:19, Galatians 4:3, Galatians 6:14, Ephesians 2:2, Colossians 2:8, Colossians 2:20, James 1:27, 2 Peter 2:20, 1 John 4:4–6, 1 John 5:4–5.

215. This seemed to be a technique that Donohue, in particular, used to try to show evangelicals as fundamentally anti-Semitic. Of course, salvation is the same for everyone, Jews and Gentiles alike. Acts 4:12 says, "There is no other name under heaven given among men by which we must be saved." The answer is, of course Jews go to Heaven. Jesus did. He's there. Most of His first followers were also Jews, and they are there, along with innumerable Jews who have lived since then.

216. George Orwell, "Politics and the English Language," *Horizon* volume 13, issue 76, April 1946.

217. John 14:6.

218. 2 Timothy 4:3.

219. Romans 8:29.

220. 2 Timothy 1:5.

221. 2 Timothy 1:8.

222. 2 Timothy 2:16.

223. Genesis 15:6.

224. Galatians 3:3.

225. Jude 3.

226. This is another reason we must not unhitch ourselves from the Old Testament. We still need God's schoolmaster of the Law to teach us that we are sinners and need a Savior.

227. Revelation 2:4–5.

228. Matthew 16:18.

229. Revelation 3:14–22.

230. Revelation 3:15–16.

231. https://randywhiteministries.org/articles/ what-southern-baptists-can-expect-from-russell-moore-and-the-erlc/.

232. https://andybraner.wordpress.com/2015/11/21/a-palestinian-farmers-life/.

233. Stephen Karetzky and Peter E. Goldman, *The Media's War Against Israel* (New York: Shapolsky Books, 1986) 12.

234. Paul Johnson, Darwin: *Portrait of a Genius* (New York: Viking, 2012) 140–141.

235. World Watch Daily, Koenig International News, "Influential Christian Leaders Speak Against Israel's Biblical Significance and Her Land," April 7, 2004, www.watch.org/showart.php3?idx =62726&rtn=/index.html&sh.

236. John G. Gager, *The Origins of Anti-Semitism* (London: Oxford University Press, 1983) 127–129.

237. John T. Pawlikowski, *Journal of Religion & Society*, "Christian Anti-Semitism: Past History, Present Challenges," http://moses.creighton.edu/ JRS/2004/2004-10.html.

238. Gene Shaparenko, "The Resurgence of 'Christian' Anti-Semitism," www. aquatechnology.net/ RESURGENCE.html.

239. Centre for the Study of Historical Christian Antisemitism, "John Chrysostom," www.hca centre.org/JohnChrysostom.html.

240. Ibid., "St. Jerome," www.hcacentre.org/Jerome.html.

241. California State University at Northridge, "Canons of the Church Council at Elvira (Granada) ca. 309 AD," www.csun.edu/~hcfll004/elvira.html.

242. New Advent, "Easter Controversy," www.newadvent.org/cathen/ 05228a. html.

243. Centre for the Study of Historical Christian Antisemitism, "Saint Augustine," www.hcacentre. org/Augustine.html.

244. For greater detail regarding the types of anti-Semitism during the Middle Ages, see: David R. Reagan, *The Jewish People: Rejected or Beloved?* (McKinney, TX: Lamb & Lion Ministries, 2017) 106–111.

245. Michael Coren, "The Reformation at 500: Grappling with Martin Luther's anti-Semitic legacy," www.macleans.ca/opinion/ the-reformation-at-500-grappling-with-martin-luthers-anti- semitic-legacy.

246. The Jewish Virtual Library, "Martin Luther: The Jews and Their Lies (1543)," www.jewish virtuallibrary.org/jsource/anti-semi tism/Luther_on_ Jews.html.

247. Ibid.

248. Jim Walker, "Martin Luther's Dirty Little Book: 'On the Jews and Their Lies: A Precursor to Nazism,'" www.nobeliefs.com/luther.htm.

249. New Hope Presbyterian Church, "An Open Letter to Evangelicals and Other Interested Parties: The People of God, the Land of Israel, and the Impartiality of the Gospel," www.new hopefairfax.org/images/ Open-Letter-To-Evangelicals-2002.pdf.

250. Ibid., 1–2.

251. Ibid., 2.

252. Ibid., 3.

253. Dennis Prager, Joseph Telushkin, et al., *Why the Jews?: The Reason for Anti-Semitism, the Most Accurate Predictor of Human Evil* (New York: Simon & Schuster, 2003).

254. For detailed information about Christian Palestinianism, see: Andrew D. Robinson, *Israel Betrayed: The History of Replacement Theology*, volume 1 (San Antonio, TX: Ariel Ministries, 2018) and volume 2 by Paul R. Wilkinson, *Israel Betrayed: The Rise of Christian Palestinianism* (San Antonio, TX: Ariel Ministries, 2018).

255. James A. Showers, "The New Anti-Semitism," *Israel My Glory* magazine, January–February 2013, 15.

256. Queenstown Bible Chapel, untitled article by Dalton Thomas, www. queenstownbiblechapel. co.nz/dr-sizer-and-the-apartheid-israel-lie.

257. Ami Isseroff, "Christian Zionism and Christians Who Are Zionists: Asset or Threat?" www. zionism-israel.com/log/archives/00000098.html.

258. World Council of Churches, "Kairos Palestine Document," www. oikoumene.org/en/resources/ documents/other-ecumenical-bodies/ kairos-palestine-document.

259. Donald E. Wagner, *Anxious for Armageddon* (Scottsdale, PA: Herald Press, 1995) 80.

260. Stephen Sizer Blog, "Sixty Academics Endorse Christian Zionism Book," www.stephensizer. blogspot.com/2008/10/sixty-academics-endorse-christian. html.

261. Alan Hart, "The New Nazis," January 13, 2009, www.alanhart.net/ the-New-Nazis.

262. Karol Markowicz, "Democrats to Israel: Go to Hell," *New York Post*, November 12, 2019, https://nypost.com/2019/11/17/ democrats-to-israel-go-to-hell.

263. Ibid. See also: Sean Savage, "Are Far-Left Candidates Pushing Democrats Further Away from Israel?" Jewish News Syndicate, www.jns.org/state-of-relations-on-the-jewish-state- how-republicans-and-democrats-have-shifted-their-support.

264. Ibid., Karol Markowicz.

265. *Times of Israel* staff, "Far-Right 'Jew Coup': Media Outlet TruNews Banned from YouTube," February 22, 2020, www.timesofisrael.com/ anti-semitic-media-outlet-trunews- banned-from-youtube-for-hate-speech.

266. Ibid.

267. Jewish Telegraphic Agency, "Conservative Pastor Says Spread of Coronavirus in Synagogues Is Punishment from God," March 29, 2020, www.jta.org/ quick-reads.

268. Ibid.

269. FLAME Hotline, "Campus Anti-Semitism Reaches New Highs—Or Lows —in America," www.factsandlogic.org/ campus-anti-semitism-reaches-new-highs- or-lows-in-america/?gclid=CjwKCAjwhOD0BRAQEiwAK7JHmIURFipr Bubl74ho6aJp3U0heBQTjeuWUxVXp8mnfGgmTUlem4yTWho C7JoQAvD_BwE. See also: ADL, "Schooled in Hate: Anti-Semitism on Campus," www.adl.org/ resources/reports/schooled-in-hate-anti-semitism-on-campus.

270. Herbert G. McCann, "Farrakhan Refers to 'Satanic Jews' While Denying He's anti-Semitic," *Times of Israel*, www.timesofisrael.com/ farrakhan-refers-to-satanic-jews-while-denying- hes-anti-semitic.

271. ADL, "Farrakhan: In His Own Words," www.adl.org/sites/default/files/ documents/assets/pdf/ anti-semitism/united-states/ farrakhan-in-his-own-words-2015-03-20.pdf.

272. Peter Dreier, *Dissent*, "Why Anti-Semitism Is on the Rise in the United States," www.dissentmagazine.org/online_articles/anti-semitism-rise-trump, 4.

273. Mattea Cumoletti and Jeanne Batalova, "Middle Eastern and

North African Immigrants in the United States," *Migration Policy Institute*, January 10, 2018, www.migrationpolicy.org/article/ middle-eastern-and-north-african-immigrants-united-states?gclid= CjwKCAjwhOD0BRAQEiwAK7JHmAMXr79iGhhN4gxkjE6m MFN6jjc_1HqlfCY3Avxm-zQoWeYbF_-2fxoCWQ4QAvD_BwE. See also: Marc Thiessen, "Why Won't Dems Slam Their Anti-Semitic Fellow Congresswomen?" *New York Post*, August 21, 2019, https://nypost. com/2019/08/21/why-wont- dems-slam-their-anti-semitic-fellow-congresswomen.

274. Maccabee Task Force, "BDS Q&A," www.maccabeetaskforce.org/bds-qa/ ?gclid=CjwKCAjwh OD0BRAQEiwAK7JHmLYzUzOiyrr5F2hfFoXnnDvNO 82fYYzL6jRcx7Q8ExNzLOD1gegF9hoCKjYQAvD_BwE.

275. *Washington Report on Middle East Affairs*, "Ten U.S. Churches Now Sanction Israel—To Some Degree, and with Caveats," www. wrmea.org/2019-march-april/ten-us-churches-now-sanction-israel-to-some-degree-and-with-caveats.html.

276. ADL, "Anti-Semitism in the US," www.adl.org/what-we-do/anti-semitism/ anti-semitism- in-the-us, 1.

277. Dreier, *Dissent*, 2.

278. ADL, "Anti-Semitism in the US," 2.

279. European Jewish Congress, "Anti-Semitism in Europe," https:// eurojewcong.org/what-we-do/ combatting-antisemitism/ antisemitism-in-europe, 1.

280. Ibid., 2.

281. ADL, "Anti-Semitism Globally," www.adl.org/what-we-do/anti-semitism/ anti-semitism-glo bally, page 1. See also: The Wilson Center, "The Rise of Global Anti-Semitism," www.wilson center.org/event/ the-rise-global-anti-semitism.

282. Ibid., ADL, "Anti-Semitism Globally."

283. Olivier J. Melnick, *End-Times Antisemitism: A New Chapter in the Long Hatred* (Tustin, CA: Hope for Today Publications, 2017) 12.

284. Ibid., 13.

285. "Bill Gates Blasted as 'Vaccine Criminal' in Italian Parliament, *The American Thinker Magazine*, https://www.thenewamerican.com/world-news/europe/ item/35756-bill-gates-blasted-as-vaccine-criminal-in-italian-parliament.

286. Dr. David Reagan, "Does God Care When We Are in Crisis?", Lamb and Lion Ministries e-newsletter, April 08, 2020.